Japan and Germany
in the
Modern World

JAPAN AND GERMANY
IN THE
MODERN WORLD

Bernd Martin

Berghahn Books
Providence • Oxford

Published in 1995 by

Berghahn Books
Editorial offices:
165 Taber Avenue, Providence, RI 02906, USA
Bush House, Merewood Avenue, Oxford, OX3 8EF, UK

Library of Congress Cataloging-in-Publication Data

Martin, Bernd.
  Japan and Germany in the modern world / by Bernd Martin.
    p.   cm.
  Includes bibliographical references.
  ISBN 1-57181-858-8
  1. Germany--Relations--Japan. 2. Japan--Relations--Germany.
3. Germany--Military relations--Japan. 4. Japan--Military
relations--Germany. I. Title.
DD120.J3M35   1995   94-42973
327.43052--dc20   CIP

British Library Cataloguing in Publication Data
A CIP catalogue record for this book is available from
the British Library.

Printed in the United States on acid-free paper

CONTENTS

ACKNOWLEDGEMENTS

This collection of essays consists of papers written – and mostly published – during the years 1977 until 1994. It was while preparing my doctoral thesis on the German-Japanese war alliance that I first came across things Japanese which I could not understand at a first glance. As a 'normal' historian, who had never been trained in Japanese studies, my research on Germany's former ally depended to a great extent on the good will and help of others, particularly specialists around the world, in both English-speaking countries and the Far East.

Several visits to Japan (and China), after the publication of my doctoral thesis and invitations to stay at the East Asian Research Center at Harvard University (1976) and St Antony's in Oxford (1982) helped to enlarge my so far limited, German-based knowledge of the Far East. Without these international contacts most of the papers would never have been written. Therefore, I owe most to those foreign experts in the United States, Britain, China, and Japan who have kindly advised me and have often had to correct me.

I would also like to thank my students who have often responded critically in seminars or in lectures to my interpretations of Japan's modern history. It is with pleasure that I recall the discussions with my graduate students, such as Gerhard Krebs, Wieland Wagner, and Paul Schenck, who have greatly enriched my knowledge with their own dissertations. I would also like to thank Dr Peter Wetzler who taught Japanese history at Freiburg University for several years and my colleagues at the department who have been close to me. They have all provided critical suggestions but, nevertheless, have often encouraged me to continue in a historical field which is commonly regarded as very exotic at German universities.

For this special collection of essays my thanks go first to all those who have helped with the difficult translations and the tedious typing of the manuscript often in two languages, first in German and then in English. I would like to thank my wife for translating some of the chapters and for her careful advice in general. Not being a historian herself, she has read all the chapters in their different stages and by persistently asking an 'outsider's' questions has helped to clarify some of the statements that seemed self-evident to me.

Furthermore, I am indebted to my secretaries for their unfailing patience in preparing the manuscript for publication. Bravely grappling with English grammatical rules Gudrun Altfeld, Regina Fischer, Svenja Hieb, and, last but not least, Sabine Schmidt worked hard on the computer and, like Stefan Knirsch, helped with the proofreading.

Finally, I am very grateful to Sarah Miles and Dr Marion Berghahn for their great help in editing and polishing up the manuscript.

Should the essays still contain errors or incorrect interpretations this will be entirely my own fault. I can but hope that this collection of essays and the views presented will encourage other scholars to take up the topics and surpass the standard presented in this volume.

Horben near Freiburg im Breisgau   March 1995

BIBLIOGRAPHICAL NOTE

Japanese names have been transcribed according to the standard English system. Chinese romanisation is based on the Wade-Giles system which was widely used in prewar days. Pinyin did not exist then.

Japanese proper names in the text appear with the family name first, the given name second. In order to avoid confusion, in notes and references Japanese authors are quoted the usual Western way: given name first, followed by the family name.

Macrons and other symbols on Japanese names and expressions have been omitted, except for the few Japanese titles quoted in the footnotes.

INTRODUCTION

With the founding of a new national state both Japan and Germany entered world politics at about the same time. The Meiji Restoration of 1868 reinstalled the Tenno as the ruling sovereign of Japan. Exactly three years later the German rulers, having jointly defeated Imperial France, proclaimed the Prussian king Emperor at Versailles and thereby founded the Reich. Imperial Germany came to an end in 1918 with the abdication of the Kaiser. Imperial Japan, having sided with the Western powers during the First World War, was finally destroyed in the Second World War; the Emperor, however, remained in his position as the symbol of the nation's entity. Japan and Germany had much in common, not only up until 1945 when the old order in both countries was crushed by the victorious powers, but even today they still seem to have – at least from their former adversaries' point of view – a lot of similarities. A united nation once more, Germany has become the leading power within the European Community. Japan likewise has been the economic giant in East Asia and will certainly take the lead in the recently proclaimed Asian-Pacific Economic Cooperation (APEC).

In 1860 the Prussian government sent an expedition under Count Fritz zu Eulenburg to East Asia in order to conclude 'unequal treaties' with Japan and China. These were the days of the only liberal interlude in the history of Prussia – the so-called 'New Era' – and an attempt to exchange the former system based on military power and authoritarian government for a new system based on free trade and supported by an economically powerful middle class who would follow the British model and engage in worldwide trade and colonial politics. The treaty of friendship and commerce with Japan that was eventually ratified (24 January 1861), but only after putting the weak shogunate government under severe pressure, provided customs duty of between 5 and 10 percent on German products exported to Japan. Prussia had joined those countries that were engaged in overseas politics in order to keep Japan – which had only recently (1853) been opened to the world by American force – economically dependent.

If Prussia had adhered strictly to this policy, the consequences for the German, as well as for the Japanese, course of history would have been enormous. German unification during the 1860s might have been achieved under the influence of a strong Prussian middle class and might have been based on liberal democratic thinking rather than on military force. Japan, on the other hand, to whose social order Western liberal thinking was completely alien, would certainly not have chosen Germany as the only model for modernisation if Prussia had offered a Western democratic system instead of the authoritarian state to which the Japanese could easily adapt.

All this, however, is mere historical speculation, all the more so as the Prussian experiment of liberalism, in domestic as well as in foreign politics, did not last long. During the course of the Prussian constitutional conflict about the monarch's prerogatives and the special position of the military, the new Prime Minister Otto von Bismarck used all of his influence to back the monarch's position and the traditional authoritarian Prussian state. The leader of the expedition to the Far East, Count Eulenburg, was appointed Home Secretary. Instead of outward expansion, from now on Bismarck pursued the aim of inner German unification based on military strength. In the Far East, Prussia, and from 1871 onwards the German Reich, was more or less represented by the flag alone. What obviously mattered most was nationally orientated power politics.

Up to the end of the German Reich in 1945, political power was always valued more highly than mercantile interests. This policy was readily adopted by Japan which had chosen Germany as its model. The Japanese pupil quickly learned from its German teacher not only how to provide home politics with a seemingly constitutional façade, but also how to be ruthless in foreign politics. The common development of both countries, Germany and Japan, that started in 1861 was based on the misguided Japanese belief in their special kinship (*Wesensverwandtschaft*) with Germany, and fitted well with the German strategy of power politics. In the end, however, it proved fatal with the two countries waging war on the rest of the world and led to violence and defeat.

Since 1945 things have changed. The tutor as well as the eager pupil have found themselves as equal partners under American tutelage. One hundred years after the first contact with Germany, Japan has achieved outstanding economic prosperity of its own. In the course of *Jimmu Keiki*, the biggest leap forward since the foundation of the state, Japanese industrial production increased within the five years between 1956 and 1961 by 2.7 times its former level. Eventually Japan overtook the Federal Republic in 1968, and the former German tutor has, in some respects, turned into the pupil. The Germans, however, have as yet failed to properly acknowledge the Japanese and their impact.

The historical similarities between Germany and Japan have frequently been termed as the 'mislead modernisation' of two 'latecomers'. Yet, not only today's social scientists but also the then contemporary discussion have differed widely as to how to assess the respective degrees of backwardness and how to rectify them. Several questions remain unanswered:

Was Japan really the model of successful modernisation that Prime Minister Kishi, in 1957, advised the Southeast Asian states to follow? No German Chancellor would defend, let alone advertise the German special way (*Sonderweg*). How are the terms of 'modern' and 'belated' to be defined with respect to German and Japanese development? When exactly did the two countries catch up with what is called the modern world: at the date of their official state foundation (Japan in 1868 and Germany in 1871) or much later with the end of the Second World War, for the outbreak of which both are to be held responsible? And what are the structural social and political similarities of the two countries that tend to be forgotten or even – in Japan – suppressed for reasons of political opportunity?

Western theory on the process of modernisation relies on British and American industrialisation as a pattern for the development of all other countries, all the more so since during the course of the Second World War the liberal democratic system proved superior to the totalitarian nationalist order of the allied Fascist countries. However, this idea of 'one world' united by capitalism is deeply rooted in Puritan Anglo-Saxon thinking and cannot be applied to the history of either Germany or Japan, let alone to countries of the developing world. Instead, a 'belated nation's' way into the modern world can only be explained by understanding its specific history. Germany's, as well as Japan's, way to national unification and to their military alliance in 1940 was determined by social factors in the first place. In both countries social structures as well as outward expansion stem from different preindustrial factors that may seem comparable only at a first glance. Any comparison, therefore, can serve only as a means to make things clear; it certainly cannot provide a valid theory on 'latecomers' in general.

In the history of Japan and Germany the differences outnumber the similarities, which, for their part, mostly come down to mere clichés. Thus, during the Meiji period the strongest similarity was seen in military virtues. Japan as the 'Prussia of the East' and Prussia as the 'German Sparta' were common stereotypes and, grossly exaggerated during the war alliance, blurred the view. Fascist propaganda in both countries did its best to discover kinship where there was none. The nonindividualist thinking of the Japanese was considered equal to the National Socialist's group-identity, the samurai's loyalty towards his feudal lord was compared to the SS member's blind obedience ('my honour is my loyalty'). Even between the Japanese art of arranging flowers (*Ikebana*) and the beauty ideal of the National Socialist young women's organisation, the *Bund Deutscher Mädel*, common female virtues would be detected. Linguists, too, cooperated by trying to derive the terms of 'Nibelungen' and 'Nippon' from a common root.[1] Those German scholars, particularly the Japanologists of the time, who had made fools of themselves by overrating similarities between the two countries, have, since 1945 tried to avoid dealing with modern Japan at all, except on a merely philological level.

The following ten essays covering one hundred years of German-Japanese history cannot detail all aspects of both countries' modernisation and their cooperation. The main theme will focus on Imperial Japan, the German perspective, however, prevailing. The essays present the picture that the Germans had of Japan and give a German researcher's view as the articles are based entirely on German source material. Japanese primary sources and Japanese books have not been consulted due to the author's lack of Japanese. However, American and, partly, British research on Japan has advanced to an unchallenged position in the world. English-language scholarly works, therefore, served as a welcome substitute to make up for the author's lack of language skills.

In place of a monograph, a collection of essays seems to be better suited for the specialised as well as for the nonspecialised reader to find their topic of interest. The essays were written between 1977 and 1994 and, with the exception of the second ('Fatal Affinities'), have been published before either in German or in English. Some duplication between chapters is inevitable, since history cannot be compartmentalised and put into pigeon holes. Each essay stands as an independent entity. They are presented in a roughly chronological order and, it is hoped, will form a coherent whole.

The original versions have been partly revised and often abridged, but not completely rewritten. The footnotes reflect the standard of the scientific Western literature and source material available at the time when the papers were first written. It was only with the collapse of the Communist order that the archives in the former German Democratic Republic were completely opened to researchers from the West. For example, the many volumes on German experts in Meiji Japan and the bulky files containing German consular reports from the same period, which were stored in the Potsdam archives, became available only after German unification. Therefore, the reader may miss references in the notes of the somewhat older papers which will easily be found in the final notes of the more recent publications or in the select bibliography at the end of this volume.

Research on the special kinship between Japan and Germany has been grossly neglected in both countries, but for different reasons. The German picture of Japan has borne traits of ambivalence, sometimes of arrogance or even of racial superiority. In general, the Germans tended to look down on the 'little yellow Japanese'[2] whom they generally did not trust, but at best admired for their exotic thrill and military success. Until recently, the exchange between the two countries has been extremely one-sided. As the Japanese have selected German devices to take over and have adapted them to their own world, their knowledge of Germany and the Germans has increased. The Germans, who clung to their traditional pro-Chinese outlook in all matters Asian, remained in more or less complete ignorance about the island empire. Japanology as a special academic discipline was established at very few universities during the interwar period and was immediately misused by the National Socialists for the political purposes of the highly favoured Berlin-Tokyo axis.[3] Sinology, like China itself, had a much better reputation in Germany, had a longer established academic tradition, and could compete by international standards with similar research institutions in other countries. As a legacy of National Socialist times and the war alliance with Japan, German research on its former ally is strictly divided between the philological approach of the language experts, the Japanologists, and the sociohistorical expertise provided by specialists who usually do not know the language.

Just the reverse applies in Japan. Research on Germany, particularly general German history or the history of the German legal system, is very common within the Japanese academic community.[4] Of all the Western countries, Germany and the Germans enjoyed the highest esteem between the time of the Meiji Restoration and the surrender of Imperial Japan. Even today Germans enjoy a better reputation than other foreigners in Japan. Old affinities from Meiji times and the early Showa period, as well as a kind of gratitude towards the former teacher (*sensei*), may account for this traditional pro-German outlook. However, it was only the Japanese who felt this special kinship between the two countries, while the Germans remained distant even when a special relationship was officially propagated.

Having lost the war for the liberation of Asia from the 'white man', however, the Japanese would rather not be reminded of the historical events which eventually led to the Pacific War. The recent historical past has been neglected at schools as well as at the universities.[5] Therefore, even Japanese students of history know next to nothing about the history of the Pacific War and one of its main roots, the German-Japanese alliance. And since there is little material left in the archives, as the relevant files were burnt by the Japanese ministries in August 1945, only very little research has been done on Japanese-German relations.[6] Even the German impact on the modernisation of Japan during the Meiji period, which used to be a favourite topic of research, has been neglected in recent times. Japan, one of the most advanced nations of our world, does not want to be reminded of the days when, by Imperial decree, knowledge had to be adopted from all over the world.[7]

Prussia, and later Germany, of course, did not serve as the only model for turning feudal Japan into an apparently Western nation. As to the number of foreign experts, those from Great Britain and America dominated, the Germans usually remaining in the third or even, behind the French, in fourth position. American engineers and specialists helped a great deal to introduce modern technical science and skills in Japan.[8] At the same time, British experts[9] guided the Japanese in building efficient ports and the railway system, and in developing a merchant fleet as well as the Imperial Navy. For decades the shipbuilding industries of Glasgow were highly dependent on orders from the newly established Imperial Japanese Navy. The Japanese exchanged art for industry, as Glasgow served as a window to Japan with museums bursting of exotic exhibits.[10] Obviously, the Anglo-Americans introduced all kinds of technical skills to the Japanese and thereby controlled industry and foreign trade in the early Meiji period.

After some time of experimenting with American, British, and French models in public sectors such as education or administration, from 1881 onwards the Japanese turned to Germany for assistance in those fields which were to remain under the control of the central government. Thus, Japanese modernisation followed two divergent paths which would not go together.[11] Modern technical training, encouraged by the British and Americans, and a restorative social order and ideology, as advised by the Germans, often caused conflict within individuals. The conduct of modern life and labour frequently clashed with premodern thinking and traditional social habits. Japanese society, therefore, did not open to the West but became more and more secluded during the interwar period.

The only way out of this dilemma, which had been caused at least partly by a dual and incoherent modernisation programme, seemed to be a policy of expansion on the Asian mainland. Taking refuge in the imperial myths of the uniqueness and godly descent of the Yamato race together with military aggression, first in Manchuria and from 1937 onward in China proper, emerged as the two sides of Japan's modern social imperialism. This nationalist deviation led to complete isolation within the international community of nations and led the Japanese Empire to search desperately for an ally who was also an outcast and in a similar position. The unholy alliance between Hitler's Germany and the Tenno's Empire which led the world into the most devastating war, resulted far more from a misguided concept of modernisation than from the international situation.

It is hoped that the following essays will contribute to a better understanding of the two nations who caused so much devastation in our century, although they will not try to excuse them. Furthermore, these contributions are intended to widen the Anglo-American view on Japan by presenting and explaining the German impact which seems to be but little known in the English-reading community.

Notes

1. The examples quoted were taken from Regine Mathias-Pauer, 'Deutsche Meinungen zu Japan. Von der Reichsgründung bis zum Dritten Reich' and from Eberhard Friese, 'Das deutsche Japanbild 1944', both in Josef Kreiner, ed., *Deutschland – Japan. Historische Kontakte*, Bonn, 1984, pp. 115–40 and pp. 265–84.

2. The phrase 'Yellow Peril' has been applied in Germany to the Japanese since 1895. See Heinz Gollwitzer, *Die Gelbe Gefahr. Geschichte eines Schlagwortes. Studien zum imperialistischen Denken*, Göttingen, 1962.

3. Herbert Worm, 'Japanologie im Nationalsozialismus. Ein Zwischenbericht', in Gerhard Krebs and Bernd Martin, eds., *Formierung und Fall der Achse Berlin-Tokyo*, München, 1994, pp. 153–86.

4. For Japanese interest in Germany, see the various contributions in Klaus Kracht et al., eds., *Japan und Deutschland im 20. Jahrhundert*, Wiesbaden, 1984.

5. See the excellent study by Ian Buruma, *The Wages of Guilt. Memoirs of War in Germany and Japan*, New York, 1994.

6. The first Japanese study on the alliance with Germany, Takeshi Haruki, *The Tripartite Pact and Japanese Foreign Policy*, Tokyo, 1964, was based entirely on documents from the International Tribunal for the Far East/Tokyo. Japanese as well as Western source material was first used by Miyake Masaki in his studies (see the select bibliography) and in his major work (in Japanese with an English summary) on the Tripartite Alliance, *Nichi-Doku-I sangokudōmei no kenkyū*, Tokyo, 1975; Hiroshi Yoshi, *Nichi-Doku-I sangoku dōmei to Nichi-Bei kankei. Tai-heiyō sensōzen kokusaikankei no kenkyū* (The Tripartite Pact and Japanese-American Relations), Tokyo, 1971. Furthermore, see Tokushiro Ohata, 'The Anti-Comintern Pact, 1935–1939', and Chihiro Hosaya, 'The Tripartite Pact, 1939–1940', both in James W. Morley, ed., *Deterrent Diplomacy. Japan, Germany, and the USSR, 1935–1940*, New York, 1976, pp. 9–112 and 191–258. Most recently, Nobuo Tajima published a thoroughly researched book on National Socialist Foreign Policy and Manchuria, *Nachizumu Gaikō to 'Manshūkoku'*, Tokyo, 1992.

7. Paragraph 6 of the Charter Oath from 1868, 'Knowledge shall be sought throughout the world so as to broaden and strengthen the foundations of imperial rule', in David John Lu, ed., *Sources of Japanese History*, vol. 2, New York, 1974, p. 36.

8. Edward R. Beauchamp and Akira Iriye, eds., *Foreign Employees in Nineteenth-Century Japan*, Boulder, 1990; Hazel J. Jones, *Live Machines. Hired Foreigners in Meiji Japan*, Tenterden, Kent, 1980; Robert A. Rosenstone, *American Encounters with Meiji Japan*, Cambridge, Mass., 1988; D. Eleanor Westney, *Imitation and Innovation. The Transfer of Western Organized Patterns to Meiji Japan*, Cambridge, Mass., 1987.

9. Oliva Checkland, *Britain's Encounter with Meiji Japan 1868–1912*, London, 1989.

10. Antonia Lovelace, *Art for Industry. The Glasgow Japan Exchange*, Glasgow, 1991.

11. Erich Pauer, 'Japanischer Geist – Westliche Technik: Zur Rezeption westlicher Technologie in Japan' in *Saeculum*, vol. 38, 1987, pp. 19–51.

PART I

THE ROOTS OF PARTNERSHIP

❧ 1 ❧

THE PRUSSIAN EXPEDITION TO THE FAR EAST (1860–1862)

When the Americans opened Japan by a show of naval force in 1853–54, the Prussian government as well as German commercial circles closely watched further developments in East Asia. But the Prussian navy proved unable to send ships on such a long voyage and had therefore to decline the task of imitating the Americans. It was with the change of sovereigns in 1858, when William I, later to become the first German Emperor, succeeded his mentally disturbed brother, that the plans for a naval expedition to the Far East were taken up again. The new liberal government of the so-called 'New Era' – the only liberal government in the history of Prussia – encouraged preparations for such an expedition. Modern vessels were built in the shipyard of Gdansk, or rather ordered in England, since the Prussians' skill in shipbuilding was not very advanced. Liberal Prussia tried to follow English liberal patterns and became the advocate of unrestricted industrial development at home and free trade abroad. This economic programme of the liberal Prussian government was enthusiastically supported by the chambers of commerce of all the other German states. By sponsoring commercial and industrial activities, Prussia, the leading military power, also tried to reach a dominant position in politics, i.e., in the question of German unification.

Furthermore, Prussian government officials as well as officers of the newly enlarged navy had dreamed of obtaining colonies in East Asia in order to keep in line with the established West European states, like England, France, and the Netherlands – thereby demonstrating the new leading position of Prussia within the German Union against the traditional claim of the Habsburgs.

First published in *The Journal of the Siam Society*, vol. 78, part 1, 1990, pp. 35–42.

The Austrian government had originally taken the lead in exploring the Far East for the Germans. The frigate *Novarra* was to be the first German warship to sail round the world between 1857 and 1859. The Austrian ship called at the port of Shanghai where it received a frenetic welcome by the local German merchant community. The Viennese, and not the Prussian government in Berlin, were looked upon as the future protector of German trade in the world. The Austrian ship even had orders to reconnoitre suitable sites for a Habsburg overseas colony for the settlement of convicts. The Nicobar Islands in the Indian Ocean and some smaller islands of the Dutch East Indies attracted the Austrians most. The Prussian-Austrian dualism over the question of German unification thus reached a worldwide dimension. But the Austrians' plans had to be dropped in 1859 after the humiliating defeat of the Habsburg monarchy in the war against France in northern Italy, and the task of representing the Germans in overseas countries was now left to the Prussians.

On 18 August 1859 a decision of the Prussian cabinet 'to send an expedition to the Chinese waters' was given royal assent. This mission was to conclude commercial and navigation treaties with China, Japan, and Siam. It was to be carried out by the two biggest and most modern armed vessels of the Prussian navy together with a supply schooner. Soon a fourth ship, a commercial sailing vessel, was chartered for the conveyance of industrial and technical samples – a kind of exposition of German industry and commerce.

Prussia was, in addition, to negotiate and conclude treaties on behalf of all the members of the German Customs Union – from which Austria was excluded – and, what was even more important, in the name of the three Hanseatic towns, Hamburg, Bremen and Lübeck, which were proud of their traditional political and commercial independence.

The expedition was to serve scientific purposes as well. Three renowned experts in the field of botany and zoology received the royal order to join the diplomats on the ships. In the final paragraph of the cabinet paper vague colonial plans were outlined. The expedition was to explore the coastlines of South America and Africa for suitable places to hoist the Prussian flag.

While the technical and naval preparations were speeded up, the former Prussian Consul-General in Warsaw, Count Fritz zu Eulenburg, was nominated *chef de mission* and promoted to the rank of plenipotentiary extraordinary of the Prussian king. In the eyes of the Ministry of Foreign Affairs, no trained diplomat seemed suitable to lead the mission. The selection of a commercial expert, like a Consul-General, again stressed the main aim of the expedition to promote German trade in East Asia. Having neither experience in diplomatic negotiations nor in talks with Asiatic delegates, Eulenburg immediately went to Paris in March 1860, after his nomination, in order to consult with both the French and the British chief negotiators of the Tientsin treaties. Lord Elgin promised the Prussians full British help in China in obtaining a treaty based on the terms of the Tientsin arrangements which, incidentally, had not been ratified by the Chinese government at that time. The French Baron Gros even encouraged the Prussian envoy to annex the island of Formosa as a Prussian colony. The French seemed very keen on having the Prussians as their allies in colonial adventures in Southeast Asia. While French troops were to invade the kingdom of Cambodia, the Germans would occupy Formosa and thus hinder both British and Chinese attempts to interfere with France's colonial acquisitions. The idea of Formosa as a German colony under Prussian administration remained a visionary goal until the Japanese took over the island in 1895.

After some sharp quarrels between the Navy Ministry and the Admiralty that reflected the rivalry between civilian and military authorities in Prussia, the ships left their Baltic home harbours in December 1859. However, the pride of the Prussian navy, the steamship *Arcona*, had to dock in England for repairs. The ships left England individually at the end of February 1860, called at a few ports in South America, and then sailed directly via the South Atlantic and the Indian Ocean to Singapore, where they met in September. Again the ships had to undergo thorough repairs with the help of British experts.

Count Eulenburg, a *bon vivant* and by no means a military man, abhorred the discomfort of a long and strenuous sea voyage. He was allowed to travel to Singapore by a short cut, on the so-called 'land route' via the Mediterranean, Suez, and the Indian Ocean. Before his departure he received a final order from the king authorizing the expedition to use military force should the necessity arise and to participate in the campaigns of the European powers against the obstinate Peking government. But the idea of Prussia becoming a military ally of Britain and France in the war against China bordered on the ridiculous, considering that Eulenburg had a mere 740 men, not all of them trained soldiers, at his disposal.

When Eulenburg received information in Singapore, where he finally had to board the small Prussian warships, that the war situation in China had not yet improved, the cautious diplomat decided to continue the voyage to Japan and avoid military adventures in China.

Having lost the small supply ship in a heavy typhoon, the expedition anchored in the bay of Edo in early September 1860. Diplomatic talks were opened immediately, but the weak shogunate government bluntly refused to sign any further treaty with Western nations which could provoke further xenophobic reactions by the Japanese people, and so strengthen rising nationalist opposition. It was only with the assistance of American and French diplomatic colleagues that Eulenburg finally succeeded in signing a commercial agreement and a treaty of friendship between Prussia and the shogun's government. The original aim of Prussia concluding a treaty on behalf of all the members of the German Customs Union, so as to show her leading position in international relations, was blocked by the Japanese negotiators. Pretending to have no idea of the complex situation of the German states and the German Union, they would consent to no more than a formal agreement between the two monarchies. A treaty between Prussia and Japan was finally signed on 24 January 1861.

The mission left Japan for the commercial capital of China, Shanghai, where one of the ships ran aground and had to be towed into deep waters, again with British and French help. Because of the Chinese refusal to succumb to the humiliating treaty of Tientsin, British and French troops entered Peking and, as an act of 'revenge', looted the city. The small Prussian expedition was unable to take part in defeating the Chinese. It was forced to wait for the outcome of the war, from which it might gain some profit. In the talks with the Chinese government, which were resumed in the spring of 1861, Count Eulenburg insisted that Prussia should be granted the same privileges which the Western powers had achieved by military victory. Negotiating a treaty with the Chinese authorities, which required both cunning and patience, proved the most difficult task Eulenburg had to take on.

Because of the recent ratification of the Tientsin treaties in October 1860, hostilities in northern China had stopped but the whole political situation remained unstable. The Chinese Emperor and his court had fled from the invading Western troops to the summer palace in Jehol. The task of dealing with the 'barbarians', with help from the newly established Ministry of Foreign Affairs (Tsungli Yamen), was left to Prince Kung in Peking. Contrary to the wishes of their governments, the French and British diplomats were rather reluctant to offer any help to the Prussians. They even tried to persuade Eulenburg not to proceed from Shanghai to Tientsin. The appearance of a fourth great European power in Peking, where Russian, British, and French diplomatic missions had already been established, might endanger the pro-Western circles within the Chinese government and eventually lead to the overthrow of Prince Kung by traditionalist court circles. On the other hand, the Western powers in China feared the Prussian (German) competition, because the Germans – without colonial strongholds – were highly regarded by the Chinese, and in those days controlled the coastal shipping trade in China almost entirely. More than 200 German sailing vessels, mostly coming from German seaports like Hamburg and Bremen, were chartered together with their German crews, bringing great profit to Chinese merchants.

Contrary to the advice of his Western colleagues, Eulenburg sent one of his attachés, Max von Brandt, later to become German minister in China, to Tientsin to start negotiations with the Chinese central government. But the local High Commissioner of the northern treaty ports, Ch'ung Hou, refused even to transfer a letter from Eulenburg to Prince Kung in Peking. The Chinese desperately tried to negotiate with the Prussians at a lower level in order to avoid the Peking government's getting involved at all. They were ready for no more than a commercial treaty applicable only to three northern treaty ports. When the German envoy insisted on an official treaty and on Prussia's right to establish a permanent legation in the capital, the negotiations almost broke down. Eulenburg ordered Brandt to proceed to Peking to force the central authorities to consent to Prussia's wishes. But Prince Kung was offended by the unauthorised visit of the German attaché and forced him to leave the city. Prussia would certainly have failed to obtain a treaty had not the Western powers finally given substantial help. The Eulenburg mission, with only the flagship *Arcona* anchoring near the Taku forts, had no military means at its disposal to force its political demands upon the Chinese as the English and French had done before.

The French especially, after first supporting the Chinese claims, now adopted a pro-Prussian case. It can be assumed that the

French consul in Tientsin and the legation in Peking did so because they had orders from Paris. The French government still wooed the Prussians as a future colonial partner in East Asia against the dominating British. When the French started to back the Prussian demands, the British could not stand back. The Chinese, still trying to play off the barbarians against each other, delayed the talks by refusing to present the credentials of the envoys and continuing to refuse a formal political agreement. Not until July, after four months of unpleasant talks, did the Chinese central government finally give in. Possible threats from the French and the British, as well as the Chinese fear of having to conclude separate treaties with thirty single German states later instead of just one now with Prussia on behalf of the Customs Union, may have helped to change the minds of the officials and of Prince Kung. The following dialogue between Eulenburg and Ch'ung Hou during the final phase of the negotiations demonstrates the resignation of the Chinese as much as the self-assurance of the Prussian envoy:

> Ch'ung: If an expression does not make sense to us, we have got to change it. The English and the French forced us to accept a treaty in their own version.
>
> Eulenburg: As long as expressions are concerned, I shall do my best and give in. However, there is nothing substantially unreasonable in the treaty.
>
> Ch'ung: This question could best be answered by Kwei Lian who was forced to sign those treaties. I would rather have my head cut off than sign such a treaty.
>
> Eulenburg: In that case we had better break off negotiations.
>
> Ch'ung: The Emperor would be right asking me why I granted to Prussia what England and France forced us to accept only after several wars.
>
> Eulenburg: I cannot but repeat that I shall not conclude any treaty unless it is based on the terms of the most favoured nation.
>
> Ch'ung: This is how one country after the other is trying to exert political pressure upon us so that in the end nothing will be left of China.
>
> Eulenburg: China is completely free to act the way she wants. If you do not want to conclude a treaty with Prussia on the terms we are offering, then do not. I now want you to answer my question precisely: Are you or are you not willing to grant me the same rights you have granted to the other powers?

Ch'ung: We cannot grant anything but what sounds reasonable.

Eulenburg: Your answer does not stick to the point. What I am asking for is only reasonable.

Ch'ung: You are trying to force upon us something we cannot consider reasonable.

Finally, on 12 August, the treaty was drafted according to the Prussian demands. The imperial seal was fixed two days before the Emperor died on 21 August. The signing ceremony took place in Tientsin on 2 September 1861. Eulenburg had gained a splendid diplomatic victory. This time the treaty was signed not with Prussia alone, but with all members of the German Customs Union. In profiting from the Western victories, Prussia succeeded for the first time in representing the German states in an overseas country.

Meanwhile, with the Prussian government's growing pride in the results of the expedition, the discussion was opened again for a permanent foothold in East Asia, such as the Western powers had. A royal order from Berlin pointed at the Solomon Islands and Formosa (Taiwan) as the most suitable places for a German colony for the settlement of convicts and emigrants from Prussia. However, Count Eulenburg could not feel easy with the idea of Prussia becoming an equal colonial partner of the British or French. He warned his government that any colonial acquisition in East Asia might result in a diplomatic estrangement between Prussia and the Western powers and would certainly endanger the recently concluded treaties with China and Japan. In order to stress his arguments Eulenburg reported that the island of Formosa was in no way suitable for any kind of Western colonization due to its intolerably hot and humid climate. Notwithstanding the protest of Prince Adalbert, Admiral-in-Chief of the Prussian Navy, who strongly favoured a military invasion of Formosa, the mission was ordered home by the civilian government.

On their way home, they were supposed to call at the capital of Siam to conclude a treaty of friendship and commerce there. The impending arrival of the Prussian expedition had been announced to the Siamese authorities by letter from China. When the second ship of the convoy, the frigate *Thetis*, anchored in the coastal waters of Bangkok on 22 November 1861, everything was ready to welcome the first German warship and her crew in the capital. The captain and his officers gladly accepted the offer to lodge in a small palace which had been assigned as the official residence for the German envoy, and to stay until Eulenburg himself appeared. The advance party of the Prussian delegation was asked to pay a formal visit to the two leading ministers, the *Phraklang*, as minister of the treasury responsible for all external affairs, and to the *Kalahom*, the so-called first minister in charge of military affairs. The following day, the fourth day after their arrival, the Prussian naval officers were granted a private audience by the first king, Mongkut, in the private chambers of the royal palace. The Germans, accustomed to the strict etiquette at the Prussian court in Berlin, were puzzled by the King of Siam personally entertaining his guests and serving each of them a glass of sherry.

The Prussians felt greatly honoured with this preferential treatment, which was not altogether due to the natural amiability of the Siamese but had some political motives too. Only ten years before, in 1852, King Mongkut and his political advisers had closely watched the second Anglo-Burmese war, which was fought over the legal status of British tradesmen and which ended by Lower Burma becoming a British colony. In order to counter the British menace from the west and from Singapore (acquired in 1819) from the southeast, the Siamese had softened the English by giving in to their commercial demands, thus signing the first unequal treaty with a Western power.

Meanwhile, the French ruler Napoleon III, who after overthrowing the republican government had made himself Emperor of France, was looking for political success in foreign affairs to stabilise the situation in France. Colonial conquest and prestigious warlike expeditions to exotic countries seemed to him a suitable means. The French, therefore, took part as Britain's ally in the Second Opium War against China (1857–60) and, in 1859, annexed Saigon as their first stronghold in Cochin-China. Since this territory officially belonged to Cambodia, which was regarded as part of the Kingdom of Siam, the French had actually encroached upon Siamese sovereignty for the first time and furthermore were preparing to extend their influence over the whole of Cambodia.

Two weeks before the arrival of the first Prussian warship the French Consul-General had handed to the Siamese government an official note enquiring about the legal status of Cambodia. The French military supported this diplomatic *démarche* by occupying some islands off the Cambodian coast. As a further demonstration of France's advanced military and naval power, the French warship *Formosa* steamed up the Menam River and anchored in the middle of Bangkok with her guns pointing at the city. Since no foreign armed vessels were allowed to enter the capital, the authorities tried to fine the French commanding officer. King Mongkut pointedly left the city in order to avoid having to receive a French delegation. Relations between Siam and France were thus tense and even further strained when the French actually occupied Cochin-China in 1862.

Therefore the Prussians, who apparently had no colonial ambitions in Asia, were regarded as potential allies by the Thai in their struggle for maintaining independence. Prussia, the third of the European great powers to appear in Siam, had so far kept a neutral position in Europe and was expected to mediate between the interests of the colonial powers, the British and the French, on the one hand and the legitimate rights of Siam on the other. The court, therefore, could hardly wait for the arrival of the Prussian plenipotentiary, Count Eulenburg. When his flagship, the *Arcona*, finally reached the roadstead of Bangkok on 15 December 1861, the reception he received resembled the greeting of a personal friend of the king.

All the members of the mission were astonished at the cordial welcome by the Thai authorities and the presents and the variety of food they were immediately offered by the royal palace. Compared to Japan and China, the negotiations in Siam went on smoothly and without any complications. From the very first day the Thai officials warned the Germans not to imitate the Western colonial powers, since colonies meant rivalries among the great powers and finally war – a prognosis which was soon proved right by the imperialistic struggles over China and the so-called punitive expeditions against the Chinese, like the Boxer rebellion. The whole atmosphere in Bangkok seems to have been very easygoing and peaceful, just the opposite of what the Prussian soldiers and diplomats were accustomed to.

King Mongkut received Eulenburg and the official members of the Prussian delegation for the first time in a private audience on 24 December 1861 in order to discover the political views of his would-be allies. When asked about the colonial plans of the Prussian government, Eulenburg, having just disobeyed an order from Berlin on this score, diplomatically replied that Prussia would in no case look for colonies in tropical areas. The king seemed relieved and commented on the answer by saying that he felt the more delighted to have won a new unselfish friend, since the old friends had recently become troublesome. Then His Majesty made some profound remarks on the nature of Western colonialism: 'First, ships are sent out to explore the unknown parts of the world. Then other ships follow for the purpose of trading. Then merchants settle down, who are either fought by the natives or who try to subjugate the native population. In short, wars emerge out of guilt and misunderstanding on both sides. The foreigners keep extending their influence until entire empires belong to them. Nowadays, there is hardly any country left for new colonies, except Oceania (i.e., the Pacific) and the islands of the South Sea. The Asian countries have been in a disadvantageous position since the norms of Western international law have not been applied to them.'

On the occasion of the official audience three days later, the court unfolded all its royal splendour in order to impress the Prussians. The guests were amazed at the exotic spectacle but – like the Prussian soldiers they were – noticed signs of disorder within the military guard of honour and the ragged uniforms the Siamese soldiers wore. In the reception hall the nobles, all of them in formal attire, and the children of the king were lying on a heavily carpeted floor while the monarch and the Prussian envoy stood up from their chairs in order to exchange the royal letters. Addressing the king in English, Eulenburg asked for friendly relations between the two countries and expressed the desire of the Prussian government to conclude a formal treaty. While opening the letter from his royal Prussian friend, King Mongkut enquired wether the German and the English languages had much in common. When Eulenburg politely confirmed this royal assumption, the King directly asked his guest about the relationship between Britain and Prussia. He was also curious to know wether they (i.e., the English and the Prussians) would assist him if further difficulties arose between Siam and other countries. Eulenburg of course grasped the hint at the French menace. Responding as a diplomat he could not but offer the friendly services of his royal sovereign should such a case arise. King Mongkut seemed pleased. In his official reply he consented to the Prussian wishes: 'We shall nominate qualified persons in order to deliberate upon and finally conclude a treaty similar to those which have been signed with the monarchs of other European countries.' In order to stress his earnest desire to come to terms with Prussia as soon as possible, the King sent a general to Eulenburg the following day. The military man again stressed the importance of friendship between neutral Prussia and Siam in her struggle with the two neighbouring colonial powers, thereby greatly admiring and praising the Prussian military as a potential future protector.

But Eulenburg did not like the idea of Prussia getting involved in political entanglements of the great powers in remote countries such as Siam. He therefore carefully avoided giving any advice. Instead of discussing world politics with his Thai hosts, he looked for Prussia's commercial advantage. Siam's new Prussian friend behaved from the very beginning rather like the old friends, the colonial European powers. Eulenburg lent his ear to the German merchant community in Bangkok and their proposals to improve trade relations to their own benefit. When the negotiations officially started on 9 January 1862, the Prussian envoy confronted the unsuspecting Thai delegation with two new demands. He insisted on quasi-legal terms of employment for Thai people working for German merchants and thus interfered with the traditional social order in Siam. After short deliberation the Thai delegation gave in on this point but steadfastly refused to grant to the Germans the right of acquiring landed property wherever they wanted. So far, the acquisition of land by Westerners had been limited to certain districts of the capital. As neither side seemed ready to compromise, the decision had to be left to the King. In order to counterbalance the French demands over Cambodia with a treaty with Prussia, the King finally had to give in. The treaty was drafted on 23 January and formally signed two weeks later, on 7 February. According to the most favoured nation clause of the other treaties Siam had been forced to sign before, the new rights granted to the Germans were automatically bestowed on the other nations too. Now all Westerners were allowed to buy land in a country where traditionally all the soil belonged to the King and native subjects could but rent it for their houses.

On the occasion of the farewell audience for his Prussian guests on 17 February, King Mongkut symbolized the weakness of his country by explaining his own feeble position: 'I have no power. I am not absolute. If I point the end of my walking stick at a man, whom being my enemy, I wish to die, he does not die, but lives on, in spite of my "absolute" will to the contrary.' The Prussian delegates ignored this remark of a king whose status and whose country they did not accept as an equal partner of Prussia and her monarch. In the eyes of the Prussians, the Thai, although friendly and patient, remained inferior natives like the Japanese and the Chinese. Before leaving the country the civilian members of the expedition went for an excursion into the countryside in order to fetch some exotic animals and plants for the zoo and the botanical garden in Berlin.

Travelling via Singapore and the Cape of Good Hope, the ships returned to their Baltic home ports, which they reached in late autumn 1862. Casualties were high, but the experience the few naval officers and sailors had gained on this long voyage proved indispensable for the strengthening of the modern German Imperial Navy after the Reich had been founded. Most of the officers were promoted to the rank of admiral and later held key positions in the German navy. Some of them even returned to the Far East when the navy finally seized some Chinese territory in 1897, and the port of Tsingtao thus became the first German colony in East Asia under the administration of the navy.

Concerning the political and commercial consequences of the Prussian expedition to the Far East, the results were rather meagre. The liberal government in Prussia had to resign because of the constitutional conflict over the army reorganisation. The liberal interlude in the history of Prussian government to promote a foreign policy on a large scale was immediately blocked by the new Prime Minister, Otto von Bismarck. For him the unification of the German states with the help of 'iron and blood' ranked before colonial experiments. Count Eulenburg, the reluctant leader of the mission, became Minister of the Interior. Instead of occupying remote islands in the Pacific he now had to fight Bismarck's opponents.

German trade with the three Asian countries was little stimulated by the commercial treaties. German industry and commerce, primarily interested in a united market at home, supported Bismarck's political aims. When this domestic market could no longer be expanded, controlling colonies and leased territories again became means in themselves in the age of imperialism. Unlike the English custom, it was always the colours that were hoisted first, in 1861–62 with the Prussian expedition, as much as in 1897 with the seizure of Tsingtao by the Germans. German trade followed the flag only very slowly and reluctantly.

The Prussian expedition to the Far East established for the first time formal diplomatic relations with the governments of Japan, China, and Siam – contacts that have endured to the present day if not always to the benefit of the respective peoples.

Bibliography

DOCUMENTS

Federal Republic of Germany

Federal Archives/Military Archives
Freibug im Breisgau.

The Expedition to Japan; The Expedition into the Chinese Waters (Die Expedition nach Japan bzw. die Expedition nach den chinesischen Gewässern).

Navy Ministry (Marineministerium), 6 vols.

Reports and Diaries of the Chief of the Mission, of the Attachés, and the Commanding Officer of the East Asian Expedition, 18 June 1860 to 2 March 1862 (Berichte und Tagebücher des Missionschefs, der Attachés und des Geschwaderchefs der ostasiatischen Expedition, 18. Juni 1860 bis 18. März 1862) 3 vols.

Private Papers of the Commander-in-Chief of the Navy, Admiral Prince Adalbert of Prussia (Handakten des Oberbefehlshabers der Marine, Admiral Prinz Adalbert von Preussen, 1848–1861, 1 vol.

Diverse files on the merchant navy, diplomatic correspondence, personal data of the officers and crews, construction of navy vessels, etc. (Verschiedene Akten über die Handelsmarine, den diplomatischen Schriftverkehr, die Personalia der Offiziere and Mannschaften, den Bau von Kriegsschiffen usw.)

Japan

Tokyo, University of Tokyo, Department of History Microfilm Collection: Historical Documents Relating to Japan in Foreign Countries. Microfilms: 6951-37-1-1; 6951-37-1-2; 6951-37-1-3; 6951-37-1-4; 6951-37-2-1; 6951-37-5-1. (Photocopies of documents relating to the Prussian expedition to the Far East, Central Archives of the German Democratic Republic, Merseburg)

China

Peking, First Archives (Palace Archives) Documents concerning Prussia, 1861, 1 volume.

Taiwan

Nanking, Taipei, Academia Sinica, Institute of Modern History, Correspondence of the Chinese Foreign Office on the negotiations with the Prussian Delegation, 1861, 3 vols.

SECONDARY SOURCES

Berg, Albert. *Die preussische Expedition nach Ost-Asien nach amtlichen Quellen.*
Vol. I: Einleitendes zum Verständnis der Japanischen Zustände. Reisebericht, Berlin, 1864.

Vol. II: Reisebericht. Anhang I (Der Vertrag mit Japan), Anhang II (Die Ereignisse der letzten Jahre), Berlin 1866.
Vol. III: Chinas Beziehungen zum Westen bis 1860. Reisebericht, Berlin, 1873.
Vol. IV: Reisebericht. Anhang I–IV, Berlin, 1873.

Boelcke, Willi A. *So kam das Meer zu uns. Die preussisch-deutsche Kriegsmarine in Übersee 1822–1914.* Frankfurt a. M., Berlin u. Wien, 1981.

Brandt, Max von. *Dreiunddreissig Jahre in Ost-Asien. Erinnerungen eines deutschen Diplomaten.* Vol. 1 and 2, Leipzig, 1901.

Delbrück, Rudolph von. *Lebenserinnerungen 1817–1867.* 2 Vols., Leipzig, 1905.

Eulenburg-Hertefeld, Graf Philipp zu, ed. *Ost-Asien 1860–1862 in Briefen des Grafen Fritz zu Eulenburg.* Berlin, 1900.

Haupts, Leo. Die liberale Regierung in Preussen in der Zeit der 'Neuen Ära', *Historische Zeitschrift* 227 (1987), pp. 46–85.

Salewski, Michael. Die Preussische Expedition nach Japan (1859–1861), *Revue Internationale d'Histoire Militaire* 70 (1988), pp. 39–57.

Spiess, Gustav. *Die preussische Expedition nach Ostasien während der Jahre 1860–1862. Reiseskizzen aus Japan, China, Siam und der indischen Inselwelt.* 2 vols. Berlin, Leipzig, 1864.

Stahncke, Holmer. *Die diplomatischen Beziehungen zwischen Deutschland und Japan 1854–1868.* Stuttgart, 1987.

Stoecker, Helmut. *Deutschland und China im 19. Jahrhundert. Das Eindringen des deutschen Kapitalismus.* Berlin (East), 1958.

Suffa-Friedel, Frank. Die preussische Expedition nach Ostasien. Verhandlungen, Verzögerungen und Vertragsabschluß, in Kuo Heng-yü , ed., *Berlin und China. Dreihundert Jahre wechselnde Beziehungen.* vol. 3. Berlin, 1987, pp. 57–60.

Wenk, Klaus. Die Beziehungen zwischen Deutschland und Thailand. In '120 Jahre Deutsch-Thailändische Freundschaft'. Hg. von der Botschaft der Bundesrepublik Deutschland in Bangkok, 1982.

Wolterstorff, Klaus. 'Die Siamesen sind ein sympathisches Volk, rechtschaffen, freiheitsliebend, und ehrenhaft'. Zum Wandel ethnischer Stereotypen in der deutschen Reiseliteratur 1690–1899, in *Festschrift 30 Jahre Deutschabteilung,* Chulalongkorn University, Bangkok, 1987, pp. 84–93.

Wyatt, David K. *Thailand. A Short History.* Ann Arbor, 1982.

Yü Wen-tang. *Die deutsch-chinesischen Beziehungen von 1860–1880.* Bochum, 1981.

FATAL AFFINITIES

THE GERMAN ROLE IN THE MODERNISATION OF JAPAN IN THE EARLY MEIJI PERIOD (1868–1895) AND ITS AFTERMATH

Inherent Predispositions of the Meiji Restoration: The Japanese Readiness to Adopt the Prussian Model

In the years 1872–73, nearly all of the members of the new Japanese government that had been formed after the coup d'état of 1868, under Foreign Minister Iwakura, travelled extensively throughout those Western countries[1] with whom the former shogunate government had concluded the shameful 'unequal treaties'.[2] The mission first visited the United States. Less than twenty years previously, in 1853, by use of military force the United States had violently ended two hundred years of self-imposed Japanese isolation and had, in 1858, forced the central government of the shogun, further weakened by the preceding act of violence, to sign the first trade agreement.[3] A prominent member of the delegation, Vice Minister for Industry Ito, in front of the Americans, who were much admired for their technological progress, left no doubt – expressing himself in perfect English – about the economic aims of the Japanese exploratory mission: 'We come to study your strength, that, by adopting wisely your better ways we may hereafter be stronger ourselves'.[4]

Practically all of the 'founding fathers' of modern Japan belonged to the military caste of the samurai, the traditional leadership élite. Their policy, initiated by the restoration of imperial rule in 1868,[5] aimed at strengthening the country and, in the long run, catching up with the technological and economic lead of the

Translated from the German by Dr Anne M. Martin.

Western powers so that Japan might achieve a position of equal status. Two model states, the United States and Britain, seemed to offer themselves for the Japanese to emulate. Both countries had already proved the strongest interest in East Asia: the United States obviously feeling another strong 'westward' urge, and Britain having previously established its trade and political predominance in China. Moreover, Ito and several other reformers had, as young samurai, received at least part of their education in the Anglo-Saxon countries.[6]

After their visit to the United States, the Japanese travellers went on a trip throughout Europe. Although of course they were primarily interested in Britain, Germany, who had become powerful after the founding of the Reich in 1871 (*Reichsgründung*), and the highly industrialized western areas of Prussia left quite a deep impression on the visitors. In France, the Japanese, with their authoritarian concepts of order, were somewhat disconcerted by the republican ideal of freedom, and in the two Anglo-Saxon countries, the United States and Great Britain, they were taken aback by the capitalist profit-orientated system. However, conditions in Germany clearly made the Japanese guests feel more at home. From the outset the powerful German state based on military victories, the patriotic feeling of national unity that seemed to characterise the relationship between the people and their leaders, and, last but not least, the powerful influence of the state bureaucracy in all fields, including economic issues, held a strong fascination for the traditional Japanese élite who were trying to stabilise their own social position by means of a programme resting on ideological restoration and, at the same time, technological modernisation.

Consequently, the delegation tried to contact the spiritual head of German state constitutionalism Rudolph von Gneist, who was teaching in Berlin, and Lorenz von Stein,[7] who held a chair in Vienna, and, of course, the Reich Chancellor himself, the renowned pragmatist of power politics. On 15 March 1873, Bismarck favoured the Japanese guests with a lesson in practical politics. According to him, one hundred years previously Prussia had been a small powerless state, comparable to Japan's present status, which had been forced to yield to pressure from and the demands of the Great Powers. Its present status of equality was the result of patriotism, as well as of defensive wars to secure its own rights. The Chancellor concluded his lesson by adding,

'Japan is in the same position today, and this is why we ought to keep very friendly relations with each other.'[8]

In fact, the attempt to consolidate the newly unified Japanese state posed two main problems which required solving, one of which was the question of how to combine the separate armed forces formerly recruited from the individual feudal domains (*daimiates*) into one modern army that would carry out the political will of the whole nation. The other problem consisted of the search for a consistent ideology, a new national identity. Anyhow, for the time being the unstable Japanese government, threatened by domestic revolts, did not have a choice. What with the technological and economic predominance of the two Anglo-Saxon countries and their manifestly strong position in the Far East, abruptly changing tack – that is to say turning away from the Western powers and towards the young German Reich instead – was completely out of the question. During the first stage of inner reconstruction, therefore, the Japanese restricted themselves to cautiously admiring and closely watching events in Germany, while at home in Japan the urgently needed experts were British and American.

After their first stay in Germany, Ito and some members of his clan, among them the two military men Yamagata and Katsura, were in favour of the Prussian modernisation concept. But opinions differed among the small leadership group in Tokyo as to what was the best way for them to modernise the country, while at the same time retaining the new influential positions they had gained by the coup d'état. For various reasons this was not easy in Japan. The country's family-orientated social structure had presumably remained more or less unchanged for centuries;[9] moreover, the Japanese isles until very recently had managed to preserve their isolation from the Western world. Much more so than today, in those days Japanese society was vertically structured in small groups, such as the village community, that were easy to control and offered the individual his or her own place and a limited amount of responsibility. Economically, too, the hamlets (*mura*) were independent. It goes without saying that the territorial order during the time of the shogunate regime, when the country was divided into about 260 feudal domains, suited the fragmented Japanese society much better than the newly propagated control state that required a collective political will and, accordingly, the political participation of all Japanese people, if it was to stand up to Western influence. However, except for a few very short periods, there had never existed any overall national and social focus of common interest; unless the country had been superficially united by a shogun appointed commander-in-chief by the Emperor for reasons of defence against foreign enemies, it had constantly been torn apart in civil wars and by the rivalries of the samurai.

The lower samurai of the southern *daimiates* (*han*) who rebelled against the Tokugawa dictatorship seemed to be confronted with the same dilemma. What in 1868 looked like the reinstatement of the Emperor to his political rights, was in fact mere fabrication as due to his god-like position, the monarch was unable to exercise the functions of a ruler. Instead, the throne served the leading oligarchy as a sacrosanct shield, behind which was hidden the dictatorship of only a few samurai, all of whom were members of the three victorious *daimiates:* Choshu, Satsuma, and Hizen. Quite in keeping with traditional social behaviour, even among the small élite of privileged leaders, the particular interests of its members ranked higher than political consensus. For the new government, making a decision involved labouring hard at achieving a compromise agreement.[10] Hence, adopting any foreign model in the course of politically and economically restructuring the country often did not so much result from sensible judgement as from rivalry; what seemed to matter most was gaining an advantage over one's rivals and strengthening one's own power base. The antagonism between the Choshu and Satsuma clans, for instance, that by the end of the Meiji period had manifested itself in antagonism between the army and the navy, prevailed throughout the history of Imperial Japan until its end was enforced in 1945.

Certainly the political culture in Japan, with its social order based on feudal allegiance, hindered the Japanese people as well as its leaders from forming a collective political will and also from concentrating one-sidedly on any one of the foreign models to copy. However, the Meiji restoration itself, and the fact that modernisation measures were taken, did correspond to the common aim of the group of reformers and in the long run made adopting the German model look like the obvious course to take.[11] Neither the political change nor the reforms had originated with the people, but had instead been induced as a consequence of an internal shift of power among the ruling warrior-class. Young, aspiring samurai had taken over in order to fortify the traditional social order against the threats of Western capitalist infiltration. Preserving the old order was in fact the reformers' sole impetus; and all the reforms – administrative, as well as economic and cultural – initiated by the state, that is to say the leading politicians and their dependants, bore defensive anti-Western marks from the beginning.

In order to beat the West at its own game, the Japanese armament and heavy industries were to be partially modernised, and apparent reforms in the fields of administration and culture were to provide a Western façade. The ruling élite's policy of intervention covered all matters of public and social concern. Obviously, the best pattern to follow seemed to be that of Prussian Germany where, too, restoration and political self-assertion had been based on 'iron and blood' instead of the 'majority vote' of the people's representatives – all the more so as the so far politically inexperienced Japanese came to recognise the more and more distinctly emerging particularities that marked the difference between Germany and the other Western countries. The predominance of the military in Germany, the military virtues that manifested themselves in the sense of duty and unquestioning obedience permeating public life and institutions, in Japan corresponded with *bushido*,[12] the samurai's traditional warrior code. As with Germany, where historical and social development had seemed to call for the armed forces' predominance to guarantee the survival of the state and the existing social order, the predominating influence of *bushido* in Japan, too, was the result of the traditional power of the samurai.

Copying from Western models in general – no matter whether Western-democratic or Prussian-authoritarian ones – could, of course, not be done only in theory, but needed the cooperation of trained experts for the transfer of a Western culture which was in any case alien. In the case of Japan, this was realised in an astonishingly short period – within one generation. When Emperor Meiji died in 1912, the aims of the founding fathers had apparently been achieved and Japan seemed the only country to have succeeded in catching up with the 'white' (Western) nations.

Adopting Western, and from 1882 onwards mostly Prussian-German, institutional models had been more or less accomplished in 1890, when the Imperial Rescript on Education[13] advocated a spiritual revival of traditional values. First referred to in that text, the amalgam of Western technological progress and Japanese moral concepts was made the official ideology of the state during the late phase of the Meiji period. Moreover, combining Western technology and Japanese thinking by transferring Western science to Japan required an academic élite, most of whom consisted of foreign experts or those Japanese who had been educated abroad.

During the period between 1868 and the turn of the century, 2,400 foreign experts took part in transforming the Japanese feudal state into a presumably modern one.[14] The largest proportion of these – one-third – were English, the Germans only came fourth – numbering 279 – behind the French (401) and the Americans (351). Due to the suspicion nourished by the Japanese of anything Western, the government, rather than temporarily release gifted young men from the strict social order at home and send them abroad for studies, called in experts from abroad to work or teach in Japan where they would be easier to control. This explains why the number of Japanese studying abroad scarcely exceeded the number of foreign experts in Japan.[15] Even basic intellectual and technological skills, or craftsmanship, were to be taught in Japan at the newly founded institutions (such as Tokyo University, founded in 1876) by foreign teachers and under Japanese supervision so that the Japanese élite-to-be would not be too closely exposed to Western influence. In its ministries too, the Japanese government employed foreigners, thereby laying the foundations of Western-orientated modernisation. Most of them were practicians, engineers, skilled workers or foremen, or else agrarian and administrative experts; and most of them came from England – the pioneer country of industrial revolution. Experts in bureaucracy – another important contingent – came mostly from France, the classic example of centralised bureaucracy; whereas teachers and educational experts for the most part came from free America.

However, listing numbers and respective fields of activity does not answer the question of whether all the foreigners employed by the Japanese were merely supposed to do their everyday work or whether they were given key positions from which they could have some real influence on modernising Japan according to their own respective national backgrounds. With more than 86 percent (539 out of 623) of those postgraduates who received a state scholarship to continue their academic education abroad being sent to Germany,[16] one may justly conclude that as a rule the Japanese scholars who brought to Japan Western research and Western science had completed their education in Germany. During the Meiji period a total of 12,235 students graduated from Tokyo University.[17] They had been taught either by foreign, mostly German, professors or by their Japanese colleagues who had absorbed Western knowledge in Germany.

At this time the experts themselves differed widely in their assessments of the lasting impression that the practical or scholarly pioneers of modernisation might or might not have left on Japan. While the highly influential American educator Griffis saw himself as a 'helper and a servant',[18] the leading British scholar in Japanese linguistics, Basil Chamberlain,[19] considered the foreign experts to be the 'creators of modern Japan'. And Erwin Baelz, probably the most famous German medical doctor in Japan, after having spent twenty-five years successfully establishing Western medicine in Japan, resignedly concluded that he had been mistaken for a 'scientific fruit pedlar' by the Japanese.[20] Indeed, in their hearts the Japanese themselves resented most of the foreigners and at times looked upon them as 'live machines'[21] to be used and then disposed of. The 'hired foreigners' (*oyatoi gaiko kujin*), as the pejorative term labelled them, were considered a necessary evil for the country to meet the Western challenge, but the sooner one could get rid of them, the better.

On the dangerous assumption of a genuine affinity between Japan and Prussian Germany, Japan preferred to 'hire' her foreigners from the Reich. A comparatively small group of German experts were offered key positions in government institutions and chairs at the newly founded First Imperial University in Tokyo. This, combined with the Japanese academic élite's postgraduate studies in Germany, left a deep impression on the Tenno's empire that, to a certain extent, can still be felt today. During the early days of the Meiji period a symbiosis between Germany and Japan had begun that was not automatically heading for but – as will be shown – did prepare the ground for the two countries' alliance during the Second World War. Under the pressure of the World Economic Crisis both their kindred social orders turned into authoritarian regimes that eventually joined in the Tripartite Pact.

Early Contacts (1862–1881):
Hidden Admiration Versus Open Superiority

Having been forcibly opened in 1854 for the first time to the Western world by the Americans, Japan caught the eye of Prussian politicians.[22] The Ministry of Commerce spotted its chance to provide a new market in the Far East for the expanding Prussian industry, thereby, at a time of reactionary politics, obliging at least the liberal trade-orientated bourgeoisie. The Foreign Ministry saw an opportunity to hoist the Prussian flag in East Asia and in this way to state its claim to equality among the Great Powers. In addition, worldwide political ambitions might add momentum to Prussia's domestic endeavours to play the leading part in solving the German question. However, these far-reaching ambitions were thwarted by lack of means. An expedition of several warships to East Asia[23] would have been much too expensive for one thing, and would also have been far beyond the capacity of the small Prussian navy that was at best suited to guard the coastal waters of the Baltic Sea.

During these early days of Prussian Far Eastern policy, some fundamental motives manifested themselves that were to characterise the German attitude towards Japan and China up to and during the Second World War. First of all, the German East Asia policy was based on power politics, which meant that domestic issues also had to be taken into account. Trade policy ranked only second. From the military point of view, despite the stationing of warships in Chinese ports from 1868 onwards, Prussia's and later on the German Reich's influence in East Asia remained negligible compared to that of the other Great Powers. Germany never shared the British procedure of world politics – let the flag follow trade – nor even its reversed version. All of those who had hoped for a considerable increase in export trade with East Asia were disappointed: German trade with the Far East never rose above 2 to 3 percent of the total export volume.[24] Only in China, and never in Japan, did commercial endeavours gain some ground shortly before the outbreak of the First World War and again towards the end of the 1930s; and in both cases they were thwarted by the respective German government's preoccupation with power politics.

Eventually, between 1860 and 1862, during the period of the liberal 'New Era' Prussia sent an expedition to the Far East. Its practical results, however, in no way corresponded to the publicity and the high expectations that the eastbound voyage evoked.[25] The shogunate government flatly refused to acknowledge that Prussia, as the leading power among the German Customs Union, was entitled to sign a treaty in the name of all the other member states. The treaty was eventually signed only with the diplomatic support of the Western powers,[26] and, like the contract with China achieved somewhat later, remained more or less as a declaration on paper. In the few Japanese ports open to foreigners, German merchants were a negligible minority,[27] and Prussian ships rarely found their way to East Asia.[28] What was more, the new Prussian Prime Minister, Bismarck, who was preoccupied with solving the problem of national unity, did not hold with, and put a damper on, any liberal world-political ambitions. Prussia's first diplomatic representative, Max von Brandt, who because of his low rank – he was only a consul – was not properly respected by either the Japanese or the other diplomats and consequently felt an urge to assert himself, was given strict orders from Berlin to always coordinate his policy with the other representatives of the treaty powers.[29]

Consul Brandt, at his forgotten outpost, thereupon took to outlining highly promising colonial projects with which to assert his own influence on the then topical issue of whether Germany was to have colonies of her own. Since the Prussian expedition, German naval circles had secretly favoured acquiring Formosa as a colony. Brandt, who knew about this, tried to shift the German interest away from the subtropical island and towards the northern Japanese isle of Hokkaido. In two voluminous memoranda[30] he tried to convince Bismarck and the admiralty staff of the natural advantages of Hokkaido and outlined plans for taking possession of the Japanese island by sending a 5,000 man landing force together with between six and eight gunboats. With typical early imperialist thinking, Brandt justified his plans for annexing Japanese territory by labelling the Japanese 'culturally incapable' and unable to cultivate the island by themselves. When the government in Berlin did not respond to these theoretical reflections,[31] Brandt took action on his own and tried to create a *fait accompli*.

During the turmoil of the civil war, the Prussian representative supported the Japanese opposition groups whom he supplied with arms.[32] This did not prevent Brandt, after the victory of the South, from engaging in talks with one of the defeated *daimyos* (feudal lords) from the North about selling their land to the Prussian Crown.[33] In order to prove that Hokkaido was perfectly suitable for German settlement, with the help of the Prussian Honourary Consul in Hokkaido a 100-hectare area had been turned into an experimental estate – 'Augustenfelde'[34] – and had been taken on a 99-year lease. Bismarck, however, reminded the consul that the treaty powers, including Prussia, had declared their neutrality[35] in the civil war. The Prussian navy was not altogether opposed to the project, but considered the present time as inappropriate. However, in case the Japanese Empire collapsed the navy would be there to take its share.[36] Although his Hokkaido project had been turned down, far from giving up, Brandt, together with the geographer von Richthofen and the navy, pursued his colonial aims on a smaller level.[37] He now looked for any islands which would be suitable for a naval base and which were outside of the new Japanese government's sphere of influence. Yet, Bismarck did not hold with these plans either. He considered the German navy too weak to 'stand its ground if in case of war it were to be seriously attacked by the enemy's probably superior armed forces'.[38] The hazardous imperialist policy of the first German diplomat in Japan was thwarted by the unexpected ending of the civil war and by Bismarck's fundamental unwillingness to engage in colonial adventures.

After the German military victory over France and the proclamation of the German Reich, almost exactly three years after the Japanese Emperor's reinstatement, the Japanese oligarchs, especially those in charge of the military, became more and more interested in Prussia's rise to power. Yamagata,[39] the military reformer of the Choshu *han* which was among the victors in the civil war, had gone on a long military inspection trip to Europe just before the outbreak of the war between Germany and France. On returning home he advocated the Prussian military system in both his reports to the Emperor and to the Privy Council.[40] But the majority of Japanese politicians preferred to stick to the French model[41] introduced in the last years of the shogunate. Adopting German military institutions obviously posed too many problems, primarily a deficient knowledge of German. Consequently, Yamagata, then Vice Minister of War, made sure that among the first Japanese scholars to leave for Berlin there were two military students: one of them, Sato Susumo, was later to become general medical officer of the Japanese army, the other, Katsura Taro, was to become Minister of War and, later, for several terms even held the office of Prime Minister.[42]

After military and medical knowledge, the first Japanese students were interested in German law and in German national economics with its stress on social reforms (*Kathedersozialismus*). The first was studied by Aoki Shuzo, who was later appointed as the first Japanese diplomatic envoy to Germany,[43] and the latter by the future Japanese Minister of Agriculture, Hirata Tosuke, who as early as 1875 was the first Japanese person to receive a German doctorate.[44] Berlin University, next to Heidelberg and Halle, became the Japanese students' most frequented school, and between 1870 and 1905 a total of 448 Japanese students were enrolled; until 1881 there had been only forty. A large number, about 30 percent, of the Japanese students at Berlin University read law and some 42 percent were students of medicine. The rest, in more or less equal proportions, read philosophy (which then included pedagogy), science, and economics or agriculture.[45]

As the Japanese Ministry of Education awarded most of its grants for studies in Germany and in particular at Berlin University, the Friedrich-Wilhelm-University, which was then ranked highest among all German universities, had a formative influence on the education of the future academic, military, and political élite of Japan. With the first Japanese students enrolling at Berlin, the subjects of medicine, law, economics, philosophy, and pedagogy, as well as the military subjects taught at the War Academy, played a significant part in imprinting the German influence on the ideological, as well as political and practical, development of modern Japan. At Japanese universities during the Meiji era, these subjects also bore the marks of German influence; they were taught either by German professors or by Japanese academic teachers who had been educated in Germany. The first German scientists to be recruited as teachers by the German diplomatic representative in Japan were two medical officers of the Prussian military. The two of them laid the foundations of Western medical training according to the German system, even including German and Latin as compulsory foreign languages.[46]

Through the 'best school in the country' (at least this is what the German representative Brandt reported to Berlin[47]), interest in German science had generally been increased among the Japanese as had their readiness to learn German.[48] At the request of the Japanese government a preparatory school was added to the medical academy, where German teachers taught German, Latin, and mathematics. For the medical academy, too, the Japanese authorities recruited more civilian medical doctors from Germany. Apparently, tensions between these civilians and the two military doctors arose so frequently that eventually, much to the astonishment of the Japanese in the medical corps, Müller and the civilian lecturer Wernick fought a duel.[49] The two military directors of the academy also confronted their Japanese hosts with their relentless demands for absolute authority, turning a deaf ear to the Japanese proposal to appoint a Japanese person to be the nominal head of the academy without any infringement on its German teaching system. Instead, insisting on their superior status, both Prussian medical officers resigned at once[50] and until their recently renewed contracts expired restricted themselves to their duties as private physicians to the imperial family. Astonishingly enough, their stubbornness did not impair the reputation of German medicine and science in general; the report[51] of the two founding fathers of modern medicine in Japan, on their establishment of the academy and its eight-year curriculum, reads like a list of stupendous success. As early as 1877, a total of 951 students attended Tokyo Medical Academy, 309 of whom had enrolled at its German department including the preparatory school.[52] Medicine and science obviously did serve, as the two medical officers put it, *'dem Deutschthume in Japan'*, and it is through medical science, as well as the military, that Germany started to influence the modernisation of Japan.

Cultural exchange between Germany and Japan only developed fully during the 1880s; its gradual beginnings during the 1870s were as yet overshadowed by deeply rooted mutual distrust and petty quarrelling over minor political issues. General ignorance about the other country prevailed even among top government officials, and some particularly ignorant German diplomatic reports gave rise to more prejudice.[53] Both the small number of career diplomats accredited to Japan as well as the German merchant community in Japan, after the unification of the German Reich, indulged in feelings of national grandeur and failed to acknowledge, let alone understand, the Japanese way of life. To the Germans Japan was a developing country, and the Japanese were considered at best eager and hardworking pupils. Most of the German interest in Japanese culture was limited to collecting antiques at random; scarcely anybody took the trouble to study Japanese language and literature. When, in 1871, the German Empire's legation was established in Japan, only one German resident spoke Japanese – and he was the official interpreter of the German legation. Even thirty years later only a few dozen Germans living in Japan spoke Japanese,[54] although from 1887 on the Department of Oriental Studies at Berlin University offered language classes so that Japanese could also be studied in Germany.

In Japan, during the period of hectic experimentation with Western models, the court nobles saw themselves as the custodians of Japanese tradition and occasionally tried to counterbalance those activities of the government that seemed to them unduly possessed with the idea of modernisation. As to Germany, the Berlin government certainly was aware of, but did not respond to, either the cautiously dropped Japanese hints at possible closer relations between the two countries or the admiration frequently expressed by the Japanese for the venerable old German Emperor. When granted his first private audience with the twenty-year-old Japanese Tenno, the German representative Max von Brandt, at the request of the Japanese Foreign Ministry, delivered to the young ruler a lengthy lecture on the duties of a monarch. The Tenno was even said to have been studying German for months and to have expressed his wish for a native German teacher.[55] However, to judge by the German diplomatic correspondence, His Majesty's concubines[56] obviously aroused more interest on the part of the Germans than did the chances of politically influencing the Japanese court. Bismarck himself refused to acknowledge formal equality of the two imperial families and preferred not to apply the title 'Their Majesties' to the Japanese Emperor and his Consort.[57]

When in 1875 the number of experts working in Japan had reached its peak at a total of 476, a report by the German legation stressed the point that 'the German influence in Japan is less important than is generally believed in Germany'.[58] The impact of the German Reich, the report went on to explain, ranked way behind that of the other Western powers, exceeding only the Russians. Based on official Japanese data, the figures in the report revealed that Max von Brandt, who in the meantime had been transferred to Peking,[59] with his dislike of anything Japanese, had never been able nor even willing to foster the modernisation of Japan with the help of German experts. Of the total of thirty Germans employed by the Japanese government, sixteen worked with the Ministry of Education, five with the Ministry of Public Works, three with the Imperial Household Ministry, and another three with the Ministry for the Development of Hokkaido. One expert[60] was employed by the Ministry of Finance, and two geographers worked in the provinces as surveyors.[61] Two-thirds, that is, 276 people, of the total number of experts were English, who, as the report complained, occupied important positions in nearly all government sections. The Ministries of War, Justice, and Education were under the control of the ninety-four French advisors. And the posts held by the Americans, however small in number, were all key positions such as well-paid advisors to the Foreign Office. The above-mentioned German report finally concluded that Japan was trying to shake off patronizing interference from abroad and to reduce the number of foreign experts. Apparently, Germany had missed her chance of taking part in the experiment of modernising Japan, an experiment that had brought the Japanese state to the verge of bankruptcy.[62] The comparatively meagre results after ten years of attempted reforms had quite a sobering effect on Western, as well as Japanese expectations.

What was lacking in Japan was an ideologically consistent reform programme. The eclectic system of borrowing from scattered sources and adopting various models at the same time – such as the attempt at restructuring the education system according to the French model – had resulted in a distortion of Japanese identity and had considerably disconcerted the public. Equally, the oligarchy's original concept of focusing the nation on the Tenno had been counteracted by too many Western reforms and had not been accepted by the population. Reestablishing the Shinto cult, according to a German diplomatic report,[63] had also failed, as had the appeals, distributed on leaflets, to the population by itinerant priests to loyally obey the newly reinstated monarch. The Satsuma Rebellion,[64] a vehement protest of former reformers against a modernisation that seemed to them rash and haphazard, seriously endangered the new central government and, what is more, laid bare the many shortcomings of the reforms especially in the military sector. Now that public respect for the Emperor had sunk to its lowest, the government, by now consisting almost entirely of members of the Choshu-clan, could no longer hide behind the imperial screen. As the new German diplomatic envoy von Eisendecher put it in a rather matter-of-fact report, 'there is not really any trace of affection, let alone devotion, for the Emperor or the Imperial Family'.[65]

The army eventually brought about a decisive turn in Japanese domestic politics by its attempt at coordinating the reforms and, at the same time, raising public esteem for the imperial family. Compulsory military service had existed since the end of 1872,[66] but could not be put into effect since the army, numbering 35,000 men in a time of peace,[67] had no room for so many more conscripts. Moreover, the troops consisting of the former *daimyos'* fighting squads had not yet been combined into one central and effective armed force; their military inefficiency had become obvious in the course of the Satsuma Rebellion. Radical military reform thus proved a vital issue to the state, in order to fend off domestic and foreign enemies.

Yamagata, who by now had risen to the post of Army Minister, felt that the time had come for him to realise his long-cherished plan of substituting the German system of military training for the French one that had been in use so far and which emphasised passive obedience and merely theoretical knowledge.[68] Also, Military Attaché Katsura, on his return from Berlin, proposed that the Supreme Command of the armed forces henceforth be separated from the jurisdiction of the War Ministry, a proposition that was carried out on the spot.[69] Yamagata at once (at the end of 1878) took over the position of Army Chief of Staff[70] and until his death in 1922 remained the most powerful military man in Japan. Reorganising the military leadership after the Prussian model meant giving up completely the French system that had provided control over the military by the civilian War Ministry. From now on civilian and military leadership were separated from each other, which meant that as in Prussia, in Japan too the military could now develop into a state within the state and exercise greater influence on politics in general.

Now that relations between the two countries had become closer, Japanese government circles apparently expected the Germans to help with the revision of the unequal treaties.[71] It was clear that the fetters binding Japanese sovereignty could only be broken with the help of Western law experts. Such help could scarcely be expected from England and France, that is to say, those countries whose own strong mercantile interests were at stake and would be threatened if the unequal treaties favouring Western trade were to be abolished. Germany, on the other hand, who in 1877 had no more than seventeen trading posts in Japan[72], obviously did not have much to lose. Therefore, through the mediation of the Japanese legation in Berlin, in October 1878 Hermann Roesler, one of the best-known German experts in administrative law and a strong supporter of social welfare, was offered a six-year contract as legal advisor to the Japanese Foreign Ministry in Tokyo.[73] There, Germany's good reputation had previously been established by highly qualified experts such as Mayet, a specialist in finances, Naumann, a geologist, and Baelz, the famous German medical doctor.[74]

When the sixteen-year-old Prince Heinrich of Prussia visited Japan in 1879–80,[75] the newly established friendly relations between the two countries were reinforced by the Japanese court's so far unheard-of interest in their Imperial German guest. A few embarrassing incidents during a hunting party, caused by the arrogance and inexperience of His Highness the German Emperor's grandson and the overzealousness of Japanese authorities, were smoothed over with the help of the Germanophile Japanese legate on home leave – although Bismarck chose to speak of the Japanese rural population as of a bunch of semisavages with murderous instincts.[76] After the disharmony had eventually been settled for good by the Tenno entertaining the German guest of honour at a private lunch,[77] the Japanese government dared to officially express its wish for German support.

Foreign Minister Inoue and Vice-President of the Privy Council Iwakura, on behalf of the whole Cabinet, professed the intention to 'seek close ties with the German Reich and to beg His Majesty the Emperor Wilhelm's government for its special friendship and for its support of Japan in her present difficult period of development'.[78] The reason given by the two spokesmen for the Japanese change of orientation towards Germany was that the American influence in Japan had been of little use and had in fact only stirred untoward political agitation against the government among the press. Bismarck, who had been against upgrading the German ministerial residence and turning it into a legation[79] – certainly the obvious thing to do – again reacted in a rather reserved way. In any case, at the top of the Japanese government the decision had apparently not been as unanimous as Inoue and Iwakura had tried to make the German diplomats believe. Opinions differed too widely on the issues of adopting an alien constitution and taking a new loan abroad.[80] When eventually the government did ask for a loan (their third foreign loan) in Berlin, the Germans refused it for formal reasons.[81] Obviously, Japan was not considered creditworthy, notwithstanding the fact that reorganising the state according to the Prussian model depended on financial support from the West. As things were, Berlin sat back to wait for the outcome of the heated debates among the Japanese on their country's future form of government.

In fact, with the military's special position established in the meantime, the internal constitutional debate had practically no choice but to decide in favour of the Prussian model. Any liberal constitution where the government and the budget would be controlled by parliament was vehemently rejected by most members of the government, especially by Ito and Iwakura. And Okuma Shigenobu,[82] Minister of Finance and the strongest advocate of a parliamentary system like the British one, was forced to resign from office on 12 October 1881 by the conservative guardians of the unique authoritarian Japanese state. On the same day, the government issued an 'Imperial Decree Promising the Establishment of a Parliament'. Doubtlessly the constitution announced for 1889 could only be based on the German model. Even though working it out was yet to pose many difficulties for Ito and his German legal advisor Roesler, the final decision was taken in 1881; Japan would remain an authoritarian state, but one with a constitutional façade.

Restructuring Public Life and Institutions after the Prussian Model: the Foundation of the Authoritarian State

The German preponderance in the modernisation of Japan reached its peak during the decade between 1882 and 1890. It began with the allegedly spontaneous foundation of a 'Society for the Promotion of German Science'[83] in Tokyo in January 1882; it was completed, in the administrative sector, with the promulgation of the Japanese constitution on 11 February 1889, and, in the ideological sector, with the 'Imperial Rescript on Education' of 30 October 1890. The era of reforms, of experimenting with Western models, was, towards the end, distinctly marked by the Japanese preference for Prussian-German solutions and consequently ended with the restoration of the imperial system together with the traditional social order. Most of the German law experts adhered to the school of conservative state constitutionalism and, like the so-called 'academic socialists', advocated a social monarchy. Therefore, they helped to stabilise a regime[84] that served the interests of a small traditional élite who were out to defend their own privileges and did not feel in the least responsible for the pauperised masses of the rural population groaning under the weight of heavy taxes.[85] To this oligarchy and their supporters, the large estate owners and big industrialists (*zaibatsu*),[86] the term 'reform' meant nothing but restoration by which they could exclude the people from political participation. The 'German measles'[87] as the British, deprived of their former influence, used to call the Japanese blind adoption of anything German, was indeed a highly contagious disease and not a harmless one either.

German experts helped to establish an authoritarian system and to provide it with an ideological superstructure. In 1895, for reasons of power politics, their dominant position came to an end, when relations between Germany and Japan became remarkably cooler because Germany had joined the Triple Alliance and had officially advised Japan to retreat from the Asian continent.[88] Their contracts expiring, most German experts went back to Germany towards the end of the Meiji period, leaving to the Japanese a politically and spiritually unfamiliar legacy.

The 'Society for the Promotion of German Science' (1882) consisted almost wholly of the small group of former students in Germany, some of whom now held leading government positions. These men of the first hour, such as Katsura, Sato, and Hirata,[89] now found themselves aligned with Imperial Prince Kitashirakawa. The Prince, who had been exiled against his will in Berlin for seven years, studying military science,[90] now seemed to be the obvious person to preside over the Society. According to the statutes of the Society, full membership required a good command of German. The main aims were to found schools in Japan after the German model and to translate, and acquaint the Japanese public with, German science and research. Most important was the fact that all of the government had joined the Society as honourary members. By Japanese standards, this was meant to be a deep enough bow to the Germans. Consequently, it was in the field of politics rather than culture that the newly founded Society had its direct impact. Even though from now on the number of students studying in Germany increased[91] and two years later (1884) the Society founded its own school in Tokyo,[92] thoroughly spreading the German language and culture among the Japanese took a much longer time. Certainly, the translations of Schiller's drama on political liberty 'William Tell' (*'Wilhelm Tell'*) and Goethe's epic on shrewdness, 'Reinecke the Fox' (*'Reineke Fuchs'*)[93] fitted in better with the feeling of a new era about to dawn in Japan than did scholarly works or scientific theory, for the reception of which Japanese intellectuals were not yet ready, as so far they had mostly been influenced by English or French culture.

Much more important was the political use that could be made of the gathering of all the Japanese experts on Germany. Their combined efforts were needed in order to tackle the difficult task of drafting the future constitution of the country, which was the most far-reaching piece of reform and had already been announced by the Tenno. The government was well aware that adopting the Prussian constitutional model would imply simultaneously coordinating, that is to say restructuring, all government institutions, especially the Ministries of Justice and Education. Therefore, the head of the 'German party', Ito,[94] only a few days after the Society had been founded, inquired of the German legation whether he himself would be welcome in Berlin in order to find out about German parliamentary institutions and the German educational system. The Japanese government, he went on to explain, had in the meantime come to the conclusion that German institutions were the most suitable for the Japanese. Quite frankly, the Japanese Foreign Minister also revealed the underlying political purpose of the reorientation towards Germany; like most of his colleagues he himself felt that German culture and education might help to 'spread loyalty and true patriotism among the Japanese and to counterbalance the all too many ultraliberalist tendencies'. In his opinion, not much good had come from Japan's former leaning on the United States, nor at present could any positive influence be expected from France. Likewise, conditions in England and Ireland, he felt, did not exactly impose themselves as an ideal model.[95]

The option was clear; in the young and aspiring German Empire the Japanese saw the model of an orderly and politically stabile society, of patriotism and, of course, the people's loyalty towards their monarch. As the head of the delegation of nine people, in 1882 Ito travelled to central Europe.[96] During his three-month stay in Berlin he attended lectures given by the renowned Professor for State Law Rudolf von Gneist and talked to several Prussian politicians. Von Gneist repeatedly expressed serious doubts about whether adopting the German constitution was advisable considering the fundamental differences between German and Japanese history and mentality. A constitution, he argued from his philosophical background of German idealism, did not simply consist of a number of regulations but rather was the living expression of a country's spirit. At the same time Gneist warned his guest not to grant parliament control over the budget, especially the military one. Emperor William I personally hinted at this sore point in the Prussian-German constitution which, in the early days of his reign, had brought about the constitutional conflict of 1862, and urgently advised the Japanese statesman to obviate such a conflict from the start by inserting the appropriate paragraphs into the constitution.[97] Indeed, from the very first drafts of the Japanese constitution article 67 did severely restrict the budgetary rights of the parliament and article 71 fixed Bismarck's so-called 'gap-theory' (*Lückentheorie*) as a basic constitutional rule.[98] Next, in Vienna Ito familiarised himself with Lorenz von Stein's ideas of a social monarchy and, in Berlin again, consulted Albert Mosse on the Prussian system of local self-government.[99] In Paris, on his way home, he met the leading Japanese expert on education, Mori Arinori,[100] with whom he discussed questions of reforming the Japanese school and general education systems after Prussian patterns. On returning to Japan Ito took over the Imperial Household Ministry. Holding the most important office at the imperial court, together with his own strong position among the Choshu Clan which dominated the government, enabled Ito, who viewed himself as 'the Japanese Hardenberg',[101] to realise the core of all reforms – the constitution – in the face of objections from both conservative, traditionalist court circles and the liberal opposition.

In 1884, the German expert in constitutional law, Roesler, who had already been working for the government and whose contract was now renewed for another six years, was assigned the position of personal adviser to Ito in matters concerning the constitution. His expert opinion was requested in a total of 160 cases. In addition, he was the only foreigner to be personally invited to take part in the discussions concerning the constitution among members of the government. Roesler, however, in contrast to Ito, was against embodying the Tenno's descent from the gods into the constitution. Instead, he preferred to limit the Emperor's prerogatives, for instance, his supreme command of the military, and clearly leave the rights of taxation and legislation with the parliament.[102] Had Roesler's ideas prevailed, the Japanese constitution would have been more democratic and more modern than its German model, and moreover, would not have left any room for new myths like the cult of the Emperor. However, Ito, as he himself admitted, needed the Tenno ideology as a kind of religious substitute in order to root in Japan a state religion comparable to the Christian religion in Western countries.[103] From the beginning the Meiji constitution thus contained an incongruity in itself, between its Western-looking legal statutes and their inherent traditional Japanese contents.

The German adviser also played a decisive part in formulating the laws concerning the houses of parliament and in creating the Privy Council that was supposed to control the government and the lower house of parliament.[104] Upon his recommendation Albert Mosse, one of the leading experts on legislation concerning local self-government,[105] was called to Japan and contributed to formulating the legal framework of the constitution.

Following the ideas of the German reformer Freiherr vom Stein, whose biography the Japanese government had had translated,[106] Chief of Staff Yamagata in particular stressed rural self-administration as an essential prerequisite for his concept of compulsory military service. The villages, the traditional folkish strongholds, were to be mobilised against the cities that were expanding fast during the Meiji period and obviously carried the seeds of all modern evils. Consequently, their self-administration was restricted, while the village was upgraded as the real nucleus of the Japanese community.[107] Before the constitution had even been promulgated the military deliberately fostered an antimodernist agrarian ideology in order to hinder the parliamentary system from developing in too liberal a fashion.

Yamagata, who had in the meantime become Minister of the Interior, for the purpose of securing the power of the state had the police force restructured according to Prussian patterns. In Tokyo, the German police officer Hoehn trained a special unit of Japanese policemen who from then on were considered to be the guarantors of law and order in the capital. Together with another Prussian court official, Hoehn also completely reorganised and enlarged the Japanese prison system[108] in order to bring it up to Western standards. What with the planned revision of the unequal treaties and the abolition of consular jurisdiction, the former dungeons needed modernising to accommodate Western convicts. Furthermore, the as yet extremely small number of criminals was expected to increase because of political delinquents. Eventually, after engaging a Prussian courtier to teach German etiquette to the Japanese Imperial Court all the necessary preparations seemed to have been made.[109]

On the mythological 'Foundation Day of the Empire' (11 February) the Tenno, by now officially a god, in a ceremony borrowed from the Prussian court ceremonial proclaimed the constitution.

The Western façade seemed to hold. However, despite all the security measures taken, the opening of the Diet was accompanied by protests from the population in the capital.[110] The German envoy in his report to Berlin spoke of the negative effects constitutionalism obviously had and expressed his hope that it would be abolished in the near future.[111] On which the young Emperor in Berlin, William II in his own nonchalant way commented: 'Those silly asses in Japan ... [abolishing the constitution B.M.] ... would be by far the most reasonable thing and will hopefully be done pretty soon, too'.[112] Both the German and the Japanese courts and leading government circles, with their military outlook, shared the same reservations against parliamentarianism and granting more civil rights to their subjects. Only a few weeks after its formal opening, the impressive building of the Diet burnt down. It had been designed in the pompous Wilhelmian style by a group of architects from Berlin and because of the swampy ground and lack of time had been built of wood.[113] What caused the fire in 1891 was never fully explained – yet, like the fire that later destroyed the Berlin Reichstag building in 1933, it might in a way be taken as a symbol of the instability of parliamentarianism, that in both countries rather resembled a straw fire.

Unlimited expansion and inner strengthening of the armed forces were guaranteed by the opportunities that the new constitution offered. What stood in the way of the swift introduction of Prussian military norms was the stubborn resistance of the French military advisers who had been employed in Japan since the end of the shogunate. The only foreign language high-ranking officers usually spoke was French, parade-ground drill followed French regulations, and officers were trained at schools modelled directly on the French military academy at St Cyr.[114] Moreover, with the lack of cadres the troops were still considered to be deficient in discipline[115] and would have been destabilised by too radical a change, their fighting strength further reduced. Therefore, the Choshu military leaders aimed at a long term compromise: the French, whose teaching methods based on passive reception were well suited to the Japanese way of learning, should remain with the troops as instructors of the ranks, but were to apply Prussian field regulations. In this way, the masses of recruits and NCOs were trained to serve as passively obedient soldiers, whereas the higher-ranking officers commanding the troops were supposed to act on the Prussian principle of individual decision and responsibility.

The indoctrination of the military with traditional values, an amalgam of Confucian virtues and the Japanese fighting code (*bushido*), was an essential prerequisite for turning the army into the 'school of the nation' and the guardian of national entity which centred upon the Tenno. An imperial ordinance for soldiers and marines, drawn up by Yamagata and proclaimed by the Emperor on 2 January 1882, contained all the basic elements of the Tenno ideology for the first time.[116] The spiritual foundations of the future policy had now been laid. Now, Minister of War Oyama together with a delegation of fifteen high-ranking military officers was sent to Europe.[117] Following orders from the government, the mission was to engage a prominent Prussian officer of the general staff who would be able to train Japanese generals in commanding large military units. The Japanese army, ideologically brought into line and under strict military discipline, was to be prepared for the great war that, due to the permanent tensions over the Ryukyu Isles and over Korea, was conceivable only against China.

Complying with Japanese wishes in Berlin, the chief of the Prussian general staff Moltke senior, ordered Major Jacob Meckel, one of the most promising younger officers of the general staff, to move to the Tokyo war academy. Although from the spring of 1885 onwards, Meckel stayed in Japan for only three years, it was probably he, of all the foreign experts, who left the deepest and longest-lasting impression on the modernisation of Japan. Personally introduced into his office by the Tenno himself, Meckel, who was able to draw upon his personal experiences from the Prussian campaigns against Austria (1866) and France (1871), trained about sixty of the highest-ranking officers in tactics, strategy, and the daily routine work of the general staff. Laying great stress on the historical background of all military sciences, he frequently gave lectures on Prussian military history. Unlike the French instructors, Meckel not only taught theoretical knowledge, but had his students practice their skills in manoeuvres that he himself supervised.[118] The Japanese army's future victories on the battlefields of Korea (1895) and Manchuria (1905) were almost certainly due to Meckel's meticulous Prussian thoroughness.

When in 1886 Katsura, a pro-German military man of the first hour who had been educated in Berlin and spoke German fluently, took over the office of Vice Minister of War, Meckel in addition to his teaching was called upon to help with the general reorganisation of the military. First, the change became evident in the soldiers' outfits; their uniforms, formerly cut in the French style, now perfectly resembled the Prussian ones.[119] For the most part Meckel's memoranda served the purpose of tightening and centralising the administration of the army, thus providing a higher degree of mobility. Upon his suggestions the army bases were reorganised, logistics and military medical service were brought up to date, and the drafting of conscripts, which had so far been handled in a rather arbitrary way, was also reorganised.[120] Moreover, Meckel wrote a few fundamental memoranda on national defence[121] suggesting amongst other things the fortification of the coastlines, which offered the German armament trust Krupp the welcome opportunity to enter the Japanese market on a large scale.[122] Refusing to renew his contract for a second time, Meckel called in another German officer who succeeded him at the war academy and ensured that teaching continued according to the rules Meckel had established.

By dividing the command of the army into three departments of equal status – the Ministry of War, the Chief of the General Staff, and the General Inspection – Meckel left a heritage that turned out to weigh heavily upon Japan. Dividing superintendences into the three sectors of administration, troop command, and training could only make sense if all three were controlled by a central power, for instance, the Emperor as Supreme Commander, together with the military cabinet. As the Tenno's god-like position left no room for him to actually interfere as Supreme Commander, this Prussian army structure further worsened the existing rivalry between different people and their respective factions. Not only was cooperation inconceivable between the army and the navy, which were linked to two different former *han* but even within the army itself rivalries and particular interests prevailed.

When blindly adopting Prussian military structures, Meckel and Katsura had failed to take into account the fundamental dichotomy between the Japanese social structure and the new constitutional façade. However, the modern Japanese army remained Meckel's personal achievement. Upon his return to Germany, the German legation reported to Berlin that Meckel had been by far the most successful of all Germans working in Japan.[124] This evaluation was later confirmed by further reports by the legation on several imperial manoeuvres, which might just as well have been held in Germany. The Japanese officers trained by Meckel regarded their former teacher (*sensei*) as the real victor in their battles against the Chinese, and ten years later against the Russians. Yet, however successful from the strategic point of view, Meckel's tactics of recklessly deploying infantry units in heavy assaults for the purpose of offensive strategy did result in the horrendous number of Japanese casualties in the battle of Mukden in 1905.[125] Likewise, during the First World War (1914–18) the German infantry tactics, which were still influenced by Meckel's theories, were largely responsible for the heavy losses in the trenches of Flanders (for instance at Langemarck). In Japan, this way of sacrificing the infantry fitted in with the traditional fighting code of the samurai that was to manifest itself, almost sixty years after Meckel had laid down his theories, in the Pacific War; facing death by fighting to the last ditch was considered much more honourable than facing captivity by shamefully yielding to the enemy and capitulating in time.

Civilian schools badly lagged behind the military 'school of the nation'. As late as in the 1890s army recruits had first to be taught elementary skills[126] before they could be trained on the weaponry. Like the military, the civilian school system had, in all respects, also followed the French model after the respective laws had been passed in 1872.[127] These laws provided eight school districts to be equally structured in an educational pyramid from elementary schools at the bottom to one university at the top (the latter never being realised). Overloaded with Western learning and hampered by rigid centralisation, the experiment failed after eight years. The confused authorities now reversed their course, and there and then in 1879 introduced the American school system. Yet, to the Japanese teachers and their pupils alike the new liberty proved even more difficult to deal with than the former French curricula,[128] so that at the same time that the decision was taken to adopt Prussian constitutionalism the second experiment in public education was cancelled. It is probable that the general Japanese disappointment with the Americans stemmed from the failed school reform. From now on, Prussia was the only model to be emulated.

In March 1882, Ito, the creator of the Japanese constitution, and Mori Arinori, who was in charge of public education, met in Paris and decided to introduce the Prussian dual school system.[129] From now on Japanese officials, supported by German experts in the Ministry of Education, carefully studied German pedagogical texts. The writings of Johann Heinrich Pestalozzi (1746–1827) with their stress on the community and the family, were readily received in Japan, as were the theories of Friedrich Froebel (1782–1852) on child pedagogy that easily corresponded with the Japanese principles of education. Most of all, however, the Japanese were interested in the German philosopher and pedagogue Johann Friedrich Herbart (1776–1841); instilling moral virtues into the young by means of teaching, discipline, and strict regimen certainly confirmed the conservative Japanese reformers' own educational concepts, all the more so since Herbart's five moral ideals obviously fitted in with the five Confucian virtues (filial piety, love, harmony, modesty, and benevolence).[130] In order to spread these teachings the German educator Emil Hausknecht, who also was an expert in elementary education, was offered a chair at Tokyo University. There, and at additional teachers' seminars, Japanese students and teachers were trained so thoroughly that Herbart's doctrines soon became the meticulously adhered to educational gospel.[131] Furthermore, Minister Mori added gymnastics to the elementary school curriculum; physical education as it had been conceived by the German Johann Ludwig Jahn (1778–1852) seemed an appropriate means by which to secure strict school discipline as well as to instill a sense of patriotic duty and prepare the pupils for military service.[132]

Having returned from his ambassador's post in London to the Ministry of Education, in 1886 Mori applied the theoretical Prussian foundations to the practice of Japanese education in several school ordinances.[133] The dual system of education in Prussia was faithfully copied: Japanese elementary schools now were to serve the same purpose as the German *Volksschule* whose foremost aim, as Bismarck had once said, was to spread sound patriotism among the masses.[134] In the field of secondary education, in Japan as in Germany the utmost amount of academic freedom and critical research was prescribed. In both countries, the mechanisms of social selection made sure that this kind of higher education remained the privilege of the happy few, the small ruling élite, and excluded lower- and middle-class children.

After the conservative reform of the content and the structure of Japanese education had been completed, it was crowned by the Imperial Rescript on Education. The idea of improving the moral education of the population and evoking among the Japanese a feeling of national unity and community originated with an educational expert who had been trained in Germany.[135] The Japanese philosopher Inoue,[136] who had just returned from a six-year study trip to Germany, wrote the official commentary, four million copies of which were published to be handed out to pupils. The Imperial Rescript on Education[137] combined Confucian family norms and the fighting spirit derived from the Shinto cult into a common behaviour code centred upon the Tenno. Up until 1945, in every Japanese school it was read out daily at the morning assembly to all pupils, who bowed in the direction of His Majesty the Tenno's Imperial Palace, and in this way soon became the religious creed of the entire nation.

The institutional and ideological foundation of the modern Japanese state and society on authoritarian structures would not have been possible without German influence and support, nor without the pro-German faction among the government who consequently relied on Prussian patterns. The 'elective affinity' with Prussian Germany certainly corresponded with the aims of the Japanese oligarchy. Once the German influence had been firmly anchored in the Japanese constitution, the military, and the educational system, not only the ruling class but also the general population identified themselves with the new system. Meiji Japan in 1889 firmly rested upon the cornerstone laid by the Germans. Summing up the work done by a comparatively small number of experts, the diplomatic envoy von Holleben, who in the course of this development had considerably increased his political influence, therefore rightly concluded: 'No other nation has achieved anything comparable here, and one may say that Japan has been more thoroughly "Germanised" than either the other powers or even most of the Japanese themselves would suspect'.[138]

Germans Acting as Transmitters of Western Sciences: Strengthening Japanese National Ideology

Adopting the Prussian system of education obviously implied opening the doors of Japanese institutions of higher education, especially the Imperial University in Tokyo, to German curricula and German professors. More than once German scholars introduced their own disciplines and established their own departments at the newly founded Tokyo University and – as the German medical doctor Baelz did for more than twenty-five years

– taught whole generations of Japanese students.[139] These German 'mandarins',[140] whose political and social outlook had been shaped by Wilhelmian Germany, saw themselves as an apolitical and impartial élite whose main task it was to protect the monarchial order and its class distinctions from subversive or foreign influences. Despite the worldwide renown of German scholarship, especially in the humanities, social sciences such as philology, history, and economics rather tended towards a narrow, nationalist outlook reducing the German Empire and its true essence to the foundation year of the German Reich, 1871, and regarding patriotism not as a natural thing but as a specifically German virtue. The hierarchical university structure, a microcosm exactly mirroring the surrounding society, reinforced the professors' self-important conviction that they were the chosen élite to spiritually and morally educate the people.

But for the exotic thrill, Japan and her institutions, which for a large part had been adopted from Germany, must therefore have seemed quite familiar to the German scholars. Here, too, politics and society were centred around an imperial house, nationalist patriotism prevailed, and recent history culminated in the glorious foundation of the new state. In Japan, like in Germany, the 'Dark Ages' had obviously been completely overcome and the newly unified national state was looking ahead to a bright future full of progress. Furthermore, a teacher (*sensei*) in Japan traditionally received almost obsequious reverence from his devoted pupils. If anything, a professor's position in Japan was even better than in Germany, as he was allowed better research facilities and received an ample salary that even the colonial lifestyle with its many servants would not use up.[141] All in all, life in Japan seemed more relaxed so that most German guest professors and experts gladly had their usual three-year contracts renewed.

In 1887–88, with a total of between seventy to eighty, the number of German experts in Japan reached its peak.[142] Proportionally large was the number of German scientists at the universities, especially at Tokyo University. Most of these were medical doctors, the history of German medicine in Japan dating back longest, that is, since 1871. In fact, Western medicine had been brought to Japan almost exclusively by German doctors, and the faculty of medicine at Tokyo University was in the hands of German professors and their Japanese students.[143] Soon the German language not only provided the technical terms of medicine but also served as the

Japanese medical colleagues' daily means of communication.[144] The progress made by the Japanese medical students either in Japan or during their postgraduate studies in Germany was enormous. Already by the end of the Meiji period Japanese medicine enjoyed worldwide renown for the results it had achieved in scientific research. Kitasato, for instance, who for many years had worked with Robert Koch, had developed vaccines against rabies and diphtheria and had discovered the bacillus which spread the bubonic plague that was especially dreaded in Asia.[145]

However, in Japan as in Germany, medicine and medical ethics seem to have been infected at an early stage with social Darwinist and racial theories. As early as 1900, Baelz, of all people, the grand old man of Japanese medicine, carried out research on racial phenomena in Hawaii,[146] which for a long time had been claimed as a Japanese possession. Later during the interwar period, Japanese anthropologists and medical doctors obviously contributed to the Japanese ideas of racial predominance by providing them with a pseudoscientific façade. In the end, in Japan as in Germany inhumane medicine unscrupulously practised euthanasia and experimented on human beings (called 'lumps of wood' – *maruta* – in Japanese.)[147]

Next to medical doctors, jurists exerted the greatest influence in Japan. Most prominent among these was Georg Michaelis, who later became Chancellor of the Reich,[148] even though, teaching at the school of the 'German Club', he did not achieve the same amount of influence as his colleagues teaching at Todai, such as the then widely known Ludwig Lönholm.[149] The 'Society for the Promotion of German Science' had founded its own school in Tokyo in 1882, to which three years later it had added a department of law. The Japanese law students were instructed in German legal norms that either had already been, or in the near future would be, adopted in Japan. By founding a German law school of its own the 'Society' tried to provide a counterbalance to the department of law at Tokyo University where, they felt, the Anglo-Saxon and French influence was still too strong and where English still served as the main language. Together with his German colleagues (the Delbrück brothers) Michaelis taught several courses in which he tried to persuade the candidates of the advantages that the German system offered. Topics such as 'The Advantages of a Judge's Position in Germany as compared to England and France' or 'Military Service – a Means of Public

Education'[150] praised the German model and moreover conveyed patriotic values.

In addition, gradually substituting German law for the Anglo-Saxon and French legal systems might enable the Japanese, so they hoped, to tackle the problem of the 'unequal treaties' and confront the relentless English on quasi-equal terms, that is to say, with the help of a legal system that was both Western and yet fundamentally different from English law. Needless to say, the English refused to accept the norms of a Romano-Germanic law code that, according to them, did not correspond to the sense of justice of most foreign residents in Japan and had been introduced for the sole purpose of undermining their position there.[151] Consequently, only when the war between Japan and China loomed on the political horizon, did the English see fit to revise the 'unequal treaties'.[152]

In the meantime, German experts in law such as Mosse and Roesler, who were employed as civil servants by the Japanese state, had drawn up most of the legal codes and their respective procedures. Even the civil law code, that had originally been shaped after the French model by a French expert and had been in effect for three years, was suspended to be reshaped after the German civil code. The strong position of the monarch that in the discussions about the constitution had been advocated by the German advisers was also now copied in the civil law code, and the family law (*ie*) decreed that the male head of the household, for better or worse, was to decide on all matters concerning the members of his family.[153]

Neither the constitution nor the family law contained the smallest trait of any democratic equality that, in the eyes of Japanese conservatives – like Hozumi[154] who had read law in Germany – would seriously have endangered the foundations of Japanese society. Liberal thinking and constitutionalism of the kind advocated by Hozumi's opponent Minobe[155] had already, during the Meiji period, had a hard time. The Tenno myth left no room for the individual's rights that, instead, were reduced further and further as the Tenno cult was made the official state doctrine. Eventually, the remains of liberal thinking were swept away to be substituted by a folkish order, at approximately the same time in both National Socialist Germany and in militarised Japan.

In the field of fine arts, too, during the 1880s a strong German influence prevailed, with the educated public literally being carried away by a reading mania. The most famous Japanese writer of the day, Mori Ogai, had, as a military doctor, spent four years in

Berlin where he learned to speak German so fluently that he not only coached his fellow officers but also translated into Japanese Clausewitz' work *On War* (*Vom Kriege*) and several German literary classics.[156] Japanese students returning from Germany brought back with them German classical music and especially folk songs[157] that soon spread throughout the country. Even the Japanese national anthem was adapted for Western instruments by the Austrian musician Franz Eckert.[158]

Since the foundation of Todai University, philosophy had been of eminent importance as the highly developed traditional Japanese philosophy had to confront the influx of Western thinking. To start with, this was marked mainly by English utilitarianism and positivism, or rather evolutionism, taught in Japan by the American philosopher Fenellosa.[159] Later, after two German professors of philosophy, Ludwig Busse and Raphael von Koeber,[160] had been offered chairs at Tokyo University, German idealism, especially its state ethics, was more widely received in Japan. Fichte, Hegel, and Kant's transcendental philosophy left the strongest impression on Japanese philosophy.[161] Inoue Tetsujiro[162] – probably the most influential philosopher of the time, who had received his education in Berlin – tried to amalgamate German idealism with the Confucian thinking of traditional Japanese schools, into a kind of Japanese moral philosophy containing nationalism and Western as well as Japanese elements. Towards the end of the Meiji period, as a commentator on the 'Imperial Rescript on Education', he became an authority on questions of moral philosophy and a strong supporter of the Tenno myth. His colleague Kato Hiroyuki,[163] Professor of Philosophy and Rector of Todai University, was mainly influenced by Darwinism and the German biologist Ernst Haeckel's anthropological teachings. Kato, who had been the first Japanese to learn German and had helped to spread the German language in Japan, even wrote some of his Darwinist treaties in German: *Der Kampf ums Recht des Stärkeren* (*The Struggle for the Predominance of the Strongest*). In Japan, too, the symbiosis of idealism and social Darwinism seems to have had its dangerous impact.

In the field of philology, too, German scholars exerted their great influence, not only by language teaching. The founder of German Japanology Karl Florenz,[164] after graduating in Indology, had attended the Japanese philosopher Inoue's lectures on Japanese history at the Oriental Seminar (founded in 1887) of Berlin University. From 1889 until the outbreak of the First World War

Florenz taught German philology at Todai and carried out research into the mythical past of Japanese history. His pioneering work, the translation of the Japanese Annals from 592 to 697, *Nihongi*, first written down in 720, made these annals available for the first time for Western research.[165] Furthermore, the images they conveyed of the Tenno's personal rule and the reform work (*Taika*) he undertook for the sake of strengthening the Japanese state certainly served the political aims of the Meiji period. By publishing the Annals, Florenz indirectly helped to justify the Tenno myth, although he himself retained his doubts about the historical truth of the legendary Japanese origins and critically commented on the authenticity of the chronicles. The outbreak of the First World War came as a shock to him, especially as the Japanese declaration of war against Germany forced him to leave the country. After Hitler's seizure of power, Florenz, who had never engaged in party politics nor been a member of the Nazi Party, nevertheless in November 1933 signed the German professors' loyalty address towards the 'Führer'. And the Dutchman Pierson's Manyoshu translation published a year before Florenz died, included Florenz's name in its dedication to Adolf Hitler. Whether as a coauthor of the work he had intentionally signed the dedication or whether his name had been added without his knowing has not yet been fully explained.[166]

Japanese political economics were deeply influenced by German Academic Socialism. Among the members of the *Verein für Sozialpolitik* (Association for Social Politics) founded in Berlin in 1872[167] were the prominent German economists Gustav Schmoller, Lujo Brentano, and Adolf Wagner all of whom, for social reasons, advocated state intervention in economic policy. The economy to them was a part of society, and economic policy consequently had to be based on social responsibility rather than capitalist market laws. Their more or less distinct political aims concentrated on two main issues: firstly, to secure the workers' loyalty to the state and knock the bottom out of socialist revolutionary ideas; and, secondly, by stabilising conditions at home, to prepare the ground for national power politics together with an increase of trade. Already the first students in Berlin, for instance Hirata,[168] had been fascinated by the doctrine of Academic Socialism, and Roesler had been called to Japan so that a prominent exponent of this academic school might contribute to the establishment of the

Meiji state. In the fields of law and economics in particular, the model of a social monarchy was to be transferred to Japan.

From 1882 onwards the German scholar Karl Rathgen[169] held a chair of constitutional law and political economics at Todai University. For eight years he propagated the theories of German political economics that due to his influence were readily accepted in Japan. In 1896 the 'Japanese Association for Social Politics', the counterpart of the German association, was founded by Rathgen's Japanese pupils.[170] One of the most prominent of these was Kanai Naboru who, after studying under Rathgen in Tokyo for five years, attended the lectures of the Academic Socialists in Berlin for another four years and eventually in 1890, following in his master's footsteps, so to speak, held a chair of law at Todai University. A pronounced opponent of liberal economics, throughout the thirty-five years of his teaching he claimed that the state should tackle social problems and the challenge of socialism – that by the turn of the century had also arisen in Japan – by taking preventive economic measures. Thought control of the masses, that is, political indoctrination, and economic control in Kanai's theory combined into the so-called 'third way' between *laissez-faire* capitalism and revolutionary socialism.

One of Kanai's pupils, Kuwata Kumazo, applied his teacher's doctrine to Japanese agriculture. After a prolonged study trip to Germany he was quite impressed with Bismarck's social legislation: 'The German social policy is an expression of the German national character'.[171] According to Kuwata, in Japan too, the state should remind itself of its social responsibilities and put an end to the growing misery of the rural population. Eventually, shortly after the turn of the century, farmers' cooperatives after the German model (*Raiffeisen*) were established by the Minister of Agriculture Hirata (who had been the first Japanese student to attend the Academic Socialists' lectures in Berlin). When economic conditions in the countryside further worsened during the early 1920s, Goto Shimpei, the leading agricultural bureaucrat, who had also spent three years in Germany, took up Hirata's ideas and changed them into a kind of national agrarian socialism that was eventually further developed into a typically Japanese form of agrarian patriarchy by the reform bureaucrats of the 1930s.[172]

History did not arouse much interest among the Japanese students in Germany; of the total of 448 students enrolled at Berlin University only eight read history.[173] Yet, the amazing amount of influence that one single academic teacher could exert in those times of rapid change can be seen in the case of history as an academic subject and its impact on politics. Minister Mori wished to introduce history at Todai University in order to bolster up higher education by a national-conservative Prussian academic discipline.[174] Though not institutionally represented in Japan, English historical research[175] discussing the Glorious Revolution from Whig and Tory historians' opposing points of view had left its marks on the Japanese constitutional debate; certainly Cromwell's 'regicide' did not fit in with the conservative Japanese social order, let alone serve as a historical model, whereas in the course of German history, at any rate, no ruler had been beheaded. In order to suppress the English influence and establish in Japan the 'German method' (the critical evaluation of source material), if at all possible, a pupil of the famous German historian Leopold von Ranke was to be engaged. Applying the German method, a critical edition of the national Japanese source material[176] was to be prepared that would strengthen the new sense of national identity, as the editing of the German medieval sources·(the *Monumenta*) had obviously done in Germany.

Through the mediation of the German historian Delbrück, Ludwig Riess, then twenty-six years old,[177] was chosen. A few years previously he had written his doctoral dissertation on medieval English constitutional law and thus obviously fulfilled the necessary condition of speaking English. For some time Riess had worked as a clerk for Ranke, which meant he was quite familiar with the grand old man's work and his method. Paradoxically enough, he was now supposed to teach the new progressive methods to 'the peoples forever standing still' (as Ranke had it). In 1887 he accepted the first Japanese chair of history that had been created especially for him at the Imperial University of Tokyo. He left in 1902 after some discord over his salary, which he considered to be too small in comparison to that of Karl Florenz.[178]

Riess immediately introduced German teaching methods, such as seminar discussions, that were completely new to the Japanese students who had been trained to listen to their teacher's words in respectful silence. He established historical criticism as the scientific way to edit source material; and on his advice the Japanese Historical Society together with its own 'Historical Review' were founded in 1889.[179] In a memorandum[180] he suggested that Japanese historical research should concentrate on diplomatic history and on collecting sources concerning Japan's foreign relations, especially her contacts with the Dutch during the days of hermetic isolation. These suggestions were readily accepted by the government, and a special institute was added to Tokyo University where archivists collected those sources and made them available for a kind of official historiography. To the present day these huge collections have not been completely edited, but the respective catalogue was finished in 1964.

So far, Confucian thinking had conceived of history as a self-contained whole where foreign relations could exist only within the framework of tributary hierarchy. Riess succeeded in breaking up this traditional concept and, in what is his main achievement, replacing it with the Western concept of diplomatic relations among sovereign states.[181] Yet, by turning the 'primacy of foreign politics' into the preponderant approach to history, Riess and his numerous Japanese pupils helped to blur the Japanese view of their own historical reality. For unlike Germany, Japan as an island country scarcely had any relations with foreign powers. Therefore, explaining the Japanese development as the result of threats imposed from abroad could not help but lead to distortions and misinterpretations of the course of Japanese history that rather resulted from domestic social conditions. Moreover, by one-sidedly concentrating on foreign politics the 'German' concept further nourished the Japanese fears of being attacked from abroad. Prevailing since the days of the Meiji Restoration, those fears contributed to the Japanese paranoia during the 1930s and again today manifest themselves in the idea of Japan having to face the rest of the world alone.[182] Both Japanese and German historians eloquently supported a powerful state and territorial expansion. Despite the critical method introduced by Riess, critical historiography did not exist in Japan until 1945. Like their German colleagues, Japanese historians neglected the sociocritical approach to contemporary history.

To judge by the small number of German scholars and government counsellors, the German influence and German interests were never strongly represented in Japan. Much rather, throughout Japan during the Meiji period the image of *gaijin* (foreigners) was connected with English-speaking persons. Nonetheless, with the Japanese court and the government from 1881 onwards deliberately opting for the Prussian way of modernisation, the Germans, placed in the right positions, were offered an unexpectedly wide range of influence, the long-term impact of which they often did not even realise. Although in 1895 Germany joined the Triple Intervention against the Japanese aspirations for power on the Asian continent, which put a damper on the official friendship between the two countries and even made Japan conclude an alliance with Great Britain (1902), the Germans maintained their predominant influence in the Tenno's empire. Meiji Japan had put on a German corset – by taking it off now she would have run the risk of collapsing.

Consequences of Choosing the Wrong Model

With the onset of fighting in the First World War, the few remaining German experts had to give up their positions, leaving behind them a heritage the impact of which its Japanese heirs certainly could not assess. However, it did not automatically lead to the two countries' eventual alliance for reasons of power politics during the 1930s. On the contrary, Japan joining the Entente clearly seemed to block the way to any German-Japanese partnership. And yet, as early as 1917, Riess, who by then had been back in Germany for fifteen years, justly described the strong similarities in the military sector: '[militarism, B.M.] ... implies a strong sense of duty that is shared by both Germans and Japanese and can always serve as a bridge'.[183]

It was a long and tortuous route, the individual stations of which cannot be described here, that led to the military alliance during the Second World War which was concluded on 26 September 1940. Such factors as the international system of powers and their respective power politics may, as catalysts, have added momentum to the process. The main reason, however, for Japan and Germany confronting the rest of the world together can be derived from their inner affinity as two 'latecomers'.[184]

Both societies were put in quasi-quarantine by their conservative ruling élites. As domestic reforms were neglected for fear of endangering the traditional order, success was to be achieved only in foreign politics. A policy of aggression and enrichment at the expense of the neighbouring nations had to make up for domestic repression and, in Japan, economic misery. Military victories seemed the simplest way for the government to justify its rule, and the Japanese victories over China (1895) and Russia (1905) helped to stabilise the Meiji government much more than all the preceding reforms had done. The German attempt to conquer Central Europe failed in the First World War, but the original war aim – to 'pacify' Europe under German rule – in many ways can be compared to the Japanese policy towards China; although for reasons of political opportunism Japan had joined the camp of Germany's adversaries, behind the scenes of the European war she tried to take over China as a protectorate.[185] Their common aims of far-reaching territorial expansion and of rounding off their respective spheres of influence, both of which were directly opposed to the aims of the Entente, induced Japan and Germany from 1917 onwards to discuss in secret talks the possibilities of a separate peace to be concluded against the Western powers' predominance.[186] The concept of a Eurasian land block, where in some way or other the crumbling Russian empire was to be forcibly integrated, surfaced in these talks for the first time. These thoughts originally stemmed from the geopolitical theories first conceived by Karl Haushofer after he had been detached to the Japanese army for some time prior to the First World War.[187]

Accepting the victorious Anglo-Saxon powers' political system would have implied granting more rights to the subjects in domestic politics and, in foreign politics, acknowledging the new international order. Both things seemed equally inconceivable to the Japanese. What 'Versailles' was to the Germans, 'Washington' was to them: establishing the political and mercantile predominance of the Anglo-Saxon powers. At the Washington conference in 1922 Japan had been forced by the combined pressure from the victorious powers to leave Tsingtao, which had been wrested from the Germans, and to abandon the tremendous influence which had been established in China during the war.[188] Instead, the Japanese Empire was made to consent to the 'open door policy' in China that merely served the interests of the economically strongest powers, the United States and Great Britain.

In domestic politics too, the Japanese could not get used to the parliamentary system that during the Meiji period had constantly been discredited and superseded by German order concepts. Although general male suffrage had eventually been introduced, in Japan even less than in the 'Weimar Republic' political parties could not attain any real political influence. Caught up in the Tenno ideology, the masses were not prepared for a parliamentary form of government based on political parties, but rather regarded the elected representatives as public nuisances. What was occasionally called the 'parliamentary interlude' during the Taisho era (1912–25) remained more or less fictitious;[189] similarly, during the Weimar Republic parliamentarianism was, to a large extent, considered nothing but a necessary evil. Lacking a sufficient political base as well as a convincing alternative programme to replace the existing social order, the political parties in both countries in fact undermined their own position. In Germany they were dissolved in 1933, in Japan they were allowed to do so themselves, while still controlled by the state, in 1940.[190] In both countries 'the people' had got rid of the 'alien' parliamentary system.

To the political and economic change of the world economic crisis both Japan and Germany reacted in a noticeably similar way. The nationalist camp, in both countries the military, saw its chance to shake off all armament restrictions,[191] and while the West was being economically weakened, to create their own self-sufficient spheres of interest. In Japan political radicalisation, to a large extent due to the agrarian misery, expressed itself in a folkish ideology of outward expansion that was put into practice by the army from 1931 onwards occupying Manchuria.[192] The quest for a 'Showa Restoration' implied radically changing the existing social order and establishing a plebiscitarian monarchy. The oligarchy, whose positions were threatened, reacted by suspending the political parties and at the same time adopting some elements of these radical ideas, a kind of Japanese 'fascism' based on agrarian myth and antimodernism.[193] *Kokutai*, the doctrine of Japanese identity centred upon the Tenno, had by the 'Peace Laws' of 1925[194] been granted official approval and protection for the first time . In the wake of the political radicalisation during the world economic crisis, it was now turned into the official state doctrine by the military who in the meantime had gained virtually complete control over the government. *Kokutai* was used as a shield to ward off subversive foreign influence.[195] Henceforth, any attempt at spreading socialist or even liberal thoughts was treated as a serious political offence.

In the field of economics Japan adopted a policy of massive intervention by the state,[196] even before Schacht and Hitler did the same in Germany. By means of deficit spending and an armament programme complying with the wishes of the military, the economy was set going again. State intervention, which had always been advocated by the theorists of social political economics in

Germany and Japan, now one-sidedly favoured the military's aspirations for power. It certainly had nothing in common with the ideal once depicted by Lorenz von Stein and Gneist of a social monarchy that, on the contrary, was now perverted into a military state dominating everything.

Both the National Socialist ideology of the German 'master race' and its manifest destiny to conquer the world as well as the 'Fundamental Principles of National Entity' (*Kokutai no hongi*)[197] officially declared in Japan in 1937 had grown from historical roots. They marked the peak of national delusions of grandeur that were eventually destroyed, or rather destroyed themselves, in the war. By their radical national totalitarianism militarised Japan and National Socialist Germany alienated themselves further from the international family of nations. Their worldwide political isolation resulting from their political structures and their comparable forms of fascism suggested their mutual approach at the military level.[198] Already the Anti-Comintern Pact (25 November 1936) by the militaries on both sides was regarded as a demonstration against worldwide British predominance and consequently almost four years later was enlarged into a military alliance against the Anglo-Saxon powers.[199] In 1940 the front lines were clearly marked between the authoritarian countries and the Western democracies. Two ideological systems fundamentally different in their evaluation of the individual, as well as in their economic systems, stood facing each other, ready to fight for predominance. With the victory of the Soviet Union over Germany, communism emerged as a new power block, and the political systems of Germany and Japan alike were shattered. In 1945 the 'special way' in world politics that Prussia, convinced of her national destiny, had started upon, to be followed by Meiji Japan, was forcibly ended, apparently for good.

The modernisation of Japan that occasionally social scientists, and also the Japanese themselves, tend to praise as the one successful model for developing countries to follow was, instead, buried under the ruins of the Second World War. In fact, total defeat was the prerequisite for the political and economic recovery that started after 1945 in both Germany and Japan under the control of the American victors.[200] Adopting an alien culture, which had been forced upon Japan since 1853 when the country was opened to the West by an American act of violence, ended in 1945 in unconditional surrender. In fact, Japan also surrendered to her own inability to critically integrate Western thinking. As the pattern of Japanese society obviously showed certain affinities with the Prussian-German one, this seemed to offer an opportunity to avoid Western influence in its Anglo-Saxon form and still become a modern nation. Consequently, from the Meiji period on, Japan sought to intensify her relations with Germany, even if the Japanese approaches always remained rather one-sided and were never wholeheartedly returned, by either Bismarck or Hitler. Moreover, opting for Germany also proved to be the wrong choice, when under Hitler the much-admired German model turned into a nightmare ending in disaster.[201] What was supposed to serve as a historical model of successful modernisation may rather serve, from the historian's point of view, as a warning against an ill-advised attempt at one-sidedly assimilating a foreign culture.

Notes

PRELIMINARY NOTE

This paper fully evaluates for the first time the source material – however scarce – available at the Political Archives of the Foreign Ministry in Bonn. In the normal diplomatic correspondence between the German legation in Tokyo and the government in Berlin, questions concerning the German influence on the modernisation of Japan were of only marginal importance. The relevant materials – for instance 130 volumes containing consular reports up to the First World War – are to be found in the former Central Archives of the German Democratic Republic, now a branch of the Koblenz Federal Archives. As employing a German expert required formal consent by the German Foreign Ministry – which did not apply to university professors probably because of the universities' autonomy – the six volumes on *German Experts in Meiji Japan* contain an abundance of such cases that in this study could only be evaluated in a selective manner. Likewise, the author during his visit to the Potsdam archives in October 1990 could not thoroughly peruse but only list the probably highly interesting consular records. Consequently, this article should be seen merely as a first attempt at dealing with a wide-ranging topic.

The following abbreviations of source material will be used:

AA/PA	Auswärtiges Amt/Politisches Archiv Bonn
BA/MA	Bundesarchiv/Militärarchiv Freiburg im Breisgau
	(RM refers to Navy materials)
BA/Potsdam	Bundesarchiv/Außenstelle Potsdam

1. Eugene Soviak, 'On the Nature of Western Progress: The Journal of the Iwakura Embassy', in Donald H. Shively, ed., *Tradition and Modernization in Japanese Culture*, Princeton, 1971, pp. 7–34.

2. Morinosuke Kajima, *Geschichte der japanischen Außenbeziehungen. Bd. 1: Von der Landesöffnung bis zur Meiji-Restauration*, ed. Horst Hammitzsch, Wiesbaden, 1976.

3. Ibid., pp. 48ff. Roger Pineau, ed., *The Japan Expedition 1852–1854. The Personal Journal of Commodore M.C. Perry*, Washington, D.C., 1968.

4. Erich Pauer, 'Japanischer Geist – westliche Technik: Zur Rezeption westlicher Technologie in Japan', *Saeculum* No. 38 (1987), pp. 19–51; here p. 37; quotation from John M. Foster, *American Diplomacy in the Orient*, Boston, 1904, p. 346 (although the quotation is probably not genuine, it does accord with the facts. The statement ascribed to Ito in Sacramento is not verified by Foster).

5. Western standard works are: William G. Beasley, *The Meiji Restoration*, Stanford, 1973, and Conrad Totman, *The Collapse of the Tokugawa-Bakufu, 1862–1868*, University Press of Hawaii, 1980. The only German study focussing mainly on economic development is Annelotte Piper, *Japans Weg von der Feudalgesellschaft zum Industriestaat*, Köln, 1976.

6. During the final years of the shogunate, between 1862 and 1867, ninety-two Japanese students were sent abroad, half of them by the Central Government (*bakufu*), the other half by some feudal lords (*daimyo*). See Ardath W. Burks, 'Japan's Outreach: The Ryugakusei', in Ardath W. Burks, *The Modernizers. Overseas Students, Foreign Employees, and Meiji-Japan*, Boulder, 1985, p. 152. Ito Hirobumi (1841–1911), who belonged to the Choshu clan residing in the south of the main Japanese isle Honshu, from May 1863 until June 1864 had stayed in England. See Albert M. Craig, *Choshu in the Meiji Restoration*, Cambridge, Mass., 1961, and Olivia Checkland, *Britain's Encounter with Meiji Japan 1868–1912*, London, 1989. The latest study, too, Edward R. Beauchamp and Akira Iriye, eds., *Foreign Employees in Nineteenth-Century Japan*, Boulder, 1990, almost exclusively refers to American and English experts. The most comprehensive Japanese study is the unpublished doctoral thesis written by Tomihide Kashioka, *Meiji Japan's Study Abroad Program: Modernizing Elites and Reference Societies*, Ph.D. diss., Duke University, 1982. The only German study so far has been published by the Japanese Institute in Cologne: Japanisches Kulturinstitut Köln, ed., *Kulturvermittler zwischen Japan und Deutschland. Biographische Skizzen aus vier Jahrhunderten*, Köln, 1990.

7. Soviak, Iwakura Embassy, p. 12.

8. BA Potsdam 51020/1: letter from the interpreter of the German minister-residence in Tokyo to the Foreign Office, of 20 November 1871: Report on the talk with Iwakura and notification about his planned visit to Berlin. Ibid., 50986: Note from the Foreign Office concerning the costs of the Iwakura mission visiting Berlin. For the period between 7 March and 29 March 1873, these costs amounted to 11,417.20 Reichsmark. Also see 'Conversation with Prince Iwakura, Marquis Ito and other Japanese Gentlemen' in Otto von Bismarck, *Die gesammelten Werke* (Friedrichsruh edition) vol. 8, Berlin, 1926, pp. 64f.

9. The two most relevant Japanese studies, by now available in German translation, too, are Chie Nakane, *Japanese Society*, Berkeley, 1970, and Takeo Doi,
'Amae. A Key Concept for Understanding Japanese Personality Structure' in R.
J. Smith and Richard K. Beardsley, eds., *Japanese Culture. Its Development and
Characteristics*, London, 1963, pp. 132–39. Referring in particular to the Japan of
today Irmela Hijiya-Kirschnereit, *Das Ende der Exotik. Zur japanischen Kultur
und Gesellschaft der Gegenwart*, Frankfurt am Main, 1988.

10. For decision making in Japan in general, see: Kiyoaki Tsuji, 'Decision Making
in the Japanese Government. A Study of *Ringisei*' in *Political Development of
Modern Japan*, ed. Robert E. Ward, Princeton, 1968, pp. 457–76.

11. See the following studies: Eberhard Jäckel, 'Der gleichzeitige Eintritt in die
Weltpolitik'; Eihachiro Sakai, 'Die Entstehung des modernen Beamtenstaates';
Bernd Martin, 'Faschistisch-militaristische Großmachtpolitik', in Arnulf Bar-
ing and Masamori Sase, eds., *Zwei zaghafte Riesen? Deutschland und Japan seit
1945*, Stuttgart, 1977. Also see the collection of essays prepared by the author,
Bernd Martin, ed., *Japans Weg in die Moderne. Ein Sonderweg nach deutschem
Vorbild?*, Frankfurt am Main, 1987.

12. Inazo Nitobe, *Bushido. The Soul of Japan. An Exposition of Japanese Thought*,
Tokyo, 1905; German edition: *Bushido. Die Seele Japans*, Magdeburg, 1937. After
studying in America, Nitobe had studied agriculture from 1888 on in Germany and in 1890 had received a Ph.D. at Halle University. See Horst E. Wittig, *Pädagogik und Bildungspolitik Japans. Quellentexte und Dokumente von der
Tokugawa-Zeit bis zur Gegenwart*, München, 1976, pp. 104ff. Also see Nitobe's
own reflexions: Inazo Nitobe et al., *Western Influences in Modern Japan. A Series
of Papers on Cultural Relations*, Chicago, 1931.

13. Wittig, *Pädagogik und Bildungspolitik Japans*, pp. 89–91 (30 October 1890).

14. Hazel J. Jones, *Live Machines. Hired Foreigners in Meiji-Japan*, Tenterden, Kent,
1980. Especially see the charts at the end of the book, pp. 145ff.

15. Exact figures are not available. See the figures referring to Berlin (note 45); a
total of nine hundred Japanese studied in America between 1867 and 1902
[Ardath W. Burks, *The Modernizers*, (c.f. note 6), p. 153]. See J. T. Conte, *Overseas
Study in the Meiji Period: Japanese Students in America*, Ann Arbor, 1983.

16. J. R. Bartholemew, 'Japanese Modernization and the Imperial Universities' in
Journal of Asian Studies, vol. 37, 1978, pp. 251–71, here p. 263. Occasionally, a
student's expected admiration for Germany changed into a critical attitude
during his stay there, as was the case with the Japanese student of humanities
Anesaki Masakaru who in 1900 started to read philosophy at Kiel. He was
shocked by William's II '*Hunnen-Rede*' ('Hun-Speech') that revealed to him the
dark side of Wilhelmian society. (William II delivered that address on 22 July
1900 when sending the German expedition corps out to crush the Boxer rebellion in China). See Sukehiro Hirakawa, 'Changing Japanese Attitudes Toward
Western Learning. Is study abroad meaningless?', in *Contemporary Japan*, vol.
28, 1969, pp. 789–806.

17. Jones, *Live Machines*, p. 24. During the period between 1876 and 1912: law
4,151; engineering 2,815; medicine 1,932; humanities 1,545; agronomy 1,118;
natural sciences 674.

18. Hazel J. Jones, 'The Griffis Thesis and Meiji Policy Toward Hired Foreigners', in Burks, *The Modernizers*, pp. 219–53; here p. 220. William Elliot Griffis, who from 1870 to 1874 was employed by the Japanese government, kept track of the foreigners employed in Japan until after the First World War.

19. Burks, *The Modernizers*, p. 221: Basil Hall Chamberlain, a brother of Houston Stewart Chamberlain, from 1874 to 1911 worked as a language teacher at the Navy Academy and as a professor of linguistics at Todai University. He translated the earliest written texts, records of the events during the olden days, *kojiki*, dating from 712, into a Western language for the first time. (C.f. the work done by Karl Florenz; see note 165.)

20. Erwin Baelz, *Das Leben eines deutschen Arztes im erwachenden Japan*, Stuttgart, 1931, pp. 120f. Also see Sukehiro Hirakawa, 'Changing Japanese Attitudes toward Western Learning. Dr. Erwin Baelz and Mori Ogai', in *Contemporary Japan*, vol. 29, 1968, pp. 138–57.

21. For the term 'live machine' and the pejorative use of the term *oyatoi*, see Jones, *Live Machines*, p. 125.

22. BA/MA: RM 1/v 2880: Memorandum of the Prussian legate to Mexico Emil Freiherr von Richthofen: 'Memorandum concerning political conditions in Japan with respect to the starting of trade relations with the empire', Potsdam, 29 September 1854.

23. For the origins and the carrying out of the Prussian East Asia expedition, see BA/MA RM 1/v 2336–2348 containing probably the most comprehensive collection of source material that has scarcely been analysed so far, but for the author's small survey: Bernd Martin, 'The Prussian Expedition to the Far East (1860–62)', in this volume.

    Based on the official four-volume report published by Albert Berg in Berlin from 1864 to 1873 (*Die Preußische Expedition nach Ostasien nach amtlichen Quellen*) are the studies by Michael Salewski, 'Die preußische Expedition nach Japan (1859–1861)', in *Revue Internationale d'Histoire Militaire*, vol. 70, 1988, pp. 39–57; and Frank Suffa-Friedel, 'Die Preußische Expedition nach Ostasien. Verhandlungen, Verzögerungen und Vertragsabschluß', in Kuo Heng-yü, ed., *Berlin und China. Dreihundert Jahre wechselvolle Beziehungen*, vol.3, Berlin, 1987, pp. 57–70. A thorough study based on the records of the Prussian Foreign Ministry stored at Merseburg (formerly German Democratic Republik) was provided by Holmer Stahncke, *Die diplomatischen Beziehungen zwischen Deutschland und Japan 1854–1868*, Stuttgart, 1987.

24. For China, see the long-term study by Udo Ratenhof, *Die Chinapolitik des Deutschen Reiches 1871 bis 1945. Wirtschaft – Rüstung – Militär*, Boppard, 1985, especially the charts pp. 56ff. For Japan, see the somewhat lengthy study by Michael Rauck, *Die Beziehungen zwischen Japan und Deutschland 1859–1914 unter besonderer Berücksichtigung der Wirtschaftsbeziehungen* (doctoral dissertation in economics and social sciences), Erlangen, 1988, pp. 405–61; and – as a survey – Erich Pauer, 'Die wirtschaftlichen Beziehungen zwischen Japan und Deutschland 1900–1945', in Josef Kreiner, ed., *Deutschland – Japan. Historische Kontakte*, Bonn, 1984, pp. 161–210.

25. Georg Kerst, *Die Anfänge der Erschließung Japans im Spiegel der zeitgenössischen Publizistik – Untersucht auf Grund der Veröffentlichungen der Kölnischen Zeitung*, Hamburg, 1953.

26. The best account of the negotiations is given by Stahncke, *Diplomatische Beziehungen*, pp. 128–47; treaty of 24 January 1861, text in Berg, *Preußische Expedition*, vol. II, pp. 223–38.

27. The oldest German trading company in Japan was Kniffler and Co., founded on 1 July 1859 in Nagasaki and opening a branch in Yokohama in 1861. Renamed as Illies and Co. in 1880, the firm still exists today; see Käthe Molsen, *C. Illies and Co. 1859-1959. Ein Beitrag zur Geschichte des deutsch-japanischen Handels*, Hamburg, 1959. Between 1859 and 1868 in Yokohama there were 193 English, 51 Americans, 19 Dutch, 16 French, but only 11 Prussians; altogether there were about 20 Germans in Yokohama in 1860; see Kurt Meissner, *Deutsche in Japan*, Tokyo, 1961, pp. 31f.

28. Meissner, *Deutsche in Japan*, p. 34. Between the end of 1861 and 1865, excluding 1863, a total of 320 foreign ships entered Yokohama port, among them only five from Prussia. Other German ships, such as those from the Hanseatic cities (Bremen, Hamburg, Lübeck), were not allowed into Japan until 1867 when the *bakufu* acknowledged the flag of the North-German Confederation (Norddeutscher Bund) (see Stahncke, *Diplomatische Beziehungen*, pp. 217f.)

29. Orders of 8 January and 8 May 1865. Bruno Siemers, *Japans Eingliederung in den Welthandelsverkehr 1855–1859*, Berlin, 1937. Siemers' study is partly based on records that were destroyed during the Second World War.

30. BA/MA RM 1/v 571 Memorandum Brandt (Berlin) to War Minister Roon of 7 February 1867; summary of a memorandum by Brandt from Kanagawa November 1865.

31. Ibid., in the records Roon only acknowledges receipt on 13 February 1867.

32. Stahncke, *Diplomatische Beziehungen*, pp. 224f.

33. BA/MA RM 1/v 867: letter from Brandt to Bismarck of 31 July 1868.

34. Rauck, *Beziehungen zwischen Japan und Deutschland*, p. 122, according to the records of the Prussian consulate in Hakodate stored in Merseburg (Augusta was the name of the German Empress, William's I wife).

35. BA/MA RM 1/v 867 Bismarck's comment on Brandt's report of 31 July 1868 (see note 33).

36. Ibid., Comment by the Navy Ministry of 11 October 1868.

37. Ibid., Memoranda by Richthofen of 10 January 1869 and 28 November 1872; memorandum by Brandt of 4 January 1873. For the context, see Wolfgang Petter, *Die überseeische Stützpunktpolitik der preußisch-deutschen Kriegsmarine 1859–1883*, Ph.D., Freiburg i. Br., 1975, pp. 188ff.

38. Hans-Ulrich Wehler, *Bismarck und der Imperialismus*, Köln, 1969, p. 192. Reichs-Chancellor's office to Foreign Office on 15 August 1873.

39. See the basic study by Roger F. Hackett, *Yamagata Aritomo in the Rise of Modern Japan 1838–1922*, Cambridge, Mass., 1971.

40. Ibid., pp. 52f and 58.

41. Ernest L. Presseisen, *Before Aggression: Europeans Prepare the Japanese Army*, University of Arizona Press, 1965, pp. 9f: At the end of 1866 the first French military mission left for Japan.

42. Rauck, *Beziehungen zwischen Japan und Deutschland*, p. 39; Masaki Miyake, 'German Political and Cultural Influence on Japan, 1870–1914', in John M. Moses and Paul M. Kennedy, eds., *Germany in the Pacific and the Far East 1870–1914*, St. Lucia, Queensland, 1980, pp. 156-81, here pp. 159f.

43. Ibid.

44. Kenneth B. Pyle, 'Advantages of Followership: German Economics and Japanese Bureaucrats, 1890-1925', in *Journal of Japanese Studies*, vol. 1, 1974, pp. 127–64, here p. 156. Pyle's little known study is by far the most thorough one, even if it deals with the economic aspect only. See below.

45. For the figures concerning Berlin see Rudolf Hartmann, 'Einige Aspekte des geistig-politischen Einflusses Deutschlands auf Japan vor der Jahrhundertwende', in *Mitteilungen des Instituts für Orientforschung der Deutschen Akademie der Wissenschaften zu Berlin*, vol. XII, 1962, pp. 463–79, charts on pp. 480f. Concerning Jena, by the same author, 'Jenas Universität und Japans Weg in die Moderne', in *Sozialistische Universität. Jena, Friedrich-Schiller-Universität* (28 April 1989).

46. Staff surgeon Theodor Eduard Hoffmann and colonel surgeon Leopold von Müller worked in Japan from August 1871 for four years. BA/Potsdam 63498: letter from the Prussian War Ministry to Bismarck from 14 July 1874: the letter reported Müller and Hoffmann had been granted a three-year unpaid leave by highest cabinet order (i.e., the Prussian King); they had left on 23 May, but had yet not returned. Ibid., Telegram German minister-resident Tokyo – Berlin of 5 August 1874: The Japanese government wishes to prolong the contract for another 15 months. Ibid., Order by King William of Prussia on 17 October 1874 prolonging the leave until 1 March 1876. Also, see (written without knowledge of the record material) Heinz Vianden, 'Deutsche Ärzte im Japan der Meiji-Zeit', in Kreiner, *Deutschland-Japan*, pp. 89–113; Werner Wenz and Arnold Vogt, 'Der Einfluß der deutschen Schulmedizin auf Japan', in Martin, *Japans Weg in die Moderne*, pp. 69–86.

47. BA/Potsdam 63498: Report Brandt-Bismarck of 12 February 1875.

48. Ibid., Report Brandt-Bismarck of 21 July 1874. Comment by the German diplomat on the two military doctors' report (that is included in the records).

49. Ibid., Reports Holleben-Bülow/Foreign Office, of 8 and 20 July and 1 August 1875. In the duel, the civilian Wernicke, a medical doctor like his challenger Müller, was slightly injured.

50. Ibid., Report Holleben-Bülow of 20 September 1875.

51. Ibid., 63499: Original report, altogether 130 handwritten pages, by Müller and Hoffmann to Bismarck, of 5 November 1876.

52. Ibid., Report of the German minister resident to Bülow of 8 November 1877. At the school and the academy a total of eleven German teachers worked; both the German and the Japanese sections were structured in the same way, and knowledge of German and Latin was requested in the Japanese section as well. Probably the only difference between the two sections was that teaching was done in the respective native language.

53. Regine Mathias-Pauer, 'Deutsche Meinungen zu Japan – Von der Reichsgründung bis zum Dritten Reich', in Kreiner, Deutschland-Japan, pp. 115–40; Adolf Freitag, *Die Japaner im Urteil der Meiji-Deutschen*, Tokyo/Leipzig, 1939.

54. For figures, see Rauck, *Beziehungen zwischen Japan und Deutschland*, p. 182.

55. AA/PA I B 8: Report Brandt-Bismarck of 13 May 1872. Ibid., Report Brandt-Bismarck of 8 March 1873. Ibid., I B 16,5: Report Holleben-Bismarck of 19 October 1875.

56. AA/PA I B 8: Report Brandt-Bismarck of 22 July 1873 about the Imperial concubines. Ibid., I B 16,9: Report Eisendecher of 27 September 1877 about an Imperial concubine giving birth to a Prince. The report was presented to William I on 8 November 1877.

57. AA/PA I B 16,6: Foreign Office to von Eisendecher (who from 1875 to 1882 was the German representative in Tokyo) on 3 March 1876. By no means was the Tenno's wife to be called 'Her Majesty the Empress' in diplomatic reports.

58. The quotation and the figures were taken from Holleben's (in 1875 chief of the Mission ad interim) two letters to Bismarck, of 18 May and 16 August 1875 (AA/PA I B 16,4).

59. For the fatal part the sinophile Max von Brandt played as a counsellor to the Foreign Office during the war between Japan and China, see Rolf-Harald Wippich, *Japan und die deutsche Fernostpolitik 1894–1898*, Stuttgart, 1987, pp. 90ff. Also see Max von Brandt's memoirs, *Dreiunddreißig Jahre in Ostasien. Erinnerungen eines deutschen Diplomaten*, vols. 1 and 2, Leipzig, 1901.

60. BA/Potsdam 63498: Letter from the Japanese legation in Berlin to the Foreign Office, of 7 August 1875: Requesting Paul Mayet as a teacher of German, Latin, and mathematics at the medical preparatory school. Ibid., 63499: Report by Gutschmid to the Foreign Office of 11 March 1879. Mayet had switched over to the Ministry of Finance. Before returning to Germany in 1893, Mayet worked for the Japanese Postal Administration and, eventually, the Ministry of Agriculture (ibid., 29746: Report Holleben-Caprivi of 16 June 1890 about foreigners in Japan). Like Roesler, Mayet earned a top salary amounting to 7200 yen a year (ibid., 63499: Report of the Tokyo legation to the Foreign Office, of 3 July 1880). While still in Japan Mayet published his book on the population of Japan (*Japanische Bevölkerungsstatistik*, Yokohama, 1888).

61. Johannes Justus Rein worked in Japan from 1873 to 1875, Edmund Naumann from 1875 to 1879. Rein wrote the first German general survey on Japan: *Japan nach Reisen und Studien im Auftrage der königlich-preußischen Regierung dargestellt*, 2 vols., Leipzig, 1881. Naumann was requested by the Japanese legation as a teacher of mineralogy and geology at a yearly salary of 3600 yen (BA/Potsdam 63498: Letter to the Foreign Office, on 1 June 1875). In Japan he achieved a certain notoriety not only for beating his students, but also coming to blows with his subordinate the topographer Otto Schmidt whom he accused of having an affair with his wife. The spectacular brawl, which had happened in the street, was dealt with by the German consular court, and Naumann was sentenced to a fine of 300 Reichsmark for intentional physical injury. The incident made it into all the East Asian newspapers (Ibid., 29744: Report Eisendecher to the Foreign Office including the newspaper clippings of 21 January 1882). However, until June 1885 Naumann kept his work in Japan as an expert topographical surveyor (Ibid., 29745: Letter Doenhoff-Bismarck of 12 May 1885). Back in Berlin, he ridiculed the Japanese attempts at modernisation; his insults were witnessed and passed on by Mori Ogai (see below) who was then staying in Berlin (see Jones, *Live Machines*, p. 86). For the German influence in the field of geography in general, see Karl Haushofer, *Der deutsche Anteil an der geographischen Erschließung des subjapanischen Erdraums, und deren Förderung durch den Einfluß von Krieg und Wehrpolitik*, München, 1914.

62. Jones, *Live Machines*, pp. 12f. Half the total budget of the Ministry of Education was spent on foreign teachers; Todai University spent one-third of its total budget on the salaries of its foreign professors.

63. AA/PA I B 16,4: Report Brandt-Bismarck, of 12 February 1875.

64. AA/PA extensive account by the German legation, B 16, 7–B 16,10.

65. AA/PA B 16,11: Report of 23 March 1878.

66. W. W. McLaren, ed., *Japanese Government Documents 1867–1889*, Tokyo, 1914, p. 17. Conscription Regulations of 3 January 1871; enlarged into compulsory military service by Imperial Rescript on 28 November 1872. *Sources of Japanese Tradition*, compiled by Ryusaku Tsunoda, Wm. Theodore de Bary, and Donald Keene, New York, 1958, pp. 703ff. AA/PA I B 8: Brandt-Bismarck on 20 March 1873: Transmitting the German translation of the rescript on compulsory military service Brandt realistically foresaw the financial problems its carrying out would cause. Presseisen, *Before Aggression*, p. 29: In his memorandum for the Emperor of 4 February 1872, Yamagata mentioned the German model.

67. AA/PA I B 16,5: Report legation Tokyo-Foreign Office, of 27 September 1875.

68. Ibid., I 16, 11: Report Eisendecher-Foreign Office, of 31 March 1878: Yamagata's plans of reorganising the army according to the German model; for years all the Prussian army regulations had been translated.

69. Presseisen, *Before Aggression*, pp. 63ff, on 5 December 1878; Miyake, *German Influence*, p. 160, wrongly dates the decision one year later.

70. Hackett, *Yamagata Aritomo*, p. 82.

71. Still the standard work: F. C. Jones, *Extraterritoriality in Japan and the Diplomatic Relations Resulting in its Abolition, 1853–1899*, New Haven, 1931. Also Tadao Johannes Araki, *Geschichte der Entstehung und Revision der ungleichen Verträge mit Japan (1853–1894)*, Phil. diss., Marburg, 1959.

72. Meissner, *Deutsche in Japan*, p. 65; later, in 1898 there were 42 trading offices; for the meagre trade relations, see Rauck, *Beziehungen zwischen Japan und Deutschland*, pp. 320ff.

73. BA Potsdam 63499: Notification to the Foreign Office by the Japanese envoy Aoki on 18 October 1878: Roesler had been engaged for five years as legal counsellor to the Japanese Foreign Office. Copy of the contract. As a yearly salary Roesler received 7200 yen. Ibid., 29744: Letter from Roesler to the Foreign Office, of 25 February 1885: His contract had been prolonged for another six years; he had just completed the Japanese commercial code. Roesler's contract was again prolonged until 31 March 1893. Although Ito would have liked him to stay on, Roesler handed in his resignation and went back to Germany, much to the discontent of the German legation (ibid., 29747: Report Gutschmid-Caprivi, of 5 April, 1893: 'After all I have known from the past about his political outlook, I'm afraid he is not very likely to use his talents in a cooperative way …'). Roesler was a pronounced opponent of Bismarck's and, as a sign of his protest against the Chancellor's fighting the Catholics (*Kulturkampf*), had converted to Catholicism. This is why official reports tended to unduly minimise his achievements in Japan. For Roesler's impact see Johannes Siemes, 'Die Staatsgründung des modernen Japans: Die Einflüsse Hermann Roeslers', in Joseph Roggendorf, ed., *Das moderne Japan. Einführende Aufsätze*, Tokyo, 1963, pp. 1–25; and Jones, *Live Machines*, pp. 103f. Also see Anton Rauscher, *Die soziale Rechtsidee und die Überwindung des wirtschaftsliberalen Denkens. Hermann Roesler und sein Beitrag zum Verständnis von Wirtschaft und Gesellschaft*, München, 1969, pp. 14–50.

74. AA/PA Japan 1,1: Report Gutschmid-Foreign Office, of 23 January 1879.

75. The Prince arrived on 23 May 1879 and left in April 1880. For a detailed report about the visit and the incident occurring during a hunting party near Osaka, see the files AA/PA Japan 1,1 and 1,2.

76. AA/PA Japan 1,2: Handwritten letter from Bismarck to William I, of 31 March 1880.

77. Ibid., Japan 1, 3: Report Eisendecher-Foreign Office, of 4 April 1880: the Tenno had invited the Prince for a private lunch on 2 April at which the ladies took part, too, for the first time at the Imperial court.

78. Ibid., Report Eisendecher-Foreign Office, of 6 May 1880. The report arrived in Berlin on 25 June and was presented to the German Emperor on 5 July (mail sent by special diplomatic courier took about five to six weeks from Japan).

79. BA Potsdam 61047: On 27 November 1879, the Japanese envoy to Berlin proposed to the Foreign Office to grant the German minister-residence in Tokyo the status of a legation. In a memorandum of 12 December 1878 the Foreign Office welcomed this suggestion that was, however, turned down by Bismarck three days later. Apparently, the Foreign Office thereupon directly addressed the Emperor. On 8 April 1880 William I promoted Eisendecher to the rank of a diplomatic envoy, thereby upgrading the diplomatic outpost to a status equal to that of the other countries' legations.

80. Ibid., Report Eisendecher-Foreign Office, of 23 September 1880.

81. Ibid., Note made by the Foreign Office on 30 March 1881.

82. Ibid., Telegram German legation-Foreign Office, of 13 October, 1881. Okuma Shigenobu (1838–1922) came from Hizen *daimiate*. In 1888–89 he was eventually allowed to join the government again as Foreign Minister. In 1882 Okuma founded the Constitutional Progress Party that was later to develop into the Minseito. For Okuma, see Yoshitake Oka, *Five Political Leaders of Modern Japan. Ito Hirobumi, Okuma Shigenobu, Hara Takashi, Inukai Tsuyoshi, and Saionji Kinmochi*, Tokyo, 1986.

83. AA/PA Japan 1, 4: Report Eisendecher-Foreign Office, of 8 March 1882, including the complete members' list.

84. Only Hartmann, *Einfluß Deutschlands*, gives a critical, if somewhat exaggerated, evaluation of the German influence in Japan.

85. For rural conditions and the lower classes, see Thomas R. H. Havens, *Farm and Nation in Modern Japan. Agrarian Nationalism*, Princeton, 1974; Ann Waswo, *Japanese Landlords. The Decline of a Rural Elite*, Berkeley, 1977; Mikiso Hane, *Peasants, Rebels and Outcasts. The Underside of Modern Japan*, New York, 1981.

86. For the concentration of industry and commerce in the hands of the *zaibatsu* that was reinforced by the privatisation of formerly state-owned enterprises, see Piper, *Von der Feudalgesellschaft zum Industriestaat*, pp. 160ff. For private enterprise see Theodor Dams, 'Die Industrialisierung Japans: Gemeinsamkeiten und Unterschiede zu Deutschland' in Martin, *Japans Weg in die Moderne* (c.f. note 11) pp. 87–138.

87. The term is quoted in an essay by the historian Ludwig Riess (see below), 'Deutschland und Japan', in *Preußische Jahrbücher*, vol. 168, 1917, pp. 203–29, here p. 203; the French spoke of *Liaison Allemande*.

88. For the Triple Intervention (Russia-France-Germany) of 6 March 1895 against the Japanese occupation of the Liaotung Peninsula (Pt. Arthur), see the comprehensive study by Wippich, *Japan und die deutsche Fernostpolitik*.

89. C.f. note 83.

90. Prince Kitashirakawa Yoshihisa (1847–95, during the Japanese invasion of Formosa). Kitashirakawa is said to have been, in 1868, the opposition candidate for the Japanese throne and consequently, after the Meiji-tenno's access to the throne, had to leave Japan. See Otto Schmiedel, *Die Deutschen in Japan*, Leipzig, 1920, p. 243 (from 1887–92 Schmiedel taught ethics at the School of the German Society). BA/Potsdam 51023: Answer from the Foreign Office, of 28 April 1875, to the Prussian War Ministry's enquiry whether the Prince would be allowed to attend the war academy and might be attached to the 'Emperor Franz Grenadiers' Regiment'. The Foreign Office had no objections, only, because of the 'polygamous habits prevailing with the Imperial Family in Tokyo' he was not to be addressed as 'His Imperial Highness'. AA/PA I B 16,11: Report Eisendecher-Foreign Office, of 15 April 1878: The Prince had returned from Berlin but because of his unauthorized engagement with a German lady had been placed under house arrest. His main occupation consisted of studying German military books.

91. See above, note 45; most renowned among them was Mori Ogai, later a famous poet, who studied medicine in Berlin from 1884 to 1888 (see below).

92. Hartmann, *Einfluß Deutschlands*, p. 474.

93. Roland Schneider, 'Literaturaustausch zwischen Japan und Deutschland' in Klaus Kracht et al., eds., *Japan und Deutschland im 20. Jahrhundert*, Wiesbaden, 1984, pp. 44–45. (*Reineke Fuchs* was translated in 1884 and was banned three years later). Michiko Minami, 'Einige Gedanken zu deutschen Übersetzungen aus dem modernen japanischen Schrifttum', in Johannes Schmidt, ed., *Deutsch-japanische Freundschaft*, Preetz, 1980, pp. 12–26.

94. AA/PA Japan 1,5: Report of the legation of 27 March 1884.

95. Ibid., Japan 1,4: Reports Eisendecher-Foreign Office, of 17 January and 7 February 1882. Both reports were presented to William I.

96. Ibid., Report Eisendecher-Foreign Office, of 5 March 1882. In order not to irritate the other powers, Ito's mission was officially named a round trip through Europe.

97. Karl Kroeschell, 'Das moderne Japan und das deutsche Recht', in B. Martin, *Japans Weg in die Moderne*, pp. 45–67.

98. Hirobumi Ito, *Commentaries on the Constitution of the Empire of Japan*, Tokyo, 1906, pp. 140ff and 148ff.

99. George M. Beckmann, *The Making of the Meiji-Constitution. The Oligarchs and the Constitutional Development of Japan 1868–1891*, Lawrence, Kansas, 1957; for Ito's voyage, see pp. 70ff. For Lorenz von Stein, see Stefan Koslowski, *Die Geburt des Sozialstaates aus dem Geist des deutschen Idealismus. Person und Gemeinschaft bei Lorenz von Stein*, Weinheim, 1989.

100. Ivan Hall, *Mori Arinori*, Cambridge, Mass., 1973. Also, see below, note 129.

101. AA/PA Japan 1,6: Report Holleben-Foreign Office, of 19 April 1886.

102. Siemes, *Einflüsse Hermann Roeslers*, pp. 8ff.

103. Siemes, *Einflüsse Hermann Roeslers*, pp. 23f. See Ito's defense of the constitution in a speech given at his hometown Hagi, on 2 June 1899. See Tsunoda, *Sources of Japanese Tradition*, pp. 676–79.

104. Siemes, *Einflüsse Hermann Roeslers*, p. 14. For the structure of the new form of government in Japan see, indispensable still today and including reprints of the most important documents, Harold S. Quigley, *Japanese Government and Politics. An Introductory Study*, New York, 1932.

105. BA, Potsdam 29745: Letter from the Japanese legation to the Foreign Office, of 30 June 1885, requesting Mosse for three-and-a-half years. Ibid., In a letter to the Emperor via the Ministry of Justice, of 22 February 1886, Bismarck advocated making an exception granting Mosse leave while keeping up his claim to re-employment and pension. Mosse was offered three more years of service in Japan, which he refused on account of his wife's bad health (Ibid., 29746: Letter from the Japanese legation to the Foreign Office, of 24 July 1890). Perhaps because he was a Jew, Albert Mosse's work in Japan was overshadowed by Roesler's (see above, note 73). Yet, in a report from 1890 (Ibid., 29746), Mosse is called a most influential German expert: until 1 April 1890 'he worked as a legal and administrative adviser to the Japanese cabinet and during that time his success was probably unequalled by any of his predecessors or contemporary colleagues, German or foreign … In any case, it is largely due to his merits that Japanese public life and institutions are being shaped after the German model and Germany has been and still is held in high esteem here.' Also see Hackett, *Yamagata Aritomo*, pp. 108f.

106. Ito had the English historian's biography, J. R. Seeley, *Life and Times of Stein*, Boston, 1879, translated into Japanese (Hackett, *Yamagata Aritomo*, p. 110).

107. Hackett, *Yamagata Aritomo*, pp. 111ff; also see the eminent study on the development of the nationalist Tenno ideology in Japan by Carol Gluck, *Japan's Modern Myths. Ideology in the Late Meiji Period*, Princeton, 1985, pp. 192f.

108. BA Potsdam 29744: Telegram Doenhoff (Tokyo) to Bismarck, of 9 April 1883, transmitting the Japanese request of a police officer from Berlin and 'an experienced and intelligent major-sergeant of the gendarmerie'. On 1 September 1884, in a letter to the Foreign Office, the Prussian Home Ministry suggested police captain Hoehn, who then stayed in Japan until March 1891. During those six years he founded a police school in Tokyo where all the top officers of the Japanese police had to attend special courses, under Hoehn's supervision. After closing the school, Hoehn made sure on wide-ranging inspection tours that the Japanese police had been organised in the Prussian way all over the country. The report by the German legation (ibid., of 6 January 1891) concludes: 'Major Hoehn is one of the very few here who can say they have left their work completed'. For a rather general survey, see Hartmann, *Einfluß Deutschlands*, pp. 470f; and Schmiedel, *Die Deutschen in Japan*, pp. 122f. Hoehn's daughter Anna, in the Protestant parish in 1885, set up a school for lacemaking to support the poor (Schmiedel, *Die Deutschen in Japan*, p. 216).

109. The Prussian courtier Ottmar von Mohl from 1887 to 1889 taught Western court etiquette to the members of the Imperial Household Ministry, whose head, in the rank of a minister, was Ito. Actually but for official receptions, Mohl did not see the Tenno himself. See his memoirs: Ottmar von Mohl, *Am japanischen Hofe*, Berlin, 1904. Also see AA/PA Japan 1,6: A private letter from Mohl to von Bülow, Foreign Office, of 7 July 1887. BA Potsdam 61050: In a report of 11 December 1892, about an audience with the Tenno, the German envoy Gutschmidt expressly appreciated Mohl's work.

110. AA/PA Japan 1,7: Report Holleben-Caprivi, of 16 December 1890 about hostile activities against foreigners.

111. Ibid., Japan 1,8: Report Holleben-Caprivi, of 13 January 1891.

112. Ibid. Already William I in 1887 had expressed the same opinion to Mohl (*Am japanischen Hofe*, p. 3): 'He had heard the Japanese Emperor was about to promulgate a constitution, which he could not understand, since parliamentarian institutions had caused such a fiasco in Prussia and Germany'.

113. Meissner, *Deutsche in Japan*, p. 72. The building burnt down on 20 January 1891. Schmiedel, *Die Deutschen in Japan*, p. 153. BA Potsdam 29745: Letter from Beckmann to the Foreign Office, of 26 February 1886: He (Beckmann) was going to Japan in order to construct several large buildings, such as the Japanese State Bank, the Diet, and several Ministries. Ibid., Telegram German legation Tokyo-Foreign Office, of 1 March 1886: Ito. Ibid.,: Telegram Holleben-Foreign Office, of 24 Sept., 1886: Together with those large buildings, Tokyo was to receive a sewage system. The planning would be done by Dr Hobrecht, communal architect in Berlin, who would afterwards come to Japan for six to eight weeks (in autumn 1882 Tokyo had been hit by a cholera epidemic, ibid., 61048, enquiry from the Foreign Office, of 17 September 1882).

114. Presseisen, *Before Aggression*, chapter 'German versus French Instruction'.

115. AA/PA Japan, Militärangelegenheiten, vol. 1: Report German military attaché-Bismarck, of 11 October 1882.

116. Hackett, *Yamagata Aritomo*, pp. 81ff; text in Tsunoda, *Sources of Japanese Tradition*, pp. 705ff.

117. Georg Kerst, *Jacob Meckel. Sein Leben, sein Wirken in Deutschland und Japan*, Göttingen, 1970, pp. 33, 50ff. Andreas Meckel, 'Jacob Meckel (1842–1906), Instrukteur der japanischen Armee. Ein Leben im preußischen Zeitgeist', in *Kulturvermittler zwischen Japan und Deutschland*, pp. 78–92; Presseisen, *Before Aggression*, pp. 100ff.

118. Kerst, *Meckel*, pp. 52ff., Presseisen, *Before Aggression*, pp. 112ff.

119. Mitsue Koike, 'Die Übernahme westlicher Kleidung in Japan', in *Saeculum*, vol. 38, 1987, pp. 113–19; here p. 116.

120. Kerst, *Meckel*, pp. 58ff; Presseisen, *Before Aggression*, pp. 120ff.

121. AA/PA Japan, Militärangelegenheiten vol. II: The memorandum 'On National Defense in Japan' ('Über die Landesverteidigung Japans') sent to Bismarck by von Holleben, on 8 August 1887.

122. Ibid., vol. I: Memorandum by the Krupp company to the Foreign Office, of 22 July 1885. Since 1868 the company had delivered a total of 273 guns to Japan, most of them for the defense of the coastlines.

123. Major Hermann von Blankenburg and Colonel Erwin von Wildenbruch, the latter teaching at the Japanese war academy until 1890 (Kerst, *Meckel*, pp. 60 and 64).

124. Report from Doernberg (Holleben's deputy) to Bismarck, of 23 March 1888, quoted by Kerst, *Meckel*, p. 97. Kerst's study is partly based on source material he used at the *Reichsarchiv* Potsdam before the Second World War, part of which were destroyed by bombs during the war. In the Potsdam records, too, Meckel is scarcely mentioned. Probably the Prussian military, on the order of the Emperor, had acted on its own without even informing the Foreign Office of Meckel's mission. Only in a letter of recommendation by the Meiji Tenno, of 18 January 1887, is there a small acknowledgement of Meckel's achievements, BA Potsdam 285, 31.

125. AA/PA Japan, Militärangelegenheiten, vol. II: Report Holleben to Caprivi, of 1 June 1890, about the big Imperial manoeuvres. After Meckel's death on 5 July 1906, he was honoured by his Japanese pupils, during the commemoration ceremony in Tokyo, as the real victor of the war against Russia that had just ended (Kerst, *Meckel*, appendix). In the battle of Mukden, the Japanese had lost about 75,000 men (15,892 dead, 59,812 wounded); the Russians 70,000 (20,000 dead, 49,000 wounded) and 20,000 captives. The number of Japanese captives has not been recorded, as there were probably none. [See R. M. Connaughton, *The War of the Rising Sun and the Tumbling Bear. A Military History of the Russo-Japanese War (1904–1905)*, London, 1988.]

126. Gluck, *Japan's Modern Myths*, p. 172. In Osaka in 1893, one-third of all the recruits were illiterate, and most conscripts could not tell left from right. In 1906, almost all of them had been to elementary school and knew a few practical skills.

127. Wittig, *Pädagogik und Bildungspolitik Japans*, pp. 81ff.

128. Michio Nagai, 'Westernization and Japanization. The Early Meiji Transformation of Education', in Donald H. Shively, ed., *Tradition and Modernization in Japanese Culture*, Princeton, 1971, pp. 35–76.

129. Ibid., p. 74, and Burks, *The Modernizers*, p. 261.

130. Gluck, *Japan's Modern Myths*, p. 127.

131. Klaus Luhmer, *Schule und Bildungsreform in Japan. Japanische Bildungspolitik im internationalen Vergleich. Erster Band: Gestaltungsfaktoren, Aufbau, Strukturwandel und Verwaltung des allgemeinbildenden Schulwesens*, Tokyo, 1972, pp. 73ff. Gluck, *Japan's Modern Myths*, pp. 110 and 127.

132. Rauck, *Beziehungen zwischen Japan und Deutschland*, p. 170.

133. Gluck, *Japan's Modern Myths*, p. 109.

134. Bismarck in the Privy Council on 30 April 1889. Quoted by Folkert Meyer, *Schule der Untertanen. Lehrer und Politik in Preußen 1848–1900*, Hamburg, 1976, p. 171.

135. Komatsubara Eitaro in 1882 belonged to the founding members of the 'Society For the Promotion of German Science'; in February 1890 as Prefect of Saitama at a Prefects' conference he suggested issuing a statement on elementary education (Gluck, *Japan's Modern Myth*, pp. 115f.); in 1910 he became Minister of the Interior and started another revision of school textbooks.

136. Inoue Tetsujiro (1856–1944) from 1884 to 1890 studied philosophy at Berlin University, especially with Eduard von Hartmann's 'Identitäts-Realismus'. In 1890 he got a chair for philosophy at Todai where he tried to amalgamate Buddhism with the teachings of Schopenhauer and von Hartmann into the so-called 'Reformed Buddhism' (Gluck, *Japan's Modern Myths*, pp. 129f). Also see Klaus Antoni, 'Inoue Tetsujiro (1856–1944) und die Entwicklung der Staatsideologie in der zweiten Hälfte der Meiji-Zeit', in *Oriens Extremus*, vol. 33, 1990, pp. 99–117.

137. German text in Wittig, *Pädagogik und Bildungspolitik Japans*, pp. 89ff.

138. AA/PA Japan 1,7: Report Holleben-Bismarck, of 14 April 1889.

139. 1876–1902, see his memoirs: Erwin Baelz, *Das Leben eines deutschen Arztes im erwachenden Japan*, Stuttgart, 1931.

140. Fritz K. Ringer, *The Decline of the German Mandarins. The German Academic Community 1890–1933*, Cambridge, Mass., 1969. For the strong German influence on and the political role of the new academic élite, see Byron K. Marshall, 'Professors and Politics. The Meiji Academic Elite', in *Journal of Japanese Studies*, vol. 3, 1977, pp. 71–97; the author does not, however, justly evaluate the German influence nor the parallels with Germany.

141. Salaries in Japan were twice as high as in Germany. The historian Riess (see note 177) for example received 470 yen a month, equalling 1555 Reichsmark (in 1887 the exchange rate was 1 yen = 3,30 RM); the linguist Florenz (see note 166) even earned 500 yen a month. For comparison, a Japanese cook received 8 yen a month, his wife sharing his work got 4 yen. Food was extremely cheap. See Schmiedel, *Die Deutschen in Japan*, pp. 66ff, and the social study by Irene Hardach-Pinke 'Die Meiji-Deutschen: Historische und soziale Bedingungen der Anfänge deutsch-japanischer Kulturkontakte in Japan', in *Saeculum*, vol. 38, 1987, pp. 76–98.

142. Rauck, *Beziehungen zwischen Japan und Deutschland*, p. 129. Only in 1888 was the number of German advisers higher than those from any other group. Jones, *Live Machines*, p. 148, lists sixty-five persons in 1888. The number of forty-three Germans in 1887 given by Hardach-Pinke, *Die Meiji-Deutschen*, is obviously too small.

143. See the table in Burks, *The Modernizers*, p. 213. Next to Baelz, the surgeon Julius Scriba must be mentioned who taught at Tokyo University from 1881 to 1905. Even today there is a memorial for the two of them on the premises of Tokyo University.

144. Hartmann, *Einfluß Deutschlands*, p. 465, note 8.

145. Werner Wenz and Arnold Vogt, 'Der Einfluß der deutschen Schulmedizin auf die Herausbildung einer westlichen Medizin in Japan', in Martin, ed., *Japans Weg in die Moderne*, pp. 69–85. Horst Hammitzsch, ed., *Japan Handbuch*, Wiesbaden, 1981. The bacteriologist Kitasato Shibasaburo (1852–1931) from 1884 to 1891 worked with Robert Koch as his pupil in Berlin. Koch visited Japan in 1908, two years before he died.

146. Baelz, *Arzt in Japan*, pp. 210f. As early as 1883, Baelz had reported on the cranial measurements of the Japanese and the Ainu in a contribution to a scientific series 'Die körperlichen Eigenschaften der Japaner' in *Mitteilungen der Deutschen Gesellschaft für Natur- und Völkerkunde Ostasiens*, vol. 28, 1883, pp. 329–59. There he proved many of the contemporary studies wrong and carefully avoided fixing special forms from which to conclude any special traits of the Japanese race.

147. For the infamous special unit '731' in Manchuria, see Peter Williams and David Wallace, *Unit '731': Japan's Secret Biological Warfare in World War Two*, New York, 1989, and Noburo Miyazaki 'Eine japanische 'Vergangenheitsbewältigung'', in Peter Pörtner, ed., *Japan Konkursbuch*, vol. 16/17, Tübingen, 1986; and Saburo Ienaga, *Japan's Last War. World War Two and the Japanese 1931–1945*, Oxford, 1979, pp. 188ff. For the Japanese war crimes, especially vivisections carried out by medical doctors, see Edward F. L. Russell, *The Knights of Bushido. A Short History of Japanese War Crimes*, London, 1958.

148. BA/ Potsdam 29745: Letter Prussian Ministry of Justice to Foreign Office of 29 May 1885: Georg Michaelis, a law court official, had been given a leave to work in Japan from August 1885 to the end of 1888. Also see Michaelis' memoirs: *Für Staat und Volk*, Berlin, 1922, chapter 7: 'Als Hochschullehrer in Japan' (As a University Teacher in Japan).

149. BA/ Potsdam 29746: Telegrams Holleben to Foreign Office, of 2 October 1889: Michaelis and the Delbrück brothers had left Japan in July 1889; their successors, the law experts Dr. Lönholm and Dr. Nippold, had arrived. Lönholm taught law at Todai from 1889 to 1907 (Schmiedel, *Die Deutschen in Japan*, pp. 121f).

150. Akio Nakai, 'Georg Michaelis und Japan', in *Studien des Instituts für die Kultur der deutschsprachigen Länder*, vol. 6, Sophia Universität Tokyo, 1988, pp. 36–39.

151. Jones, *Extraterritoriality*, p. 102.

152. Ibid., pp. 175–86; Aoki-Kimberly Treaty of 16 July, 1894. The revision of the unequal treaties was finally realized on 4 August 1899.

153. AA/PA Japan 1,7: Report Holleben to Bismarck, of 3 January 1890. Prime Minister Yamagata had announced to Holleben that all Japanese law codes were to be reshaped after German patterns. For the work of the law experts, see Kroeschell (note 97), and Nobuyoshi Toshitani, 'Japan's Modern Legal System. Its Formation and Structure', and by the same author, 'Family Policy and Family Law in Modern Japan', vols I and II, both of them in *Annals of the Institute of Social Science*, vol. 17, University of Tokyo, 1976, pp. 1–50, vol. 20, 1979, pp. 95–141, vol. 21, 1980, pp. 130–76.

154. Richard H. Minear, *Japanese Tradition and Western Law. Emperor, State, and Law in the Thought of Hozumi Yatsuka*, Cambridge, Mass., 1970, pp. 31ff. (From 1884 to 1889 Hozumi had studied in Heidelberg, Berlin, and Straßburg.)

155. Frank O. Miller, *Minobe Tatsukichi. Interpreter of Constitutionalism in Japan*, Berkeley, 1965.

156. Saizo Yoshida, 'Jacob Meckel und Mori Ogai', in Schmidt, *Deutsch-japanische Freundschaft*, pp. 56–59. Mori translated Lessing's 'Emilia Galotti' in 1889, and Kleist's work in 1890. See *Japan-Handbuch*, p. 1092.

157. Walter Giesen 'Musik und Ongaku: Bilanz der Ignoranz', in Kracht et al., *Japan und Deutschland*, pp. 167–88. The Japanese were especially fond of 'Rorerai' (Die Loreley).

158. Meissner, *Deutsche in Japan*, p. 28; and Hans Molisch, *Deutsche Kulturarbeit in Japan*, Vienna, 1926; the Rector's inaugural address at Vienna University on 29 October 1926, p. 90. (The Austrian professor of medicine Molisch taught in Japan from 1922 to 1925.) BA Potsdam 29746: In a letter of 13 November 1888 the Japanese legation asked the Foreign Office to send a musical director to Japan to conduct the Navy Band. The Chief of the Admiralty on 21 December 1888 ordered the oboist Gustav Arpe to Japan (ibid.).

159. Doris Croissant, 'Fenellosas "Wahre Theorie der Kunst" und ihre Wirkung in der Meiji-Zeit (1868–1912)', in *Saeculum*, vol. 38, 1987, pp. 52–75. *Japan-Handbuch*, 'Philosophie', pp. 1295–396.

160. Ludwig Busse (1862–1907) from 1887 to 1892 held a chair of philosophy at Todai; he represented the philosophical school of metaphysical realism that had been influenced by Herrmann Lotze (1817–1881). His successor was Raphael von Koeber (1845–1923) who took Busse's chair from 1893 and seems to have worked in Japan until his death.

161. Rudolf Seidl, 'Die deutsch-japanischen Kulturbeziehungen auf dem Gebiete der Wissenschaften', in *Ostasiatische Rundschau*, vol. 20, 1939, pp. 242–44, and 299–300.

162. See above, note 136.

163. Kato Hiroyuki (1836–1916) in 1861 had been given a telegraph as a present by the Eulenburg mission, and in order to use it he had to learn German. From 1877 to 1886 and again from 1890 to 1893 he was Rector of Todai. See David Abosch, *Kato Hiroyuki and the Introduction of German Political Thought in Modern Japan, 1868–1883*, unpublished Ph.D. dissertation, University of California, Berkeley, 1964.

164. Kentaro Hayashi, 'Ludwig Riess, einer der Väter der Geschichtswissenschaft in Japan', in *Bonner Zeitschrift für Japanologie*, vol. 3, 1981, pp. 31–45, here p. 35.

165. Karl Florenz (1865–1939), *Japanische Annalen A.D. 592–697. Nihongi (Buch XXII–XXX)*, Tokyo, 1903.

166. 'To Adolf Hitler, the Personification of Goodwill and the Master of Well-Timed Action'. The book, vol. IV of a collection of poetry was published by Bull's in Leiden. As the preface is dated 1938, the 'well-timed action' must be the incorporation (*Anschluß*) of Austria. The Dutchman Pierson was a well-known senior fascist and had dedicated the preceding volume to Mussolini. Dedicating the book to Hitler had an aftermath in that the OAG (German East Asian Society) Prize, awarded for the first time in 1986, and originally named after Florenz as the founder of German Japanology had to be renamed into 'OAG Award', even though the Society was probably more deeply involved in national socialism than Karl Florenz. See Herbert Worm, 'War Karl Florenz ein Verehrer Hitlers? Eine deutsche Preisverleihung in Tokyo', in *Nachrichten der Gesellschaft für Natur- und Völkerkunde Ostasiens/Hamburg*, vol. 144, 1988, pp. 29–49. For the involvement of German Japanology with the National Socialist ideology, see Herbert Worm, *Japanologie im nationalsozialistischen Deutschland*, in Gerhard Krebs and Bernd Martin, eds., *Formierung und Fall der Achse Berlin-Tokyo*, München 1994, pp. 153–86. For Florenz' scholarly achievements, see the contributions to the conference in Hamburg in 1985, in *Nachrichten der Gesellschaft für Natur- und Völkerkunde Ostasiens/Hamburg*, vol. 137, 1985.

167. Dieter Lindenlaub, *Richtungskämpfe im Verein für Sozialpolitik*, Wiesbaden, 1967.

168. See above, note 44.

169. BA/Potsdam 29746: Report from the German legation (Holleben) to Caprivi on foreigners in Japan. According to the report, Rathgen returned to Germany against Japanese wishes. Karl Rathgen (1856–1921) was Schmoller's brother-in-law. From 1882 to 1890 he held a chair of state law and administrative law at Todai. See Karl Rathgen, *Japans Volkswirtschaft und Staatshaushalt*, Leipzig, 1891.

170. For the following, see Pyle, *German Economics*, and recently Kiichiro Yagi, *Wirtschaftswissenschaften und Modernisierung Japans. Einführung und Institutionalisierung der Wirtschaftswissenschaften in Japan 1860–1925. Diskussionsbeiträge* No. 13 (Institut für Entwicklunspolitik der Universität Freiburg im Breisgau, 1990) and Wolfgang Schwentker, 'Fremde Gelehrte: Japanische Nationalökonom und Sozialreformer im Kaiserreich' in Gangolf Hübinger und Wolfgang Schwentker, eds., *Intellektuelle im Kaiserreich*, Frankfurt am Main, 1993, pp. 172–97. For a general account, see: Chuhei Sugiyama and Hiroshi Mizuta, eds., *Enlightenment and Beyond. Political Economy Comes to Japan*, Tokyo, 1988.

171. Pyle, *German Economics*, p. 147; the quotation is to be found in the treatise Kuwata published in 1896 shortly before leaving for Germany: 'Der Staat und die Soziale Frage'.

172. See Havens, *Farm and Nations*, and Richard J. Smethurst, *A Social Basis for Prewar Japanese Militarism. The Army and the Rural Community*, Berkeley, 1974.

173. Hartmann, *Einfluß Deutschlands*, pp. 480f.

174. Hayashi, *Ludwig Riess*, and Leonard Blussé, 'Japanese Historiography and European Sources', in P. C. Emmer and H. L. Wesseling, eds., *Reappraisals in Overseas History*, Leiden, 1979, pp. 193–224; here pp. 200ff.

175. Hiroshi Imai, 'British Influence on Modern Japanese Historiography', in *Saeculum*, vol. 38, 1987, pp. 99–112.

176. For those aspects of national history that suggested combining the 'German method' with the anti-Confucian school of historiography towards the end of the shogunate, see Ulrich Goch, 'Die Entstehung einer modernen Geschichtswissenschaft in Japan', in *Bochumer Jahrbuch zur Ostasienforschung*, vol. 1, 1978, pp. 238–71.

177. Ludwig Riess (1861–1928) from 1887 to 1902 taught history at Tokyo University. For fear of running into difficulties in Germany because of his mixed marriage (his wife was Japanese) especially as he was a Jew, he left his family in Japan and returned to Germany alone. In Berlin he taught at the University and the War Academy, but he led a secluded life until his death. In 1940 his dissertation was published in English in second edition in Cambridge (Hayashi, *Ludwig Riess*, p. 36).

178. See above, note 164.

179. Imai, *British Influence*, p. 110.

180. Blussé, *Japanese Historiography*, p. 200. For the following, too, see that excellent study.

181. See Wieland Wagner, *Japans Außenpolitik in der frühen Meiji-Zeit 1868–1895*, Stuttgart, 1990.

182. Blussé, *Japanese Historiography*. For the search for identity of today's Japanese, see Irmela Hijiya-Kirschnereit, *Ende der Exotik*, and Nelly Naumann, 'Identitätsfindungdas geistige Problem des modernen Japan', in Martin, *Japans Weg in die Moderne*, pp. 173–92.

183. Ludwig Riess, 'Deutschland und Japan', in *Preußische Jahrbücher*, vol. 168, 1917, pp. 203–29, here p. 229.

184. See two of the author's numerous studies on German-Japan relations: Bernd Martin, 'Japans Weg in die Moderne und das deutsche Vorbild: Historische Gemeinsamkeiten zweier verspäteter Nationen', in Martin, *Japans Weg in die Moderne*, pp. 98–114; and 'Die deutsch-japanischen Beziehungen während des Dritten Reiches', in Manfred Funke, ed., *Hitler, Deutschland und die Mächte. Materialien zur Außenpolitik des Dritten Reiches*, Düsseldorf, 1976, pp. 454–70; revised and reprinted in Karl-Dietrich Bracher et al., eds., *Nationalsozialistische Diktatur 1933–1945. Eine Bilanz*, Bonn, 1983, pp. 370–89.

185. 'Twenty-one Demands' of 18 January 1915; English text in David John Lu, ed., *Sources of Japanese History*, vol. II, New York, 1974, pp. 107–9. Also, see Marius B. Jansen, *Japan and China: From War to Peace, 1894–1972*, Chicago, 1975, pp. 209–23.

186. Akira Hayashima, *Die Illusion des Sonderfriedens. Deutsche Verständigungspolitik mit Japan im Ersten Weltkrieg*, München, 1982.

187. Karl Haushofer (1869–1946) as a Bavarian officer in 1909–10 had been transferred to the Japanese army and afterwards travelled large parts of East Asia. Upon his return he published the geopolitical German books, *Dai Nihon*, Berlin, 1913, and *Geopolitik des Pazifischen Raumes*, Heidelberg, 1913. From 1924 on he edited the periodical *Zeitschrift für Geopolitik* that strongly advocated a worldwide German-Japanese alliance based on geostrategical concepts and influenced the National Socialists' policy of alliances concerning East Asia.

188. Sadao Asada, 'Japan's "Special Interests" and the Washington Conference', in *American Historical Review*, vol. 57, 1961, pp. 62–70; and Thomas Buckley, *The United States and the Washington Conference 1921–1922*, Knoxville, 1970.

189. Peter Duus, *Party Rivalry and Political Change in Taisho Japan*, Cambridge, Mass., 1968; Bernard S. Silberman and H. D. Harootunian, eds., *Japan in Crisis: Essays on Taisho Democracy*, Princeton, 1974.

190. On 12 October 1940 Konoe, then Prime Minister, founded the 'Imperial Rule Assistance Association' that soon absorbed all political parties. The foundation of such a unified mass movement clearly followed National Socialist patterns. For the debates among the different groups of the Japanese government, see Gerhard Krebs, *Japans Deutschlandpolitik 1935–1941. Eine Studie zur Vorgeschichte des Pazifischen Krieges*, two volumes, Hamburg, 1984, pp. 548ff.

191. In 1930 the Japanese navy tried to cancel the decisions on armament restriction that had been renewed at the London Naval Conference and to start on a rearmament programme of a battle fleet according to the example set by Tirpitz. See the contribution to this volume: 'Japan and Germany on the Path towards War'.

192. Takehiko Yoshihashi: *Conspiracy at Mukden. The Rise of the Japanese Military*, New Haven, 1963.

193. See the author's comparative study, chapter 6, 'Three Forms of Fascism', in this volume.

194. Richard H. Mitchell, *Thought Control in Prewar Japan*, Ithaca, N.Y., 1976.

195. Klaus Antoni, 'Kokutai. Das "Nationalwesen" als japanische Utopie', in *Saeculum*, vol. 38, 1987, pp. 266–82.

196. See chapter 4, 'Japan During the World Economic Crisis. Big Business and Social Unrest', in this volume.

197. Robert King Hall, ed., *Kokutai no hongi. Cardinal Principles of the National Entity of Japan*, Cambridge, Mass., 1949, excerpts in Tsunoda, *Sources*, pp. 785ff.

198. See Martin, *Deutsch-japanische Beziehungen*.

199. Theo Sommer, *Deutschland und Japan zwischen den Mächten 1935–1940*, Tübingen, 1962; James William Morley, ed., *Deterrent Diplomacy. Japan, Germany, and the USSR 1935–1940*. Selected translations from 'Taiheiyo senso e no michi; Kaisen gaiko shi', New York, 1976; and the study by Krebs, *Japans Deutschlandpolitik*.

200. There is only one comparative study, by Arnulf Baring and Masamori Sase, *Zwei zaghafte Riesen?*

201. Bernd Martin, *Deutschland und Japan im Zweiten Weltkrieg*, Göttingen, 1969.

List of the German diplomatic representatives in Tokyo, compiled after Hans Schwalbe and Heinrich Seemann, eds., *Deutsche Botschafter in Japan, 1860–1973*, Tokyo, 1974.

1. Graf Friedrich Albrecht zu Eulenburg (1860–1861)
2. Max von Brandt (1862–1875)
3. Karl von Eisendecher (1875–1882)
4. Otto Graf von Dönhoff (1882–1885)
5. Theodor von Holleben (1886–1891)
6. Felix Freiherr von Gutschmid (1892–1897)
7. Casimir Graf von Leyden (1898–1900)
8. Emmerich Graf von Arco-Valley (1901–1906)
9. Alfons Freiherr Mumm von Schwarzenstein (1906–1911)
10. Arthur Graf von Rex (1911–1914)
11. Wilhelm Solf (1920–1928)
12. Ernst-Arthur Voretzsch (1928–1933)
13. Herbert von Dirksen (1933–1938)
14. Eugen Ott (1938–1942)
15. Heinrich Georg Stahmer (1943–1945)

PART II

JAPAN'S SOCIAL IMPERIALISM

❧ 3 ❧

THE POLITICS OF EXPANSION OF THE JAPANESE EMPIRE

NEO-IMPERIALISM OR PAN-ASIATIC MISSION?

Japan's politics of expansion from the emergence of modern Japan during the Meiji Restoration to the present time have produced highly conflicting interpretations. One of the major works on international relations in the Far East after 1918 – Akira Iriye's *After Imperialism: The Search for a New Order in the Far East*[1] – suggests that the era of imperialism came to an end with the First World War. This point of view has many advocates among revisionist historians of modern Asia, especially in the United States. They interpret the period leading up to the Pacific War mainly in terms of a political antagonism between the United States and Imperial Japan. This view lacks an awareness of the increasing radicalisation in both socialist and fascist directions that characterised Japan's domestic politics during the interwar years. What also tends to be neglected is the fact that the European powers, including Germany, maintained their strong positions in the Far East throughout the 1920s and 1930s. Although as early as 1901 the Japanese socialist, Kotoku Shusui, published a fundamental treatise on imperialism anticipating J. A. Hobson's theory which appeared the following year,[2] the specific origins and effects of Japanese imperialism have received scant attention in the West. Europe continued to be seen as the sole source of territorial expansionism, and neither the realities of modern East Asian history nor the debates among champions and opponents of imperialism in Japan were fully taken into account. Japan was regarded

---

This chapter is a revised version of a translation by Christian Sonntag and Dr Jürgen Osterhammel, which was originally published in Wolfgang J. Mommsen and Jürgen Osterhammel, eds., *Imperialism and After*, London, 1986, pp. 63–82.

as an altogether peculiar country to which the concepts of Western social science, including that of imperialism, could by no means be applied. At best, Japanese expansionism was explained as the retarded stirrings of a 'latecomer' on the international scene, in other words, as a kind of derivative imperialism in a nation prone to imitating foreign models in all conceivable respects. This view is still almost as widespread today as it was several decades ago.

This chapter will attempt to survey imperialist tendencies in Japanese society and foreign policy over a period of more than one hundred years, paying special attention to connections between the various sources and external manifestations of Japanese imperialism. After a few remarks concerning the particular preconditions of Japanese imperialist policies, a four-stage model of their evolution will be suggested. Finally, each of the four stages will be discussed in terms of current Western theories of imperialism.

National Determinants of Japanese Imperialism

The expansionist policies of Imperial Japan, which culminated in the occupation of Southeast Asia and collapsed with the empire's unconditional surrender in September 1945, were primarily determined by endogenous factors, the impact of the international system taking second place. Japan's social order was rigid even by Asian standards,[3] its small and atavistic élite totally committed to defending the system and obstinately opposed to reform of any kind. Unless Japan could somehow integrate itself into the capitalist world order, the situation could only lead to a war with the West. After more than two hundred years of hermetic seclusion from the outside world, the static order of the Tokugawa shogunate – a kind of centralistic military dictatorship – was challenged by the superior American navy in 1853 and confronted with the consequences of an unequal commercial treaty forced upon the shogun's government. The European powers quickly followed suit with similar treaties. As a result, the Japanese market was exposed virtually unprotected to industrial imports from the West. Japan, like China at the same time, seemed to be wide open for the more advanced Western nations to make political inroads.[4] But, in contrast to the lofty caste of Chinese literati who despised Western progress and Western material achievements, the traditional

Japanese warrior-élite, the samurai, rose to the challenge. Determined to defend Japan's national identity and their own long-established right to privilege and leadership, this group engineered an internal shift of power in 1868: the shogun system was eliminated, and the god-like emperor was reinstated as the central political authority endowed with absolute power. The so-called 'renewal of the Meiji period', sometimes even referred to as the 'Meiji Revolution', was in reality a restoration, stemming from a will to preserve the existing social order.[5]

The social system of vertically stratified small groups, the hierarchical principle of loyalty embedded in the system of child-like devotion of inferiors towards the paternal benevolence of their superiors (*oyabun-kobun*),[6] and hence the harmony of a village-centred social order were to be protected against the divisive and corrupting influence of the Western 'barbarians'. At the same time, traditional values and norms of behaviour were to be preserved in order to guarantee the position of power and the claim to leadership of a premodern élite. During and after 1868 a body of dictatorial leaders emerged, hiding behind the sacred shield of the allegedly omnipotent and god-like emperor. It recruited its members from the three focuses of power which were alternately to dominate the country until 1945: the military, the court circles, and the civil politicians (later to evolve into party politicians) who had close ties with the big merchants.

The oligarchy committed itself to a programme of modernisation that was basically nationalistic and defensive. From the very beginning, its principal aim was the establishment of an efficient, heavy industry along with the necessary infrastructure. Only thus, was it thought, could a military force be created that would rank equally with that of the West. Foreign experts were hired to help the government in building model factories and initiating pilot projects, which were later sold to the *zaibatsu* (literally, money cliques) already in existence, thus strengthening their hold on the market. From the start, there was a dual economy in Japan. Alongside a few large modern enterprises, there were a multitude of small family workshops which continued the preindustrial tradition of highly developed craftsmanship. They soon found themselves in a position of semifeudal dependence on the modern corporations which were able to dictate prices and terms of delivery to them. The family firm of medium size which played such a decisive role in the industrial development of the West was absent in Japan and, with it, the politically assertive bourgeois entrepreneur. Neither a bourgeois stratum nor a horizontally integrated working class developed in Japan during the period of industrialisation.

Two main problems had to be overcome for the ambitious programmes of industrialisation and militarisation to succeed: a scarcity of natural resources and a lack of capital. Those raw materials required for establishing heavy industry (minerals, coal, and, later, oil) were often available only in insufficient quantities or not at all, and were also of inferior quality. Since most of these raw materials and essential machinery had to be imported from Western countries, increasing exports had to take top priority in economic policy. After the First World War, textiles and other products of light industry made up the bulk of exports. During the preceding period, agriculture not only had to supply most of the goods which Japan sold abroad, it also bore the burden of financing almost the entire economic development. Peasants had to pay a fixed tax in cash which amounted to 18 percent of the value of their crops.[7] The revenue derived from this tax, together with the proceeds from the export of silk, contributed decisively to financing early industrialisation. There were only two foreign loans during the early Meiji period[8] because the Japanese government wanted to minimise opportunities for Western interference in the domestic economy.

Although enforced modernisation transformed the country into a great power within one generation, the social costs were considerable. Above all, agriculture was ruined, a sector that as late as during the Pacific War provided employment for more than half of the population. Serfdom had been abolished in 1871. Even so, a small stratum of big landlords kept the peasants in a position of quasi-feudal tenancy. As a result, social disaffection and unrest were smouldering among the impoverished peasants. In the cities, the small artisans, totally dependent on the large enterprises, formed a potentially restless element. Industrialisation dictated from above endangered the village community, which had always been seen as the hub of Japanese society; it threatened to reduce the mass of the people to a materially and politically deprived proletariat. It was therefore inevitable that, as industrialisation proceeded, Japan sank deeper and deeper into a dichotomy between traditional concepts of legitimacy and traditional social norms on the one hand, and the reality of a conflict-ridden society on the other. Most of the social and political conflicts in modern

Japan can be traced back to this fundamental separation between traditional social and moral values and the harsh world of incipient and superficial industrialisation. For the people and the leadership alike, the only way to bridge this gap was to escape into a mythical nationalism, which was rooted in the peasant masses, but which could also be manipulated from above.

Classical (Competitive) Imperialism

The Japanese ruling élite never abandoned the battle cry of the Restoration: 'rich country – strong army'. Politics of all kinds were governed by the supreme goal of attaining parity with the Western powers. The strengthening of the nation was to be achieved by a build-up of heavy industry which, in turn, would supply an army based on compulsory military service.

The beginning of Japan's policy of expansion and thus of Japanese imperialism dates back to the preindustrial period. In the early 1870s, the pros and cons of territorial expansion had been fiercely debated within the small circle of the Meiji 'founding fathers'. The compromise reached at that time led to the first, albeit cautious, steps being taken on the path of imperialism. While the majority of the government were on their first official mission abroad (Iwakura mission) to negotiate a revision of the unequal treaties, their colleagues in Tokyo were planning the invasion of Korea. The rationale for their plan was twofold. First, Japan was to share in the partition of China (which claimed suzerainty over Korea) on an equal footing with the Western powers. Secondly, the energies of the restless samurai class were to be deflected abroad in a war of conquest. In numerical terms, the strength of the samurai class was considerable. Together with their families, the samurai comprised about 4 to 5 percent of the population: a total of approximately two million people. After the abolition of the feudal fiefs in 1871 this class lost its social functions, and ways had to be found to fit it into the new order.

Having hastily returned from Europe, the members of the Iwakura mission, impressed by what they had seen abroad, vehemently opposed all military adventures.[9] In their view, which eventually prevailed, Japan should concentrate its energies on domestic development before territorial annexations could be contemplated. The samurai class would be of greater use to the country if its virtues and abilities could be made to serve administrative and economic reform at home rather than being wasted in a bloody military gamble.

Japan's activities abroad were, therefore, limited to the annexation of the Ryukyu Islands (Okinawa) in 1872, a punitive expedition against Formosa in 1874, and the forcing open of the Korean port of Pusan two years later. Although not very significant in themselves, these moves foreshadowed the double thrust that was to characterise Imperial Japan's expansion in the following decades: first, via the Korean peninsula to the Asian mainland, and secondly, over the chain of islands extending from Formosa towards Southeast Asia. The two leading clans of the Meiji Restoration, Choshu and Satsuma, favoured the northern and the southern strategy respectively. Henceforth, the rivalry between these two clans shaped the conflict over the direction of imperial expansion. It later turned into an antagonism between army (Choshu) and navy (Satsuma) that continued right up to the Pacific War.

The constitution of 1889, which largely followed the Prussian model,[10] marked the outward culmination of the Meiji reform and seemed to set Japan on the track towards a Western-style constitutional state. However, the Imperial Rescript on Education[11] of the following year represented an ideological retreat from this position, demanding a return to Confucian values and emphasising the idea of the Japanese as the chosen people, thus indicating that Japan was again turning its back on the West. All the prerequisites for a belligerent foreign policy were now present: military power, an indigenous ideology, and the end of domestic reform. Japan was prepared to join the imperialist struggle for China and to strive for equality with the Western powers. The Japanese systematically enhanced their influence at the Korean court and, having secured British diplomatic backing,[12] went to war with China over Korea. When in 1895 Japan imposed harsh peace terms on the defeated Chinese Empire, it unwittingly furthered the interests of Western imperialism. The acquisition of Formosa and the Pescadores as well as the lease of the Liaotung Peninsula encouraged the European powers to fulfil their own ambitions. Even the Americans arrived on the scene as guarantors of free trade with China – a role which they had arrogated to themselves. The huge 'indemnity' of 230 million taels[13] – almost twice the amount of the Japanese state budget at that time – ruined China's public finances and increased its financial dependence on the Western powers.

Nevertheless, Japan failed to gain the equality it desired in the international arena. The emptiness of Japan's claim to be a major power was exposed when the Triple Intervention of France, Russia, and Germany forced it to give up the leased territory in Southern Manchuria.

It was the victory over tsarist Russia in 1905[14] that finally established Japan's hegemony in Southern Manchuria and paved the way for the annexation of Korea five years later. Imperial Japan now assumed a new role as leader of the Asian peoples' anticolonial struggle against their white masters. On the other hand, the Western powers could no longer deny Japan recognition as a great power in its own right. In 1911 tariff autonomy was finally attained and a protectionist foreign-trade policy implemented forthwith.[15] At the time of the Emperor Meiji's death in 1912, Japan seemed to be at the peak of its domestic strength and international standing.

Agrarian Socialism versus Capitalist Expansion: Ideological and Economic Motives behind Japan's 'Manifest Destiny'

It was not until the First World War that Japanese imperialism acquired unequivocally aggressive features. The military victory over the Germans at Tsingtao, in conjunction with the unexpected wartime boom in domestic industry, induced the leaders in Tokyo to launch a diplomatic surprise attack on China. The Twenty-One Demands of January 1915 are remarkable in that for the first time in the history of Japanese expansion, economic concerns were paramount. Japan demanded control over China's raw materials, its infrastructure, and its administrative apparatus.[16] As the Western powers were involved in the European war and therefore could not provide the support requested by China, the weak government of Yuan Shi-k'ai gave in to Tokyo's ultimatum and conceded most of Japan's demands. Even the United States, which was to acknowledge Japan's special position on the Asian mainland in the Lansing-Ishii Agreement of November 1917,[17] offered no help.

At home, an unprecedented economic upturn stimulated the concentration of industry and doubled the industrial labour force from one to two million.[18] At the same time, social unrest increased, especially in urban areas where it erupted in the rice riots of the summer of 1918.[19] Influenced by the Russian Revolution, the Japanese proletariat gained political self-confidence and shifted to the left, demanding higher wages, social benefits, and last but not least, more political rights. One way out for the oligarchy would have been to channel social and political discontent into expansionist adventures. This failed, however, because the Western powers were determined to restrict Japan's position to that of an imperialist junior partner. At the Versailles Conference, the Japanese demand for racial equality was rejected by the colonial powers. At the Washington Conference of 1921–22,[20] Japan had to abandon its privileges in Shantung province (the former German sphere of interest) and, furthermore, to agree to a limitation of its naval armaments to maintain a ratio of 3:5:5, in relation to the United States and Britain. In addition, the alliance with Britain[21] was abandoned in favour of collective treaties reaffirming the status quo in the Pacific and the 'open door' in China. In both nationalist and socialist circles in Japan these agreements were denounced as the 'Japanese Versailles'. The exclusion of the Japanese from immigration into the United States which came into force at the same time added to this sense of national humiliation. The social-imperialist policy of distracting attention from internal tensions by imperialist adventures abroad was thus sabotaged by the Western powers.

The domestic crisis deepened after the collapse of the wartime boom in the spring of 1920, and the government found itself compelled to introduce reforms. Moreover, the shift to party Cabinets in 1918 and the introduction of universal male suffrage in 1925 resulted in a corrupt symbiosis of party politicians and business leaders rather than in a genuine democratisation of the country.[22] The Peace Preservation Laws of the same year[23] put heavy penalties on all political activities that were deemed dangerous to the imperial system (*kokutai*); in effect, they amounted to a ban on socialist and even liberal political parties. 'Taisho democracy' meant little more than a shift of power from the Meiji founding fathers who had been close to the court, many of whom were now dead, to professional politicians and business circles.

An unstable economy with widely fluctuating prices and stagnant real incomes was the hallmark of the 1920s. The population continued to grow, and the increase had to be absorbed by the agrarian sector. Agriculture suffered heavily after the government, anxious to pacify the restless urban masses, opened the market to cheap imports of rice. The Ministry of Commerce and Industry which was founded in 1925,[24] was looking for foreign models. American rationalisation of production and Germany's state-controlled economy of the First World War were those recommended by Kishi Nobusuke, a young ministry official who had undertaken a series of study trips abroad.[25] Even before the onset of the Great Depression, the state was called upon to manage the economy and to curb the allegedly selfish activities of big business. Demands of this kind were chiefly voiced by military and social-revolutionary groups. However, they went unheeded in parliament, where 55 percent of the members of the lower house (in 1930) were known to be closely affiliated with powerful economic interests.[26]

The military, which prided itself on being the creator and guardian of the nation's greatness, had been affected by budget cuts and attacked the capitalist alliance of politicians and industrial magnates. Since the majority of the conscripts and about half of the officers came from the impoverished peasantry, they were easily won over by nationalist agitation clamouring for anticapitalist revolution and imperialist expansion.[27] The 'General outline of measures for the reorganisation of Japan', written by the socialist Kita Ikki in 1923,[28] envisaged an uprising from below and the creation of a Great Asian Empire comprising India, Australia, and Eastern Siberia. Parallels with fascist movements in Europe are obvious, although Kita was not influenced by them. The various nationalist groups were united by the call for the restoration of direct imperial rule. Under the impact of the Great Depression, this turned into something of a religious creed.

The mismanagement of monetary policy by the *zaibatsu* led to an acute depression as early as 1927. Whereas the big industrial corporations weathered the crisis fairly comfortably (if only at the expense of the small suppliers), the slump had disastrous effects on agriculture, especially from 1929 onwards when the American market could no longer absorb Japanese agrarian exports. Rural Japan suffered unparalleled impoverishment: only a third of all peasant households earned a modest income from agriculture. Most farmers had to try to find other means for eking out a living; a considerable number rented out their daughters on the flourishing red-light districts of the cities. Since the government was closely allied to the *zaibatsu*, it did nothing to counter the growing misery, thus providing an opening for the anticapitalist and social-revolutionary opposition movement that was led by the army.

The occupation of Manchuria had long been prepared for by army circles and was finally carried out in September 1931. It was an openly imperialistic act of aggression, fuelled by nationalistic motives and initiated against the wishes of government and industry. The army or, more precisely, the officers of middle rank, transformed Manchuria into their territorial power base and used it as a laboratory for testing their ideas about state socialism and economic planning. Just as the pauperised classes within any society resist material deprivation, Japan as a 'have-not' nation claimed its share of the world's natural resources. In 1931 Imperial Japan threw off its role as a junior partner of the old-established imperialist powers and openly challenged the Western nations as well as Republican China, which was gaining strength under the government of the Kuomintang. The Manchurian Crisis dealt a heavy blow to the international order created at Versailles; it presaged a military showdown with the West.

Having eliminated the party Cabinets and having reduced the influence of the *zaibatsu* (in several ways, including political assassination), the army dominated the various leadership factions between 1932 and 1936. Yet, it was unable to implement its aim of a planned economy. The *zaibatsu* kept aloof from acts of political violence at home and abroad, and refused to cooperate with the military in Manchuria. Court and navy circles, too, shrank back from openly antagonising the Western powers and attacking Soviet Russia. They preferred peaceful penetration of Southeast Asia, where those raw materials which were not available in Manchuria could be found: oil, bauxite, rubber, and certain kinds of minerals.[29]

From 1932 onwards, the government resorted to a policy of deficit spending, thus bringing army and industry closer together once again in Japan. The military benefited from a programme of large-scale armaments: between 1932 and 1936 the military budget increased two-and-a-half times.[30] During the same period, heavy industry overtook light industry as the focal point of Japan's industrial structure. Within four years the production index rose by 60 percent.[31] By 1935 Japan had overcome the depression, but the growing demand for raw materials could be met only by an increase in exports. Beginning in 1934 Japan infiltrated Britain's traditional markets for consumer goods (above all, cotton textiles) in Southeast Asia and Latin America using methods of under-selling that were widely denounced as dumping. Britain retaliated by raising its tariffs, as did the United States. Japan was forced to fall back on markets at home, limited as they were, and in its colonies. So, in 1935 the government had to choose between two options: to expand the domestic market for consumer goods by implementing a programme of social reform, or to go ahead with plans for further social-imperialist expansion overseas.

The final decision was strongly influenced by a putsch of young officers on 26 February 1936. It was Emperor Hirohito himself who helped to defeat the coup when he sided with industry and the navy, declared himself against any attempt to install a fascist-authoritarian system from below, and insisted on draconian punishment for the insurgents. Seizing the opportunity, the navy and industry tried to have their plan of a southward expansion adopted as government policy. The attempt failed, and in the Cabinet decision on the 'Fundamental principles of national policy'[32] of 7 August 1936, the southern thrust was only referred to as one of two alternatives, the other being an army attack against the Soviet Union.

The issue was resolved when war broke out with China in July 1937. The army seized upon one of the almost routine skirmishes with Chinese troops on the outskirts of Peking and expanded it into a full-scale military action. The intention was to push for a speedy and spectacular victory so as to unite the battered nation as one large family behind the Tenno, and then to put into effect the army's ideas of revitalising the economic and political order. The government of Prime Minister Count Konoe Fumimaro, however, representing as it did the traditional upper class, grasped the opportunity to keep the unruly army busy in the field of honour. The army's thrust was deflected southwards, towards central China, and the army's hopes for an early peace were disappointed.[33] The war in China was escalated not by the army, but by the traditional oligarchy acting together with the court, the navy, and industry.

Since the First World War a fundamental antagonism had become apparent between, on the one hand, the army which held anticapitalist views and spoke out for the disadvantaged masses and, on the other, the traditional élite with its close ties to big business. This contrast was now submerged by a wave of belligerence and chauvinism. Within the alliance between the army and the wealthy ruling class that was forged during the war against China, the army played a subservient role; the true masters were the *zaibatsu*. From 1937 onwards, two modes of imperialism that had initially been opposed to each other formed a strange symbiosis: a mythical and vainglorious brand of nationalism, and a carefully calculated policy of using overseas expansion as a safety valve for domestic tensions. The traditional oligarchy never deviated from the rational pursuit of their own interests. In the final analysis, it was they who kept the upper hand over the idealistic military men.

Illusions of Liberation and Realities of War: The Greater East Asia Co-Prosperity Sphere

The War Mobilisation Laws of 1 April 1938 gave the state absolute control over both entrepreneurs and workers, at least in theory. But in reality, official regulation only strengthened the dominant role of big business, whose representatives held all the key positions in cartels and other industrial associations. They and their allies from the traditional oligarchy sabotaged any attempt made by reformist officials, such as Kishi Nobusuke, the Deputy-Minister of Commerce and Industry, to subordinate the egotistical and profit-orientated behaviour of the *zaibatsu* to the imperatives of national armament, and to put state commissioners in charge of industrial production.[34] The government instead accommodated the *zaibatsu* by promulgating the Major Industries Association Ordinance of September 1941.[35] It gave the chairmen of the various industrial control committees, most of them *zaibatsu* representatives, the final say in matters concerning compulsory mergers, pricing, and raw material quotas. Although this vertical organisation of arms production corresponded to Japan's social structure, it was to prove a fatal and irreversible mistake. It allowed the *zaibatsu* full scope to further their own selfish interests, which were opposed to the requirements of warfare. By the end of the war, they owned more than 70 percent of all bank deposits and controlled more than 50 percent of industrial production; during the war years they had been able to increase their capital more than fourfold.[36] The process of economic concentration and the aggrandisement of the *zaibatsu* had a decisive influence on Japan's internal development and also on its foreign relations, in particular on its policy towards the territories which were occupied during the war. Japanese propaganda was fond of hailing China as an Asian brother nation, but from its very beginning, the military campaign was conceived and conducted as a war of annihilation. The aim was to ruthlessly destroy China's society and culture and to reduce the country to the status of a colony. Political control of the conquered territories was taken out of civilian hands and given to the military whose only way of achieving 'pacification' was by brutal force. The *zaibatsu* and the government were partners in the Central China Development Company and the North China Development Company which took over the entire economy of the occupied areas and, within a short time, ruined it completely.[37] The realities of Japanese rule in China made all the slogans of Pan-Asiatic liberation sound utterly cynical. The Japanese were even unable to develop a political concept for China that would have gained them the collaboration of the weak Chinese ruling class.

At home, remodelling the nation along national socialist lines was a much-debated topic. Since 1938 vigorous efforts had been made to form a party of national unity. It finally materialised in October 1940 after Japan had joined Nazi Germany and Fascist Italy in the Tripartite Pact of 27 September 1940.[38] The Imperial Rule Assistance Association and its numerous branches, such as the Greater Japan Patriotic Industrial Movement that included both workers and employers, were used as instruments to bring about national unity in view of the anticipated war with the Western powers. Central to the ideological war effort was the Showa Research Institute which was mainly staffed by former socialists and which had served as a think tank for Konoe.[39] It moulded the various nationalist currents into a coherent ideology of Greater Japan, centring on domestic social reforms and the creation of a self-sufficient empire in East and Southeast Asia. The very eclecticism of Japanese nationalist and expansionist socialism, this strange amalgam of totalitarian and fascist views with ideals of socialist reform, can also be interpreted as a strained attempt to harmonise social tensions. Socialists, even communists, militant farmers, small craftsmen, big capitalists, traditional court circles, and former party politicians could all come together under the same ideological roof, which was hardly more than a camouflage designed to glorify imperialist aggression.

The Greater East Asia Co-Prosperity Sphere was officially proclaimed in August 1940. Its envisaged borders were delineated in negotiations with Germany in the following month. The new *Lebensraum*, anticipated in the writings of Kita Ikki, was to include India, Australia, New Zealand, and the Pacific Islands as far east as New Caledonia.[40] This programme of conquest reflected the views of industry, but also of court circles and the navy. The army's northern strategy – a direct strike at the Soviet Union – was finally laid to rest as a result of Japan's defeat in border clashes with the Red Army, and because of the supposedly friendly relations between Hitler's Germany and Stalin's Russia. The southern strategy was expected to lead to the carving out of an unassailable and autarkic regional base that could be used as a stepping-stone towards the status of a world power. Little heed was paid by the self-deluded strategists of the empire to the fact that Japan's industrial capacity amounted to only 10 percent of that of the United States.

After successful operations, the originally limited military plans were modified in the spring of 1942 to include India and Australia as well.[41] Euphoric about their easy victories during the opening months of the Pacific War, the military overruled the diplomats' plans for consolidating Japanese rule in the occupied countries. Projects for an economic transformation of the former European colonies came to nothing. Conquest and occupation soon gained a momentum of their own, all the more so since the Japanese troops had to live off the subjugated areas. Raw materials of military significance were seized immediately, but a bottleneck in shipping capacities allowed only a fraction of them to be sent to Japan. The goods shipped from Southeast Asia to Japan in 1942, that is, before American submarines controlled the sea routes, amounted to a mere 15 percent of overall Japanese imports and were thus decidedly below prewar levels.[42]

The new masters proved unable to fill the gap left by the 'whites' who had been expelled or interned. Instead of elevating Japan to the 'light of Asia', as the official commentary on the outbreak of war would have it,[43] an ignorant occupation force caused economic havoc in the 'liberated' territories. Famine raged in Southeast Asia; the entire economic life of the region regressed to the level of subsistence production and barter trade.[44] Even if Japan did not succeed during the Pacific War in becoming the hub of East Asian trade, the occupation had profound and long-lasting consequences in the region. Of particular importance was the destruction of the plantation economy which put an end to the traditional trade between the colonies and their mother countries. After the war, this almost inevitably led to a new economic orientation towards the former occupying power. The war thus laid the foundation for today's system of trade in East Asia with Tokyo at its centre.

As the war dragged on, it became more and more apparent that the Japanese economy needed a thoroughgoing refurbishment if it were to stand up to the economic and military might of the West. The performance of the arms industry was disappointing; basic supplies for the civilian population were totally inadequate; the administration disintegrated into utter chaos. Put on the defensive, in 1943 the leadership changed both its occupation strategy and economic organisation at home. The Philippines, Burma, and the government of Free India were granted independence in 1943, and Indonesia during the last days of war. Yet, this was all too obviously dictated by the hopeless military situation and did not win over the Asian peoples to the Japanese cause. Economic reform, masterminded at the newly created Munitions Ministry by Kishi Nobusuke, the Japanese counterpart to Albert Speer, met with greater success.[45] The *zaibatsu* were deprived of their influence, and production was organised horizontally rather than in the traditional vertical manner. Factories in certain branches of industry were placed under government supervision, and their output was limited to one type of product only. Owing to modern management methods Japan was remarkably successful in manufacturing tankers, aircraft, and the necessary electronic equipment. Arms production finally peaked in September 1944. Much of the economic revival in postwar Japan was based on these wartime reforms and especially on those branches that had reached a high level of technological sophistication during the war. After Kishi eventually became Prime Minister in 1957, he successfully continued the reconstruction of the economy, relying on the Ministry of International Trade and Industry (MITI), which developed directly from the Munitions Ministry. Between 1957 and 1960, Kishi's economic policy culminated in the most rapid development since the foundation of the state.[46]

Japan's Hegemony in East Asia: the Continuity of Economic Expansion in the Postwar Period

The capitulation of Imperial Japan on 2 September 1945 was an act of military surrender, but not of political and social self-denigration. Government, administration, and even the institution of the Tenno remained in existence, even though the American High Command insisted on its authority to issue orders to the 'Son of Heaven'. The victors came to Japan with a carefully prepared programme of reform and reeducation: those responsible for the war were to be put on trial, the country was to be liberated from feudal relics, and a democratic order was to be introduced. The American administrators, many of whom had a New Deal background, regarded the eight leading *zaibatsu*, the court, and a few thousand big landowners as the forces behind Japan's aggressive war policy.[47] In fact, despite devastating bombardment of their factories, the *zaibatsu* had survived the war as its true winners. Striking evidence of their purely profit-seeking behaviour and their close involvement with the traditional leadership is provided by the fact that the *zaibatsu* and the government divided among themselves the remaining supplies during the interregnum between the armistice (15 August 1945) and the arrival of the Americans (2 September 1945). Within two weeks, stores of iron, steel, aluminium, food, machine tools, and raw materials valued at approximately $4,000 million (US) vanished without trace.[48] Civilian and military authorities destroyed a large number of files that might have proved incriminating;[49] many people simply disappeared or, with official connivance, acquired new names to avoid persecution. Thus, the Japanese prepared to undermine overzealous American reforms.

In any event, only those reforms were carried out which were either imposed by the occupation authorities – the new constitution being the chief example – or which had already proved to be overdue during the war. The original American plan involving a radical purge of the ruling élite, the dissolution of the *zaibatsu*, and a reorganisation of the economy according to Western principles of industrial relations, was foiled by the tenacious obstruction of those potentially affected. In general, the Japanese ruling élite remained intact beyond 1945 to a much larger extent than that of the 'Third Reich'. In the main trial of war criminals, held in Tokyo from 1946 to 1948, seven of the twenty-eight defendants received death sentences and were executed; former Foreign Minister Hirota Koki was the only civilian among them. In further military trials some 920 people were condemned to death and executed.[50] The political purges, by contrast, were relatively harmless: of a total of 210,288 people removed from their positions, 80 percent belonged to the military and only 16.5 percent were civilian politicians. The all-powerful bureaucracy, where only 1,809 people (0.9 percent) of all personnel temporarily lost their jobs, escaped virtually unscathed. The same was true for industry where 1,898 people (0.9 percent) were purged.[51]

Nevertheless, the occupation brought about a significant shift in the composition of the ruling élite. The court was deprived of its political function, the big landowners were expropriated during the land reform, and the alleged villains – the military – were singled out for punishment. The locus of power now shifted to industry and the bureaucracy. This new and numerically larger élite, however, remained committed to the same conservative and nationalistic values that had guided the traditional oligarchy.[52] What was new after the war was that the leadership now managed to reconcile these traditional norms with Western pragmatism. As in the Meiji period, Japan after 1945 opened itself to the West only as far as was deemed necessary to achieve equality with the advanced industrial nations. Now, however, the competition was economic rather than military.

The moving spirit behind this policy of covert restoration and its foremost representative was Yoshida Shigeru, a leading politician in postwar Japan who had once, as a diplomat, pushed for the Japanese takeover in Manchuria.[53] Now his policy was to reject all reforms initiated by the Americans, or, if this could not be done, to distort them into a Japanised form. His chosen instrument was the loyal and omnipotent bureaucracy. The dissolution of the *zaibatsu*, decreed by the Americans in 1947, was abandoned only a year later.[54] In the meantime, however, the old family-owners had been replaced by experienced industrial managers. In a way, this meant that the *zaibatsu* were nationalised and put under direct state supervision. In 1949, the MITI was put in charge of the economic reconstruction programme. A protectionist foreign-trade policy and underhand bureaucratic manoeuvres were used to shield economic reconstruction. Import restrictions were lifted as late as 1971, under direct pressure from other countries.[55] By then, Japanese industry had a firm grip on the domestic market and was penetrating foreign markets all over the world, and Japan had developed into the second strongest industrial power behind the United States. Today Mitsubishi, the former armaments *zaibatsu*, is the world's largest corporation. The six largest enterprises in Japan effectively control 21 percent of the turnover in the private sector and 23 percent of total share capital; they employ 10 percent of the permanent work force.[56]

The political cornerstone of the alignment between industry and bureaucracy was laid with the founding of the Liberal Democratic Party (LDP) in October 1955.[57] Neither liberal nor democratic, the ruling party is a loose coalition of all kinds of conservative groups. It could well be described as an authoritarian alliance of corrupt parliamentary factions. More than 54 percent of LDP members of the Diet are themselves employers or closely connected with business interests.[58] Just as in the interwar period, the conservatives today reinforce their position with an antisocialist ideology that gives overriding importance to the nation's greatness and to what is seen as the welfare of the people. Since socialists and communists are even more divided among themselves than the LDP, and since they lack financial support from big business that would enable them to buy votes, as is customary in Japan, they are unlikely to assume political power unless the entire system undergoes fundamental change. The present government tends to glorify the country's imperialist past rather than to maintain a critical distance from it. The Tenno myth is being revived and there are moves to give greater power to the Emperor in a revised constitution. History books used in schools blatantly falsify the recent past and monuments are being erected for leaders who were condemned as war criminals.

While the national unity of the Japanese is often admired in the West, the former victims of Japanese nationalism are highly suspicious of Japan's reemergence as a major power. Tokyo's foreign and economic policy towards the countries of East and Southeast Asia has strengthened rather than dispelled distrust of the deeds and intentions of that 'chosen' nation. Today Japan regards the former Greater East Asia Co-Prosperity Sphere as a source of raw materials and as a market for industrial exports. Neither the Japanese government nor the big private corporations have undertaken long-term and costly development projects which might have contributed to autonomous economic development in those countries. The question of reparations had not been settled in the peace treaty of San Francisco and was left to bilateral agreements; Japanese businessmen were able to influence them so as to secure maximum advantage for the domestic economy. Loans were extended on conditions that were more beneficial to the Japanese economy than to the recipients. Southeast Asian countries have run up growing deficits in their trade with Japan; the gulf has widened between developed Japan and underdeveloped Southeast Asia.

Japan gives practically no economic aid for training professionals and skilled labourers. The number of students from the poorer Asian countries who are studying at Japanese universities is negligible, partly because of a shortage of grants, partly on account of latent racial discrimination that keeps away undesired foreigners.[59] Vice versa, there are hardly any Japanese experts engaged in aid projects in Southeast Asia, as the people in those countries have shown themselves to be persistently hostile to the Japanese. Japan's contribution to international development aid does not reflect its economic strength; contributing only 0.26 percent of its GNP (in 1980), Japan was well below the average of 0.34 percent.[60] The Southeast Asian countries today merely serve as a peripheral area for Japan's expansionist capitalism; they are kept in their present state of underdevelopment by means of 'structural violence'. This state of affairs goes virtually unchallenged in Japan. Even the socialists, who like to regard themselves as the Asiatic conscience of the nation, tolerate this kind of informal imperialism,[61] just as in the past they gave their open support to formal militarist expansion. Then, as now, the honour and greatness of the nation seemed to be at stake.

The economic and social system of contemporary Japan appears to be somewhat unstable.[62] The economy could not withstand a drastic recession because the capital market would collapse instantly. Japan has managed to build up and maintain its economic hegemony only at the expense of its international environment: of the dependent Third World countries, of the Americans who are still suffering from a guilt complex towards Japan, and also of the Europeans who have so far taken little notice of the working of the Japanese system.

Japanese Imperialism: A Theoretical Perspective

Neither classical theories of imperialism nor those derived from the contemporary social sciences can do full justice to the unique prerequisites of Japanese imperialism and to its historical development. In particular, those theories have to be ruled out which focus too strongly on Europe as the source of imperialist expansionism. Japan's building of formal and informal empires was largely initiated and sustained by internal forces. While this process is characterised by a strong underlying continuity, it has passed through four stages.

The period from 1868 to 1915, when the Twenty-One Demands were presented to China, was marked by preindustrial capitalism which proceeded cautiously and was careful to seek British cover. Its aim was to elevate Japan to equal rank with the West. Disorientation and discontent among the people in the course of precipitate modernisation converged with the inclinations of the ruling oligarchy, resulting in a desire for a strong and united nation, inspired by time-honoured values and virtues.

In the second stage, lasting from 1915 until the outbreak of the war with China in 1937, nationalism spread among the people as economic conditions took an unfavourable turn, especially in the agrarian sector. The leadership was put under mounting pressure. During the Great Depression nationalist attitudes and sentiments were infused with elements of social-revolutionary utopianism which were particularly popular among the middle ranks of the army. The occupation of Manchuria was an early attempt to put these ideas into practice. Reacting against popular pressure, the traditional élites and the representatives of big business drew closer together in an effort to channel the nationalism fermenting among the people into a programme of southward expansion. Nationalism from below and manipulative social-imperialism from above jointly resulted in the war with China.

During the third stage, from the beginning of the hostilities with China in 1937 to the end of the Pacific War, an aggressive military expansionism was unleashed which soon was no longer amenable to rational control from above. It resulted in plunder and fierce repression of the occupied areas. The idea of the Greater East Asian Co-Prosperity Sphere lost its original idealistic and anticolonialist overtones and degenerated into cynical propaganda. Several factors combined to defeat Japan's self-proclaimed mission: the inability of a backward-looking élite to introduce reforms, the 'unpatriotic' behaviour of the *zaibatsu* which totally failed to contribute to the war effort, and the military set-backs of the war.

The fourth stage began in 1952. Elements inherent in all of the three earlier forms of imperialism can be traced as constituents of the informal trade imperialism that has come to characterise the postwar era. Again, control is exercised from the top and the masses give their tacit support. This sort of informal imperialism is part and parcel of the present social and economic system and is likely to continue as long as prosperity can be maintained.

Of the classical theories of imperialism, Joseph A. Schumpeter's ideas about imperialism being an 'atavism of ruling aristocracies' serving the 'preservation of feudal structures'[63] appears to fit the Japanese case most closely. The postwar period can also be analysed in terms of the theory of state monopolistic capitalism.[64] Japan surpasses all other Western nations in the degree to which the state manipulates the economy. If there is one continuous thread which links the Meiji founding fathers to the oligarchs of the first half of the twentieth century and these, in turn, to today's élite of bureaucrats and business leaders, it is the desire to preserve the traditional social structure and defend a political system that has constantly denied real participation to the majority of the people.

The 'eccentric approach', as advocated by Ronald Robinson,[65] does not really explain the characteristics of Japanese expansion. In the Japanese case, there was no transition from formal and colonialist imperialism to informal economic penetration. Apart from Korea and Taiwan, the empire did not possess colonies. Since its colonial policies aimed at repeating the process of modernisation that had taken place in the mother country,[66] they cannot be compared with those of the Western powers. Moreover, the brutality that accompanied Japan's expansion and the claim to cultural leadership *vis-à-vis* the people in occupied China ruled out the emergence of collaborationist élites. As far as allegiance was pledged to the Greater Asian Co-Prosperity Sphere by nationalist circles in the conquered areas, they did it from pragmatic motives and in expectation of Japan's ultimate defeat which would allow them to get rid of their 'yellow' colonial masters who had already replaced the 'white' ones.

In postwar Japan itself, the debate about imperialism has been dominated by the official views of the communist and socialist parties. Little progress has been made in these circles since the communist analyses of the interwar period. As early as 1927 the Comintern labelled Japan 'the most threatening imperialist power in East Asia' and described the Pacific region as 'a central battleground for the imperialist powers'. In 1932 the term 'absolutist military and feudal imperialism' was coined to account for characteristics of Japanese society.[67]

Japan's defeat seemed to have destroyed imperialist tendencies. The debate now focused on American imperialism. Japan's economic imperialism as it is displayed in Southeast Asia is usually ignored by the socialist or communist theorists, or minimised by regarding it as a result of Japan's dependence on the United States. Attempts made by some economists to develop Marxist explanations in the tradition of Lenin and Hilferding[68] met with as little response as did liberal efforts to build upon the ideas of Max Weber.[69] Given the overwhelming influence of American economic theory, those approaches remained limited to circles outside the academic mainstream.

As before the war, the conservative ruling groups prefer to see Japan's expansion on the Asian mainland neither as aggression nor as imperialism, but rather as a gradual 'advance'.[70] As one Japanese Foreign Minister said, when confronted with the accusation that Japan had in the past behaved as an imperialist power: 'If that was "imperialism", then it was glorious imperialism'.[71]

Notes

Parts of the present chapter are based on some of the author's previous publications on modern Japanese history: 'Restauration – Die "Bewältigung der Vergangenheit" in Japan', *Zeitschrift für Politik*, vol. 17 (1970), pp. 155–170; 'Aggressionspolitik als Mobilisierungsfaktor: Der militärische und wirtschaftliche Imperialismus Japans 1931–1941', in F. Forstmeier and H.-E. Volkmann, eds., *Wirtschaft und Rüstung am Vorabend des Zweiten Weltkrieges* (Düsseldorf, 1975), pp. 222–44; 'Japans Kriegswirtschaft 1941–1945', in F. Forstmeier and H.-E. Volkmann, eds., *Kriegswirtschaft und Rüstung 1939–1945* (Düsseldorf, 1977), pp. 256–86. For a survey of recent research see 'Japans Weg in den Krieg. Bemerkungen über Forschungsstand und Literatur zur japanischen Zeitgeschichte', *Militärgeschichtliche Mitteilungen*, vol. 23 (1978), pp. 183–209, and 'Japan und der Krieg in Ostasien. Kommentierender Bericht über das Schrifttum', *Historische Zeitschrift*, special issue no. 8 (1980), pp. 79–220.

1. Cambridge, Mass., 1965. See also A. Iriye, *Power and Culture: The Japanese-American War, 1941–1945*, Cambridge, Mass., 1981.

2. *Imperialism: The Specter of the Twentieth Century*. The book was first published in Japanese in 1901. See F. G. Nothelfer, *Kotoku Shusui: Portrait of a Japanese Radical*, Cambridge, 1971, pp. 82–87. J. A. Hobson, *Imperialism: A Study*, was published in London in 1902.

3. For the peculiarities of Japanese society, see: C. Nakane, *Japanese Society*, Berkeley, Calif., 1970; T. Doi, *The Anatomy of Dependence*, New York, 1973.

4. See the stimulating, but not always convincing, book by F. V. Moulder, *Japan, China and the Modern World Economy. Toward a Reinterpretation of East Asian Development, ca. 1600 to ca. 1918*, Cambridge, 1977.

5. The standard account is W .G. Beasley, *The Meiji Restoration*, Stanford, Calif., 1972. See also J. W. Dower, ed., *Origins of the Modern Japanese State. Selected Writings of E. H. Norman*, New York, 1975.

6. J. W. Bennett and I. Ishino, *Paternalism in the Japanese Economy: Anthropological Studies of oyabun-kobun Patterns*, Minneapolis, Minn., 1963.

7. W. W. Lockwood, *The Economic Development of Japan: Growth and Structural Change, 1868–1938*, Princeton, N.J., 1954, p. 98. On the agrarian order see A. Waswo, *Japanese Landlords: The Decline of a Rural Elite*, Berkeley, 1977.

8. The first loan of 3 million yen was originally granted to the shogunate for the purpose of building Japan's first railway line (Tokyo to Yokohama); it was actually paid to the Meiji government. The second loan of over 10.7 million yen was used for paying the pensions of the samurai from 1872 onwards. See G. C. Allen, *A Short Economic History of Modern Japan, 1867–1937*, 3rd ed., London, 1972, p. 41.

9. See the memorandum by T. Okubo, 'Reasons for opposing the Korean expedition', in R. Tsunoda et al., eds., *Sources of Japanese Tradition*, New York, 1957, pp. 658–62. For the debate, see I. H. Nish, *Japanese Foreign Policy, 1869–1942: Kasumigaseki to Miyakezaka*, London, 1977, pp. 21–25.

10. So far there is no comprehensive study on Prussia-Germany's influence on the modernisation of Japan. For the legal system, see N. Toshitani, 'Japan's modern legal system: its formation and structure', *Annals of the Institute of Social Science, University of Tokyo*, vol. 17 (1976), pp. 1–50. For the German impact on military organisation, see E. L. Presseisen, *Before Aggression: Europeans Prepare the Japanese Army*, Tucson, Ariz., 1965. For German influence on the constitution of 1889, see J. Siemes, *Hermann Roesler and the Making of the Meiji State*, Tokyo, 1968.

11. Extracts from both documents in D. Lu, ed., *Sources of Japanese History*, vol. 2, New York, 1974, pp. 66–71.

12. H. Conroy, *The Japanese Seizure of Korea, 1868–1910*, Philadelphia, 1960.

13. 200 million taels in the original peace treaty of Shimonoseki, a further 30 million taels indemnity payment for Japan's retrocession of the Liaotung Peninsula after the Triple Intervention. Cf. Nish, *Japanese Foreign Policy*, pp. 39–41.

14. S. Okamoto, *The Japanese Oligarchy and the Russo-Japanese War*, New York, 1970.

15. F. C. Jones, *Extraterritoriality in Japan and the Diplomatic Relations Resulting in its Abolition, 1853–1899*, New Haven, Conn., 1931; Nish, *Japanese Foreign Policy*, pp. 46–50.

16. Reprinted in Lu, ed., *Sources of Japanese History*, vol. 2, pp. 107–9.

17. See Nish, *Japanese Foreign Policy*, pp. 111–18.

18. Lockwood, *The Economic Development*, pp. 38–39.

19. J. Halliday, *A Political History of Japanese Capitalism*, New York, 1975, pp. 70–72.

20. T. H. Buckley, *The United States and the Washington Conference, 1921–1922*, Knoxville, Tenn., 1970.

21. I. H. Nish, *Alliance in Decline: A Study in Anglo-Japanese Relations, 1908–1923*, London, 1972.

22. P. Duus, *Party Rivalry and Political Change in Taisho Japan*, Cambridge, Mass., 1968.

23. R. H. Mitchell, *Thought Control in Prewar Japan*, Ithaca, N.Y., 1976.

24. C. Johnson, *MITI and the Japanese Miracle: The Growth of Industrial Policy, 1925–1975*, Stanford, Calif., 1982, pp. 83–84.

25. Ibid., p. 103. For a biography of Japan's leading industrial bureaucrat, see D. Kurzman, *Kishi and Japan: The Search for the Sun*, New York, 1960.

26. A. E. Tiedeman, 'Big business and politics in prewar Japan', in J. W. Morley, ed., *Dilemmas of Growth in Prewar Japan*, Princeton, N.J., 1971, pp. 267–316.

27. B.-A. Shillony, *Revolt in Japan: The Young Officers and the February 26, 1936 Incident*, Princeton, N.J., 1973, p. 20. See also T. R. H. Havens, *Farm and Nation in Modern Japan: Agrarian Nationalism, 1870–1940*, Princeton, N.J., 1974.

28. Extracts in Lu, ed., *Sources of Japanese History*, vol. 2, pp. 131–6.

29. Only six percent of total Japanese imports of iron ore originated from Manchuria. Cf. Lockwood, *The Economic Development*, p. 524.

30. H. T. Patrick, 'The economic muddle of the 1920s', in Morley, ed., *Dilemmas of Growth*, p. 250.

31. Allen, *Short Economic History*, p. 139.

32. J. B. Crowley, *Japan's Quest for Autonomy: National Security and Foreign Policy, 1930–1938*, Princeton, N.J., 1966, p. 190.

33. Ibid., p. 358.

34. Hoshino Naoki, president of the Cabinet Planning Board, and Kishi, Deputy-Minister of Commerce and Industry, both drew up plans for a state-controlled economy. Both were charged with 'red thinking' and forced to resign at the beginning of 1941. See Johnson, *MITI and the Japanese Miracle*, pp. 150–2.

35. E. B. Schumpeter, *The Industrialization of Japan and Manchukuo, 1930–1940*, New York, 1940, pp. 686, 793, 820; J.B. Cohen, *Japan's Economy in War and Reconstruction*, Minneapolis, Minn., 1949, p. 32.

36. K. Ikeda, *Die industrielle Entwicklung in Japan unter besonderer Berücksichtigung seiner Finanz- und Wirtschaftspolitik*, Berlin, 1970, p. 129; T. A. Bisson, 'The *zaibatsu's* wartime role', *Pacific Affairs*, vol. 18 (1945), pp. 355–68.

37. Cohen, *Japan's Economy*, p. 42. For the Japanese occupation of North China, see L. Li, *The Japanese Army in North China, 1937–1941: Problems of Political and Economic Control*, London, 1975. From the Japanese point of view: J. W. Morley, ed., *The China Quagmire: Japan's Expansion on the Asian Continent, 1933–1941*, New York, 1983, pp. 292–3, 326–7, 428ff.

38. For an analysis, based on Japanese sources, of Japan's orientation towards Germany, see G. Krebs, *Japans Deutschlandpolitik. Eine Studie zur Vorgeschichte des Pazifischen Krieges*, Hamburg, 1984.

39. M. Fletcher, *The Search for a New Order: Intellectuals and Fascism in Prewar Japan*, Chapel Hill, N.C., 1982.

40. For the full English text of the decision taken by the Inner Cabinet and reconfirmed by the Liaison Conference of 19 September 1940, see T. Sommer, *Deutschland und Japan zwischen den Mächten 1935–1940*, Tübingen, 1962, pp. 509–24.

41. B. Martin, *Deutschland und Japan im Zweiten Weltkrieg*, Göttingen, 1969.

42. Cohen, *Japan's Economy*, p. 69.

43. 'Commentary on the imperial declaration of war', in Tsunoda et al., eds., *Sources of Japanese Tradition*, pp. 799–801.

44. J. C. Scott, 'An approach to the problems of food supply in Southeast Asia during World War II', in B. Martin and A. Milward, eds., *Agriculture and Food Supply in World War II*, Stuttgart, 1985, pp. 269–82.

45. Johnson, *MITI and the Japanese Miracle*, pp. 157–97.

46. 'Jimmu Keiki'. Between 1956 and 1961 industrial production and mining increased 2.7-fold. Big business finally reestablished its dominance. See H. Hammitzsch, ed., *Japan-Handbuch*, Wiesbaden, 1981, cols. 2077–8.

47. T. A. Bisson, *Japan's War Economy*, New York, 1945, p. 7. (Bisson served on the U.S. Government Committee on Economic Warfare.)

48. Halliday, *A Political History*, p. 162.

49. Interview with Colonel S. Nishiura by the author, Tokyo, 13 August 1969. Nishiura was in charge of burning the files of the War (Army) Ministry in August 1945. After the war, being an expert on the lost material, he became head of the Historical Division of the Ministry of Self-Defence.

50. R. H. Minear, *Victors' Justice: The Tokyo War Crimes Trial*, Princeton, N.J., 1971; P. R. Piccigallo, *The Japanese on Trial: Allied War Crimes Operations in the East, 1945–1951*, London, 1979.

51. H. H. Baerwald, *The Purge of the Japanese Leaders under the Occupation*, Berkeley, Calif., 1959, pp. 80ff.

52. An excellent study on the continuity of the political élite in Japan was written by the former secretary of the German Embassy in Tokyo, K. F. Zahl: *Die politische Elite Japans nach dem Zweiten Weltkrieg*, Wiesbaden, 1973.

53. J. W. Dower, *Empire and Aftermath: Yoshida Shigeru and the Japanese Experience, 1878–1954*, Cambridge, Mass., 1979.

54. Halliday, *A Political History*, pp. 175ff.; J. G. Roberts, 'The "Japanese Crowd" and the *zaibatsu* restoration', *Japan Interpreter*, vol. 12 (1979), pp. 384–415.

55. Johnson, *MITI and the Japanese Miracle*, pp. 275–304.

56. R. Gaul et al., *Japan-Report. Wirtschaftsriese Nippon – die sieben Geheimnisse des Erfolgs*, Munich, 1982, pp. 190–3.

57. N. Thayer, *How the Conservatives Rule Japan*, Princeton, N.J., 1969.

58. Ibid., pp. 323–32: A. Dettloff and H. Kirchmann, *Arbeitsstaat Japan – Exportdrohung gegen die Gewerkschaften*, Reinbek, 1981, p. 108.

59. J. Halliday and G. McCormack, *Japanese Imperialism Today: 'Co-Prosperity in Greater East Asia'*, New York, 1973, p. 69; H. Hammitzsch, ed., *Japan-Handbuch*, col. 86. In 1969 there were only 563 students from underdeveloped countries enrolled at Japanese universities, most of them from Africa and the Near East. In 1974, the majority of the 2,000 foreign students in Japan came from Europe and the United States.

60. E. Wilkinson, *Japan ist ganz anders. Geschichte eines grossen Missverständnisses*, Königstein, 1982, p. 195.

61. Hammitzsch, *Japan-Handbuch*, p. 421.

62. Halliday, *A Political History*, p. 297: 'bicycle-economy' (if it slows down, it collapses). See also Z. Brzezinski, *The Fragile Blossom: Crisis and Change in Japan*, New York, 1973; F. Gibney, *Japan: The Fragile Superpower*, New York, 1975.

63. J. A. Schumpeter, 'Zur Soziologie der Imperialismen', *Archiv für Sozialwissenschaft und Sozialpolitik*, vol. 46 (1918–19), pp. 1–39, 275–310.

64. See M. Dobb, *Organisierter Kapitalismus. Fünf Beiträge zur politischen Ökonomie*, Frankfurt am Main, 1966.

65. See Ronald Robinson, 'The excentric Idea of Imperialism, with or without Empire', in W. J. Mommsen and J. Osterhammel, eds., *Imperialism and after, Continuities and Discontinuities*, London, 1986, pp. 267–89.

66. E. Chen, 'Japanese colonialism in Korea and Formosa: a comparison of the system of political control', *Harvard Journal of Asiatic Studies*, vol. 30 (1970), pp. 126–58; G. H. Kerr, *Formosa: Licensed Revolution and the Home Rule Movement, 1895–1945*, Honolulu, 1974; G. Wontroba and U. Menzel, *Stagnation und Unterentwicklung in Korea: Von der Yi-Dynastie zur Peripherisierung unter japanischer Kolonialherrschaft*, Meisenheim, 1978. R. H. Myers and M. R. Peattie, eds., *The Japanese Colonial Empire, 1895–1945*, Princeton, N.J., 1984.

67. H. Hammitzsch, ed., *Japan-Handbuch*, pp. 419–20.

68. T. Sekine, 'Uno-Riron: a Japanese contribution to Marxian political economy', *Journal of Economic Literature*, vol. 13 (1975), pp. 847–77.

69. Hammitzsch, *Japan-Handbuch*, col. 2374.

70. This propaganda term was used at the time of the Sino-Japanese War of 1937–45. It was revived in 1982 in officially licensed textbooks for schools. The Chinese vehemently protested against this falsification of history.

71. Foreign Minister Shiina Etsusaburo in 1966, quoted in A. Axelbank, *Black Star over Japan: Rising Forces of Militarism*, New York, 1977, p. 123.

❧ 4 ❧

JAPAN DURING THE WORLD ECONOMIC CRISIS

BIG BUSINESS AND SOCIAL UNREST

Before the Pacific War, according to Western standards, Japan was neither a developing country, at the 'take-off' stage of economic development, nor an industrialised land. Japanese modernisation was uneven and superficial at that time.[1] On the surface the world economic crisis had similar effects as in the West: the rapid fall of prices on the world market led to a drop in industrial production, to a shrinkage of agricultural exports, and consequently to a perceptible decline in the real income of the work force. The people, in turn, reacted to the material deterioration of living standards with political militancy. However, contrary to contemporary events in Western industrialised states, this political radicalisation was not to be seen in the cities in armies of unemployed, which did not exist in Japan. Rather, it was manifested in the countryside in a union between the farmer-peasant folk-class and revolutionary military circles. This was a purposeful union between the army, whose traditional self-evident role as the guarantors of the social order based on the emperor as a living god had been shaken by foreign influences,[2] and the farmers – the protectors of the patriarchal social customs practiced at the time. In September 1931 it enabled the army to take possession of Manchuria against the wishes of government leaders and the important businessmen closely associated with them.[3]

First published in German as 'Die Auswirkungen der Weltwirtschaftskrise in Japan', in Dietmar Rothermund, ed., *Die Peripherie in der Weltwirtschaftskrise: Afrika, Asien und Lateinamerika 1929–1939*, Paderborn, 1982, pp. 197–227. Translated by Dr Peter Wetzler.

This forcible annexation of a foreign territory upset the international status quo established at Versailles and was the beginning of the politics of open revisionism. It was not so much a direct reaction to the economic depression started by the United States, as primarily an expression of the latent opposition existing in Japan since the founding of the modern state between the oligarchic leadership and the masses. The manifest outbreak of this antagonism, which can also be regarded as a class conflict between a traditional, numerically small governing élite and the politically unemancipated declassed masses, constituted a specifically Japanese answer to the worldwide economic crisis and the accompanying domestic problems in Japan. The peculiar political and economic form that the Depression, which began in Japan two years before the stock market crash in New York, took as well as the special way it was overcome cannot be explained by retrospective socioeconomic determinism. One must look for a plausible explanation in the self-conceived role of the governing class, the interlacing character of their affairs, and the traditional, premodern norms which determined the reaction of the people.

The extraordinary character of developments in Japan before, during, and after this economic crisis can only be understood in the context of her unique social order,[4] a social order which is unusual even by Asian standards. The dichotomy between the oligarchy grouped around the imperial court – concerned foremost with preserving the system – and the people – functionally exposed to the technical-industrial transformation taking place – emerged during the Meiji Restoration and grew parallel with the increasing degree of industrialisation. With the Meiji Restoration in 1868 the Emperor was reinstated as the prototypical centre of national political ideology. But traditional social norms emphasising the descent of the Japanese people from the gods on the one hand, and the necessity of technological advancement according to Western standards on the other, intensified social alienation as the government increasingly pushed outward conformity to the nations of the West, which was deemed essential. Both areas clashed frequently, both in the actions of the individual and at the pinnacle of the state. The gap between the rationalism of technology and traditional moral behavior, which from the Western point of view appears irrational, finally became unbridgeable due to the effects of the world economic crisis. It could only be covered by socioimperialistic chauvinism insofar as the rigid government leaders did not balance the sociopolitical order with a degree of modernisation. On the other hand, considering the protesting masses impregnated with rural values, a stable political order would have been difficult to achieve by means of only a few social reforms.

The continuing economic crisis in Japan between 1927 and 1932 was in reality the crisis of a society that had been modernised on the surface only, and too hastily at that. The repercussions of the world economic crisis, especially the loss of the American export market, worked simply as catalysts. A clear answer was demanded to the question of whether Japan would follow its own traditional way of sociopolitical development with the help of an expanded sphere of dominion, or if it would conform to Western parameters and thereby submit to Western commercial and political hegemony.

Basic Historical and Social Conditions of Economic Development in the Meiji and Taisho Eras up until 1926

The ossified feudal rule of the shogun, a type of military dictatorship by the Tokugawa family who possessed about one-fourth of the tillable land in Japan, had been worn down by social changes over two-and-a-half centuries of rule, and was not equal to the challenge presented by military pressure from the United States to open the country to foreign trade. From 1854 onwards the Western nations had secured commercial advantages in unequal treaties with the weak shogunate in Edo, the Tokyo of today. Japan, like China, was supposed to become a half-colonised market for industrial consumer goods. Against this threat to national integrity and what was perceived as an insult to the unbroken unique 'way of Japan', a stream of opposition grew among the middle-class samurai under the slogan, 'Revere the Emperor and expel the barbarians.' Together with the merchants who constituted the lowest social class in the Tokugawa Neo-Confucian feudal system and the leaders of 'outside' (*tozama*) feudal territories in the southwest, they deposed the shogun in the years 1867 to 1868 and reinstated the Emperor, still in his minority, as the nominal leader of the nation. The Emperor had been 'banned' to Kyoto, that is, from the corridors of power in Edo, during the Tokugawa Period.[5] This revolution from above, by which means the Emperor came to his role as an integrating force in politics, a role which lasted until 1945, was restorative in intent. The Western system, regarded as superior, was supposed to be adapted to as quickly as possible in the areas of state organisation and economic planning, with the result that the patronising dominance of the West could be terminated. Through national determination, the centralised state structure and the inherited ethic of working for the benefit of the community, there arose in Japan, entirely in contrast to China, the necessary preconditions for rapid, self-organised, and, for the most part, self-financed industrialisation.[6] The inherent Japanese *leitmotiv* of national self-assurance set the priorities in their economic development as building a powerful, heavy industrial complex, extending shipping networks, and later, constructing a railway system at home, as well as building up an army equal to the military establishments in the West.[7] Other reforms, like those in state administration or the system of justice,[8] were functionally subordinated to industrialisation for the purpose of self-preservation, meaning defence against the West. Social and sociopolitical reforms from which the masses might have profited were deemed superfluous until long after the First World War, and remained distinctly secondary in importance until the demise of Imperial Japan in 1945.

The state promoted model plants and pilot projects, for example, the building of a coastal shipping network,[9] through financial subsidies and the recruitment of Western specialists. With this initiative the foundation of a disparate economic order was laid in which a few large, modern, and well-equipped enterprises stood alongside the mass of small urban handworkers and primitive farm operators. The privatisation of the large enterprises promoted by the government was carried out such that the *zaibatsu*, powerful family controlled combines, were well served. They had largely financed the overthrow of the Tokugawa regime and used this opportunity to build up family holding companies.[10] The oligopolisation of the Japanese economy and its control by a few families presents, alongside its disparate structure, another essential characteristic of the peculiar development of Japan which was dictated by domestic social pressures.

This defence-orientated industrial build-up was financed on the back of the ostensibly freed peasantry. Up until the end of the feudal regime the peasants were burdened with a tax-in-kind of 30 to 40 percent of their harvest. After the Restoration the new state demanded that, regardless of the harvest, they paid a monetary property tax which at first amounted to 25 percent and later 18 percent of the average gross income.[11] The number of independent farmers declined steadily until about 1910. Many had to sell their land and sank to the status of a tenant farmer or agricultural worker. A new class of wealthy landowners emerged. They held about one-half of the peasant population in slave-like dependency, demanding up to 50 percent of the harvest through tenancy agreements which were not regulated by law.[12] Only about one-third of the peasants worked their own land exclusively, and with an average holding of only one hectare per family, they too remained dependent on the large landowners who controlled the villages and the countryside until 1945.[13]

The ambivalence of an economic policy which disregarded the agricultural sector of the economy soon affected domestic politics. The peasantry, the base of the Japanese social order, was gripped by a process of pauperisation which finally threatened to dissipate not only rural society but the entire state system. However, in the area of national foreign affairs this concept of industrialisation brought the hoped-for successes: in the military confrontations with China (1895) and Russia (1905), Japan was victorious, and as a result, prior to the First World War she was regarded without dispute as the leading major power in the Far East. The industrialised nations of the West accepted the parity of Japan in commercial and political relations, and before the turn of the century had agreed to the revision of the unequal treaties.[14] As a much-courted ally[15] in a coalition against Germany, at the end of the Meiji era, after only two generations of nation-building, Japan stood, with her apparent power in foreign affairs, at the zenith of the great nations. The reverse side of this growth process that emphasised power politics – the consequences for the general population – was not recognised and at first was not perceptible. It lay in the growing national debt, which included steadily rising military expenditure, amounting in 1913 to around 50 percent of the national budget.[16] This included increased credit from overseas capital markets[17] and a steadily growing foreign trade balance-of-payments deficit.[18] The resulting cycle of inflation was also abetted by doubling the issue of bank notes.[19]

A convulsive national financial crisis seemed inevitable as the First World War broke out, but Japan reaped extraordinary profits as a supplier to the Allies. Japan went from being a debtor to creditor of the Western nations during the war. Industrial production rose some 80 percent, and the number of industrial workers grew from around 1.1 to 2 million.[20] Japan experienced an export boom not only with armaments but also with traditional export items of the prewar period – textiles and simple commercial goods. As a result of the economic and political withdrawal of the Western powers from East and Southeast Asia during the war, Japan made decisive inroads into the markets of China, the Dutch East-Indies, and British-controlled India.

Only large concerns profited from the economic upswing set in motion by the war. They were able to extend their positions as market leaders and controllers such that they paid out dividends to their stockholders of up to 80 percent.[21] Economic policy during the war, bound as it was to both national prestige and the profit mania of the *zaibatsu*, ignored the needs of the workers, and also those of the peasantry. Private consumption rose only slightly because industrial production was orientated toward export. Due to rising inflation real incomes remained stagnant.[22] The *zaibatsu* also maintained the price index at an artificially high level through the banks which they controlled, so that by 1919 there was once again a slight deficit in the export trade balance-of-payments.[23]

Unrest among the masses in the cities due to the unsatisfactory supply of foodstuffs, the so-called 'rice riots', brought about political concessions. Party cabinets were formed, and universal suffrage for men was granted;[24] but these measures had no effect on economic policy. After the overheated war economy collapsed in March 1920, economic instability became the hallmark of the 1920s.[25] Growers' prices in the overworked area of agriculture rose and fell, in part, but not only, as a result of rice imports forced by the government in answer to the unrest in the cities.[26] The secondary level of the economy stagnated generally in the decade before 1930; the dominant sector of Japanese industry, textiles, was able to register a slight gain during this time; by contrast, production in the metal manufacturing industries declined.[27] The increase in the population, which reached nine million in the 1920s, including three million new workers, was absorbed in the agricultural and service sectors of the economy. The latter was the only area of the economy which registered a high rate of growth.[28]

The governments of the 1920s, which were stabile as such, did not see fit to erect a constructive economic programme that could have promoted something akin to the consumer-orientated industries in the West, which created an expanded domestic market through the stimulation of the buying power of the masses. The external prerequisites for the politics of economic consolidation were certainly present: the nation had come out of the Great War as a victor and ally of the Western powers and had overcome her inferior status. The armament restrictions of the Washington Naval Conference of 1922 led to a perceptible reduction in military spending.[29] The political course emphasising national self-affirmation against the West could have been abandoned. But the oligarchs and the Japanese people manipulated by them in this anti-Western modernisation process were unable to manage such a change of course. The entire state structure was based on the nationalism kindled in the Meiji Restoration and the predestined role of the Japanese people in Asia. Nationalistic circles, which were to be found particularly in the army but also at court, in the political parties, and in business, thought the gains which had been achieved were insufficient. Japan's withdrawal from China, relinquishing the Tsingtao territory taken from the Germans,[30] arms limitations, and the prohibition of Japanese immigration in California[31] and Australia were all perceived as national insults, and were used to incite strong nationalistic feelings. These recitations of the prejudices against Japan found resonance mainly amongst the broad masses from which the government and business had withheld improvements in material well-being. The numerous lower middle-class populations in the large cities, small manufacturers and merchants, as well as the impoverished peasantry were organised under army guidance into influential reserve and youth associations during the 1920s. They had a protest potential which could be easily mobilised to promote nationalistic aspirations in a political economic crisis. Instead of removing the social sources of discontent, government leaders promoted national collectivisation.[32]

The cardinal mistake, substantiated today, of Japanese economic policy after the First World War was their failure to follow, in a consequent manner, a policy of deflation and to devaluate the yen.[33] Individual government leaders cannot be blamed for these incorrect decisions; rather, they were a result of socially prescribed national structural conditions. National prestige and the nationalism of the people prohibited a devaluation of the Japanese currency, which, moreover, could have stimulated the export-orientated industry. A correct policy of scarce money in order to depress the, according to international standards, excessively high wholesale price levels,[34] and to make consumer goods more attractive to the home market, was obstructed by the dominant power in the economy, the *zaibatsu*, with the help of the numerous credit institutions that were dependent on them. Through the credit policy that they controlled, these large holding companies were able to take over many insolvent concerns during the 1920s. In this way they expanded their traditional business activities in heavy industry and export trade to other areas, such as trading in agricultural products and the vitally important artificial fertiliser necessary for Japan's intensive farming methods.[35]

Through election bribes, the corruption of individual representatives, and also the nomination of their own candidates, the *zaibatsu* gained increasing influence with the political parties and both houses of parliament. The 58th Diet constituted in 1930, during the economic crisis which was already in full swing, represented a high point in the corrupt symbiosis of parliament and big business. In both the lower and the upper house, the largest ever number of people belonging to business circles held office – 55 and 45 percent of the representatives respectively.[36] This powerful economic lobby controlled all of the economic and social committees in parliament, and was able to block every reform bill which was contrary to the business interests of the large enterprises.[37] Both of the major political parties, the Seiyukai and Minseito, cooperated to the same degree with industry, but with different branches,[38] and they discredited themselves in the eyes of the materially deprived voting public. The torpid political and social system in Japan was, similar to the Tokugawa shogunate before the restoration, undermined and without basis among the people. Just as political slogans advocating a restoration of imperial rule had brought about the overthrow of the shogun, so in the latter half of the 1920s, prior to the definitive start of the oncoming economic crisis, renewed calls came for a Showa Restoration and direct rule by the young emperor Hirohito.[39] Social conflicts, which had taken hold due to the modernisation programme of the government, could not be parried by the traditional élite in the reform-hostile system. Likewise, they could not be articulated politically by the masses who were overcome by irrational nationalism, but only channeled into the religious missionary fever propagated about the Yamato race.

Industry and Agriculture in Crisis, 1927–1932: The Impoverishment and Militancy of the Masses

The illogical policy of cheap money, for which the profit-hungry *zaibatsu* were responsible, led to a bank crash in April 1927.[40] This brought about a financial crisis in Japan which was unrelated to the world depression that began over two years later. The world economic crisis actually only worsened an already existing national economic crisis of Japan's own making, but it offered propaganda the possibility of diverting attention away from the self-inflicted character of this calamity. The United States, simultaneously an ideal model and rival, was responsible for the collapse of the national, as well as the international, economic order.

The *zaibatsu* controlled over half of all the deposits in Japan's 6,498 banks.[41] Since there were no binding regulations about minimum reserves, and no state or local protection for private savings deposits, a number of the large banks had overextended their credit lines. In addition, this credit was spread insecurely over a small number of borrowers. In 1927, as the banks were finally supposed to redeem credits issued after the Kanto earthquake in 1923,[42] the Peers Bank and the Bank of Taiwan failed and had to close. The only way the government could quell the storm of depositors on the credit institutions was to declare bank holidays and issue new credit to the insolvent big banks. Due to these financial support measures, the state went deeply into debt, debts that had doubled twice over by 1937, the year of the outbreak of the war in China.[43] Moreover, the bank crisis destroyed the public's confidence in the credit institutions and in the government's money policies. However, the anticapitalist resentment against the financial machinations of the banks, in collusion with the *zaibatsu* and government, did not enable the forcing through of a stronger banking law. Even if the number of banks declined,[44] they continued to serve the *zaibatsu* as a willing steering mechanism for the economy. Special institutes like the Bank of Chosen were state-controlled institutions serving Japan's imperialist policies in Korea and Manchuria.[45]

Japanese society, with its basic patriarchal structure – vertical arrangement and loyalty concepts orientated on parent-child (*oya-bun-kobun*) relationships – as these socialisation norms were adopted in the industrial world,[46] was better able to deal with an economic recession than Western society, which was centered on the individual and rationally organised horizontally, that is, in classes. Unemployment, insofar as there was any, was dealt with in a form of 'under employment', because people who lost their jobs could return to their families in the country, join the army of city street vendors, or become small tradesmen. Not working and demanding welfare support from the state, which in any case was nonexistent, was not in accord with the Japanese ethic of work and industriousness, and would have branded a person as an outsider and drastically reduced his social status. Collective pressure to devote one's working power to the benefit of the family or some other small group took precedence in Japan over the sparse material proceeds from such alternative types of work and hindered the growth of a mass of unemployed persons.

Also, the disparate structure of Japanese industry, the co-existence in close proximity of large concerns and small dependent suppliers, proved to be extremely flexible. The hardest effects of the crisis were softened, at least for the regular employees of the large companies. Since only around 21 percent of all industrial workers were employed in firms with more than one hundred employees, and these firms accounted for 35 to 40 percent of Japanese production,[47] the number of workers and levels of production in these factories could be maintained even during the economic crisis. The large concerns transferred all of the effects of the economic crisis, for example, lower prices and shrinking production, to the small companies. The small family companies, which mainly produced half-finished individual components[48] for big firms where the final production, quality control, and sales activities took place, were dictated new business terms, usually meaning price reductions. This, in turn, reduced their already none-too-high profit margins. If the suppliers did not acquiesce to the demands of the big companies, the latter, with the help of the banks who were dependent on them, possessed sufficient means to drive a company into insolvency and buy it out or make it more compliant. Depending on their particular economic interests and pressure from the competition, the *zaibatsu* in particular applied one means of persuasion or another, and even during the economic crisis they were able to further solidify their dominant market position. The brunt of the suffering in industry during the crisis was born by around three million small enterprises. In some cases up to three people worked up to sixteen hours a day, and were nevertheless unable to secure a livelihood for their families.

The income structure of the working population, including those living in the countryside, revealed in 1930 a gap between the top earners and the broad vegetating masses, uncharacteristic of both the industrialised countries of the West and the traditional Asiatic agrarian economies. Although a uniform distribution of the national income would have given each Japanese household 1,400 yen per year, only 7.1 percent of all households actually reached this, at the time, imposing figure. The rich families profited from the catastrophic economic developments and accumulated capital such that 0.2 percent of the households in Japan pocketed 10 percent of the total national income. By comparison, 56 percent of the households had to make do with an income of under 400 yen per year.[49]

Organised political protest from the labor unions or help from the political parties was not to be expected. Rigid controls suppressed any aspirations toward changing the imperial system, meaning the existing state and social order. The Peace Preservation Law of 1925,[50] enacted together with the granting of universal male suffrage, had an especially stifling effect. To be sure, the number of people arrested, most for only a short time, for political dereliction – defined as 'dangerous thoughts' – reached its high point from 1932–3.[51] However, only a small minority of these people came from the lower-income classes. Most came from among the leftist students and the numerically small middle class in the cities. A free labour movement in Japan was constituted only under the most difficult of circumstances because skilled workers were tied to patriarchic company unions. They were not threatened by dismissal and saw no reason for protesting. The mass of small tradesmen were engaged in a murderous, competitive battle with each other during the crisis, and regardless, were difficult to organise. Of the 12 million people employed in commerce, industry, and the service sector in 1931, only 370,000 workers, i.e., less than 3 percent, were organised in free unions.[52] The depoliticised masses in the cities therefore only constituted a muffled protest potential, which could only be mobilised to a limited extent with anticapitalistic and sociorevolutionary phrases. Despite many material curtailments, life in the cities,[53] which was not to be compared with the drudgery of farm work, was not circumscribed by the customary social group norms of the villages. Even the economic crisis could not resuscitate these norms in urban areas. This began only after the destruction of the cities toward the end of the Second World War.[54] By contrast, among the people in the countryside sociorevolutionary utopian ideas arose and the basic social values of the village were reinforced due to the unequally hard repercussions of the economic crisis.

The 5.5 million Japanese farm families, in which about half of the population and 40 percent of all working people lived, in 1928 realised a meagre average profit of 308 yen per year, and in 1930 the average farm family budget showed a deficit of 77 yen.[55] Only a third of all rural households showed modest profits. Much of the rural population, meaning a large proportion of Japan's total population, experienced a progressive deterioration in living standards. Many individual families were only able to survive through indenturing or selling their underage daughters to bordellos in the cities, or to those owned by the army. The entertainment districts in the cities experienced a boom in business during the world economic crisis,[56] and it is estimated that in the 1930s one in ten of Japan's adolescent females worked for their families in these areas, which were frequented by the upper classes. In this way prostitution became a modern form of serfdom for the politically disenfranchised and materially deprived lower-class peasants.

The crisis in agriculture, which threatened the minimal existence of so many, had come about through the drop in prices since 1927 of the farmers' most important products – rice and silkworm cocoons. Producer prices were kept artificially high during the First World War, and they had already fallen by some 30 percent between 1919 and 1921. They fell again between 1927 and 1932, when the depression in the countryside reached its high point, by another 30 percent on average, and were thus 40 percent of their 1919 level.[57] The drop in export prices[58] of raw silk had especially severe consequences for Japanese agriculture, and at the same time also had a bad influence on Japanese foreign trade in general. Silkworm cultivation was a lucrative activity in the agricultural sector of the economy, especially since mulberry bushes require no intensive cultivation, as is the case with rice. About 17 percent of all agricultural production came from this area, in which 40 percent of the farmers were engaged.[59] The silk exports, 96.7 percent of which went to the United States, still accounted for 36.3 percent of all Japanese exports in 1929.[60] Japan's agricultural economy and a large part of her foreign trade hung quite literally upon on a silk thread. This thread was broken at the end of 1929 when the American market dried up as a result of the Great Depression, and when simultaneously synthetic fibre began its conquest of the world as a cheaper substitute. Over two-thirds of the retrenchment of Japan's total exports in 1930, a 31.5 percent reduction in comparison to the previous year, was due to the shrinking market for raw silk.[61]

Japan itself was not predisposed to even partially absorbing the excess production, despite the steep decline in raw silk prices and with them the prices for finished silk products.[62] Due to the extremely low incomes of the people and consequently their lack of buying power, a market for high-style consumer goods and luxury items could not develop in Imperial Japan. With respect to private consumerism, Imperial Japan stood so far in arrears in comparison with the industrialised nations of the West,[63] that this degree of underdevelopment far exceeded her attained degree of modernisation. The social structure, with the huge gap between the poor and the extremely small number of wealthy people, which expanded further during the economic crisis and subsequent recovery during the 1930s,[64] as well as the oligopolisation of the economy in a typically Japanese fashion with the growth of the family holding companies, was responsible for the fact that a domestic consumer market could not develop. Foreign trade, built up and patronised by the government for national defence purposes during the Meiji Period, gave priority to securing the raw materials required by heavy industry. The priority of national defence against the West and with it the compulsion of external economic assimilation with the industrialised nations, dictated the alignment of the economy towards producing exports. As in the case of silk, the Japanese economy, as steered by the oligarchs, produced not for the needs of its own people, but for promoting national growth, meaning the realisation of the greatest possible profits for a few large firms. The *zaibatsu*, through whom the house of Mitsui handled 20 percent of Japan's foreign trade,[65] preferred to sell for large profits overseas in order to invest in the new profit-promising chemical and electrical industries. Family-, i.e., company-related interest in profits for the *zaibatsu* from exports,[66] resulting in speculation and corruption, did not as such coincide any longer at the end of the 1920s with national interests in foreign trade and armaments. The economic crisis revealed to broad segments of the population that the desire for profits of a few seemed to take precedence over national interests. As a result, the call for a restorative recovery of Japanese consciousness was accompanied by calls for a nationalisation, or at least strong state control, of the giants of industry.[67]

The governing party cabinets, intimately involved with the economic magnates, were unable to solve the national, economic, and social crises. The state's reaction to the decimation of Japanese economic life was decided by the interests of big business, and in the end worsened the crisis. The government of the Minseito, led by Prime Minister Hamaguchi with Finance Minister Inoue, initiated the basic economic policy of returning to the gold standard, together with the deflationary economic policies which served this goal.[68] The second largest of the *zaibatsu* at that time, Mitsubishi, fully backed this programme, because if it proved successful the position of the company with respect to its rivals – Mitsui and Sumitomo – would be strengthened. Because Mitsubishi was primarily engaged in heavy industry, the promotion in radical army circles of the nationalisation of the large industry concerns caused the *zaibatsu* to work even more closely with the government in order to ensure the freedom of their business activities in the future.

The other large industrial firms also appeared to be interested in a reduction of wholesale prices, which by comparison to international standards were still too high.[69] As a precondition of reviving exports, they also approved the policy of scarce money. The announced measure of linking the yen to gold could also expect to meet with national acclaim, because Japan would once again achieve parity with the two leading industrial nations of the world, the United States and Britain. But the time chosen to realise this measure could not have been less favourable because the expanding American economic crisis, which had grown in the meantime, limited Japan's most important export market. Moreover, the yen, overvalued in comparison to the dollar,[70] made Japanese products in the United States excessively expensive. The precipitous fall of export prices for Japanese raw silk of over 60 percent within one year was therefore also the result of the Tokyo government's erroneous monetary policy.[71]

Although the wholesale index fell as expected, from 152.2 in January 1930 to its lowest level of 111.0 in October 1931,[72] the hoped-for rise in exports did not take place. Instead, the export and import statistics fell further in 1931 after their drastic decline in the first year of the world economic crisis. Agriculture was the principal bearer of the suffering brought on by the depression and would remain so until 1935, but from 1931 heavy industry, coal, steel, and the machine-tool industries were also affected by the decline in exports. They experienced a slight reduction in orders, but at around 10 percent this cannot be compared with the losses in the agricultural sector.[73] In order to prevent further losses, the big businesses availed themselves of their political connections and also made structural reforms to bring about savings in production,[74] options which were not open to the farming population. In 1930 the opposition Seiyukai Party began to attack the government for imposing cuts on the military budget. In particular, the navy demanded that Japan should free itself of the armament restrictions imposed by the London Naval Conference of 1930. Japan should embark on a sizable expansion of her naval forces.[75] Mitsubishi supported the government, but her competitors supported the opposition that began to form in 1930, which favored the economics of increased armaments. This opposition demanded an increase in state expenditures and cheaper credit. Japanese economic policy was, therefore, not so much based on rational concepts as on premodern, prestige-orientated group loyalties. It was characterised by feudal-like battles between cliques.

If big business attempted to manipulate state institutions for its own profit, in a like manner the army represented the people in the villages. The occupation of Manchuria in 1931 by the Japanese units stationed there was supposed to thwart the corrupt symbiosis of big business and government which had grown worse due to the material challenge presented by the economic crisis. This invasion was to lead to an independent, state-controlled economic system which included an advanced level of industrial nationalisation as well as an anticapitalist, romantic agrarian programme for the restorative restructuring of the entire society. Big business, the traditional *zaibatsu*, distanced themselves from the army's act of violence and the programme on which it was based.[76] The government, on the contrary, was obliged to sanction after the fact the annexation of a foreign territory, if it did not wish to provoke an armed insurrection at home. The confrontation between the military representing those advocating a folkish restoration and the *zaibatsu* as the vanguard of an industrial revolution was never conclusively decided in Imperial Japan. Between 1932 and 1936 the army temporarily achieved ascendancy principally due to the failure of the government's economic policies and because the *zaibatsu* had completely compromised themselves.[77]

Great Britain's retreat from the gold standard, which occurred by chance three days after the Mukden Incident,[78] sounded the death knell for the cabinet's economic policies. Instead of immediately freeing the Japanese yen from the gold standard, the government watched passively as 58.5 percent of her currency flowed out into gold as a result of monetary speculation.[79] The Mitsui concern played an important role in these transactions and thereby in the depreciation of the value of Japanese currency, through its hasty dollar buying in the expectation that the yen would be uncoupled from gold.[80] The government capitulated before the national emotions released in Japan by the international crisis concerning Manchuria and the financial chaos which they themselves had brought about. At the end of December 1931 the cabinet resigned leaving the field to the opposition Seiyukai.[81] Although the new government immediately began an effective programme in order to lift the nation out of the depression which had bottomed out at the end of 1931, the ill-conceived economic policy had created a heated sociorevolutionary climate in Japan. Political assassinations were carried out by nationalistic fanatics intent on doing away with those apparently responsible for the nation's misery. Victims included the Finance Minister in the previous cabinet, Baron Dan, the chief manager of Mitsui, and Prime Minister Inukai himself. These killings indicate the extent of the violent sociopolitical emotions convulsing the people. The governing coalition of big business and party politicians was not, in the long run, equal to the situation.[82]

Overcoming the Crisis: Economic Concentration and the Rule of the Military Technocrats

The world economic crisis became a permanent problem in the 1930s in the industrialised nations of the West, especially in the United States and the developing countries dependent on her. It was only overcome in the early years of the Second World War.[83] However, the Allies' future wartime adversaries, Germany and Japan, were able to achieve a more rapid, astonishingly similar economic recovery. In both countries, with the help of a restorative, folkish, basically antimodern ideology, economic recovery was made a national priority. The leaders of both states, the National Socialists as well as the military autocrats, saw domestic economic recovery simply as a necessary precondition for achieving their announced goals. State-financed credit, the promotion of the armament industries, consolidation of the most important branches of industry, and planning for economic self-sufficiency characterise the economic development of both nations during the 1930s.[84] The political opposition since 1933 between the authoritative remonstrating 'have-not' countries and the Western industrial nations, coincided with a much graver antagonism between the two camps' economic orders which was laden with more important consequences. It pressed with imminent inevitability toward a military confrontation.

The credit and overseas economic policy of the new Finance Minister Takahashi,[85] who had held office since December 1931, for the most part anticipated the policies followed by his counterpart in Germany, Schacht, one year later. For reasons of national prestige an open policy of inflation was rejected in Japan as well as in National Socialist Germany. Instead, the current deflation was to be overcome by an increase in credit in the form of public bonds through a type of artificial fund raising. As a prerequisite for this reflationary policy, the new government uncoupled the yen from gold in order to stem any further outflow of currency, and to reopen the most important export market for the industries that were to be revived – the United States. Within a year the overvalued yen sank more than 60 percent *vis-à-vis* the dollar.[86] Japanese products, low-priced in any case, henceforth could be offered on the American market for half their previous prices. They were without competition, and with these lowest of prices the Japanese made up for the lack of buying power which had been caused by the depression.

The central element of Takahashi's reflationary policy was the issue of public promissory notes which were sold by the state to the Bank of Japan. With the paper money received, the state contended with increased expenditures, especially in the military's budget. The Bank of Japan in turn sold the promissory notes on the open credit market and thereby mobilised fallow money in the economy. But the original idea, to call in the 'swap for the future' after the economy had been stimulated and prevent it from overheating, was not realised. Unproductive armament manufacture proved to have laws of its own. At home and in foreign trade, constant increases were demanded which could only be financed through increasing the state debt, i.e., with the help of the printing press and inflation. The raising of the limit, authorised by Takahashi, on the amount of money that could be issued by the Bank of Japan for public bonds from 120 million to 1 billion yen could not be rescinded.[87] During his period in office, which was brutally ended in the attempted putsch of 26 February 1936,[88] the amount of money in circulation climbed by a further 500 million yen.[89] The creation of cheap loans was also well served by the fact that the Bank of Japan lowered its interest rate three times in 1932 alone. The interest rate stood at 7 percent at the time when the economic crisis reached its peak in Japan, and it fell to 4.7 percent by the end of 1932 and finally stood at 3.29 percent in 1937.[90]

Deficit spending by the state from 1932 onwards led to a rapid growth in the nation's expenditure. The volume of this expenditure doubled within the six years from 1931–6.[91] The lion's share of this increase, around 62 percent, went to the military. By comparison only 14 percent was marked for social projects, and 7 percent for refurbishing Japan's infrastructure, agriculture, and other services.[92] The military budget, which at 455 million yen in 1931 constituted slightly less than 30 percent of the total budget, rose in the following fiscal year alone to 687 million yen – 38 percent of all state spending. In 1936 it was two-and-a-half times the 1931 level, and already constituted almost half of the Tokyo government's budget.[93]

This government spending policy favouring the military satisfied the zaibatsu, who controlled the armaments sector of the economy. At the same time, it accorded with the national desire for security against the challenge from the West, and was welcomed by the technocrats on the general staff, the so-called 'German group', with their sociopolitical model of a resolute peasant warrior state in arms.[94] Nevertheless, the state's support measures, like her entire credit policy, mainly benefited the big businesses which controlled marketing and finance policy. Therefore, the needs of the rural population, despite lively debate in parliament, were ignored, and continued as themes in the propaganda slogans of the young army officers and similarly leftist students. The murder of the new Prime Minister, Inukai, in May 1932 by radical officers[95] was to destroy the alliance of big business and the civilian government which still, simply under the name of a different party, dominated politics, and open the way to the socialisation of Japan. These political murders swept away the parliamentary system, which had never established itself among the voters, but big business defended its independence in the new professional cabinets. As at the time of the rebuilding of the economy, big businesses were able to compromise the new politicians. Political reorganisation had no direct influence on the economic revival, which, as before, remained in the hands of Finance Minister Takahashi. Only the ensuing dominance of the military at the pinnacle of the government ensured that the revived economy would serve functionally to militarise the entire nation.[96]

The necessity for increased imports of raw materials for the armaments industry could only be met by an increase in the exports which had fallen dramatically during the economic crisis. Because Manchuria, which had been annexed by the army and was also administered by her, was supposed to be primarily a resettlement area for the impoverished rural population of the home country, its own industrial development stagnated. As a result, raw material imports[97] from this area only slightly reduced Japan's dependence on the Western industrial nations and their colonies.[98] The steel manufacturing industry, the backbone of any armament economy, was 85 percent dependent on deliveries of raw materials, which came either as scrap metal from the United States or in the form of ore from the British Commonwealth or the Western-controlled areas of China. Except for the low-quality coal for domestic consumption mined in Japan itself, energy producing raw materials had to be imported: coal for blast furnaces from northern China, and oil from the Dutch East Indies and the United States.

Japanese refineries were unable, and in part were not sufficiently advanced technically, to produce enough high-grade aircraft gasoline and special lubricants to meet domestic needs.[99] Up to 90 percent of these fuels and lubricants, which are vital for any modern army and in particular to modern navies, had to be imported. Japan was 100 percent dependent on foreign suppliers for bauxite, for the basic material for aircraft construction – aluminium, for cotton – the raw material of Japan's largest industry even in the 1930s, and also for wool and synthetic fibers. Japan was almost completely dependent on foreign suppliers for special ores, lead, zinc, tin, and nickel, as well as tungsten, which largely came from the Southeast Asian colonies of the European powers.[100]

The main Japanese exports, after raw silk lost out as her most important foreign-trade item, were cotton products and products from those industries manufacturing inexpensive, low-quality, mass-produced goods. With the help of cheap credit, the most important export industry, textiles, was fitted out with the most modern machines available and mechanised to a high degree. Technical innovation, raising productivity, and the consolidation of production reached a high point in the cotton industry during and immediately after the economic crisis.[101] The textile makers took advantage of the excessive supply of cheap labour coming from the rural areas and indentured adolescent girls to work for them, who were then confined to the factory and nearby company dormitory grounds.[102] Since skilled long-term workers were no longer employed in these factories, the real income of the textile workers sank by over 60 percent.[103] With these unrivaled, extremely low salaries, which hardly affected the budgets of the companies, together with practical freedom from taxes – the average tax for this industry was 4.3 percent[104] – and export subventions from the government, the Japanese cotton industry was able to pitch their products on the world market at the lowest possible prices.

This export offensive, regarded as 'dumping' by the Western powers, led to a permanent trade war between Japan and Britain's colonies in West Africa and South Asia. Great Britain abrogated the treaties between her colonies and Japan in 1934, and set quotas for the import of Japanese textiles. Japan answered with a 'Law for the Protection of Foreign Trade'. It enabled the state to limit or completely suspend temporarily, as a countermeasure, trade with specific nations at any time.[105] The government's customs policies supported this export offensive and protected the home market from undesirable Western competition. The average duty on imported goods rose from 17.2 percent in 1929 to around 24 percent in 1931. In order to protect the industrial expansion programme, in 1932 customs duties were raised by 35 percent. Moreover, a special tax on luxury items was levied. Duties on imported rice, which in conjunction with the build-up of the armaments industry was supposed to be grown in Japan, were raised to six times their previous levels. In the same manner, producers of cellulose, automobiles, and chemical products were protected from foreign competition by raising tariff barriers. By contrast, customs receipts for the import of raw materials were inconsequential.[106]

State protectionism for the export industry as the guarantor of heavy industrial expansion coincided with state-directed economic measures for the concentration of these industries, which for reasons of national defence enjoyed special protection. The development of the Japanese economy tended strongly in the direction of state-monopoly capitalism, which was vehemently advocated by the army. However, instead of the state the *zaibatsu* were supposed to assume the leadership of this monopoly. This policy was encouraged by the government, and finally it was ruthlessly exploited during the war from 1937 onwards.

A Major Industries Control Law was passed in the Diet with the support of the dominating business lobby there, and went into effect in August 1931.[107] Although the partly ruinous, competitive struggle between the small firms dependent on the big businesses could have justified such state intervention, the new law did not provide for the control of big business, rather it promoted their concentration to the detriment of the smaller firms. The law provided for production and price agreements in the fields designated by the government as large industries, only when more than half of the companies in a particular field desired such. The remaining companies could be forced to join the agreement through a directive from the Finance Ministry. The law was amended twice in a manner benefiting the large concerns,[108] resulting in the relaxation of government regulation. The ministry merely warned companies about overly high prices, and only in one case forced a price reduction, from the cement cartel.[109]

The significance of the law lay not in its direct effects. It was important because it provided government sanction for the cartels and syndicates which already existed, or had been formed since the beginning of the economic crisis. The law encouraged the formation of more of these organisations – there already existed cartels in the iron-working industries for anthracite, sheet metal, steel plates and metal alloys. Also, in the chemical industry, a cartel had been formed in the lucrative production of artificial fertilisers. By 1936 cartels had been formed in the textile industry, paper processing, sugar manufacture, coal production, cement manufacture, and among the breweries.[110] Strategic key industries were finally taken over by the state and fused together.

In January 1934 the 'Japanese Iron Manufacturing Company' was created by a fusion of the state Yawata Works[111] and the six largest enterprises in the country. The government controlled around 80 percent of the capital, with the remainder under the control of the *zaibatsu*. About 96 percent of the country's raw iron production, 52 percent of the steel manufactured, and 44 percent of all finished steel products from that time onwards came from this state enterprise.[112] A law passed in the same year put the oil industry under complete state control.[113] The state also increased its support of the manufacturing and export corporations legalised in 1925. From 1933 it became possible to forcibly integrate outsiders into these corporations. The number of export corporations more than doubled by 1936, and the increase in manufacturing corporations was even greater.[114]

The process of economic concentration legalised by the state led to a structural shift in the economy away from textile manufacturing to heavy industry. Modern branches of industry expanded greatly, for example, the chemical industry which was never affected by the recession. Machine, machine-tool, and the shipbuilding industries also experienced high rates of growth. The textile industry, which in 1931 still employed over 50 percent of all industrial workers, was overtaken in 1936 by the metal manufacturing and chemical industries with respect to the number of workers employed.[115] The absolute number of industrial workers, which had remained roughly constant during the 1920s at around 4.5 million, rose by 1940 to around 6.8 million.[116] The production index rose over 60 percent between 1931 and 1936,[117] and in 1935 the number of employees in most fields of industry exceeded the previous high point before the economic crisis, which had been reached in 1925. The economic crisis was conclusively overcome in 1935, but at the cost of giving priority to the armaments industry and acceding to the political hegemony of the military.

The profits from the economic recovery were quietly turned over to the *zaibatsu*, who had receded into the background of public life. If average profits in industry were 10 percent, the *zaibatsu's* profits came close to 20 percent during this recovery period.[118] Except for the few at the very top of the pyramid, the working masses dependent on wages went away empty-handed, because real incomes declined until 1936.[119] The army of small businessmen and manufacturers in the cities vegetated at the edge of a minimum existence, now legally dependent on the state or big business. Up until 1935 most of the rural population still lived below the poverty line. Although the government subsidised agriculture, the amounts were only noticeable in the propaganda. Military spending came to 942 million yen in 1934, and in the same year agriculture subsidies, for half the Japanese population, reached an all time high of 83 million yen.[120] Until 1936 a coalition of interests made up of industrialists and large property owners blocked, in both houses of parliament, all proposed laws which might have lightened the material distress in the countryside, such as legal regulation of lease agreements or state control of artificial fertiliser prices.[121] The young officers revolt in February 1936,[122] which presented the greatest threat to the imperial system and was a highly revolutionary attempt to overthrow the government; a foreign policy linked to National Socialist Germany in the same year; and the escalating conflict with China which could only lead to the war which broke out in the summer of 1937 – these constituted the political price paid by an inflexible, reform-hostile Japanese society for an economic recovery which was successful on the surface, but was socially a complete disaster.

Conclusion

The course of modernisation laid out in 1853 was raised to the status of a state programme with the Meiji Restoration in 1868. It was carried out according to Western models and an anti-Western ideology with inviolate ideals directed toward national independence. Japanese modernisation was aligned toward a confrontation with the industrialised world which could only be finally settled by a war. Imperial Japan's leaders were bound in their political maneuvering to the primacy of unassailable national greatness and to their inherited traditional value system. The parameters of their decisions, particularly in the area of economics, were prescribed by social constraints.[123] The putative economic forces in Japanese history reveal themselves to be self-constructed barriers on the path to modernisation.

Japan exported and built up her industry not out of the necessity of survival, but due to the unquestioned priorities of her government leaders – a heavy industrial build-up with a nationalistic, expansionist orientation without any consideration for the social necessities of the people. The ideology entertained by the oligarchs, in close symbiosis with the other power centres of Imperial Japan, likewise controlled the nation's politics and economics. The world economic crisis only deepened the cracks and contradictions which characterised the social structure of the country, and encouraged radical political groups to attack the system. As with the formation of international alliances,[124] the world economic crisis which emanated from the United States acted, in the socioeconomic area, as a catalyst. Nation-state concepts coupled with political resentments left over from the First World War burst onto the scene as a result of the crisis. Their perpetuity, concealed until 1929, indicates that the world order created in 1918 was only a temporary one which would have collapsed with any sort of crisis. After the breakdown, brought on by the First World War, of the old order in international, as well as economic, quarters, the interwar period became an era of permanent politico-economic crisis – not only in Japan – which reached a high point in 1929–30. The inability of the Western industrialised nations to solve the crisis, as well as the apparent success ascribed to Germany and Japan, can be explained by the basic structural differences in these respective societies. The opposing concepts of politicising the economy as in the autocratic fascist states and the preeminence of economics over politics as in the Anglo-Saxon nations clashed,[125] and the outcome of the Second World War decided this confrontation in favour of the latter, liberal-capitalistic order, at least for a large part of the world.

Notes

1. Two further essays correspond with and respectively continue the topic of this essay: Bernd Martin, 'Aggressionspolitik als Mobilisierungsfaktor. Der militärische und wirtschaftliche Imperialismus Japans 1931–1941', in Friedrich Forstmeier and Hans-Erich Volkmann, eds., *Wirtschaft und Rüstung am Vorabend des Zweiten Weltkrieges*, Düsseldorf, 1975, pp. 222–44; 'Japans Kriegswirtschaft 1941–1945', in Friedrich Forstmeier and Hans-Erich Volkmann, eds., *Kriegswirtschaft und Rüstung 1939–1945*, Düsseldorf, 1977, pp. 256–86.

2. Richard J. Smethurst, *A Social Basis for Prewar Japanese Militarism. The Army and the Rural Community*, Berkeley, 1974.

3. Takehiko Yoshihashi, *Conspiracy at Mukden. The Rise of the Japanese Military*, London, 1963.

4. Chie Nakane, *Japanese Society*, Berkeley, 1970.

5. William G. Beasley, *The Meiji Restoration*, Stanford, 1973.

6. For theories of 'late developers' which are still stimulating with regard to the Japanese starting situation, see Alexander Gerschenkron, *Economic Backwardness in Historical Perspective*, Cambridge, Mass., 1962, pp. 6–30. For a comparison between Japan and Germany, see Reinhard Bendix, 'Preconditions of Development: A Comparison of Japan and Germany', in Reinhard Bendix, *Nation-Building and Citizenship. Studies of Our Changing Social Order*, New York, 1964, pp. 177–213. Gustav Ranis, 'Die Finanzierung der wirtschaftlichen Entwicklung Japans', in Rudolf Braun et al., eds., *Industrielle Revolution. Wirtschaftliche Aspekte*, Cologne, 1972, pp. 237–52 (English translation: 'The Financing of Japanese Economic Development' in Kazushi Ohkawa et al., eds., *Agriculture and Economic Growth: Japan's Experience*, Tokyo, 1970, pp. 37–47); Kotaro Ikeda et al., eds., *Die industrielle Entwicklung in Japan unter besonderer Berücksichtigung seiner Wirtschafts- und Finanzpolitik*, Berlin, 1970, pp. 29–65; Kinichiro Sakurai, *Financial Aspects of Economic Development of Japan, 1868–1958*, Tokyo, 1964, is in part apologetic about the finance policies of the banks, which were dependent on the *zaibatsu*.

   Foreign loans on a large scale were first accepted after the turn of the century, especially during the war with Russia, 1904–5. In 1867, i.e., before the Restoration, the government borrowed 3.5 million yen in London to finance the first railroad in Japan between Tokyo and Yokohama. Later in 1872, 10.7 million yen was borrowed in London to finance the commutation of the stipends of the feudal lords. G. C. Allen, *A Short Economic History of Modern Japan 1867–1937*, London, 3rd ed. 1972, p. 41.

7. Roger F. Hackett, *Yamagata Aritomo in the Rise of Modern Japan 1838–1922*, Cambridge, Mass., 1971. (Field Marshall Yamagata was the outstanding military man of the Meiji Period. He instituted universal compulsory military service. Later as *genro* he was a member of the Privy Council, and was an influential politician until his death. For example, the *genro* – foremost oligarchs among the oligarchs – nominated prime ministers for sanction by the emperor. The last *genro*, Prince Saionji Kimmochi, continued to function in this capacity until late in the 1930s.

8. George Akita, *Foundations of Constitutional Government in Modern Japan 1868–1900*, Cambridge, Mass., 1967. Annelotte Piper, *Japans Weg von der Feudalgesellschaft zum Industriestaat*, Cologne, 1976. For the new system of justice: Nobuyoshi Toshitani, 'Japan's Modern Legal System: Its Formation and Structure', in *Annals of the Institute of Social Science*, University of Tokyo, vol. 17, 1976, pp. 1–50. The civil law code modelled after that of Germany came into effect in 1898 in Japan, two years before it was officially promulgated in Imperial Germany.

9. Thomas C. Smith, *Political Change and Industrial Development in Japan. Government Enterprise, 1868–1880*, Stanford, 1955. Yasuzo Horie, 'Modern Entrepreneurship in Meiji-Japan', in William L. Lockwood, ed., *The State and Economic Enterprise in Japan*, Princeton, 1965, pp. 183–208.

10. For a company history of the largest of the *zaibatsu*, Mitsui, see: Oland D. Russell, *Das Haus Mitsui*, Zürich, 1940.

11. William W. Lockwood, *The Economic Development of Japan. Growth and Structural Change 1868–1938*, Princeton, 1954, p. 98. (The tax was assessed at 3 percent of the value of the land, which in turn was set at 8.5 times the value of a single harvest. The average value of a harvest was often overestimated, and in the beginning the property tax often came to 33 percent. In 1877 the tax rate was reset at 2.5 percent the value of the property. Inflation served to lighten somewhat the tax yoke of the peasants until 1898, when the tax rate was raised again to 3.3 percent.)

12. Ibid., p. 26. Reginald P. Dore, *Land Reform in Japan*, Oxford, 1959. See the tables on pp. 175 and 176. According to these tables, in Japan in 1941 there were (including Okinawa) around 5.5 million peasant families of whom: 1.7 million or 31.2% were landowners; 1.2 million or 20.7% were both landowners and tenant farmers, owning over 50% of their land; 1.1 million or 20% were both landowners and tenant farmers, owning under 50% of their land; 1.5 million or 27.7% were tenant farmers. With a total of around 5.9 million hectares of cultivated land, the average size of a plot was slightly over one hectare per family (Dore, p. 27, data from August 1947 census).

13. Only around 3,000 large landholders owned more than 50 *cho* (1 *cho* = 0.99174 hectare), meaning slightly less than 50 hectares. They constituted the most powerful groups politically in the countryside and controlled, for the most part, the Seiyukai political party and the parliament through their representatives (Dore, pp. 30 and 86ff).

14. Lockwood, *The Economic Development of Japan*, pp. 13 and 538.

15. An alliance with Great Britain was formed in 1902, Ian H. Nish, *The Anglo-Japanese Alliance*, London, 1966; with France in 1907 (Frank W. Iklé, 'The Franco-Japanese Agreement of 1907: Seedbed of Diplomatic Revolution and Midwife to World War I', in James B. Parsons, ed., *Papers in Honor of Professor Woodbridge Bingham*, San Francisco, 1976, pp. 39–54.

16. Lockwood, *The Economic Development of Japan*, pp. 35, 292. The statistics on military spending vary depending on whether pensions and repayment of debts are included, or only pure budget spending is given. For dependable data, see the tables in Hugh T. Patrick, 'The Economic Muddle of the 1920s', in James W. Morley, ed., *Dilemmas of Growth in Prewar Japan*, Princeton, 1971, pp. 211–66, here pp. 250f.

17. Lockwood, *The Economic Development of Japan*, p. 36. Overseas loans came to 98 million yen in 1903, before the war with Russia. In 1913 they had climbed to 1.5 billion yen and constituted more than half of the national debt.

18. Ibid. For authoritative tables on total foreign trade: 'Monthly Data, 1913 to 1940, for Japanese Imports and Exports, Exchange Rates in London and New York, and Wholesale Price Indices for Japan, England and the United States', in the appendix (slipcase) of Elizabeth Boody Schumpeter, ed., *The Industrialisation of Japan and Manchukuo 1930–1940. Population, Raw Materials and Industry*, New York, 1940.

19. Lockwood, *The Economic Development of Japan*, p. 36, between 1900 and 1913.

20. Lockwood, *The Economic Development of Japan*, pp. 38ff. Allen, *Economic History*, pp. 97ff. The latter notes a growth of the industrial work force from 948,000 to 1.6 million, but includes only enterprises with over five workers.

21. Gerd Hardach, *Der Erste Weltkrieg* (Geschichte der Weltwirtschaft im 20. Jahrhundert, vol. 2) Munich, 1973, p. 279. On the bribery scandals which involved *zaibatsu* companies like Mitsui, see Russell, *Haus Mitsui*, pp. 256ff.

22. Lockwood, *The Economic Development of Japan*, p. 41.

23. Allen, *Economic History*, p. 229. Imports: 2,173 billion yen; exports: 2,099 billion yen.

24. Peter Duus, *Party Rivalry and Political Change in Taisho Japan*, Cambridge, Mass., 1968, pp. 125ff.

25. Lockwood, *The Economic Development of Japan*, p. 41. The wholesale-price index reached its high point in March 1920, 321.5 (1913 = 100), and it fell to 205.6 by December of the same year. Compare data, Schumpeter, *Industrialisation of Japan*, table 4.

26. Thomas R. Havens, *Farm and Nation in Modern Japan. Agrarian Nationalism, 1870 to 1940*, Princeton, 1974, pp. 135ff. Agricultural prices fell some 20 percent between 1919 and 1921. Rice imports, which amounted to about one-third the marketed rice, pressed down prices and quieted the small handworkers in the cities, the centre of the 1918 rice riots.

27. Teijiro Uyeda, *The Growth of Population and Occupational Changes in Japan, 1920–1935*, Tokyo, 1936, Annex for tables divided according to industry branches. Also, Irene B. Taeuber, *The Population of Japan*, Princeton, 1958, p. 87.

28. Uyeda, *Growth of Population*, p. 13; Schumpeter, *Industrialisation of Japan*, p. 481. The amusement sector of the economy alone absorbed about half a million new workers between 1920 and 1930. Over half of these were women, who constituted 63.7 percent of the hotel and restaurant work force. See note 56 below.

29. See Wm. Roger Louis, *British Strategy in the Far East 1919–1939*, Oxford, 1971, pp. 79–108 for the Washington Naval Conference, Britain's previous cancellation of the alliance with Japan, and the setting of the fleet tonnage ratio of 5:5:3 (USA:GB:Japan).

30. Charles B. Burdick, *The Japanese Siege of Tsingtau. World War I in Asia*, Hamden, Conn., 1976.

31. Roger Daniels, *The Politics of Prejudice. The Anti-Japanese Movement in California and the Struggle for Japanese Exclusion*, Berkeley, 1962.

32. Smethurst, *Social Basis*, p. 39: in 1926 with the support of both parties and the government, a type of four-year vocational school was established by the army, mainly in rural areas. The school was to prepare school leavers with training for the nation, for military service. The four-year curriculum provided for 800 hours of education, including 400 hours of paramilitary training and 100 hours of moral education.

33. Patrick, *Economic Muddle*, p. 234. This is his central thesis.

34. Ibid., p. 233, and Schumpeter, *Industrialisation of Japan* (Monthly Data), 1928, show the wholesale-price index in Japan was about 170 (1913 = 100), while in the United States it was under 140 and Great Britain slightly over 140.

35. Lockwood, *The Economic Development of Japan*, pp. 58 and 515; Allen, *Economic History*, pp. 100ff; Schumpeter, *Industrialisation of Japan*, pp. 625ff. In 1905 the *zaibatsu* controlled 23 percent of the total capital market; in 1941, 58 percent. Mitsui also traded agricultural products, including eggs, milk and fruit. (Schumpeter, p. 634.) See Norbert Voack, *Die japanischen 'Zaibatsu' und die Konzentration wirtschaftlicher Macht in ihren Händen*, dissertation, Erlangen-Nürnberg, 1962, pp. 56ff.

36. Arthur E. Tiedemann, 'Big Business and Politics in Prewar Japan', in James W. Morley, ed., *Dilemmas of Growth in Prewar Japan*, Princeton, 1971, pp. 267–316, here p. 280. Johannes Hirschmeier and Tsunehiko Yui, *The Development of Japanese Business 1600–1973*, Cambridge, Mass., 1975, p. 172.

37. For example in 1929 a law authorising state monitoring of artificial fertiliser was rejected, as was in 1931 a tenant law in preparation since 1920. Takekazu Ogura ed., *Agricultural Development in Modern Japan*, Tokyo, 1963, pp. 129ff, p. 224. Instead, in 1932 a law was introduced which compensated the banks for losses in silk exports, while in contrast the parliament called on the farmers in the same year to institute self-help measures. (Ibid., pp. 171f, pp. 214f.)

38. Mitsui supported the stronger Seiyukai, behind whom the navy generally stood. On the other side, there were close connections between Mitsubishi, the Minseito, and the army. Voack, *Die japanischen Zaibatsu*, p. 83, and see below.

39. The most radical theoretician of the Showa Restoration was Kita Ikki. See his published essay, 'General Outline of Measures for the Reorganization of Japan', excerpted in David J. Lu ed., *Sources of Japanese History*, New York, 1974, 2 vols, vol. 2, pp. 131–36. For a comparison of this programme with that of the National Socialists and fascists, see Bernd Martin, 'Zur Tauglichkeit eines übergreifenden Faschismus-Begriffes', in *Vierteljahrshefte für Zeitgeschichte*, Munich, 1981, vol. 29, pp. 48–73; English version in chapter 6 in this volume.

40. Lockwood, *The Economic Development of Japan*, pp. 58ff; Patrick, p. 240.

41. Lockwood, *The Economic Development of Japan*, p. 217. Compare with note 33 above.

42. For the policy of cheap money after the Kanto earthquake on 1 September 1923, in which a large part of Tokyo was destroyed by fire and 100,000 people died, see Allen, *Economic History*, p. 102; Schumpeter, *Industrialisation of Japan*, p. 885.

43. Patrick, *Economic Muddle*, p. 250, table.

44. Ibid., p. 241, table: shows the decline in the number of banks from 6,498 in 1927 to 3,946 in 1938.

45. Lockwood, *The Economic Development of Japan*, p. 517.

46. John W. Bennet and Iwao Ishino, *Paternalism in the Japanese Economy. Anthropological Studies of Oyabun-Kobun Patterns*, Minneapolis, 1963.

47. The following table was compiled by the author from Lockwood, *The Economic Development of Japan*, p. 204, and Patrick, *Economic Muddle*, pp. 220f (census of 1930).

Company Size (number of employees)	No. of Companies	No. of Employees	(%)	Percentage of Total Production
Independent				
One-Man	665,533	665,533		
1–4	512,271	2.2 mil	58.3%	20–25
5–99	59,643	988,456	20.8%	40
100–499	2,178	504,512	10.6%	
Over 500	413	494,761	10.4%	35–40
	1.2 mil.	**4.7 mil.**		

48. Schumpeter, *Industrialisation of Japan*, pp. 543–66 for a detailed description of the small suppliers.

49. The following table from Lockwood, *The Economic Development of Japan*, p. 272.

Income/Year Y	No. of Households	(%)	Total Income (mil. Y)	% of National Income
Over 1 mil.	19	–	32	0.4
50,000–1 mil.	1,739	–	276	3.2
10,000–50,000	22,674	0.2	596	6.8
3,000–10,000	145,360	1.2	1,010	11.5
1,200–3,000	723,141	5.7	1,542	17.6
800–1,200	1,087,343	8.6	1,096	12.5
400–800	3,500,000	27.8	2,142	24.5
200–400	4,888,000	38.8	1,711	19.6
0–200	2,232,000	17.7	335	3.8

50. Richard H. Mitchell, *Thought Control in Prewar Japan*, Ithaca, N.Y., 1976.

51. Ibid., p. 142. In 1933, 14,622 people were put under arrest for short periods of time.

52. Allen, *Economic History*, p. 125. Jerome B. Cohen, *Japan's Economy in War and Reconstruction*, University of Minnesota Press, 1949, p. 283, sets the highest number of workers organised in free unions at 420,000 in 1936, but this climb in the number of unionised workers runs contrary to the trend toward militarisation.

53. Sepp Linhart, 'Das Entstehen eines modernen Lebenstils in Japan während der Taisho Periode (1912–1926)', in *Saeculum*, vol. 25, 1974, pp. 115–127.

54. See Martin, 'The End of the Old Order: Social Change in Japan during the Pacific War', in this volume, chapter 5.

55. Havens, *Farm and Nation*, p. 137.

56. Ibid. For a more detailed, if moralising and puritanical, view, Harry E. Wildes, *Japan in Crisis*, New York, 1934, pp.130ff. See, too, Tsutomu Ouchi, 'Agricultural Depression and Japanese Villages', in *The Developing Economies*, vol. 5, 1967, pp. 597–627. See note 28.

57. Havens, *Farm and Nation*, pp. 135f; Patrick, *Economic Muddle*, p. 217.

58. Schumpeter, *Industrialisation of Japan*, pp. 511ff, p. 825, p. 831, p. 893; Allen, *Economic History*, p. 117. The average price per picul (132 lbs.) of raw silk:

Date	Price (Y)
Prior to the First World War	800–900
1920	1,191
1923	2,150
1929	1,420
Oct. 1930	540
June 1932	390

59. Lockwood, *The Economic Development of Japan*, p. 94; Patrick, *Economic Muddle*, p. 219.

60. Schumpeter, *Industrialisation of Japan*, p. 207; Lockwood, *The Economic Development of Japan*, p. 45.

61. Schumpeter, *Industrialisation of Japan*, p. 207.

62. Allen, *Economic History*, pp. 115ff.; modified opposing position in Lockwood, *The Economic Development of Japan*, p. 189, pp. 305ff. Also, untenable in this form, Alan H. Gleason, 'Economic Growth and Consumption in Japan', in William W. Lockwood, ed., *The State and Economic Enterprise in Japan*, Princeton, 1965, pp. 391–444.

63. M. K. Bennett, 'International Disparities in Consumption Levels', in *American Economic Review*, vol. 41, 1951, pp. 632–49. For the period 1934–38 Japan was number 10 among the 31 nations investigated, about equal with Italy and Cuba, but ahead of the Soviet Union and the other Asian nations.

64. Patrick, *Economic Muddle*, pp. 221ff; Lockwood, *The Economic Development of Japan*, pp. 272ff. Interest, stocks and leases constituted in 1930 about one-third of the national income in Japan; in the United States it was only 20 percent. G. C. Allen, *Japanese Industry: Its Recent Development and Present Condition*, New York, 1940, p. 97; real incomes sank on the average between 1932 and 1936 by around 10 percent.

65. Schumpeter, *Industrialisation of Japan*, p. 633; Russell, *Haus Mitsui*, p. 285, maintains that Mitsui controlled even 40–50 percent of Japan's foreign trade between 1932 and 1935.

66. In 1929 the *zaibatsu* reached the height of their political and economic power. Allen, *Economic History*, p. 134.

67. See the program of Kita Ikki (note 39) and the proposals for agrarian nationalism by Gondo Seikyo, Tachibana Kozaburo, and Kato Kanji in Havens, *Farm and Nation*, pp. 190ff, 233ff, 275ff.

68. Schumpeter, *Industrialisation of Japan*, p. 629, pp. 891ff; Patrick, *Economic Muddle*, pp. 253ff; Lockwood, *The Economic Development of Japan*, pp. 63f.

69. Patrick, *Economic Muddle*, p. 233 (table). The 1929 wholesale-price index: USA: 137.9, Great Britain: 137, Japan: 166.1; 1930, USA: 125.1, Great Britain: 119.9, Japan: 136.7 (1913 = 100). See, too, table 5 in Schumpeter, *Industrialisation of Japan*, Annex.

70. Schumpeter, *Industrialisation of Japan*, Annex: During the period when the yen was linked to gold, 11 January 1930 to 13 December 1931, the exchange rate was 100 yen = $49.38. In 1928 and 1929 the rate was 100 yen = $45–$47.

71. See note 58 above.

72. Schumpeter, *Industrialisation of Japan*, Annex. At 111.0 the wholesale index in Japan in October 1930 was still far above that of the United States, 100.6, and Great Britain, 96.8.

73. Schumpeter, *Industrialisation of Japan*, table 106, p. 484. In 1930 the steel industry accounted for 10 percent of Japan's total industrial production; in 1931

only 9.1 percent. In machine tools, production sank from 10.6 percent to 8.9 percent of national production.

74. Raising productivity through increased mechanisation and energy consumption. See Schumpeter, *Industrialisation of Japan*, pp. 647ff. However, in comparison to the West, Japan remained behind in organisation and production. The net production of Japan's factories in the 1930s was 25 percent of that of similar German works and 17 percent of comparable American factories. With 61.8 hours, the Japanese worker had the longest working week. Japan's degree of mechanisation at 1.7, measured according to available figures on H.P. per worker, was also far behind that of the United States (4.8), Great Britain (2.4,) and Germany (2.4). Lockwood, *The Economic Development of Japan*, pp. 175ff.

75. See chapter, 'Japan and Germany on the Path towards War', in this volume.

76. Schumpeter, *Industrialisation of Japan*, p. 644.

77. For the reorganisation of the *zaibatsu* firm Mitsui and its new publicity tactics after the murder of the head of the company Baron Dan on 5 March 1932, see Tiedemann, *Big Business*, pp. 299ff.

78. September 21, 1931. The Japanese army staged a bomb explosion on the railway line near Mukden and used the incident as a pretext for the military occupation of Manchuria.

79. Patrick, *Economic Muddle*, pp. 255ff.

80. Tiedemann, *Big Business*, pp. 289f.

81. On 11 December 1931 the cabinet of Wakatsuki Reijiro (Minseito) resigned after the Minister of the Interior left the party due to public indignation about *zaibatsu* currency speculation. Schumpeter, *Industrialisation of Japan*, p. 896. The following cabinet was headed by Inukai Tsuyoshi of the Seiyukai.

82. Finance Minister Inoue was murdered on 9 February 1932, Dan one month later (note 77). In the elections of 20 February 1932 the Seiyukai had campaigned with the slogan 'Minseito = Depression, Seiyukai = Boom' and achieved a landslide victory. For the domestic and foreign political developments, see James B. Crowley, *Japan's Quest for Autonomy. National Security and Foreign Policy 1930–1938*, Princeton, 1966, pp. 171ff.

83. Bernd Martin, 'Amerikas Durchbruch zur politischen Weltmacht', in *Militärgeschichtliche Mitteilungen*, vol. 2, 1981, pp. 57–98.

84. See note 75.

85. Ikeda, *Industrielle Entwicklung*, pp. 104ff.

86. The exchange rate of 100 yen = $49.38 (November 1931) sank to $20.72; after the American devaluation of the dollar on 1 February 1934, 100 yen fluctuated at about $29. This rate was maintained until 1939. Schumpeter, *Industrialisation of Japan*, table 4, Monthly Data.

87. Ikeda, *Industrielle Entwicklung*, p. 107; Allen, *Economic History*, pp. 90ff. In March 1939, 2.4 billion yen was in circulation.

88. Takahashi attempted – like Schacht in Germany – to stop the rearmament after the economy had been stimulated with help from this sector. Both finance experts prepared, against their respective wills, the way for military expansion. Takahashi was murdered by young army officers at the beginning of the February 26th putsch due to his criticism of increasing military spending. Schacht fell out with Hitler in 1937 and was dismissed.

89. From 1,330 billion yen to 1,870 billion yen. See Allen, *Economic History*, p. 138.

90. Schumpeter, *Industrialisation of Japan*, p. 902, table.

91. Ibid., p. 16, table; Patrick, *Economic Muddle*, p. 250, table. The statistics differ in these two sources because Schumpeter defined more narrowly state expenditures and her table is based on official data from that time. Nevertheless, the rapid rise of expenditures is readily evident in both.

92. Patrick, *Economic Muddle*, p. 257, lists a rise in government spending between 1930 and 1935 of 946 million yen. The missing 17 percent was used to service the debt.

93. See the tables, which differ slightly, in, Cohen, *Japan's Economy*, p. 5; Schumpeter, *Industrialisation of Japan*, p. 16; Patrick, *Economic Muddle*, p. 250. The data in the text are from Schumpeter.

94. For the 'German group' around T. Nagata and later the war premier H. Tojo, see chapter 8, 'Japan and Germany on the Path towards War', in this volume.

95. Crowley, *Japan's Quest*, p. 172 (May 15).

96. For a detailed explanation, see Martin, 'Aggressionspolitik'.

97. Lockwood, *Economic Development*, p. 533. Only six percent of Japan's total iron imports came from Manchuria.

98. For the dependence of Japanese industry on raw material imports, see the table for 1930 in, Lockwood, *Economic Development*, p. 388; likewise for the following percent data.

99. Cohen, *Japan's Economy*, pp. 22ff, pp. 133ff; Schumpeter, *Industrialisation of Japan*, p. 365.

100. During the first phase of the Pacific War, from the surprise attack on Pearl Harbor (7 December 1941) to the seizure of Burma (March 1942), Japan nearly achieved economic self-sufficiency with respect to raw materials. With the exception of nickel in early 1942, Japan had at its disposal more than enough of all of the raw materials necessary for her industries. (Martin, 'Kriegswirtschaft') The advance into the Coral Sea in May 1942 had, as its final goal, taking possession of New Caledonia and the nickel mines there for Japan's new economic and political empire. For strategy discussions among Japanese leaders, see Bernd Martin, *Deutschland und Japan im Zweiten Weltkrieg*, Göttingen, 1969, pp. 135ff and p. 139.

101. Schumpeter, *Industrialisation of Japan*, pp. 568ff.

102. Ibid., pp. 655ff. For the indenturing and confinement of young peasant girls in the textile factories, see a report on a visit to such a factory by Helen Mears,

'The Way of the Gods', in Jon Livingston et al., eds., *The Japan Reader, vol. 1, Imperial Japan 1800–1945*, New York, 1973, pp. 413–24.

103. Patrick, *Economic Muddle*, p. 223; Allen, *Economic History*, p. 97, p. 221, table. The following is a real salary index for textile workers, which in 1926 = 100:

Date	Index
1929	114
1930	127
1931	137
1932	128
1933	122
1934	121
1935	120
1936	115

104. Cf. the articles by Ranis (see note 6): Between 1928 and 1932 the average tax burden in agriculture, measured according to net income, was 9.7 percent; in industry, 4.3 percent. Also, Lockwood, *Economic Development*, p. 524. In 1933 taxes on personal incomes, industrial profits, and property still brought in about the same amount as the tax proceeds from *sake*. Tax reforms were made first in 1940. For this, see Saburo Shiomi, *Japan's Finance and Taxation 1940–1956*, New York, 1957.

105. Martin, 'Aggressionspolitik', p. 230; also for a contemporary justification of this policy, see Isohoshi Asahi, *The Economic Strength of Japan*, Tokyo, 1939, especially pp. 171ff on foreign trade.

106. Lockwood, *Economic Development*, p. 541; Schumpeter, *Industrialisation of Japan*, pp. 737f.

107. Schumpeter, *Industrialisation of Japan*, pp. 686f; Tiedemann, *Big Business*, p. 283. In the parliamentary committee which prepared this law, four of the nine members were from the *zaibatsu*.

108. Schumpeter, *Industrialisation of Japan*, pp. 686f. In March 1933 a directive was passed which stipulated that upon demand individual firms were to send production figures to the government. With this order, the companies not included in a control agreement could be forced to reveal their productivity. In July 1936, on the insistence of the big businesses, the prerequisites for building control organisations were changed. Formerly, half of the companies in an industrial branch had to vote for establishing a control organisation. Now a control organisation could be formed when the companies accounting for half the production in a branch desired it.

109. Ibid., p. 690.

110. Ibid., pp. 691ff; see also pp. 719ff for tables on the control committees formed up to July 20, 1936, and p. 723 for tables on 'other cartels'.

111. Lockwood, *Economic Development*, p. 224; Schumpeter, *Industrialisation of Japan*, p. 480.

112. Schumpeter, *Industrialisation of Japan*, pp. 602f; Cohen, *Japan's Economy*, p. 26.

113. Cohen, *Japan's Economy*, p. 23; Schumpeter, *Industrialisation of Japan*, p. 775 (Petroleum Industry Law).

114. Schumpeter, *Industrialisation of Japan*, pp. 759ff for the export corporations, pp. 760ff for the manufacturing corporations.

115. Schumpeter, *Industrialisation of Japan*, p. 484, table.

116. See the table in Taeuber, *Population of Japan*, Annex.

117. Allen, *Economic History*, p. 139; compare with the tables on industrial production in Schumpeter, *Industrialisation of Japan*, p. 482.

118. Russell, *Haus Mitsui*, p. 288; Lockwood, *Economic Development*, p. 275. In the years 1930–36 the nation's income was proportioned out as follows: Proprietors (industry and agriculture) 36.5 percent, employees 40.1 percent, other types of income (property, interest, pensions) 23.4 percent. Thus wage costs as a proportion of the net value of all industrial products in Japan (1934) was only 27.4 percent, while in Germany (1936) it was 32.0 percent, and in the United States (1937) it came to 40.2 percent. Lockwood, *Economic Development*, p. 276. Social insurance for employees was practically unknown and available only on a private basis.

119. See note 103.

120. Schumpeter, *Industrialisation of Japan*, p. 734, table; Lockwood, *Economic Development*, pp. 528f. For the military budget, see note 93. Ogura, *Agricultural Development*, p. 404, notes that the funds were used for public works in rural areas, but the profits were pocketed by the construction industry.

121. Ogura, *Agricultural Development*, p. 225. The artificial fertiliser producers' cartel (see also Schumpeter, *Industrialisation of Japan*, p. 706) steadily drove prices up. In 1936, after the failure of the young officers' revolt, a law providing for state price controls on artificial fertiliser, which had failed in 1935, was passed. The price remained constant until 1945 because the state paid the producers the difference.

    The problem of leasing agreements was first taken up by the Diet after the outbreak of the war with China (The Agricultural Adjustment Act of 1938). It was finally resolved in 1942 with the 'Food Control Law' which provided for a two-fold price system for the state purchase of rice – one for farmers who worked their own land and one for large property owners. See Bernd Martin, 'Agriculture and Food Supply in Japan during the Second World War' in Bernd Martin and Alan Milward, eds., *Agriculture and Food Supply in the Second World War*, Ostfildern, 1985, pp. 181–205.

122. Ben-Ami Shillony, *Revolt in Japan. The Young Officers and the February 26, 1936 Incident*, Princeton, 1973.

123. See for the theoretical implications, Bendix, *Nation Building*, p. 208.

124. See Josef Becker and Klaus Hildebrand, eds., *Internationale Beziehungen in der Weltwirtschaftskrise, 1929–1933*, Augsburg, 1980.

125. See Martin, 'Amerikas Durchbruch zur politischen Weltmacht', in note 83.

❧ 5 ❧

THE END OF THE OLD ORDER
SOCIAL CHANGE IN JAPAN DURING THE PACIFIC WAR

The Tenno System: Irrationality and Inefficiency of a Premodern Ruling Class

On 1 April 1945 one of the biggest Japanese national papers, *Asahi*, tersely commented on the country's war efforts: nine-tenths of it 'cannot be said to be definitely on a rational basis'.[1]

In fact, the chaos in the administration, the war economy, and even in military strategy was not, in the first place, a consequence of the large-scale American bombardment of Japanese towns that had begun at the end of 1944, but much rather resulted from the ruling élites' traditional style of leadership before and during the war. The clash between the premodern ethical norms of the Tenno system, supported by a small élite on the one side and technological progress on the other, cried out for immediate administrative reforms; and the ensuing dichotomy set the scene for the conflicts that during the 1930s were manifested as political murder, attempted military coups, and, as a consequence, foreign political aggression. From 1937 on, civilian groups – not the military – deepened the conflict with China in order to divert the tensions between the preindustrial élite and the impoverished agrarian population into belligerent chauvinism.[2]

As a consequence of the Meiji Restoration[3] the Japanese ruling élite had established itself in a quasi-dictatorial oligarchy, which recruited its members from among the three then most important

First published in German as 'Sozialer Wandel in Japan während des Zweiten Weltkrieges und seine Folgen für die Nachkriegszeit', in Waclaw Dlugoborski, ed., *Zweiter Weltkrieg und sozialer Wandel, Göttingen*, 1981, pp. 364–84. Translated by Dr Anne M. Martin.

political power centres: the court nobility, consisting of a few influential family clans; the military, who were under no civilian control and viewed themselves as the guarantors of the nation's self-determination; and civilian party politicians, who were closely linked with business circles. According to the constitution shaped after the Prussian model, the Emperor was considered the supreme integrating authority. However, because of his mythological descent from the gods, the Tenno could not directly interfere with politics. Instead, he served as the spiritual focus of the empire to unite the nation into one large family. The members of the oligarchy, where during the mid-1930s the military had achieved predominance,[4] developed the imperial system into a cohesive all-encompassing ideology. With the help of the military, the nation was to preserve a political system that above all guaranteed the privileges of the traditional élite.

Unable to cope with the problems of the modern world, the ruling class desperately tried to preserve its power by engaging in belligerent expansion. Having started on the way to suppression in domestic politics and aggression in foreign politics, there was no return, unless the oligarchy resigned. Hence, the survival of the imperial system and its ruling élite was as directly dependent on the victorious outcome of the war, as was the National Socialists' leadership in Germany. When defeat was imminent, the Japanese, as well as the German leaders, lapsed into dogmatic fatalism.

At a time when the imperial system was most loudly professed in public, it was destroyed from within. Despite the impression of unity and despite the deeply rooted consensus on social patterns, there was no denying the fact that the Japanese government system was the clumsiest and most inefficient of its day. Decisions were taken within a labyrinth of inner political groups and subgroups, following semifeudal rituals and evading personal responsibility. Even among top government officials, prestige and status were the guidelines to be followed, which mirrored the patriarchal rural order of collective harmony. Consequently, as all of these groups constantly blocked each other's way, fundamental decisions regarding politics as well as priorities during the war mostly ended in mere compromise phraseology.[5] In its political and, from 1941 onwards, military confrontation with the Western states, the Japanese Tenno system was bound to be defeated. Worst of all proved to be the impact of the army's premodern feudal way of thinking and acting on the political and military fate of the country. The army's *bushido* fighting code with its stress on military virtues[6] was no match for the American strategy that rationally made use of its material superiority. During the course of the war, *bushido* proved more and more senseless and in fact brought the nation close to physical annihilation. The strongest pillar upon which the imperial system rested, the Japanese military, in particular the army, had by the end of the war badly compromised itself. As a matter of course, when the armed forces surrendered in 1945, the whole patriarchal system based on the Tenno's manipulated god-like nature broke down. The political purges effected by the American forces of occupation concentrated on former military personnel, who made up 80 percent of all people screened.[7] This meant the end of the armed forces' political influence. With the revision of the constitution, the court and the traditional nobility, too, lost their political power.

Together with the imperial system, the power monopoly of the oligarchy had been partly destroyed by the outcome of the war and had finally been broken by the American occupants. Out of the three former centres of political power, only the civilian administrative élite was left, with its bureaucratic apparatus and its close ties with economic interests. The bureaucrats were thus spared the reeducation measures imposed by the Americans. Hence, it was this bureaucratic and economic élite, comparatively large in number, that best survived the collapse of 1945.[8] Consisting of former middle-ranking executives who had been under the control of the oligarchy, this group of experts now replaced the oligarchs and their premodern values. As to their backgrounds and education, the new leading class certainly fitted in with the traditional social patterns of Imperial Japan; yet, on the other hand, as responsible administrators they had proved their ability to cope with the demands of the modern world, thus mastering both faces of Japanese reality – the deeply rooted traditions, as well as the problems of the new industrial society. From this social stratum emerged the new political and economic leaders of the country, such as Prime Minister Yoshida, which meant that the postwar government still bore the marks of the former authoritarian structures and of nationalist conservative thinking. The new élite's traditional origin and their roots in Imperial Japan made the year of defeat, 1945, seem less radical a break. After the war, the social pyramid was deprived of its peak as the premodern élite resigned. In their stead, new cadres from industry and the civilian government took over. Technocrats were to lead the way to economic recovery in a country whose population had scarcely been touched by social change.

The Industry: National Efficiency versus Monopoly Interests

Before the old ruling class was forced to resign, any attempts to break up the traditional, irrational structures obviously remained fragmentary. This also applied to the war economy, which played as decisive a part in the outcome of the war as did the combat forces. Under the influence of the old élite, the industrial top management was unable to cope with the problems of the war economy. Yet, the beginnings of administrative reform, which was imposed in the difficult situation of war and resulted in a huge production increase, contained the nucleus of and showed the way to the stupendous recovery of the Japanese postwar economy. Certainly, it was not the Japanese economy itself that failed to meet the demands of modern technical warfare – within a year, in 1944, the shipyards built more tankers than had been available at the beginning of the war.[9]

Those technocrats who advocated total economic mobilisation[10] to confront the highly mechanised forces of the Western states remained powerless against the influence of the traditional holding companies, the *zaibatsu*. Certainly from 1932 onwards, regardless of the *zaibatsu*, bureaucratic experts along with high-ranking army and navy personnel had succeeded in building up heavy industrial complexes in Manchukuo, at the time controlled by the army. Any plans, however, to have the economy controlled by the state and factories managed by state commissioners failed because of the stiff resistance of the proprietors and their mouthpieces, the parliamentarians, most of whom had close affiliations with the industrialists.

Bills such as the Hoshino Plan[11] of September 1940, based on the German economy of the 1914–1918 war, were never given a chance in parliament. Instead, the oligarchy complied with the *zaibatsu*'s wishes, and on 1 September 1941 the 'Major Industries Association Ordinance' was passed by the Diet. So-called 'Control Councils'[12] imposed forced mergers within the different branches of industry, thereby transferring the chaos that reigned at the top level of government to the level of industrial management. In this way, the war economy, too, was now vertically structured and based on the principles of patriarchal care (on the part of the *zaibatsu*) and loyal submissiveness (on the part of small firms) according to the traditional family or group model of Japanese social structure in general. This step turned out to be an irreversible mistake for the whole of the war industry; in fact, it helped to hasten defeat.[13] From now on, coordination on a horizontal level was made impossible; for example, factories belonging to different industrial branches could hardly cooperate in producing the specific parts needed for large armaments such as guns and aircraft. The associations were controlled by the *zaibatsu* families, and since there was no higher level of authority to direct the production, they felt free to produce whatever best served their own interests, regardless of what was needed at the front. Stockpiling raw materials and wasting or even selling on the black market[14] such rare materials as aluminium that could no longer be obtained were as typical of the *zaibatsu*'s economic policy as was their aversion to taking risks and their hostility to technical innovation. No matter what the costs of production or what goods were produced, the state guaranteed a 6 to 8 percent dividend[15] without being able to directly influence armament production.[16]

Moreover, in the conferences between the leaders of the government and of the army and navy, decisions on the war's economic priorities were hindered by the military's ignorance, their rivalries, and their blind belief in victory. In order to supply the industry with raw materials and the population with agrarian products, Japan as an island country had to rely on her maritime connections with the conquered regions. Yet, no priority whatsoever was given to building ships, especially tankers for the transport of oil from the South Sea, so that as early as 1942, while raw materials were piling up in the ports of the occupied territories, in Japan the production of urgently needed goods had to be reduced.[17]

Only after the military's self-confidence had been shaken by several defeats, and the *zaibatsu* had started thinking about the impact of possible defeat on their own monopoly, did the voices of those economic and military experts succeed in making themselves heard, requesting thorough reorganisation of the Japanese war economy according to the Western model. Eventually, in

March 1943,[18] Prime Minister Tojo was authorised by Imperial Decree to issue directives concerning the war industry. As a result of the Prime Minister's widened range of authority over selfish company interests, in 1944 industrial production concentrated on shipbuilding (especially tankers) and electronic equipment. Another Imperial Decree, of November 1943, went even further by establishing a 'Munitions Ministry'[19] that was originally meant to act as the top administrative organ of the whole war economy. But because of the *zaibatsu*'s intervention, its control was limited to the production of airplanes, which to the *zaibatsu* themselves seemed to involve too many risks. However, it was in this field of industrial production that, for the first time in Japan, the traditional vertical structure was relinquished to be replaced by a horizontal production system that had the final product in view. Under Kishi Nobusuke, the Japanese counterpart to the German Minister for Armament, Albert Speer,[20] 671 factories and a total of 1.5 million workers experienced for the first time the Western way of management which left no room for traditional Japanese rituals of decision making, but where, instead, orders were given and had to be carried out.

Not least because of the experience he had gathered during the war, Kishi, the prototype of the modern Japanese manager, was later able as Japanese Prime Minister (1957 to 1960) to establish the country's economic predominance in Asia. During the war, the highest growth rate of Japanese armament production was achieved in the sectors of airplanes, tankers, and electronic equipment,[21] where technical and administrative innovation was effected by the government – always at the expense of the *zaibatsu*. Those branches that had been modernised during the war according to the Western model were able to maintain their standards after 1945 and were to lead the way in the Japanese export offensive. The development during the war made it clear that the *zaibatsu*'s pursuit of their own selfish profit interests and their overpowering, direct economic influence would inevitably have to be restricted by stripping the owner families of all their power. After the American occupiers' attempt at disentanglement,[22] the former *zaibatsu* companies were no longer run as family enterprises. Instead, closely linked with the political and economic administrative cadres of postwar Japan, they were, in a way, nationalised, their particular interests subordinated to the common aim of economic recovery.

Agriculture: Increased Productivity through Reform

Despite the huge increase in industrial production during the 1930s – between 1932 and 1936 the production index rose by 50 percent[23] – agriculture in Japan predominated throughout and even beyond the Second World War. More than half the population lived in the countryside, and about 50 percent of the working population were employed in agriculture.[24] For the most part these were women and old people, since many young men migrated to the cities. The proportion of female farm labour reached its peak during the last years of the war when the conscription rate rose fast.[25] Yet, because of most farmers' semifeudal dependency and the partition of the land in small allotments, Japan was not self-sufficient in food supply. Some 22 percent of rice – the essential staple food in Japan – had to be imported. Together with sugar and soybeans – equally essential – these food supplies came from the Japanese colonial possessions of Taiwan and Korea and from officially independent Manchukuo.[26] Moreover, the Meiji oligarchy had enforced the industrialisation of the country by imposing high taxes on agriculture,[27] which resulted in the utter impoverishment – unimaginable by Western standards – of more than half the population.

As a consequence, militant agrarian protest arose after the First World War, and during the 1930s sociorevolutionary nationalist movements and agrarian romanticism spread fast. The army, which considered itself the mouthpiece of the deprived, took up those ideologies and used them in its struggle for power before the beginning of the war.[28] Despite all this, the government, closely linked with the interests of big industry, could not see any reason for taking any supporting measures or inducing structural reforms in agriculture. Instead, about 50 percent of the farmers, who because of their dire poverty were commonly called 'water drinkers', remained as tenants at the mercy of their estate managers while the landlord lived far away in one of the big cities. The rent to be paid by the tenant was in most cases not even settled by a contract and could amount to 60 percent of his income, to be delivered in kind. About 20 percent of the farmers partly rented and partly owned the land they cultivated; only 30 percent owned all of their land.[29] After the leading oligarchs, these landowners, totalling around 3,500, were indirectly one of the most influential groups in the country.[30] They controlled the upper house and with

the help of bribery ensured that, for the most part, the rural population voted for the Seiyukai Party, which was closely connected
with and supported the interests of the landholders and big business.[31] As in Germany, the political alliance between the agrarians
and the *zaibatsu* in Japan aimed at preserving the traditional social
order, but instead – again as in Germany – it helped to increase the
political radicalisation of the masses.

With the beginning of war in China in 1937, potential political
disturbances in the countryside had to be quelled, and at the same
time the feudal system needed modernising in order to increase
the rate of self-sufficiency in supplying foodstuffs. Despite its antimodern traditionalist ideology, the army, most of whose members
up to the middle ranking officers came from rural backgrounds,
strongly advocated modernisation. In answer to pressure from the
army, which was worried about the alarmingly poor health of its
rural conscripts, by the end of 1937 the government for the first
time granted loans on generous terms for 1 million tenant families
to buy land.[32] Two years later, state control of lease agreements
was intensified, and rents were lowered and frozen. In addition,
the market value of the land was fixed in order to prevent speculation and to hinder the estate owners from buying back the
land.[33] Yet, it was only the dual price system, which provided different prices for the rice grown by the farmers themselves and the
rice the landowners received as payment in kind from their tenants, which shook the economic basis of the big estate holders. As
self-grown rice achieved 40 percent higher prices, cultivation was
intensified, and for the first time farmers enjoyed modest prosperity,[34] all the more so since unlike the landowners they were not
subject to the food-rationing system.

Fear of endangering the rural substance of the nation with the
effects of the war led the Tojo government to decree an agrarian
law in 1943.[35] Based on the model of the Russian agrarian reform
(Stolypin),[36] this law in the course of twenty-five years was to
guarantee survival of the middle-sized farms and dissolve the
landowners' large estates. The radical agrarian reform carried out
by the American occupation force, which is generally regarded as
the core of all the reforms,[37] had in fact been initiated by the Japanese military. Certainly, the latter's main purpose – reestablishing
an agrarian society – was not shared by the American occupiers,
but with the large estates divided up, the rural population's political discontent was also relieved. As a result of the reforms, the

proportion of those employed in agriculture after the war dropped to between 20 and 25 percent. Today, Japanese rice production is self-sufficient, and Japanese farmers are the strongest supporters of the country's conservative government.

Mobilising the Masses: Restoring Traditional Values

Unlike Germany, in Japan the organisation of the nation for the purposes of war did not require the creation of any special institutions of 'folkish' community (*Volksgemeinschaft*). Instead, the traditional rulers could rely on the existing social patterns; all that was required was the strengthening of those ties with the active support of the population. Eliminating Western ideas of the individual's role and of personal and individual responsibility thus proved comparatively easy. The Japanese society needed no *Gleichschaltung* (bringing into line) in the German way; only such Western imports as propaganda techniques and the mass media had to be adapted and brought into line.[38] The monopoly of the state news agency 'Domei' and the Press Law of 1937 ensured that any 'dangerous thoughts' of Japanese journalists educated in Western countries disappeared from the newspapers. Furthermore, newspapers were drastically reduced in variety, as well as in number, by forced mergers. In fact, today's concentration of the press and its conformist outlook – there are no opposition papers except for a few unimportant communist ones – as well as the political conformism of the state-run radio and television broadcasting companies[39] can be traced back to the nationwide mobilising process before the outbreak of the Pacific War. The politically expedient uniformity of the media – then imposed by the traditional oligarchy – today serves the conservative élite as a welcome means to ward off unpleasant criticism.

As a result of the antiliberal and antiparliamentarian campaigns launched by the army against the pernicious influence of the West, in the autumn of 1940 (it was not an accident that this coincided with the conclusion of the Tripartite Pact) the political parties were forced to dissolve. In their stead, the so-called Imperial Rule Assistance Association was founded.[40] Rejecting the Western model of political parties and instead entrusting the nation, like an extended family, to the paternal care of the divine Emperor better suited the Japanese and their patriarchal social patterns. As it turned out, the

'Association' amounted to not much more than the politically negligible assembly of a motley crowd of discontented and jealous
party politicians. Despite this, until the end of the war it remained
the official umbrella organisation comprising all of the newly
established Greater Japanese patriotic groups. When in April 1942,
during a period of overwhelming military victories, the only
wartime elections for the Diet were held, 81 percent of the voters
in comparatively free voting supported the new organisation
which seemed to meet their desire for harmony.[41] Nor did the
political reforms imposed by the Americans after 1945 succeed in
establishing the Western system of distinctive political parties
with clearly defined political programmes. Now, as then, political
parties in Japan either resemble vertically structured large groups
or split, as with today's Liberal Democrats, into rival factions that
instead of expressing their voters' demands, rather pursue the
aims of different groups among the ruling élite.[42]

Under the patronage of the Home Ministry and of the Ministry
of Industry and Trade, from 1939 onwards patriotic industrial
unions were built up and eventually, in November 1940, were
united in the compulsory 'Greater Japan Patriotic Industrial
Movement',[43] the Japanese equivalent of the National Socialist
Arbeitsfront (Labour Front). These new Japanese institutions, too,
relied on the traditional patterns of subservience, discipline, and
harmony. The promise of equal rights for employees and employers soon turned out to be a mere propaganda slogan, as the board
was always made up of employers. Furthermore, as there were no
labour disputes,[44] this alleged arbitration panel was never called
upon for mediation. Instead, conceiving the company as one big
family in typically Japanese fashion, this institution steered Japanese workers away from the heresies of class-conscious Western
trade unions and socialised them to serve the common good, that
is, the ruling élite's interests. Actual control of these war-bound
socialising institutions lay with the bureaucrats of the Home Ministry. During the war, the bureaucracy – the future élite of the
country – had already provided for its instruments of power that,
if not in their traditional form, did survive after 1945 and shaped
the subservient ethics and the sense of duty of the postwar working class. Japanese workers had learned to accept their employers
as masters and, at the same time, to feel responsible for the common well-being of the nation.

Another measure taken in preparation for war was the establishment in 1940 of the neighbourhood associations which on the surface resembled the National Socialist block system.[45] They, too, proved an excellent means of socialising the family, the nucleus of Japanese society, for the concerns of the extended national family. In the cities in particular, groups of ten to twenty families were formed; their spokesman was elected by the group, but had to be confirmed by the mayor, who in those days was appointed by the Home Ministry. In this way, the ministry that was responsible for national stability was able to extend its control to the individual family. The neighbourhood associations, above which so-called community councils were established,[46] dealt primarily with those tasks that the state considered beyond its reach, such as social care, civil air defence, fire fighting, the prevention of crime, and, of course, political indoctrination. From October 1942 onwards, the approximately 1.3 million neighbourhood associations also saw to the distribution of rationed foodstuffs. In this way, the single family was connected with national priorities and, what is more, was made aware of the neighbouring family's concerns and of neighbourly help, which in the Japanese society was a completely new experience. So efficiently did the neighbourhood associations and the community councils work that they were kept up by the Americans for another one-and-a-half years as useful administrative networks on a low level.[47] After about seven years they had managed to overcome the single family's feeling of isolation among the anonymous masses of the big cities, and had instilled a sense of community within the residential districts or quarters[48] which is still to be felt today. Furthermore, these common neighbourhood efforts, together with the dress regulations ordered by the government during the war,[49] helped to level the differences between rich and poor.

Based on traditional norms, the Japanese nation acquired a sense of unity that was not achieved by any of the other belligerent countries, since in Japan all official attempts at strengthening the feeling of community could rely on preindustrial concepts of social order and were readily accepted by the masses. In order to foster the ideal of a benevolent, patriarchal leader caring for the members of his extended family, the Japanese state from 1938 onwards initiated social welfare legislation that in 1943 culminated in a national health service system.[50]

Only the background of restorative national mobilisation can explain the patience of the Japanese population, their self-denial bordering on apathy, that made them endure the hardships of war. Regardless of the future of the country as well as of the needs of the population – who from 1944 to 1945, clearly had to make do with less than the minimum subsistence level[51] – the comparatively small upper class of Imperial Japan was able to pay for the war at the expense of 'the man in the street' without suffering the slightest loss to their own service conveniences or their own pleasure. At this time, when industry and agriculture were desperately short of labour, the government ordered 1.3 million people who were employed in the entertainment industry, among them 74,000 geishas, to apply for more useful positions related to the economic war efforts,[52] an order that was, however, quite often circumvented. In comparison with any other country at war, in Japan the supply of consumer goods to the population was most drastically reduced,[53] black-market prices soared the highest, and the average citizen had to make do without even his or her most basic needs being fulfilled.[54] Nevertheless, there was no upheaval nor even any estrangement between the population and its ruling class. Instead, the traditional norms proved strong enough to unite the nation for the purposes of war, as well as for recovery after the war.

Women at War: Traditional Roles and New Responsibilities

The authoritarian fascist states of the 'World Political Triangle' (*'Weltpolitisches Dreieck'*) defined themselves as male-dominated societies where women were confined to hearth and home and their place in life was restricted to bringing up the children of the family. In the European fascist countries this premodern, strict partition of roles had been overcome in the course of history, particularly during the First World War, and consequently had to be artificially restored. Not so in the traditional society of Imperial Japan, where the female role of being a servant or even, especially in the lower classes, a slave to her husband had never been questioned. According to the Family (House) Law (*Ie*)[55] effective until 1945, women, including their property, legally remained under the tutelage of the respective male head of the household, that is to say, their husbands, their elder brothers, or their fathers-in-law. A divorce could de facto only be obtained by a man; any divorced woman, no matter what had been the cause of her divorce, would certainly be ostracised, which of course would never happen to a man. The male section of the upper class did not take monogamy too seriously; financial means permitting, a man quite often kept concubines who occasionally were even accepted by his legal wife as members of the household. Not only socially inferior to men, women were also deprived of political rights. Only in 1946 were they included in the general suffrage.[56]

Far from shaking the concepts of the female role, the war, with all of its demands on the individual, merely altered the surface appearance of female behaviour patterns. The recruitment of female labour for the purposes of war[57] is an example of how the Japanese state succeeded in keeping up its traditional social structure with its fixed social norms, while at the same time assigning to the individual new tasks that required adjusting to, at least on the surface. It was probably the Japanese women who, most of all, experienced the discrepancy between the internalised old values and the new everyday tasks which had to be fulfilled. Even in today's modern industrial society the gap has been widening between the deeply rooted, traditional female behaviour patterns and the new practical demands on women. Compared to Western standards, discrimination against women is much worse in Japan.[58]

Prior to and during the war, women in the countryside usually toiled away as the slaves of impoverished farmers. About 40 percent of Japanese women held regular jobs, 90 percent of which were related to agriculture. Middle-class and upper-class women as a rule did not go to work, but looked after their household and children. The proportion of female industrial labour even in 1944, that is, at the the the peak of armament production, amounted to no more than 24 percent.[59] These were mostly young, unmarried women who had to live in barracks owned by their factory and do inferior jobs for half the wages of their male colleagues. Most of them came from pauperised farmers' families and had been sent to the factory in order to make their contribution to the family income. Some impoverished farmers even sold their daughters to army brothels.[60]

According to the results of a government inquiry in 1944, the shortage of labour in the armament industry could have been overcome by employing more women.[61] However, for obvious reasons female labour resources were not made use of, nor were more foreign workers from Asian countries employed.[62] For employing more women would inevitably have posed the question of equal rights; and employing more foreign workers might have endangered the Japanese feeling of group identity, all the more so since the Japanese, because of their Tenno's divine origin, considered themselves to be superior to any other nation, even other Asian ones. Compulsory labour service for women was never taken into consideration. This is why, between 1940 and 1944, the proportion of female employees in the armament industry rose by only 10 percent.[63] General Tojo, Prime Minister during the war, advocated that a woman's natural mission in life was to be with her household, and Mrs Tojo, mother of seven children, launched a state campaign to increase the birth rate. In fact, of all the countries at war, only Japan kept her marriage and birth rates constant throughout the war. Demographic shifts, therefore, resulted only from direct impacts of the war on the population.[64]

State organisations, such as the 'Greater Japanese Women's Association',[65] were more or less unnecessary, even as propaganda instruments. In any case, by the end of the war women had taken over where men were no longer available. The neighbourhood associations were often managed by women; and when, in the spring and summer of 1945, 10 million people fled from the bombardment of the large cities into the countryside,[66] women mastered tasks that traditionally had been ascribed to men only. Much more than in the cities, women in the countryside had infiltrated previously all-male domains, such as running the farm and acting as patriarchal authorities. However, as with Germany, during the last year of the war, the impact of women's efficiency on social change in general is difficult to assess, since the women themselves felt that they were only doing their duty in an emergency situation, which did not affect their concepts of the female role as such. Nonetheless, even if traditional relations between men and women remained unchanged, the war did bring about some legal as well as professional changes for women. As in the European countries after the First World War, women had to be granted legal and political equality in Japan after the Second World War. The general attitude towards professional women has changed slightly, too; at least today a young Japanese woman is expected to go to work before getting married and contribute to the country's economy.[67] The war had revealed the resources of female labour, and the male-dominated society could not help acknowledging women's capabilities. As a result, the range of jobs open to women was widened while at the same time the traditional family-orientated norms were restored. In this way, a large number of partially 'modernised' young women were made available to help with the country's economic recovery during the 1950s.

Conclusion: Technological and Institutional Change and Social Restabilisation – Japan's Rise to Economic Power after the War

After the war the Tenno system was abolished, the military were vanquished, and the large-estate owners were deprived of their power – these were decisive changes in Japanese society brought about directly or indirectly by the course of the war or by its outcome. In fact, the only group which emerged victorious from the military defeat and with their social status confirmed were the experts in bureaucratic and economic administration. Social change in the proper sense of the term, concerning basic values and structures, did not take place. Rather, traditional social behaviour was restored during the war and – as if to ward off the consequences of modern war – was even more deeply internalised by the population. The masses had only been partially and superficially modernised.

Between 1937 and 1945 the Japanese armed forces had recruited about 12 million men, that is, 80 percent of all those fit for military service;[68] these included, especially towards the end of the war and for auxiliary services, school pupils from the age of ten upwards and students. In this way, the majority of the male population were, for a certain amount of time, removed from their traditional patriarchal surroundings and were exposed to the military system of strict orders and unquestioning obedience. This meant that for them, the familiar norms based on collective harmony were – at least temporarily – abolished for reasons of military urgency. Furthermore, the conscripts were trained to handle weapons and equipment the technical standard of which by far exceeded that of the tools used by the small farmer or craftsman. Additionally, another 1.5 million skilled workers were forced to work in the branches of the armament industry that were under the control of the Munitions Ministry;[69] they, too, got used to dealing with Western technology as well as Western norms and management.

The Japanese male population – roughly comparable in number to the German one – suffered only about 25 percent of the German casualties.[70] All those who survived the war underwent a process of outward modernisation that increased their learning ability and flexibility while at the same time leaving the old social patterns intact. The same applies – to a limited extent – to the female population, who also had to adapt to the demands of modernisation without giving up their traditional role patterns. This is why, for the economic recovery of the country, the bureaucracy as a new ruling élite could now rely on a progressive, skilled labour force in the shipbuilding, electronic, and machine-tool industries, and on the masses of workers whose discipline and subservience had been reinforced during the war, and who at the same time were ready to accept Western innovation in technology and administration.

Notes

1. Thomas A. Bisson, *Japan's War Economy*, New York, 1945, p. 184.

2. For details, see Bernd Martin, 'Aggressionspolitik als Mobilisierungsfaktor. Der militärische und wirtschaftliche Imperialismus Japans 1931 bis 1941', in Friedrich Forstmeier and Hans Erich Volkmann, eds., *Wirtschaft und Rüstung am Vorabend des Zweiten Weltkrieges*, Düsseldorf, 1975, pp. 230ff.

3. Standard works on the Meiji Restoration are William G. Beasly, *The Meiji-Restoration*, Stanford, 1972; and John W. Dower, ed., *Origins of the Modern Japanese State. Selected Writings of E. H. Norman*, New York, 1975; and the first German study by Annelotte Piper, *Japans Weg von der Feudalgesellschaft zum Industriestaat. Wandlungsimpulse und wirtschaftliche Entwicklungsprozesse in ihrer politischen, geistigen und gesellschaftlichen Verankerung*, Köln, 1976.

4. This culminated in 1936 with the putsch of the Tokyo garrison; see Ben-Ami Shillony, *Revolt in Japan. The Young Officers and the February 26, 1936 Incident*, Princeton, 1973.

5. See Yale C. Maxon, *Control of Japanese Foreign Policy. A Study of Civil Military Rivalry 1930–1945*, Berkeley, 1957, Reprint Westport, Conn., 1973; and Nobutaka Ike, *Japan's Decision for War. Records of the 1941 Policy Conferences*, Stanford, 1967.

6. See Inazo Nitobe, *Bushido: the Soul of Japan*, Tokyo, 1969, first edition in 1905, first German translation in 1937; and the chapter on 'The Military: Authoritarian and

Irrational' by Saburo Ienaga, *Japan's Last War, World War II and the Japanese, 1931–1945*, New York, 1978; first Japanese edition in 1968.

7. Hans H. Baerwald, *The Purge of Japanese Leaders under the Occupation*, Berkeley, 1959, p. 82ff; for a comparison of the purges in Japan with the ones in Germany, see John D. Montgomery, *Forced to be Free. The Artificial Revolution in Germany and Japan*, Chicago, 1957.

8. Karl F. Zahl, *Die politische Elite Japans nach dem Zweiten Weltkrieg*, Wiesbaden, 1973.

9. See Bernd Martin, 'Japans Kriegswirtschaft 1941–1945', in Friedrich Forstmeier and Hans-Erich Volkmann, eds., *Kriegswirtschaft und Rüstung 1939–1945*, Düsseldorf, 1977, pp. 256–86; for the most important collection of dates on the Japanese war economy, see United States Bombing Survey (USBB), *The Effects of Strategic Bombing on Japan's War Economy*, Washington, D.C., 1946; a standard work on Japanese economy during and shortly after the war: Jerome B. Cohen, *Japan's Economy in War and Reconstruction*, Minneapolis, 1949.

10. The most eminent thinker of the so-called 'German Group' among the general staff, to which Tojo Hideki also belonged, was Nagata Tetsuzan, who from 1934 was head of the Political Bureau of the Army. Advocating a total armament with the necessary supplies, Nagata was assassinated on 12 August 1935 as he sought cooperation of the heavy industry for his programme. See chapter 8, 'Japan and Germany on the Path towards War', in this volume.

11. Martin, 'Aggressionspolitik', pp. 239ff.

12. Martin, 'Kriegswirtschaft', p. 261.

13. Bisson, *Japan's War Economy*, pp. 60ff; Bisson, as an expert on Asia, served as a member of the American Government Board of Economic Warfare.

14. USBB, p. 122; and Cohen, *Japan's Economy*, p. 74; an official report in mid-1943 revealed that the yearly output of aeroplanes amounted to no more than between eight and ten thousand. But fifty-three thousand would have been possible if 45 percent of the aluminium available had not been used up for the production of consumer goods or had simply disappeared on the black market. Cohen seems quite right in saying (p. 209): 'Rarely in the annals of history has a group of military planners, who were privileged to elect the time and method of starting a war, ever exhibited greater stupidity.'

15. Cohen, *Japan's Economy*, p. 18; H.T. Oshima, 'Japan's New Economic Structure', *Pacific Affairs*, vol. 15, 1942, pp. 261–79, here: pp. 267 and 277.

16. The Cabinet Planning Board, under Admiral Suzuki Teiichi, which was in charge of the coordination of the war economy, was quite often given wrong figures by the army and the navy.

17. Martin, 'Kriegswirtschaft', pp. 269ff.

18. Imperial Ordinance of 17 March 1943. Bisson, *Japan's War Economy*, pp. 248f. quotes it in the English translation.

19. For the full text, see Bisson, *Japan's War Economy*, pp. 251ff.: 'Major Provisions of the Munitions Company Act'. As the army and the navy could not agree on how much of their responsibility they were to yield to the new ministry, it

could only take up its work on 15 January 1944. For details, see Martin, 'Kriegswirtschaft', pp. 276f.

20. See the interesting biography by Dan Kurzman, *Kishi and Japan. The Search for the Sun*, New York, 1960.

21. See the figures in USBB, p. 181 and p. 222; and Cohen, *Japan's Economy*, p. 240.

22. See Corwin D. Edwards, 'The Dissolution of the Japanese Combines', *Pacific Affairs*, vol. 19 (1946), pp. 227–40. With respect especially to postwar development, see Norbert Voack, *Die japanischen 'Zaibatsu' und die Konzentration wirtschaftlicher Macht in ihren Händen*, Diss. Rer. Pol., Erlangen-Nürnberg, 1962.

23. Martin, 'Aggressionspolitik', p. 229.

24. Most reliable demographic information in Irene B. Taeuber, *The Population of Japan*, Princeton, 1958; here p. 87: table on: "The industrial structure of the economically active population. 1920–1955"; and pp. 70ff.: on the fluctuations of the population.

25. Ibid., p. 94: Figures for 1940; and Martin, 'Kriegswirtschaft', p. 281.

26. Cohen, *Japan's Economy*, p. 368f.

27. See the titles listed in note 3.

28. Basic studies complementing each other: Thomas R. H. Havens, *Farm and Nation in Modern Japan. Agrarian Nationalism, 1870–1940*, Princeton, 1974; and Richard J. Smethurst, *A Social Basis for Prewar Japanese Militarism. The Army and the Rural Community*, Berkeley, 1974.

29. An excellent monograph: Reginald P. Dore, *Land Reform in Japan*, Oxford, 1959, here: p. 19.

30. Ibid., pp. 24f., 41, 87; and Bisson, *Japan's War Economy*, VII.

31. For the history of the political parties in the 1930s, see Gordon M. Berger, *Parties out of Power in Japan 1931–1941*, Princeton, 1977.

32. Thomas R. H. Havens, *Valley of Darkness. The Japanese People and World War Two*, New York, 1978, pp. 97f. (this is the only thoroughly reliable Western survey of the domestic front in Japan during the Second World War that is based on Japanese source material).

33. Ibid., p. 98 (in December, 1939), and Dore, *Land Reform*, p. 112.

34. Dore, *Land Reform*, p. 22 and p. 114 (table on the price paid by the state for rice cultivated by farmers themselves and for rice sold by the large estate holders).

35. Ibid., p. 112.

36. For the Russian Prime Minister Peter Arkad'evi Stolypin's agrarian reforms in 1906, see Constantin v. Dietze, *Stolypinsche Agrarreform und Feldgemeinschaft*, Leipzig, 1920; and J. Naetzold, *Wirtschaftspolitische Alternativen der Entwicklung Rußlands in der Ära Witte und Stolypin*, Berlin, 1966.

37. For the actual course of the reform, see the study by Dore; for the American self-evaluation, see the memorandum on "Two Years of Occupation – Political Government Section" in the documentation by W. Benz, Amerikanische

Besatzungsherrschaft in Japan 1945–1947, in *Vierteljahrshefte für Zeitgeschichte*, vol. 26, 1978, pp. 265–346, here: p. 344.

38. Ienaga, *Japan's Last War*, pp. 97ff.; Havens, *Valley of Darkness*, pp. 20ff.: The campaigns to purge Japan of dangerous Western thoughts were eventually intensified during the war. The Japanese language was purified by removing its – even then – numerous Anglicisms, the Bible was banned, and from 1943 English was no longer taught as a foreign language.

39. For the conformity of today's Japanese news media, see the correspondent to the *Süddeutsche Zeitung* Gebhard Hielscher's critical comment on Japan, 'Gesellschaft und Innenpolitik in Japan und der Bundesrepublik', in Arnulf Baring and Masamori Sase, eds., *Zwei zaghafte Riesen? Deutschland und Japan seit 1945*, Stuttgart, 1977, pp. 559–615, here: pp. 614f. His verdict is confirmed by K. F. Zahl, for many years Secretary of the German Embassy in Tokyo and a noted authority on Japan, in his excellent study on the Japanese postwar élite: Zahl, *Politische Elite Japans*, p. 179: 'All daily papers with large circulations – except only for the communist *Akahata* – have been and still are controlled by the conservative policy and its particular interests; their apparent opposition against the government is due to business tactics much rather than their editor's genuine political beliefs.'

40. Berger, *Parties out of Power*, pp. 313ff.: Though outwardly based on European fascist models, the movement decidedly distanced itself from these. (Also see Martin, chapter 8, 'Japan and Germany on the Path towards War', in this volume.)

41. Havens, *Valley of Darkness*, p. 60: 361 total of 464 members of parliament belonged to the 'Imperial Rule Assistance Organisation'. Ienaga, *Japan's Last War*, p. 213: The election results were appealed in court and were eventually annulled in March 1945; political consequences, however, did not ensue.

42. For the attempts of the Americans, see Supreme Command Allied Powers (SCAP) Government Section, ed., *The Political Reorientation of Japan. September 1945 to September 1948*. 2 Volumes, Washington, D.C., 1949; Reprints St. Clair Shores, Michigan, 1968, Westport, Conn., 1970, pp. 338ff. For the Liberal Democratic Party, see Nathaniel B. Thayer, *How the Conservatives Rule Japan*, Princeton, 1969, and the study by Zahl, *Politische Elite Japans*.

43. The only Western study based on Japanese studies, most of them communist, is Z. Vasiljevová, 'The Industrial Patriotic Movement. A Study on the Structure of Fascist Dictatorship in War-Time Japan', in Vlasta Hilská and Zdenka Vasiljevová, *Problems of Modern Japanese Society* (Acta Universitatis Carolinae, Philologica Monographia XXVII) Praha, 1971; and Havens, *Valley of Darkness*, pp. 55ff.

44. Cohen, *Japan's Economy*, p. 286; and Ienaga, *Japan's Last War*, p. 209. According to both authors, giving different figures, in 1944 there had been a total of 216 resp. 296 labour disputes officially registered with 6,000 resp. 10,000 persons involved.

45. On 11 September 1940. See Havens, *Valley of Darkness*, pp. 37ff. and pp. 76ff. For the legislation, see Nobuyoshi Toshitani, 'Family Policy and Family Law in Modern Japan', in *Annals of the Institute of Social Science* (University of Tokyo), vol. 20, 1979, pp. 91–125. The system of collective family unions came from

ancient China (Pao Chia) and had been transferred to Japan during the seventh century; until the Meiji Restoration it was known in Japan under various names and served the authorities to receive information about and exert control over the individual. From 1863 to 1940 this system did not exist officially. During the 1930s, however, the army, in mobilising the rural population (in the veterans' unions and youth organisations), took up the tradition of the premodern unions of collective liability. The army's political information network was not based on the new local administration boundaries fixed by the Meiji Restoration (the *mura*, where several villages formed an administration district), but instead on the former outline of the Japanese village that was, on the whole, only of moderate size and was socially structured into several large families. See Smethurst, *Social Basis*, pp. 50ff.

46. In 1943 the community councils were integrated into the local administrative systems, which intensified direct control by the Home Ministry. See Havens, *Valley of Darkness*, p. 80.

47. Benz, *Amerikanische Besatzungsherrschaft*, p. 278, and *Political Reorientation of Japan*, pp. 284–88: The abolition of the Tonari-Gumi system.

48. In the course of early Meiji administrative reforms, the Japanese towns had been artificially divided into *ku*-areas (city quarters) subdivided into *cho*-areas (smaller districts), which hindered a sense of historically grown community from developing. Much rather, the newcomers to the cities, most of whom came from the countryside, stuck to their old concepts of the villages' social order that, consequently, could be easily revived during the war in the newly created neighbourhood associations.

49. Havens, *Valley of Darkness*, pp. 15ff. From 1939 on, Western cosmetics and Western clothes for women were forbidden, to be replaced by the *monpe*, Turkish-style trousers. Western permanent waves, too, were considered decadent, and hairdressers were only allowed to style their customers' hair in exactly three rows of curls. On 11 October 1940, Western dance music and Western dances were forbidden, and dance halls in the cities were closed. Men, too, were advised to exchange Western-style clothes for a simple uniform outfit (a close-buttoned jacket and cotton trousers). In the beginning, these dress regulations were generally neglected; however, with the strict rationing of textiles during the war, they imposed themselves.

50. Toshitani, *Family Policy*, pp. 106ff; Ienaga, *Japan's Last War*, p. 228; Havens, *Valley of Darkness*, pp. 40ff. A decisive motive for state-controlled health care was the steadily deteriorating health of the recruits. During the war, about 10 percent of them were completely unfit for service, another 30 percent were fit for service only in case of emergency, so that only 60 percent of the young men remained available for military service. During the 1920s and 1930s the percentages looked much better (see Smethurst, *Social Basis*, p. 72).

51. Martin, 'Kriegswirtschaft', pp. 279f.

52. Cohen, *Japan's Economy*, pp. 312.

53. Of all the countries at war, Japan suffered the biggest cuts in consumer goods expenditure: 30 percent. See Cohen, *Japan's Economy*, p. 354.

54. From the end of 1944 on, dire necessity and even starvation menaced the country, especially the urban areas. In 1945 the average daily food supply per person amounted to no more than about 1,680 calories, the minimum subsistence level being 2,165 calories. (Cohen, *Japan's Economy*, p. 386). For the insufficient food supply, also see Ienaga, *Japan's Last War*, pp. 192ff., and Havens, *Valley of Darkness*, pp. 116ff. Consequently, prices on the black market were exorbitant: in July 1945 they amounted to twelve times the prices fixed by the state, and already in November 1944, rice on the black market cost seventy times its state-fixed price. See Cohen, *Japan's Economy*, pp. 362ff.

55. N. Toshitani, 'Japan's Modern Legal System: Its Formation and Structure', in *Annals of the Institute of Social Science*, vol. 17, Tokyo University, 1976, pp. 1–50; here: pp. 36ff.

56. In the parliamentary elections on 10 April 1946, women were, for the first time, given suffrage because of the new Election Law of 17 December 1945. Reprint of the law in *Political Reorientation of Japan*, pp. 822–45. The new Family Law of 22 December 1947 granted legal equality to women (see ibid., pp. 1076–87).

57. Thomas R. H. Havens, 'Women and War in Japan, 1937–1945', in *American Historical Revue*, vol. 80, 1975, pp. 913–34.

58. Joyce Lebra et al., eds., *Women in Changing Japan*, Boulder, Col., 1976; Renate Herold, *Die Blume am Arbeitsplatz. Japans Frauen im Beruf*, Tübingen, 1980.

59. Havens, *Women and War*, pp. 917ff.

60. Ienaga, *Japan's Last War*, p. 190: High-ranking officers even took prostitutes with them to the battlefields, where, as for instance during the battle of Okinawa, they were taken into the trenches and exposed to violent death.

61. Havens, *Valley of Darkness*, p. 110.

62. Cohen, *Japan's Economy*, p. 326: A total of about 1.5 million Koreans worked in Japan; 667,684 of them had been contracted between 1939 and 1945. Korea, however, had been annexed to Japan and thus, legally speaking, 'belonged' to Japan. But there were only about 31,000 Chinese workers in Japan. These 'foreign workers' were given two-year contracts. Most of the Chinese and 94,000 Koreans worked as slave labour in underground mining. Havens, *Valley of Darkness*, p. 104, lists 1.3 million Koreans for the time between 1937 and 1945, and 38,000 recruited Chinese. These figures would equal 4 percent of the total labour force, compared to 20 percent of foreign labourers in Germany. Concerning Korean workers, their number seems to be overestimated, probably counting all the Koreans registered in Japan. Ienaga, *Japan's Last War*, pp. 169ff, calculated estimates which give the number of 6,830 Chinese and about 60,000 Koreans who did not survive their employment in the Japanese war industry, but who died of either exhaustion or starvation or in one of the numerous mining accidents. After a strike of the Chinese 'slaves' in the Hanaoka Copper Mines (Akita prefecture) on 30 June 1945, 400 of the 850 Chinese involved were shot then and there. Not least because of the use of forced labour in Japan, the production output of the coal mines amounted to much less than in any other industrialised country: in Japan in 1944 the average miner produced 119 tons of coal, in Great Britain 269 and in the United States 1,430 (see Cohen,

Japan's Economy, pp. 348f.). Outside of Japan, white prisoners of war were put to work in a similar way as the Koreans and the Chinese, so that 27 percent of them did not survive. For details about Japanese war crimes, see Edward F. L. Russell (Lord Russell of Liverpool), *The Knights of Bushido: The Shocking History of Japanese War Atrocities*, New York, 1958.

63. Havens, *Women and War*, p. 918. During the same period in Germany where, too, a woman's place in life was supposed to be her home, the number of female industry workers remained more or less constant. See Dörte Winkler, *Frauenarbeit im Dritten Reich*, Hamburg, 1977, especially the statistics provided in the supplement.

64. Havens, *Valley of Darkness*, pp. 135f, and Taeuber, *Population of Japan*, p. 355: Between the censuses of 1 October 1940 and 22 February 1944, the population on the Japanese isles increased by 4.7 million.

65. Havens, *Women and War*, p. 915. Before the end of the war, in June 1945, the union was dissolved.

66. For the mass exodus from the cities, see Havens, *Valley of Darkness*, pp. 154–72.

67. See the conclusions drawn by Havens, *Valley of Darkness*, p. 198 and Ienaga, *Japan's Last War*, pp. 226ff.

68. Martin, 'Kriegswirtschaft', p. 284.

69. Ibid., p. 277.

70. In an official statistic of 1949, their number is said to be 299,485 (Ienaga, *Japan's Last War* p. 202, and Cohen, *Japan's Economy*, p. 408). This refers to the civilian population only; the number of casualties among the soldiers cannot be calculated exactly. Altogether, only about a quarter of all recruits, that is, 2 out of 8 million, saw combat action. At the end of August 1945, between the armistice and the official surrender, the official statistics of Japanese casualties together with many other documents were destroyed. The Japanese figure of 1.5 million soldiers killed between 7 December 1941 and 15 August 1945 seems too high. According to American studies based on the evidence given by high-ranking Japanese military, about 459,000 Japanese soldiers were killed. In any case, one may rightly assume that more of the Tenno's soldiers died because of malnutrition, diseases, starvation, and accidents than on the battlefield – yet more proof of the military and political leadership's ignorance and carelessness during the Second World War (for the figures, see Taeuber, *Population of Japan*, pp. 333ff).

PART III

THE EMERGENCE OF THE 'FASCIST' ALLIANCE

✤ 6 ✤

THREE FORMS OF FASCISM

JAPAN – ITALY – GERMANY

When the German philosopher and historian Ernst Nolte published his famous book *Der Faschismus in seiner Epoche* (1963) some thirty years ago, this title was wrongly translated into English using the phrase *Three Faces of Fascism*.[1] A more accurate translation would have been *Fascism in Its Time*, because Nolte regarded the interwar period as the breeding ground for European fascist movements, which spread first in Italy (Mussolini's *fascisti*) then in France (*Action française*), and finally in Germany with Hitler's movement (*Nationalsozialismus*). Nolte has interpreted fascism as a uniquely European phenomenon, as a kind of Pan-European movement, or better still, as a mental disorder of European intellectuals who were unable to come to terms with the results of the First World War and who had been deeply shocked by the emerging materialistic mass society of our modern world. In contrast to Marxist interpretations, for Nolte fascism can be best explained by reference to the intellectual superstructure. Although the following outline cannot compete with Marxist theories on fascism or even with Nolte's profound study on the ideology of fascism, I shall follow neither of these interpretations. My modest aim is just to compare the early stages, henceforth referred to as the different phases of the movement, and the regimes of those three countries who joined in an ideological alliance in 1936–37, the Anti-Comintern Pact, and who, in 1940, concluded a military alliance and finally fought the entire world in the Second

---

This chapter is a revised version of an article first published in German as 'Zur Tauglichkeit eines übergeordneten Faschismusbegriffs. Ein Vergleich zwischen Japan, Italien und Deutschland', in *Vierteljahrshefte für Zeitgeschichte*, vol. 29, 1981, pp. 28–53. Translation by the author.

World War. The following remarks are intended to break up the narrow perspective of interpretations of fascism which have been limited to Europe. Rather than provide a new theory of 'what does fascism mean?' I would like to give some new facts and information and, at least I hope, to state some new conclusions.

Comparabilities in the Phases of the Movements: Programmes and Responses

A comparative view of the movement phases – in Japan these were rather periods of militant mobilisation[2] – must start with the key documents. These documents either had an official party-political character and deliberately aimed at politically integrating the people, or they originated from individuals having similar intentions. In analysing their contents, the long-term causes, which are rooted in a country's national history, should be separated from any short-term factors resulting from the First World War.

In fascist ideologies, internal enemies and foreign enemies are amalgamated through propaganda into common objects of hatred. A programmatic threat against the material victors of the First World War can be observed in the early stages of all three movements. This threat was directed against the Western democracies as well as against the revolutionary product of the war, Russian communism. Put into words as a programme, this threat necessarily led to a common front against the Western powers, as well as against the Soviet Union. Eventually, this common contempt for liberalism, for which the Western democracies stood, and for communism, represented by Soviet Russia, resulted in the Tripartite Powers' fighting against these two enemy camps during the Second World War.

Which documents offer a key to the understanding of the early stages of the fascist movements and show those programmatic guidelines leading directly into war? In the case of Germany, they are the NSDAP (*Nationalsozialistische Deutsche Arbeiterpartei*) party programme dating from 1920 and Hitler's book *Mein Kampf* (*My Struggle*) written four years later. Both documents indicate a self-contained ideology and a comparatively high and systematically planned degree of organisation in the movement.

However, no such document can be found for the early stages of Italian fascism. The fascist movement in Italy never had a programme comparable to that of National Socialism. Mussolini's ideas, when the party was founded in 1919, and the party programme[3] of the same year did not gain any public response despite being modelled on the specific social and political questions of Northern Italy. In the general elections of November 1919 the fascists obtained no mandate. Later on, Mussolini often changed his views for tactical reasons. As a result, the programme lacked any rational base. Instead, the spark which initiated fascism in Italy lay in the Irredentist nationalism and was ignited in Gabriele D'Annunzio's Fiume adventure. The march on Fiume,[4] nowadays Rijeka, was a reaction against the Paris Peace Conference, which refused to award this city to Italy. In addition to the march, there arose a social substratum created by the First World War. It consisted of mercenaries, adventurers, and ardent nationalists and created for itself the myths and rites of a national rebirth under a self-nominated leader, all within the given Mediterranean city structure. This example was to be widely emulated in Italy and was to find worldwide attention. As the motley crowd of desperados was bound together by various vague emotions rather than a programme, conclusions can only be drawn from the ideas that their spiritual father and leader D'Annunzio expressed in his speech of 4 May 1919 in Rome, which met with considerable national response.[5]

Rhetorical pathos and historical transfiguration were widely substituted for rational arguments as the poet and former air force captain D'Annunzio proceeded to sanctify war as being a manly deed, as an end in itself. He called for a crusade against the small shopkeepers, the indecisive, the hesitant, and also against the bankers and merchants, and the Paris triumvirate of Wilson, Lloyd George, and Clemenceau. This crusade was to liberate the Irredenta from Fiume (Rijeka) to Ragusa (Dubrovnik). Mussolini copied the content and the style of D'Annunzio's often repeated Fiume appeals,[6] as well as that of the militia and its liturgy. So, at the birth of fascism, domestic and foreign policy were mingled in a highly irrational way.

In contrast to the National Socialists' systematic planning, Italian fascism, during its early three-and-a-half year phase, was characterised by a blind, emotional activism and heroic overestimation of its own capabilities. Created by D'Annunzio in Fiume, the strength of the Italian movement was, to a great degree, connected with the leader's charisma and his continuous dialogue with the people. Traditional patterns of social behaviour explain, at least partly, the public response enjoyed by the fascist movement regardless of social barriers. In Italy, these patterns cannot be separated from the formative influence of Mediterranean Catholicism nor from the urban masses' habitual political orientation towards patriarchal leadership.

In Germany, any political leader had to fit in with the authoritarian Prussian tradition. This figurehead, in contrast to its Italian counterpart, had to be remotely grand and of seemingly dogmatic preciseness. The political symbols of identification and the ideological concepts used by the German, as well as by the Italian, movements were part of the peoples' cultural heritage. They merely had to be transformed for the purposes of one person's claim to power, or for the purposes of a fascist party or group who supported this person. In Japan, such basic structures, which have been termed prefascist, dominated to the extent that a similarly visible transformation was not needed. Whereas Hitler and Mussolini had to revive and cunningly develop the rites of a national community (*Volksgemeinschaft*), these rites were already firmly rooted in Japan and did not allow for far-reaching changes. Japan's fascism based its programme on premodern social structures, which had barely been touched by industrialisation. It, therefore, contained many more restorative and traditional elements than the Italian and German movements, which were, to some extent, 'revolutionary' in their goals.

In 1919, still under the influence of the First World War, a manuscript entitled 'General Outline of Measures for the Reorganisation of Japan'[7] was written in Asia's then cultural focus and melting pot, Shanghai. Published in Manchuria in 1923, this outline became the handbook of political rebels in Japan, even though a publication of the Japanese variation on the *Mein Kampf* theme was banned in Japan until 1945. The author, Kita Ikki, had at first hoped for an emancipatory, independent revolution in Asia. After the Chinese pseudorevolution, as well as the Western powers' imperialistic attitudes, had disappointed him, he drafted the principles of an 'oriental socialism' averse to Western ideas. His demands for the elimination of the political system based on the Japanese oligarchy and their wealth and his intention to substitute for this system a social dictatorship headed by the Tenno were as radical as any of the views held by Hitler or Mussolini.

However, any influence of European models on Kita's writing has to be ruled out. According to Kita, the Emperor, who for almost 2,600 years had represented the identity of the nation, was to suspend the constitution, dissolve the parliament, and declare martial law. Deserving men, free from party or economic connections, were to be directly elected by the people to the position of cabinet ministers and were thereby to function as the executors of the imperial will. A similarly elected Diet was to be the people's representative organ. But its function was merely to counsel and to applaud. On the whole, Kita's discourses about the structure of the state remained vague. As the Emperor played no part in daily politics, he would have been overburdened by the sudden weight of dictatorial powers.

However, the detailed social demands, which were the nucleus of Kita's programme, did represent a threat to the ruling class. The Emperor was to set a good example by restoring the property of the imperial family to the state. Kita wanted the value of an individual's property to be limited to the rather high figure of one million yen. Extensive landed property was also to be reduced. The land thus obtained by the state was to be given to its lease-holders on the basis of a fixed rental rate. Large businesses and industries were to be nationalised and subordinated to planning ministries. Workers were promised regulated wage agreements, profit sharing, and an eight-hour working day; the small farmers, a decent income; and women, equal rights. A social policy was to provide for free health care, equal opportunities in education and old-age pensions, as well as for an overall social security scheme.

Kita did not want these truly revolutionary demands – some of which have not been carried out in Japan even up to the present day – to be realised within Japan proper. Instead, these changes were to be effected, with the help of the military, in a greater Japanese empire including eastern Siberia, India, and Australia. Therefore, the military and the system of universal conscription were of utmost importance to Kita's views. The military was to be the ideological and political spearhead of a revolution directed against the pernicious influences of the white race in Japan, as well as in East Asia. This interlacing of internal social tensions and their diversion into an aggressive foreign policy, which were clearly established in Kita's policy, were comparable, for example, to Hitler's statements in *Mein Kampf*. In Japan, these aims were pursued by the revolutionary nationalists, mostly radical officers of lower rank, up to the coup d'état in February 1936.[8]

The traditional ruling circles, headed by the court, defeated the violent attempt to assume power from below. On Hirohito's insistence, the ringleaders were shot, among them Kita. Despite its failure, the coup signified a decisive turning point in the political and social development of the country. It has, therefore, often been interpreted as the transition from the phase of the movement to institutionalised fascist rule. This assumption is based on the fact that the oligarchy could no longer afford to ignore the programme and goals of the movement led by revolutionary-minded officers who had allied themselves with the pauperised small tenant farmers and the other victims of the Great Depression – hard-hit small businessmen and tradesmen. Within the same year, the demands for expansion were integrated into a fundamental programme on national policy[9] and were partly realised in an international agreement, the Anti-Comintern Pact.

When one compares the response to the political statements of Hitler, D'Annunzio (Mussolini), and Kita within the ranks of the movements themselves, as well as within the general political public, it is surprising to find that Hitler's ideas attracted little attention, even though almost half-a-million copies of his book had been sold before he came to power. On the other hand, Kita's thoughts, which could not be published in Japan, were common knowledge to the politically aware public. In Italy, rhetorical appeals from the fathers of fascism were perfectly suited to the general mood of the population. The National Socialist ideology however, as it finally was formulated by Hitler, corresponded to a much lesser degree to the political and social realities in Germany, than did the comparable Italian or Japanese versions. Hitler's ideology instead seemed to be more of an artificial product. It was, therefore, in need of an external crisis – the repercussions of the Great Depression – and it had to be backed by a tough party organisation before it gained any significant political impact.

The historical prerequisites of all three programmes were different, as each of them was obviously determined by specific national traditions. They can be compared only in very general terms with the help of theories on modernisation. Despite this, in Italy, Germany, and Japan the political and social problems emanating from premodern structures and values were combined during the period of the First World War into a conglomerate of prefascist doctrines. These crude ideas were first formulated on the fertile ground of the immediate postwar situation, with all of its social upheavals, and were fanatically pursued by individuals and small groups who could not be politically integrated. Without the First World War and its direct consequences, the premodern burdens of the respective societies would not have been absorbed in revolutionary and utopian programmes, but would instead have slowly been removed by way of reforms.

The contents of these programmes, deliberately kept vague, reflect international insecurity and individual uprooting, both of them characteristics of periods of upheaval. All three movements took refuge in a mythical past of national grandeur and racist homogeneity. The Latin race and the Imperium Romanum,[10] the Germanic cult and the Aryan race, the supposedly godly descent, and the leadership claim of the Yamato race,[11] were points of reference by which the movements and their followers could claim cultural preeminence and racial superiority. The points of the various programmes are based on these historical fictions. They can best be described as the negation of the then existing economic and political systems, in other words, as the negation of both the liberal-capitalist and the communist systems. According to each nation's past, elements of socialism, nationalism, and communism were combined in a seemingly consistent ideology. Fascist ideologies did nothing but borrow heavily from the political and social movements which emerged in Germany, Italy, and Japan after the First World War. It was necessary for the ideology to be vague in order to overcome class distinctions and attract as many people as possible.

Overriding importance must be attributed to the agrarian romanticism inherent in all three programmes. It reflects an irrational yearning for premodern times in societies which had been totally altered by the Great War. The ambivalence between tradition and progress to be found in the programmes later developed, during the consolidation phases of the regimes and the Second World War, into antagonism between dogma and rational power politics. It indicates the fundamental contradiction within the fascist concept: the final goal of a safe and sound agrarian world was to be reached by means of forced industrialisation. This millenarian hope for a standstill of history reveals itself in National Socialist ideas, as well as in the plans of the Japanese revolutionaries adopted by the governing circles in Tokyo in 1936. Hitler,

Himmler, and the Japanese Prime Minister General Tojo[12] persisted in pursuing an agrarian resettlement plan even after it became clear that the war had been lost. The differences between their concepts, however, can be found in the respective social preconditions.

In Japan, there existed a connection between prefascist rural concepts on the one hand, and the existing social structure on the other. This was because about 50 percent of Japanese society was agrarian, and because its traditional village structure produced behavioural patterns that made the country, in essence, appear as one big village. The NSDAP, on the contrary, despite all its propaganda of 'blood and soil', was an urban-orientated party. Since only 20 percent of the German population were employed in agriculture, the ideal of a rural Germany was a fiction from the very beginning. In the National Socialist agrarian programme, reality and theory were highly contradictory. In Japan, they generally corresponded. Italian fascism, due to its opportunistic orientation, never emphasised agrarian concepts.[13] Italy's rural proletariat, which remained on the lowest social level, was won over by the regime, or at least neutralised, by means of a few social laws and by propaganda campaigns for land cultivation and the promised emigration to the African empire.[14] Even though Italy, like Japan, was predominantly agrarian, Italian fascism chose the road to industrialisation which, in Japan, was regarded as a necessary evil only to be tolerated for a period of transition. Agrarian romanticism obviously took a different shape in each of the three countries and therefore cannot be fully explained in terms of structural history.[15]

The glorification of war went hand-in-hand with the propagated restoration of the peasant class, with a rejection of Western concepts concerning individual rights and international laws, and with an animosity towards communist-like 'egalitarianism'. Even during the phase of the movement, war was already viewed as a means in itself. Fighting and the readiness to offer one's own life even without understanding the reasons started to play an important role. Man was to prove himself the new superior human being in street-fighting as well as later on the battlefield. Therefore, public life became entirely militarised and the education system was totally controlled by the regime. Both militarisation and national integration led to the externalisation of domestic problems, to an offensive attitude towards the international environment.

Prussian history provided National Socialism with traditional martial values. In Japan, the samurai, even though they had been deprived of their power, had passed on the feudal fighting code *bushido*[16] to the new Imperial Army. *Bushido* achieved such a deep indoctrination that drafted Japanese soldiers preferred death or suicide to captivity. In Italy, the lack of fighting spirit was replaced by the propagandistic transfiguration of the unification campaigns and the battles of the First World War.[17] Later on, Italian propaganda appeared artificial, not only to Italy's enemies but to her allies, too.[18] Yet, all of the three movements axiomatically adhered to Clausewitz' maxim, 'War is the father of creation and the mother of culture' (*'Krieg ist der Vater der Schöpfung und die Mutter der Kultur'*) – one of the mottoes of Japanese militarists. Nevertheless, fascist propaganda contained a declaration of war to domestic, as well as to external, enemies. From the early stages of the respective phases of the movements, fascism meant war. This bound Germany, Italy, and Japan closer together than the other programmatic items they had in common.

The organisation of the fascist movements, according to the principle of totalitarian leadership, derived logically from their programmes. The political structure – a leader, a party movement, and party-controlled organisations – became characteristic of Italy and Germany. But both elements, the leader and the political party, were paradoxically rooted in the same concept of Western institutions. For example, the Japanese constitution of 1889[19] had been consciously built up as a mere façade. Behind it, the Emperor system could be preserved. Therefore, it was necessary only to remove the Western façade in order to uncover the existing structure of the people and the imperial leader. It goes without saying that Emperor Hirohito cannot be compared to Hitler or Mussolini, even if the German leader proceeded on this assumption.[20] But it is a fact that the Tenno was manipulated by the militarists, and from 1936 by the entire oligarchy, into the fictive role of an absolute monarch, so that he could fulfil the function of a national figure of integration. The government was able to exercise dictatorial powers in the name of the Emperor. Since the Emperor's will was regarded as sacred, government decisions could neither be revoked nor criticised.

In Japan, there was no need for a fascist peoples' party. The prevailing social habits rallied the people behind the throne. The Japanese army did not, as is often stated in Western literature, form a substitute party. It did indeed form the avant-garde of political change and served as the voice of the rural substrata, from whence stemmed a great number of the army's officers.[21] The army also systematically mobilised the nation for war with the help of recruiting and youth organisations. But lastly, the ideology and structure of the military were but a mirror of the people's hopes and of their rural patterns of social behaviour. Party and people were identical in Japan. The army merely made its organisation available but did not, as did the movements in Italy and Germany, have to create a national community. The 'Imperial Assistance Association', which was founded in October 1940, was nothing but a tool in the hands of the bureaucracy in order to mobilise the population for war. As a new façade, this structure was primarily the result of the Tripartite Pact. The military alliance concluded with Italy and Germany forced the Japanese to adjust their inner political structure to those of their European partners. Prince Konoe, chairman of the new association, denied any similarities with the plebiscitarian fascist movements in Europe. The Prime Minister stated in public that in Japan there had always been 'one sovereign – one people',[22] which soon became a political slogan.

A comparison of programmes and responses to the three movements clearly shows the discrepancies between visionary concepts and given realities. The gulf between idea and reality was widest in German National Socialism, due to the high degree of development in both society and industry, and it was narrowest in Japan. Italian fascism moved between these two poles. The *Duce* understood the art of obscuring opposites and contradictions in emotional verbosity.

Incomparabilities during the Period of the Regimes: The Establishment and Maintenance of Power

The immanent similarities of the three movements become even more evident when comparing their instruments of power during the periods of the regime. At the same time, the extent of terror needed to uphold power can serve as a measure of the differences between them. The regime which least corresponded to the development of its society, the National Socialist one, needed the most severe protective measures and dealt with numerous opponents in the most radical manner. In contrast to the National Socialist regime, the systems in Japan, and in a different way in Italy, could to a large extent do without terror because they could rely on a relatively large consensus of the population. By definition, fascism and terror appear as twins. Often, extensive terrorist methods are described as one of the essential characteristics of fascism. But the synonymous use of the terms corresponds primarily to the views expressed by German political opponents during the Nazi period. The 'classic' definition of fascism, promulgated by the Comintern in 1933 (Dimitroff-formula), generally identified fascism with terror, which, by speaking of an 'open terroristic dictatorship', does not apply to the Italian and Japanese forms of fascism. The German, Italian and Japanese fascist regimes can be best distinguished in their systems and methods of exercising power.

In order to compare, one must look at those laws and ordinances by which fascism assured and strengthened its claim to power in the face of its declared opponents and hidden enemies. The so-called government of national revolution in Germany, Hitler's coalition cabinet, meant the start of a 'new era' with severe, immediately implemented interferences in the citizens' constitutional rights and with the abolition of the separation of powers. The emergency decrees of 28 February 1933 (for the protection of the people and the state) and of 23 March 1933 (the enabling act and the laws against treachery) were within the framework of the Weimar constitution. But they legalised the terror of the Nazis and forced the courts to take a hard line. The state of emergency in Germany became the state of normality. The Italian decrees concerning the 'powers of the head of state' and the laws on 'public safety' and 'for the defense of the state' from 1925–26[23] are comparable with the emergency laws of the Nazis in their political intention – not, however, in their effects. For Japan, the provisions of the 'Peace Laws', first decreed in 1925, have to be consulted.[24] All these legal and illegal actions are comparable in their genesis: they were all carried out by conservative coalition partners. Hitler and Mussolini could never have passed such laws by relying only upon their parties. The majority of the old political élites had to consent. They did and thereby – in the long run – eliminated themselves.[25] In Japan, political opposition had already been eliminated by the laws which the traditional leadership had passed as a preventive measure, together with granting suffrage to the male population. Hence, it goes without saying that any socialist opposition had been prevented from forming.

In Germany and Italy, the conservatives were alarmed by the growing political power of organised labour. In Japan, the ruling class feared liberal and leftist groupings, which emerged after the First World War. All conservative coalition partners of fascism held the erroneous belief that the respective movements, boasting of their revolutionary deeds, would mature with political responsibility and would lose their revolutionary drive during a transitory phase in which the political landscape would be purged of irksome leftists. This concept of 'taming' was, in all three states, to turn into its opposite. Papen did not, as he boasted, engage Mr Hitler, rather Hitler soon was to use his predecessor merely as the conservative figurehead of his politics. Italian fascism was neither to be integrated into the old system nor, as the traditional Italian upper class deceived themselves in the 1920s, was it 'cultivated'.[26] On the contrary, fascism cultivated its own image on the back of its allies. Likewise, the calculation of Japanese court and business circles did not add up. Their wish, after the 1936 coup, to integrate the sociorevolutionary hotheads by allowing them to participate in politics led instead to a growing influence of the military. As in Italy and Germany, in Japan, too, the political development towards authoritarian government cannot be understood without taking into account the cooperation of the traditional élites.

In all three countries, industry played an important part in the phase when the alliance of traditional powers with the fascist movements was concluded. At the beginning, the attitude of business circles towards fascist groups was generally reserved or even negative because of the socialist undertones in the programmes. But once the new movements proved capable of an alliance, the industrialists urged cooperation in order to eliminate the labour organisations and their programmes. Business was able to make use of the *mésalliance*, at the price of renouncing open political activity, by realising its endeavours within the new political structures. Only by abolishing the socialist items of the fascist programmes did the taming concept of industry work out. The alliance between capitalism and fascism meant profit for both. In all three countries, industry obtained high growth rates during a previously unmatched period of concentration. The three regimes were strengthened in their claim for power by the support of industry. The economy of all three countries was soon geared to and subordinated to the goals of expansion pursued by military means. But industry gained a differing degree of influence over the preparation and the conduct of war. In Germany, the primacy of politics was essentially preserved,[27] due to the radical form of ideology, in Italy, there existed a kind of equilibrium between the two,[28] whereas in Japan, industry won, after 1941, a slight superiority and had a decisive influence on the way the war was started and fought.[29]

The respective contents of the emergency laws reflect conservative concerns as well as fascist goals. As a kind of coalition agreement, these laws also permit conclusions about the intensity of the national crisis out of which they emerged. Hitler's dictatorship was to a much greater degree ensured by ordinances of the *Reichspräsident*, the decree for the 'protection of the people and the state', and the emergency ordinances following the blaze of the *Reichstag*, than by the enabling act, which merely concluded these dictatorial decrees. The suspension of constitutional rights put each citizen at the mercy of the Nazi storm troopers, the SA. The coalition of the so-called national government did not refrain from threatening all those who dared to oppose their instructions with the death penalty and, with the stroke of the pen, reinstated hanging for high treason and rioting offences, even though the death penalty had been de facto suspended since 1926.[30] Special courts were set up three weeks later which were to handle so-called political offences. These special courts had only one chairman and worked according to a simplified code of criminal procedure. Summary jurisdiction, by which 3,853 persons were tried for high treason alone in 1933,[31] debased justice to the rank of a beadle for the Nazi regime. By demonstrating loyalty and harshness, German justice gave up its independence. This is reflected by the frightening number of almost 12,000 death sentences[32] which ordinary courts passed in the period from 1938 to 1944 and which were carried out. The increase in the number of offenses for which the death penalty was compulsory, from three in 1932 to 42 in 1943, demonstrates the growing terror of the regime and the zeal of the judiciary power to serve as the prolonged arm of the Nazis.

A comparable massive intimidation of the individual, as well as of the entire population, by means of terror and ruthless justice similar to Germany's never existed in Italy or in Japan. The radicalism of the National Socialist ideology, the severity of the economic and sociopolitical crisis in the Reich, and the conservatives' deep-rooted fear of a revolutionary upheaval from the left culminated in the terror of the Nazi regime. Only the

National Socialist movement had such a totalitarian claim over its adherents during the phase of the movement, a claim that was ruthlessly extended to compromise the entire population after the seizure of power.

Compared to the totalitarian German system, Mussolini's political role was confined to that of a participant in a complex power structure, which included, next to the fascist organisations, the monarchy, the church, and the association of industrialists. The coalition in Italy was much more balanced; the *Duce* and his party did obtain leadership functions, but the fascists were never able, though they loudly postulated it, to realise a totalitarian claim of the state on the individual citizen. A crisis endangering the regime, the Matteotti crisis,[33] was needed and used by the fascists in order to convince the traditional powers, first of all the monarchy, to appoint the *Duce* as the head of state, responsible only to the king. The parliament lost its control over the cabinet, but kept, even if through a very complicated procedure, the right of legislation until 1938 when it was finally abolished. Even though Mussolini's coup d'état of 1925–26 meant the first step in the direction towards a totalitarian state, neither his procedure nor the surrounding circumstances are comparable to Hitler's initial measures. Italian socialists and communists still retained their seats in the deputy chamber after four years of fascist rule. In Germany, the majority of them were detained in concentration camps a month after Hitler came to power.

The Italian decree concerning public security was, accordingly, moderate.[34] Although provisions gave the police greater rights for the surveillance of political suspects, imprisonment of six months was the highest penalty. At the same time, the decree contained details on the deportation of political prisoners carried out within the Italian government's jurisdiction. The deportation took place within the motherland or in the colonies and could not exceed a maximum of five years. In this ancient Roman way, the fascist regime silenced its socialist or communist opponents. Whereas the National Socialists murdered about 20,000 members of the Communist Party (KPD),[35] the communists in Italy survived at the same time in remote exile[36] and waited for their return to politics, which was made possible after Italy's surrender in 1943. Even the Italian special court[37] can hardly be looked upon as the citadel of a totalitarian state. From 1927 on, political offences were judged in front of a court that from its composition and code of procedure represented a military court. But until its dissolution in 1943, this court pronounced only 31 death sentences and seven life sentences, both to be carried out, from a total of 5,319 cases.[38] Clad in the robes of military judges, the Italian justice system did not allow itself to become the agent of fascist politics.[39]

The Japanese 'Peace Laws' were, comparatively speaking, most harmless of all. Actually they were police ordinances. This underlines, once again, the unity of the people and the governing oligarchy. The general consensus about the aims of national policy was much stronger in Japan than in Italy. Any kind of serious opposition, like the socialist parties in Germany, was completely lacking in Japan. At the suggestion of the members of parliament, a peace law was worked out by the ministries concerned. This law was meant as an accompanying measure to universal male suffrage and furthermore was attributed the function of protecting the existing party landscape from disagreeable socialist or even communist intruders. In May 1925, it was passed by parliament with an almost unanimous vote.[40] Efforts at destroying the Emperor system (*kokutai*), which was equated with an assault on the existing private property order, were to be punished with imprisonment of up to ten years. This first law already provided for total exemption from penalty for all those offenders who voluntarily gave themselves up to the authorities.

Within the given social order of Japan, which saw the nation as a big family around the Emperor, leftist intellectuals or communists appeared to be simply misled. Nothing but mere gentle pressure from the state was considered necessary to set them back on the right path. Political opponents in Japan were neither, as in Germany, criminalised or exterminated, nor, as in Italy, deported, but rather reintegrated into society. Punishing meant resocialising. Of about 66,000 persons arrested in the period from 1925 until the outbreak of the Pacific War, only about 8 percent (5,500) were tried by the public prosecutor, because most of them renounced their heresies while still in police custody.[41] A total of over 95 percent of people proven guilty of subversion bent under the pressure of society, in which ostracism was considered to be worse than the death penalty. Even though the peace laws had been extended to cover illegal actions of groups and provided death penalties for ringleaders, the courts sentenced only a few people who refused to revoke. With one exception, death sentences were not passed in order not to create martyrs.[42] The highest number of arrests was recorded in 1933 and led to a renewed revision of the law. Henceforward, a limited protective custody was allowed and the supervision of political suspects intensified in Japan, presumably following the German and the Italian examples. However, prisoners held in protective custody were not subject to concentration camp treatment, but were given over to places of ancient Japanese tradition, shrines and hospitals.

In 1940, a written recognition of the Tenno's divinity became compulsory in order to regain freedom. Since all Western ideas were to be eradicated, civil rights were further restricted in Japan from May 1941 onwards, and special departments were set up in the judiciary system that were to pursue dangerous Western thoughts. Nevertheless, communist renegades fought for the Emperor during the Pacific War. Only 37 unrepentant communists, sentenced to long terms of imprisonment, were kept in custody in 1943. More severe terror proved unnecessary in Japan because the population fully identified itself with the system of government even in its militarised form. The Peace Laws, which were seldom used against conspiracies of the radical right, strengthened the omnipotence of bureaucracy and smoothed the path for the takeover by the militarised movement. Measured against Western standards, Japan represented a closed society with a dictatorial system of power, which the Japanese themselves did not consider as interfering much with the habitual collective norms of behaviour.

Concluding Remarks

A concept of fascism which declares terror to be a constituent of any fascist regime is, according to the aforesaid, applicable only to Germany. It unduly magnifies the exercise of power in fascist Italy, and completely disregards historical realities in Japan. Fascism as a general term is suitable at best for the movement phases of the three fascisms. As a comprehensive term for the periods of the regimes, the expression is not adequate since it does not do justice to the completely different forms of exercising power and control. To use the term fascism for what happened in Germany only too easily ends, as has often been pointed out, in minimising National Socialism.[43] Subsuming the racist measures to exterminate the Jews and Slavs, which were taken only by the Nazi regime, under a general concept of fascism leads to a distorted picture, to a forced combination of incomparable dimensions. The comparison of Mussolini's rule with that of the German 'Führer' shows considerable defects, too, and does not bear empirical research. Including Japan – the third power – in this comparison entirely deprives the collective term 'fascism' of its meaning historically. This reduces the term to a mere formula as does using the term of antifascism as a slogan against capitalism in daily politics. It, therefore, seems to be in keeping with historical reality, as well as with the way the regimes in Berlin, Rome, and Tokyo saw themselves at the time, to abandon the worn-out concept of fascism. Instead, the Hitler regime should be characterised as National Socialist, the *Duce's* Italian regime as fascist, and the Japanese government as a restorative anti-Western system with objectively fascist traits in the eyes of Westerners, yet not seen as such by the Japanese.

Notes

1. This article is a shortened version of the German original published in 1981. As it was assumed that the academic reading public would know about the standard works on the rise of National Socialism and the Hitler regime, the footnotes do not cover these works, but rather concentrate on the history of 'fascism' in Italy and Japan. With the flood of new books and articles on the topic, interpretations of fascism could be updated and rewritten all the time. However, there are but very few comparisons of the three 'fascist' ideologies and the three countries where they emerged more or less separately. This article was one of the first attempts; the latest has been presented by a historian from New Zealand: Paul Brooker, *Three Faces of Fraternalism. Nazi Germany, Fascist Italy, and Imperial Japan*, Oxford, Clarendon Press, 1991. As Brooker entirely relies on English material, he does not refer to 'foreign' publications such as the German version of this article.

2. Henry A. Turner, ed., *Reappraisals of Fascism*, New York, 1975, pp. 199–214; George M. Wilson, "A New Look at the Problem of Japanese Fascism", originally published in *Comparative Studies in Society and History. An International Quarterly*, vol. 10 (1967/68) pp. 401–12.

3. Mussolini's speech of 23 March 1919 and the 'programme' of 6 June 1919 in English translation in Charles F. Delzell, ed., *Mediterranean Fascism 1919–1945*, London, 1970, pp. 7–14. Later, too, the PNF (*Partito Nazionale Fascista*) never achieved the same degree of ideological unity as the NSDAP (*Nationalsozialistische Deutsche Arbeiterpartei*). The three main streams of Italian fascism, that

by fiercely attacking and hampering each other made Mussolini's dictatorial predominance possible, can be connected – though in a rather simplifying way – with their respective periodicals: (a) *Politica* – the periodical of the nationalists, the conservative élites under F. Coppola and A. Rocco; (b) *Vita Italiana* – the voice of the radical petit-bourgeois wing under Giovanni Preziosi and Roberto Farinaci; (c) *Critica Fascista* – the mouthpiece of the intellectual revolutionary wing and of the futurists under Guiseppe Bottai. See Franz X. Augustin, *Zur Rezeption des Nationalsozialismus im italienischen Faschismus 1930–1936* (Masters thesis), Freiburg i.Br., 1979.

4. On 12 September 1919 troops of the Ronchi garrison that had previously been stationed in Fiume and had been removed, after quarrelling with the local population, or rather the Western allies' occupation forces, marched back to Fiume under the command of D'Annunzio. The personal rule of the poet and First World War air force officer lasted until 25 December 1920. Fiume is generally regarded as the birthplace of fascism. Franco Gaeta, *Nazionalismo Italiano*, Napoli, 1965, pp. 166f.: Fiume, 'the place and the movement where and when all the factors came together … that undermined the liberal state.' Angelo Tasca, *Glauben, Gehorchen, Kämpfen. Aufstieg des Faschismus*, Vienna, 1969, Italian first edition Florence, 1950, pp. 71f.: D'Annunzio was the father of the 'alliance between expansion policy, nationalism, and antiparliamentarism'. Much the same in Hans-Ulrich Thamer and Wolfgang Wippermann, *Faschistische und neofaschistische Bewegungen*, Darmstadt, 1977, pp. 174ff.; Edward R. Tannenbaum, *The Fascist Experience. Italian Society and Culture 1922–1945*, New York, 1972, p. 30. For the Mediterranean roots of 'original Fascism' as compared to National Socialism, see Wolfgang Sauer, 'National Socialism. Totalitarianism or Fascism?' in: *American Historical Review*, vol. 73 (1967), pp. 404–24, here pp. 421ff.

5. 'Gli ultimi saranno i primi' in: Gabriele D'Annunzio, *Il Sudore di Sangue. Dalla Frode di Versaglia alla Marcia di Ronchi*, Rome, 1930, pp. 29–68. Similar in sense is the speech of two days later, on 8 May 1919. Its text in Gabriele D'Annunzio, *La Penultima Ventura. Scritti e discorsi fiumani*. A cura di Renzo De Felice, Rome, 1974, pp. 52–58. For the response to the speech of 4 May 1919, also see Tasca, *Glauben, Gehorchen, Kämpfen*, pp. 57f.

6. For Italian studies on Fiume, see the bibliography by Salvatore Samani and Luigi Peteani, eds., *Bibliografia Storica di Fiume*, Rome, 1969. Excellent in connecting biography with political and social history is the study by Michael A. Ledeen, *The First Duce. D'Annunzio at Fiume*, Baltimore, Maryland, 1977. The differences between D'Annunzio and Mussolini are pointed out by Renzo De Felice, *D'Annunzio Politico*, Bari, 1987. Despite these differences, which became obvious after the Fiume adventure, D'Annunzio and his activities in Fiume lost nothing of their decisive influence on the genesis of the fascist movement. At the same time, the national hero succeeded in refusing all attempts by the fascists to use him as a figurehead during their dynamic phase and the efforts of the conservative circles who would have welcomed his temporary dictatorship in order to tame fascism.

7. Extracts in David John Lu, ed., *Sources of Japanese History*, New York, 1974, pp. 131–6. Also see George M. Wilson, *Radical Nationalist in Japan, Kita Ikki*

1883–1937, Cambridge, Mass., 1969. For more references, see the survey by Bernd Martin, '"Japans Weg in den Krieg". Bemerkungen über Forschungs-stand und Literatur zur japanischen Zeitgeschichte', in: *Militärgeschichtliche Mitteilungen*, vol. 23 (1978), pp. 183–209; and by the same author, 'Japan und der Krieg in Ostasien. Kommentierender Bericht über das Schrifttum', in: *Son-derheft No. 8., Historische Zeitschrift "Literaturbericht zur Geschichte Chinas und der japanischen Zeitgeschichte"*, Rolf Trauzettel, Bernd Martin, eds., München, 1980, pp. 79–220.

8. Bernd Martin, 'Aggressionspolitik als Mobilisierungsfaktor. Der wirtschaft-liche und militärische Imperialismus Japans 1931–1942', in: Friedrich Forst-meier and Hans-Erich Volkmann, eds., *Wirtschaft und Rüstung am Vorabend des Zweiten Weltkrieges*, Düsseldorf, 1975, pp. 222–44. For the February putsch, see Ben-Amin Shillony, *Revolt in Japan. The Young Officers and the February 26, 1936 Incident*, Princeton, 1973.

9. 'Fundamental Principles of National Policy', passed the Hirota Cabinet on 11 Aug. 1936; its text in Lu, *Sources*, Vol. II, pp. 138ff.

10. See the basic fascist statement of 1932, 'The Doctrine of Fascism', in: *L'Enciclo-pedia Italiana*; German translation in Ernst Nolte, ed., *Theorien über den Faschis-mus*, Köln, 1967, pp. 205–20. Article 13 of the second section, which was written by Mussolini himself, says among other things: 'The Fascist State is an embodied will to power and government; the Roman tradition is here an ideal of force in action' (translated by Delzell, in: C. F. Delzell, *Mediterranean Fascism*, p. 105). See Luigi Preti, 'Fascist Imperialism and Racism', in: Roland Sarti, ed., *The Ax Within. Italian Fascism in Action*, New York, 1974, pp. 187–207. The polit-ical rapprochement with Germany in 1936 implied adjusting domestic policy as well. In the 'Provisions for the Defense of the Italian Race' of November 1938 (English translation in Delzell, *Mediterranean Fascism*, pp. 178–83) to a large extent the 'Nuremberg Racelaws' were adopted not only out of consid-eration for their German partner, whom Italy needed for her imperialistic expansion plans, but also for reasons of domestic policy as the economic effects of the campaigns in Ethiopia threatened to erode the fascist regime. The standard work on the Jews in Italy is Meir Michaelis, *Mussolini and the Jews. German-Italian Relations and the Jewish Question in Italy 1922–1945*, Oxford, 1978.

11. The main theorist of the Japanese claim of Pan-Asian leadership, based on the superiority of the Yamato race and its descent from the gods, was Okawa Shumei. He was the founder of 'Yuzonsha' and 'Jimmukai' – small groups of ultranationalist conspirators – and was closely connected with Kita Ikki who had ideologically prepared and helped to organise the February incident of 1936 (also see above). In the American War Tribunal, Okawa was considered to be one of the main war criminals (grade A), but the charge against him was dropped because of his (genuine or faked) mentally diminished responsibility. There is, as yet, no biography on Okawa in any Western language. See George M. Wilson, 'Kita Ikki, Okawa Shumei and the Yuzonsha', in: *Papers on Japan*, vol. 2, Cambridge, Mass., 1963, pp. 139–81. Kita's professed allegiance to Greater East Asia, in English translation, in Joyce C. Lebra, *Japan's Greater East Asia Co-Prosperity Sphere in World War II. Selected Readings and Documents*, Oxford University Press, 1975, pp. 36–40.

12. Prime Minister General Tojo in the Diet in 1943; Tojo is quoted in Masao Maruyama, 'The Ideology and Dynamics of Japanese Fascism', in: Masao Maruyama, *Thought and Behaviour in Modern Japanese Politics*, London, 1963, p. 47. For the role and the function of the pauperised farmers in the political radicalisation of the 1930s, see the basic works of Thomas R. H. Havens, *Farm and Nation in Modern Japan. Agrarian Nationalism 1870–1940*, Princeton, 1974, and Richard J. Smethurst, *A Social Basis for Prewar Japanese Militarism. The Army and the Rural Community*, Berkeley, 1974.

13. In Germany, as well as in Italy, those social strata that had supported the respective movements felt deceived after the movements came to power. In Germany, it was the petit-bourgeois middle class whose ambitions were thwarted; in Italy, the rural population of Northern Italy had played a decisive part in the victory of fascism and felt betrayed after 1922. The terror of the 'Squadrists' against organised farm labour in Northern Italy in 1920–22 suited the large estate owners who made use of the fascist movement, as did the small owners and tenants who felt threatened by socialist collectivism slogans. See Tasca, *Glauben, Gehorchen, Kämpfen*, pp. 109ff. Also see the regional studies by Paul Corner, *Fascism in Ferrara 1915–1925*, Oxford University Press, 1975, and Anthony L. Cardoza, *Agrarian Elites and the Origins of Italian Fascism. The Province of Bologna 1901–1922*, Phil. diss., Princeton University (University Microfilms), 1975.

14. Tannenbaum, *Fascist Experience*, pp. 105ff; Alberto Aquarone, 'A Closing Commentary. Problems of Democracy and the Quest for Identity', in: E. R. Tannenbaum and E. P. Noether, eds., *Modern Italy. A Topical History since 1861*, New York, 1974, p. 371.

15. According to Franz Borkenau, fascism accelerated the industrialisation of backward Italy: Franz Borkenau, 'Zur Soziologie des Faschismus' (first published in 1932), in: Nolte, *Theorien*, pp. 156–81; this statement is confirmed by Renzo De Felice (see above) and Jens Petersen, 'Faschismus und Industrie in Italien 1919–1929', in: *Gesellschaft. Beiträge zur Marxschen Theorie*, vol. 7 (1976), pp. 133–89, Roland Sarti, *Fascism and the Industrial Leadership in Italy 1919–1940. A Study in the Expansion of Private Power under Fascism*, University of California Press, 1971, und Thamer/Wippermann, *Faschistische Bewegungen*, p. 227.

16. Inazo Nitobe, *Bushido. Die Seele Japans. Eine Darstellung des japanischen Geistes*, Magdeburg, 1937; first published in Japanese in 1905; a German translation was prepared shortly afterwards, but apparently failed to catch a publisher's attention then and was only published much later, during the time of National Socialism; English edition: *Bushido. The Soul of Japan. An Exposition of Japanese Thought*, Tokyo, 1969.

17. Not much research seems to have been done on the relationship between the army and the fascist militia on the one side, and the fascist state and Mussolini on the other side. For the cooperation during the first years of fascist government when the fascist militia, which on 14 January 1923 had officially been integrated into the state, acted as the ideological spearhead of the regular troops, see Giorgio Rochat, 'The Fascist Militia and the Army 1922–1924', in: Sarti, *Ax Within*, New York, 1974, pp. 43–56.

18. Maruyama, *Thought and Behaviour*, p. 48: A memorandum of the War Ministry ('The True Meaning of National Defence: its Consolidation Advocated', 1934) began with Clausewitz's motto.

19. Fundamental commentary by one of the 'fathers' of the Meiji Constitution: Hirobumi Ito, *Commentaries on the Constitution of the Empire of Japan*, Tokyo, 1906; Reprint Westport, Conn., 1978. For the undermining of parliamentarism during the 1930s, see the anthology by George M. Wilson, ed., *Crisis Politics in Prewar Japan*, Tokyo, 1970.

20. The author's interview with Ambassador Eugen Ott in Munich on 11 June 1966: Apparently Ribbentrop phoned Ott in Tokyo to find out how often the Japanese Emperor attended the receptions in the German embassy, as Hitler was willing to accept invitations by the Japanese embassy only on a reciprocal basis. For the Tenno and the Japanese court's indirect rule, see David A. Titus, *Palace and Politics in Prewar Japan*, New York, 1974.

21. See Havens, *Farm and Nation*, and Smethurst, *Social Basis*; also see James B. Crowley, *Japan's Quest for Autonomy. National Security and Foreign Policy 1930–1938*, Princeton, 1966.

22. Politisches Archiv, Auswärtiges Amt Bonn, Japan – Deutschland: Report German Embassy, Journal No. 880 of 13 November 1940 on the new political structure in Japan ('Neue politische Struktur Japans'). Also see the monograph by Gordon M. Berger, *Parties out of Power in Japan 1931–1941*, Princeton, 1977.

23. English translation of these laws in Delzell, *Mediterranean Fascism*, pp. 62ff (the laws of 24 December 1925; 6 and 25 November 1926).

24. Reprint of the law of 11 May 1925 in Lu, *Sources*, p. 117. For the effects of the 'Peace Laws', see the monograph by Richard H. Mitchell, *Thought Control in Prewar Japan*, Ithaca, N.Y., 1976.

25. Lu, *Sources*, p. 115: Law of 5 May 1925 on the elections for the Lower House. See note 9.

26. Renzo De Felice, *Der Faschismus. Ein Interview von Michael A. Ledeen*. Mit einem Nachwort von Jens Petersen, Stuttgart, 1977, pp. 40ff. For the attitude of the organised nationalists, the Associazione Nazionalista Italiana founded in 1910, towards rising fascism, see Wilhelm Alff, 'Die Associazione Nazionalista Italiana von 1910', in: Wilhelm Alff, *Der Faschismus und andere Aufsätze zur Zeitgeschichte*, Frankfurt am Main, 1971, pp. 51–95. Giorgio Amendola, too, dates the birth of fascism at the time directly preceding the First World War, when, according to him, nationalism formed a reaction to domestic social tensions caused by industrialisation, leaving its nostrum of imperial expansion as a heritage to the fascists' foreign political programme. Giorgio Amendola, *Der Antifaschismus in Italien. Ein Interview von Piero Melograni*. Mit einem Nachwort von Jens Petersen. Stuttgart, 1977; first Italian edition Rome, 1976.

27. This is Tim Mason's statement which, on the whole, applies to the time between 1933 and 1938: Tim Mason, 'Der Primat der Politik. Politik und Wirtschaft im Nationalsozialismus', in: *Das Argument*, No. 8 (1966) pp. 473–94. However, numerous papers delivered at the International Conference on Social Change During the Second World War – the Axis Powers and the

Occupied Regions ('Sozialer Wandel im Zweiten Weltkrieg – Achsenmächte und besetzte Gebiete') in Bielefeld, 14 to 18 June 1979, came to the conclusion that after Austria had been annexed to the Reich (*Anschluß*) and the economy had been 'organised', industry went far beyond the usual degree of profit-orientated participation with the regime, thus adding economically to the political stabilisation of the National Socialist system. It remains doubtful whether the term of 'state monopoly capitalism' can be applied to characterise the close cooperation of large industry, military administration, party officials, and the conservative bureaucratic élites in the economic occupation of West and North European regions, all the more so since in the occupation of Slavonic countries procedures were quite different and antagonisms openly manifested themselves. For the Conference papers: Waclaw Dlugoborski, ed., *Zweiter Weltkrieg und sozialer Wandel*, Göttingen, 1981.

28. Karin Priester, *Der italienische Faschismus. Ökonomische und ideologische Grundlagen*, Köln, 1972; Sarti, *Ax Within*; Petersen, *Faschismus und Industrie*; Ernst Nolte, 'Die "herrschenden Klassen" und der Faschismus in Italien', in: Wolfgang Schieder, ed., *Faschismus als soziale Bewegung. Deutschland und Italien im Vergleich*, Hamburg, 1976, pp. 183–203. Not much research has been done so far on the complex of the armaments industry and fascist expansion. See Angela Raspin, 'Wirtschaftliche und politische Aspekte der italienischen Aufrüstung Anfang der dreißiger Jahre bis 1940' in: Forstmeier and Volkmann, eds., *Wirtschaft und Rüstung*, pp. 202–21, and Giorgio Rochat, 'L'esercito e il fascismo', in: Guido Quazza, ed., *Fascismo e Societi Italiana*, Torino, 1973, pp. 89–124. According to Rochat, the Italian State spent 27 percent of its budget on the military between 1929 and 1934, 21 percent between 1935 and 1938, and 20 percent from 1939 to 1940. However, it is likely that at least part of the state expense for the economy has to be added to the money spent for the military.

29. Bernd Martin, 'Japans Kriegswirtschaft 1941–1945', in: Friedrich Forstmeier and Hans-Erich Volkmann, eds., *Kriegswirtschaft und Rüstung 1939–1945*, Düsseldorf, 1977, pp. 256–86.

30. The death penalty was carried out only in certain murder cases: six persons in 1927, two in 1928, one in 1930, and four in 1932 (see Großer Brockhaus, 1934).

31. See the chapter on 'Recht und Justiz' in Martin Broszat, *Der Staat Hitlers*, München, 1969, pp. 403–22. In 1933 alone, there were 11,156 trials for political crimes and 9,529 sentences effected (ibid., p. 408).

32. Ibid., p. 420: in 1938, 23 death sentences were confirmed, in 1943 there were 4,438, and 2,015 for the period between January and August in 1944.

33. Giacomo Matteotti, a member of the Socialist Party, was murdered on 10 June 1924. Although the Fascists denied any responsibility, they were generally regarded as the murderers. As a consequence, the members of the Socialist Party and the Partito Popolare (the Catholic party) left the parliament and settled on the Aventin in order to demonstratively renounce cooperation with the fascists. Mussolini was shocked and seemed helpless. But when a coalition between the two parties, for which the Socialists strived, failed because of the Vatican's veto, Mussolini accepted the challenge, and for the first time asserted his dictatorial position. See: Antonio G. Casanova, *Mateotti. Una vita per il*

socialismo, Milano, 1974, and Adrian Lyttelton, *The Seizure of Power. Fascism in Italy 1919–1929*, London, 1973.

34. Delzell, *Mediterranean Fascism*, pp. 64ff.

35. Horst Duhnke, *Die KPD von 1933 bis 1945*, Köln, 1972, p. 525

36. For the places of exile, see the remarks by Amendola, who had been an exile himself: Amendola, *Antifaschismus*, p. 18. Also see Tannenbaum, *Fascist Experience*, pp. 141f., and Dante L. Germino, *The Italian Fascist Party in Power. A Study in Totalitarian Rule*, New York, 1971, first published in 1959. According to C. Friedrich's concept of totalitarianism, Germino's study tries to explain Italian fascism as a totalitarian state and thereby possibly overdraws reality in the camps (ibid., pp. 141f.). Personal memories in Ignazio Silone, *Bread and Wine*, London, 1936.

37. Delzell, *Mediterranean Fascism*, pp. 67–70: text of the law in English translation. Also see Germino, *Italian Fascist Party*, pp. 117ff: on the political police, OVRA (Opera Volontaria per la Repressione Antifascista), and the Special Tribunal.

38. Adriano dal Pont, Alfonso Leonetti, Pasquale Maiello, and Lino Zocchi, *Aula IV. Tutti i processi del tribunale speciale fascista*, Roma, 1962, reprint Milano, 1976. All these authors had been tried by the special court, and they all confirm that they were treated in a comparatively lenient way. Amendola (*Antifaschismus*, p. 132) claims that about 4,500 of persons sentenced were communists, but does not prove his statement.

39. Basically, the special court was a court-martial. It consisted of a president who had to be a general or an admiral of the military or the militia, five militia officers of a consul's rank, and one or more vice-presidents who were generals or admirals. The special court was responsible to the War Minister; its proceedings and sentences more or less corresponded to the military penal code, which meant that the death penalty could be imposed for offences against §§ 104, 107, 108, 120, 252 (conspiracy against the State, betrayal of secrets, rioting); see the original texts in Luigi Franchi, ed., *Codice Penale e di Procedura Penale*, Milano, 1908. But according to § 6 of the law concerning the special court, the judges were free to substitute a 15- to 30-year prison sentence for the death penalty. Obviously, this alternative was quite often made use of. Tannenbaum, too, confirms the integrity of the Italian law courts and their judges, who had to be party members. Tannenbaum, *Fascist Experience*, p. 72.

40. Peter Duus, *Party Rivalry and Political Change in Taisho Japan*, Cambridge, Mass., 1968, p. 205.

41. Kazuko Tsurumi, *Social Change and the Individual. Japan Before and After Defeat in World War II*, Princeton, 1970, pp. 41ff.

42. Ozaki Hotsumi, the informant of the German spy Richard Sorge, was the only civilian Japanese person who was sentenced to death and executed during the war. Saburo Ienaga, *The Pacific War. World War II and the Japanese, 1931–1946*, New York, 1978; first published in Japanese in 1968, p. 113. For the case of Richard Sorge, see Chalmers Johnson, *An Instance of Treason. Ozaki Hotsumi and the Sorge Spy Ring*, Stanford, 1964.

43. Karl Dietrich Bracher, 'Julius Leber', in: H. J. Schultz, ed., *Der zwanzigste Juli – Alternative zu Hitler*, Berlin, 1974, p. 153. By the same author, 'Kritische Betrachtungen zum Faschismusbegriff', in: Karl Dietrich Bracher, ed., *Zeitgeschichtliche Kontroversen. Faschismus, Totalitarismus, Demokratie*, München, 1976; Maruyama, *Thought and Behaviour*; Takeshi Ishida, 'Elements of Tradition and Renovation in Japan during the "Era of Fascism"', in: *Annals of the Institute of Social Science*, Tokyo University, No. 17 (1976); and Ienaga, *Japan's Last War*, pp. 112ff., clearly distinguish between the Japanese form of 'fascism' and the murderous terror regime of German National Socialism, which did not shrink from genocide. Also see De Felice, *Faschismus*, pp. 89ff, who sees fundamental differences between fascism and National Socialism, and Amendola (*Antifaschismus*, p. 18): 'Why then should we draw the picture of a totalitarian fascism similar to Nazism that destroyed its opponents?'; Amendola, *Antifaschismus*, p. 156: 'To my opinion fundamental differences exist between the two. I have difficulty in seeing in fascism, as it is frequently done today, a special structural type of state power. Two possibilities offer themselves: Either we accept an approach, which, however, we have outgrown, that explains fascism as one of the stages of imperialism on its way to the proletarian revolution; or else we share a different approach that acknowledges the specific characteristics of each form of fascism […] and understands it as the result of its respective historical background.'

❧ 7 ❧

GERMANY BETWEEN CHINA AND JAPAN
GERMAN FAR EASTERN POLICY OF THE INTERWAR PERIOD

B etween the wars, the Japanese Empire slowly shifted away
from the coalition of the victorious powers of Versailles
towards an alliance, finally signed in September 1940, with Germany and Italy. While neo-Imperialistic Japan gradually became
an enemy of the Western powers, nationalist China advanced to
the position of an ally, until in 1943 it was recognised as one of the
four big powers whose obligation it supposedly was to guide the
world to eternal peace.

Actually, the weak Chinese central government in Peking had
declared war on Germany on 17 August 1917.[1] But that decision
was made under severe pressure from the Americans. From the
Chinese point of view, it was intended to counter Japanese imperialism rather than to engage in war with Germany. After the
seizure of Tsingtao,[2] the Tokyo government had unveiled its
future goals on the Asian mainland by confronting Peking with
the ill-famed 'Twenty-One Demands'. By allying themselves with
the Western cause of democracy and by obtaining a seat at the
peace conference, China hoped to be treated as an equal partner,
expecting to influence the revision of the treaties with the colonial
powers and to regain full sovereignty over the Chinese territory.

When this attempt failed at Versailles, China refused to sign
the peace treaty with Germany. Once more, it should be borne in
mind that this step was not directed against the German people,
but served as a means of pressure against the Japanese and the
Anglo-Americans. Since there had never been any express hatred
against Germany in China, and since the Peking government did

---

This chapter is a revised version of an article first published in *Festschrift on the 50th
Anniversary of Academia Sinica*, Institute of Modern History, Nanking/Taipei, 1978.

not treat German nationals as citizens of an enemy country, the war was terminated through a unilateral declaration on the part of China in September 1919. Only about two years later, in 1921, German merchants regained their prewar position in China.

China and Germany, as well as the Soviet Union, were all outcasts of the Versailles peace settlement. The possibility of these countries joining forces in the field of international relations was enough to raise distrust among the Western powers. Therefore, when China and Germany reached an agreement in May 1921 in order to reestablish normal diplomatic relations, the German Republican Government had to give up all former special rights granted to Germany in China. For the first time in modern history China was treated as an equal partner in a treaty with a major Western power. By giving up her extraterritorial rights, Germany gained in prestige and made an immense profit. Chinese nationalists began to look upon Germany as an ally in the fight against the Anglo-American world dominance and highly admired the rapid German recovery after the defeat in the Great War. The stage seemed to be set for friendly relations between the young Chinese republic and the even younger German republic. However, World War Two again saw the two countries in hostile camps, since Germany preferred to sign an alliance with Imperial Japan, which by then had become China's arch enemy.

These developments raise important questions, such as whether certain long-range political or social factors as, for instance, the modernisation from above effected through a conservative governing class that had never been challenged by a revolution, were decisive steps in the transformation of both Germany and Japan into authoritarian states, whose approach to solving issues was similar because of the integral logic common to both systems,[3] or whether, on the contrary, these similarities stemmed from the traditional conflict of interest among comparatively autonomous political and economic groups. It could also be asked whether the politics of other powers, especially the Anglo-American influence, determined these developments. In which way did the political leadership of Germany and Japan, especially that of Adolf Hitler in Germany,[4] influence this rapprochement? Or was this 'alliance without a backbone'[5] just the casual product of a momentary decision arising, on the German side, from Hitler's restlessness and, on the Japanese, from political stubbornness of the militarists ruling the country?

As it was, both Japan and Germany actually added certain secret amendments to all their agreements which were often contradictory to the expressed content and which left each one free to act against the other's vital interest and – even in regard to military defence – to follow their own 'sacred egotism'. Thus, they seemed incapable of any real partnership as practised by the Anglo-American war coalition, or even of any real strategic or political agreements like the ones within the heterogeneous alliance between the Soviet Union and the Western powers.

In Japan the social conflict between the lower echelons of society and the traditional governing oligarchy, which dominated the state as well as the economy, was politically institutionalized by the Meiji Restoration.[6] But for a certain time this conflict was covered up by the imperialistic power politics before and during the First World War. In the 1920s, racial discrimination against the Japanese by the Anglo-Americans and the Nine Powers' Treaty, which forced Japan to acknowledge the 'open door policy' in China, were criticised by nationalist groups, mostly officers of petty rural origin, who envisioned a socioimperialist policy of living space (*Lebensraum*) in East Asia that seemed vitally necessary for Japan.[7]

Since the Japanese army consisted in large part of conscripts of rural origin – with the exception of the navy which favoured the recruitment of skilled craftsmen of urban background – and since Japan still remained an agrarian country, slogans such as 'direct actions' met with a favourable response in the army. In 1931, the troops stationed in Manchuria felt encouraged to act on their own.[8] This was a blow directed against the coalition of capitalists and upper classes, which, due to its policy of deflation, was held responsible for the impoverishment of farmers and small craftsmen. The parliamentary system, which had been stabilised during the 1920s, was destroyed in 1932 when its opponents, court circles and nationalist die-hards, united and when the main leaders of the democratic capitalist polity were assassinated. The internal radicalisation and the rising influence of the army – uncontrolled by any parliament or ministers – forced Japan to take an intransigent attitude towards the Manchurian crisis. Finally, on 27 March 1933, this resulted in the country leaving the League of Nations.[9] This occurred four days after the German Reichstag had approved the enabling law (*Ermächtigungsgesetz*). Although in Geneva Germany had voted against the Japanese aggression in Manchuria, the timely coincidence of these two facts was to be of some importance for the two countries later on.

The Weimar Republic looked upon Japan as a party to the oppressive Versailles treaty. Mutual relations were restricted to mere diplomatic formalities and some – though small – trade on the basis of a trade agreement dating from 1927. Even though Japan, from 1931 onward, shared the German attitude towards the question of reparations, the *Wilhelmstraße* (German Foreign Ministry) officially remained neutral in its Far Eastern policy. Nevertheless, the German export industry, which foresaw the future market in China, the Foreign Ministry, and the German military stuck to their de facto pro-Chinese outlook.[10]

Sun Yat-sen,[11] the father of the Chinese Republic, had visited Germany on a number of occasions before the First World War. He considered the German national unification, brought about by Bismarck's appeal of 'iron and blood', rapid industrialisation, and direct state encouragement of the economy as relevant models for the development of China. Sun even looked for direct German aid and German advisers. But shortage of money on the side of the Chinese and fear of allied intervention on the German side ended those first endeavours.[12] However, Sun Yat-sen's desire for a closer relationship between Germany and China was also shared by high ranking Kuomintang officials, among others by Chiang Kai-shek and Dr. Chu Chia-hua.

The precise nature of the origins of the German advisory group, which was finally established in Nanking in December 1928, will remain mysterious as long as Chinese documents on that subject are classified.[13] Therefore, the following analysis, which is primarily based on private German papers, may be subject to correction. Chu Chia-hua, who studied engineering at the Berlin Metallurgical Institute during the war and who received a German doctorate, became the main sponsor of German interests in China. Until 1938, when the German advisers were finally called back, Chu served the German group as a friend and ubiquitous liaison between the Chinese government and military circles and the Germans in China.

In 1926, as acting president of the Sun Yat-sen University in Canton, Chu sent a telegram to his former German professor, requesting estimates for factories, primarily munitions plants, apparently for construction in the Canton area. Finally, the powerful though clandestine coalition of German rightist industrialists and retired officers of the monarchy, who had worked well together during the war, sent Colonel Max Bauer on an inspection trip to China.[14] Bauer, who had been Ludendorff's (former German Chief of Staff) right hand, was notorious for his rightist political opinions. He was even forced to flee Germany after he had supported the armed plot of Kapp to overthrow the government of the Weimar Republic. However, this did not seem to influence either side: not only did the Germans regard him as the proper person for a business inspection of China, but the ex-colonel was immediately befriended by Chiang Kai-shek and was entrusted by him with a mission to Germany in order to select a staff of military and civilian advisers. Although Bauer and the advisory group were never supported by the German War Ministry (*Reichswehrministerium*) or the German Foreign Office, they were trusted by Chinese as well as German nationalists and heavily criticised by their democratic counterparts in both countries. Despite his political opinions, Bauer laid the foundations for German aid to the Chinese and contributed remarkably to the reorganising and modernisation of the Kuomintang revolutionary armed forces.[15]

Thus, the Germans helped to stabilise the Chinese central government of Chiang Kai-shek,[16] a fact which in the long run was, of course, contrary to Japanese interests. Only slowly could Hitler and certain National Socialist groups shift the German Far Eastern policy from China towards Japan. In general, the Japanese were regarded as narrow-minded and were mistrusted because of their tendency toward technical imitation. This deeply rooted resentment against them could never be completely dispersed by any pro-Japanese propaganda.

Hitler, who in his programme *Mein Kampf* actually never said anything about his future East Asian policy, was now forced through his anti-Bolshevist policy at home and abroad to look for new allies. For him, the *Reichswehr*, the Foreign Minister, and certain economic groups, a continental alliance with a Far Eastern power, in addition to a German-English front, seemed an ideal means to encircle the Soviet Union. The only question was with which of the two, Japan or China, the Reich should form an alliance.

Yet, for the time being, the German relations with these two countries were overshadowed by the National Socialist racial doctrine, which, of course, was resented by both of them. Asian diplomats frequently intervened in Berlin and forced the ministries to influence the Party in order to change the crude, so-far used differentiation between Aryans and non-Aryans into one of Aryans and Jews.[17]

Hitler made all of his decisions, before and during the war, according to his conviction that the 'German master race' had to find its way to world power on its own, without the help of the 'yellow' race. Only as long as there was nothing concretely planned between Germany and the Far Eastern empire did Hitler welcome Japan as his associate against the Soviet Union and, from 1940, against the United States. Neither the future Foreign Secretary Ribbentrop, nor the German military, nor the industrialists shared Hitler's racial prejudice. This, plus divergent interests among these groups, further hindered a unified German political attitude towards East Asia.

Although the Japanese army officers greatly admired the German dictatorship, the German-Japanese rapprochement was actually initiated by leading National Socialist groups, and, in particular, by Hitler himself. Hitler sponsored a formal recognition of Japanese-dominated Manchuria in order to outmaneuver the traditional 'China-lobby'. These were: the pro-Chinese Foreign Ministry, as well as army generals, who were interested in China as a territory for military experiments after the collaboration with the Red Army had been suspended, and a strong China lobby within the armaments industry. On the other hand, Hitler was supported by the newly appointed ambassador to Tokyo (Dirksen), by Rosenberg's office, and by Fritz Thyssen, who hoped to build heavy industry combines together with the Japanese in Manchuria.[18] However, Foreign Secretary von Neurath together with the Reichswehr and those industrial groups who profited by the arms trade with China prevented Hitler from changing the Far Eastern policy too quickly.[19]

Obviously, Hitler's pro-Japanese policy could not be realised by traditional diplomatic channels. This task could only be fulfilled by a newly created institution consisting of Party members and businessmen who were interested in trading with Japan. Joachim von Ribbentrop, since April 1934 Hitler's special envoy in questions of disarmament together with his office 'Büro Ribbentrop'[20] – a kind of rival party organisation to the established Foreign Ministry – seemed to be best suited for creating the worldwide anticommunist alliance aimed for. Ribbentrop made sure of the help of the German navy, whose obvious weakness made it lean towards the sea powers Britain and Japan. In his first contacts with certain Japanese naval groups in January 1935, Ribbentrop used Dr. Hack,[21] a German armament lobbyist, who had had success with some business transactions between the Heinkel aircraft works and the Imperial Japanese Navy.

Despite the different opinions on the parity of naval forces, which the Western powers had denied, the Japanese admiralty stuck to a policy of reconciliation with the Anglo-Americans who were regarded as economically superior. For this reason, these German feelers were rejected, but were, as it seems, taken up by the Japanese army. Apparently, both sides took some steps which were finally to lead to the Anti-Comintern Pact. The Japanese army, represented in Berlin by the fervently pro-German military attaché Oshima, had become aware of the pro-Japanese activities of certain persons around Hitler. Exploiting these tendencies was considered to be useful in two ways: first, the German influence in China might be neutralised, or even withdrawn, by an agreement with Germany, and second, Japan might thereby gain an ally against the Soviet Union who endangered the Japanese position in Manchuria. On 17 September 1935 Oshima suggested to Hack to try to intensify the German-Japanese collaboration which was to be worked out without the help of the two foreign offices.

Oshima took Ribbentrop into his confidence and – only a few days later – presented a handwritten draft plan for a pact. The German envoy Hack informed both Admiral Canaris, then head of the intelligence service and Blomberg, the Minister of War, about the Japanese propositions. Without hesitation, Canaris agreed to an anti-Soviet front, which originally was to include Great Britain, Germany, Poland, and Japan. Blomberg, on the other hand, did not want to endanger the German position in China by such an alliance. But since the Japanese army had also tried to use the Germans as a mediator between Japan and China,[22] it seemed possible that China would be included in the formation of such a pact. For this reason, Blomberg decided to give up his opposition. The basic ideas of the alliance, especially its anti-Comintern tendency, had been fixed by the end of November 1935. Hitler himself – against the opposition of the Foreign Ministry – had approved of this draft in a discussion with Ribbentrop.[23]

On 25 November 1936 the treaty was signed in Berlin. This delay of almost a year can be explained by an officers' rebellion in Tokyo and by the changing situation in world politics. In addition, in 1936 both partners thought it advisable to add some secret amendments which would convert the treaty into a military defence pact against the Soviet Union.[24] The latter had entered into a defence alliance with Outer Mongolia and had ratified the pact with France which had been signed in May 1935. Finally, the Spanish Civil War had also broken out.

Nevertheless, the German-Japanese rapprochement was preceded by a loan agreement with China,[25] which the Reichswehr and the Foreign Ministry advocated, and by an agreement with Manchuria[26] that had also been sponsored by the traditional diplomacy. Thus, by signing the Anti-Comintern Pact, Hitler and those who shared his pro-Japanese outlook, gained in influence, but could in no way predominate the Far Eastern policy of Germany.

Only the Japanese army, which regarded National Socialism as a model in domestic politics, recklessly approved of the alliance. The officers even tried to enlarge the armament production by imitating the National Socialist 'Four Years' Plan', by intensifying their state control system, and by further suppressing the few remaining civil rights.[27] Since the army gained much political influence by signing the Anti-Comintern Pact, the government in Tokyo to a certain extent gave way to the army's wishes. But the so-called 'quasi-war economy' increased the discontent among the working classes who, in the last free elections before the war with China began, clearly voted for a parliamentary system.

In order to break the opposition in Japan and to unify the people behind the emerging alliance between the military and big business, another rather important political incident was useful: namely, the outbreak of fighting in China in July 1937. This event had been prepared long in advance, a fact which demonstrates the domestic concerns from which it derived its political raison d'être. This war, euphemistically called a 'conflict', was welcomed by the Japanese navy because it changed the direction of continental expansion from Soviet Russia southward towards the promising raw material holdings of French Indochina and the Dutch East Indies. With this war, the Japanese army definitely supported economic imperialism, and the initial conflict between the interests of the army on the one side, and the navy and business on the other side, was overcome in the common chauvinism of war.

The army, instead of preparing for war against the Soviet Union – as was proposed in the Anti-Comintern Pact – pursued its ends in China. There it was confronted, ironically enough, by élite Chinese troops that had been trained and armed by German military advisers. By 1936 the German influence in Kuomintang China was visible everywhere. Had the war not broken out in July 1937, the German impact might have been even greater. Colonel General Hans von Seeckt, who had reorganised the small German armed forces after the humiliating defeat in the First World War, promulgated German interests in China to an extent quite unknown until then. During his brief term of office as German chief adviser from 1934–35,[28] he won the complete confidence of Chiang Kai-shek. He was even granted the privilege of issuing orders on behalf of the Marshal. As a German nationalist and military man Seeckt propagated two purposes: 1) reestablishment of Germany as a world power by strengthening her international position, and 2) support for a united and modernised China.

From Seeckt's as well as from the other military advisers' point of view, China was to become a strong anticommunist bulwark as well as a reliable trading partner and finally a political ally of the Reich. Barter agreements served the economy of both countries best. German armament exports to China boomed, German heavy industrial enterprisers like Otto Wolff signed contracts for the construction of railways, and the huge chemical concern IG Farben gained a monopoly in China, as did German firms specialising in electronic equipment, like Siemens. In 1932 Germany ranked fifth in the total value of Chinese imports; the Reich rose to a 17 percent share on total Chinese imports in 1936, which placed her second, less than only one percentage point behind the United States.[29]

On the other hand, in 1937 Germany received from China 72 percent of her total imports of tungsten, which is of utmost importance for any high quality steel production and which as raw material is not to be found in Germany itself. Last but not least, the gap between German food production and consumption could be closed through imports of soya beans without spending any foreign currency which the Reich was always obliged to draw on when importing foodstuff from West European countries.[30]

Although the Germans for their own purposes stressed heavy industry and communications as the key to national sovereignty and economic progress, this concept was not altogether self-serving.

It had forged Germany into a great nation and was regarded as the only relevant model for China's development by the German advisers as well as by most of the Kuomintang leaders.

German advisership and Chiang Kai-shek worked hand in hand. Both were dependent upon each other. But to maintain that approximately one hundred German advisers were responsible for modernising China and for strengthening the political position of the Marshal would be an exaggeration. However, denying all German influence in China would clearly contradict the historical facts and the contemporary statements of Chinese officials who, as late as 1941, openly declared German military help to be the only practical military assistance that China had ever received.[31]

The prolonged resistance of Chinese forces against the Japanese in Shanghai in 1937 should be regarded as a symbol of China's reconstruction. The then German chief adviser General Alexander von Falkenhausen[32] completed several strategic plans and offered suggestions for the battle of Shanghai as well as for the building up of various lines of defence all over China which apparently concurred with the Marshal's own intentions.

But the struggle on the Asian continent caused the Reich, like the other great powers, to take sides. Since the Japanese invasion of Manchuria, the United States strongly opposed any change in the status quo in the Far East and, consequently, supported China's claims. Germany, however, after trying in vain to reconcile the belligerents,[33] decided to support Japan. The recall of the German military advisers from China and formal recognition of Manchuria in early summer 1938[34] marked the real turning point in Germany's Far Eastern policy.

The Japanese aggression had already disrupted any regular exchange of goods with China. Therefore, German industry expected economic advantages in China as soon as Japan consolidated its occupation. But the manner in which the Japanese behaved as an occupying force and, in particular, their proclamation of a 'New Order in East Asia' quite clearly aimed at eliminating any 'white', German, or Anglo-American influence in Asia. The Japanese Empire was to become the leading Far Eastern power at the expense of the other Asian countries.[35]

These aims were bound to provoke the Soviet Union, as well as the United States and the European colonial powers. Thus, Japan's revisionist power politics coincided with the National Socialist leaders' intentions to incorporate Austria and the Sudetenland into the Reich, which meant taking risks in Europe that could be compared to those the Japanese took in Asia. After Italy's signing the Anti-Comintern Pact, Ribbentrop transformed the alliance into an anti-British one, yet without completely losing its anti-Russian character.[36]

Border clashes at the Soviet-Manchurian frontier,[37] which caused the Japanese army heavy losses, made the Japanese government increasingly desire a military alliance of the 'world political triangle', Berlin–Rome–Tokyo. Yet, preparations were delayed because of the solid opposition of the Imperial Navy, which did not want and, in fact, had never wanted, a full-scale war against the Western powers. Finally, Hitler's pact with Stalin and the outbreak of war in Europe definitely ended any attempts at converting the Anti-Comintern Pact into a military alliance. The Japanese government, especially the army, which had always favoured a close relationship with Germany, was deeply offended by the Germans' egotistic way of acting which did not fit in at all with the idea of cooperation in the struggle against communism. With regard to international politics, Japan found herself completely isolated and was forced to readjust her politics at a time when the war against China assumed a vast scale.

While German-Japanese relations deteriorated, Chinese advances in Berlin which attempted to reestablish the traditional friendship met with a favourable response. Secret ammunitions support, either via the Trans-Siberian railroad or by ship via Hanoi, and invitations for retired German officers to resume their work as advisers against the Japanese hinted at a mutual rapprochement.[38] Even after the signing of the Tripartite Pact (27 September 1940) the German government strove for a peaceful settlement of the Sino-Japanese war. The mediation of Foreign Secretary Ribbentrop in November 1940 was accepted, according to German source material, as a basis for negotiations by both belligerents.[39] But Ribbentrop's efforts were doomed to fail when Hitler finally decided to subdue Soviet Russia and thereby gave the fatal blow to the dream of a Eurasian anti-imperialistic bloc.

Without the war in China and the clear decision of the United States in favour of China, Japan would probably have remained neutral during the Second World War, or might even have joined Germany's enemies. But the Japanese oligarchy was incapable of making concessions in the China question which would have been the precondition for any political reorientation. The traditional ruling class had made the cult of the Emperor and Japan's sacred mission in Asia their programme. If it failed, this would have necessarily destroyed the privileges of the ruling economic and military circles surrounding the court. The primacy of a stable domestic order, to which Japanese foreign policy had always been subordinated, prevented the Tokyo oligarchy from improving relations with the Western powers. On the contrary, the Japanese widened the conflict with China in order to confront the 'white powers' – whose interests for the moment were fixed upon the war in Europe – with a *fait accompli* in East Asia.[40]

Talks with Chiang Kai-shek were bound to fail because of the Japanese government's incapacity for any internal or external compromise. Furthermore, the inauguration of the Chinese puppet-government under Wang Ching-wei[41] intensified the conflict with the United States. Thus, Germany again seemed to be Tokyo's only possible ally in her policy of imperialism. The German troops' lightning victory in Poland was admired by the Japanese army. For the first time, the pro-Western naval and economic groups doubted the military force of the European colonial powers. Besides, the agreements between Germany and the Soviet Union had improved Japanese-Soviet relations. The German Foreign Secretary, who, unlike Hitler, regarded the agreement with the Soviet Union as a definitive act, tried on his second visit to Moscow to bring about a mediation between Japan and Russia. Ribbentrop aimed at including the Soviet Union as a territorial link to Japan and thereby wanted to enlarge the 'world political triangle' to a Eurasian continental bloc. By this worldwide coalition, the British Empire was to be overpowered.

After the Germans' rapid success in the West and after the Dutch forces had surrendered (15 May 1940), the Tokyo government considered an arrangement on an anti-British basis with the Germans as an urgent task. But Japanese feelers did not meet a favourable response in Berlin. Hitler, full of resentment against the 'yellow' Japanese, disdainfully called them 'Johnny-come-latelies' (*Erntehelfer*), who in the shadow of the German victories did nothing but try to enlarge their own territorial sphere of influence. As long as there was any hope of the British giving in during the summer of 1940, all Japanese approaches were rejected. Because then, with the help of the English as a 'junior partner', the white man's rule in East Asia would be stabilised, and Japan's influence could be checked.[42]

Due to the unfavourable outcome of the 'Battle of Britain' and due to the strong American commitment to the British Isles, Hitler then listened to the Japanese proposals. A special envoy, later to become the German ambassador to Tokyo, Stahmer, within no time negotiated a 'preventive defence alliance' with the Japanese. This Tripartite Pact, signed on 27 September 1940, aimed in the first place to discourage the United States from entering a two-front war and to abandon Great Britain in her apparently desperate isolation. Hitler now viewed Japan in terms of a political stronghold against the United States, but not, it must be emphasised, as an ally against the Soviet Union as he had done once before, when signing the Anti-Comintern Pact.[43]

However, the German government, without regard for her Asian partner, planned to attack the Soviet Union.[44] After 22 June 1941, only Ribbentrop, like his Japanese colleague Matsuoka, strongly advocated a Japanese intervention in the war with Russia in order to maintain a territorial link. But on the German side Hitler – from his racist point of view – resisted the participation of the 'yellows' in subduing the 'inferior Slavonic hordes'. In Tokyo even the anticommunist groups within the army, with the South-east Asian raw materials before their eyes, favoured the invasion of Southern Indochina instead of an attack in the North.

The Japanese southward advance led to an embargo on oil, imposed by the United States. This caused the Imperial Navy, which up to then had delayed the decision of engaging in war, to join the army's concept of conquest. On 8 September 1941 the Imperial Conference, the supreme governmental council, agreed upon a tentative decision to make war. But only at the end of November, when strategic plans had been finished, were consultations begun with the Germans about joining the war against the United States. About sixty hours before the Japanese attack on Pearl Harbor, the German decision to take part was transmitted to Tokyo. This decision, however, taken by Hitler himself, of joining a war without even knowing where and when it was to begin, for the first time did not spring from a free choice of Hitler, but from military necessity. For the *Blitzkrieg* had come to an unexpected standstill at the outskirts of Moscow. Taking the step into the unknown, into a war that had not been prepared for in any way, not even by the military, against the strongest Western power seemed to be a method for keeping the American war effort contained in the Pacific in order to allow for a second attempt to conquer the Soviet Union without Japanese assistance.[45]

While the Japanese army and the German navy were busy planning military cooperation via either the Soviet Union or the Indian Ocean, Hitler stubbornly opposed any Japanese assistance against the Red Army[4] until the decisive German defeat at Stalingrad. On the Japanese side, the Imperial Navy concentrated on the decisive defeat of the American Pacific fleet, which finally led to the disaster at Midway (4–7 June 1942).

During the time of the war alliance, only the repeated Japanese attempts at mediating a separate peace between Germany and the Soviet Union were of some political impact.[47] But Hitler refused any mediation, although Mussolini had been supporting these endeavours from 1942 on. Even Soviet peace feelers that were attempted in Stockholm in 1943 could not shake Hitler's axiomatic conviction that communism must be defeated.[48] Similarly fixed were the Japanese leaders in defending the 'Greater East Asia Co-Prosperity Sphere' against the Americans' leap from island to island in the Pacific. They, too, did not even consider the possibility of a compromise with China or even peace talks with the Anglo-Americans until the military situation, as in Germany, left no choice but unconditional surrender.[49]

Within a democratic and capitalistic world order, National Socialist Germany and semifeudal Japan had been drawn together because of their traditional social structure. The development of historically backward states towards authoritarianism necessarily made these countries incapable of any selfless cooperation. The differences between Germany and Japan were covered over by joint declarations of force and the initial military victories won by the partners independently of each other. Any real cooperation or clearly formulated joint aim was unimaginable. Yet, from their adversaries' point of view the Tripartite Alliance could not be looked upon as a mere declaration. It decisively influenced the formation of worldwide political fronts during the 1930s as well as the allies' war coalition and, later on, the mistrust among the victorious powers which emerged in the Cold War after 1945. The accusation of 'world conspiracy' brought forward against Germany and Japan at the Nuremberg and Tokyo war tribunals, however, was based on the same fiction that the German and Japanese propaganda had claimed for themselves – their overestimation of each other's military and economic capacities.

But the final question may be asked, although it can never be answered: What course might history have taken if Germany had stuck to her traditional pro-Chinese policy and if the Reich had aided China in her struggle for sovereignty against Japanese aggression until final victory?

Notes

1. For German-Chinese relations in World War One and during the 1920s, see: Chi Chen, *Die Beziehungen zwischen Deutschland und China bis 1933*, Hamburg, 1933; Carlton L. Wood, 'Die Beziehungen Deutschlands zu China', dissertation Heidelberg, 1935; Djen Djang Feng, *The Diplomatic Relations between China and Germany since 1898*, Shanghai, 1936; Reprint Taipei 1971; Lorne E. Glaim, 'Sino-German Relations, 1919–1925: German Diplomatic, Economic, and Cultural Reentry into China after World War I', unpublished dissertation, Washington State University, 1973. Still unsurpassed: Beverly D. Causey, 'German Policy towards China 1918–1941', unpublished dissertation, Harvard University, Cambridge (Mass.), 1942. For a general survey, see: Udo Rathenhof, *Die Chinapolitik des Deutschen Reiches 1871–1945. Wirtschaft – Rüstung – Militär*, Boppard, 1986.

2. For German colonial rule in China, see: John E. Schrecker, *Imperialism and Chinese Nationalism. Germany in Shantung*, Harvard University Press, 1971; for a military account of the German-Japanese combat, see: Charles B. Burdick, *The Japanese Siege of Tsingtau. World War One in Asia*, Hamden, Conn., 1976. On German source material, see: Bernd Martin, '"Gouvernement Jiaozhou" – Forschungsstand und Archivbestände zum deutschen Pachtgebiet Quingdao (Tsingtau) 1897–1914', in: Kuo Heng-yü and Mechthild Leutner, eds., *Deutschland und China*, Munich, 1994, pp. 375–93.

3. Barrington Moore, *Social Origins of Dictatorship and Democracy. Lord and Peasant in the Making of the Modern World*, London, 1967, and – much better: Reinhard Bendix, 'Preconditions of Development: A Comparison of Japan and Germany', in: Reinhard Bendix, *Nation Building and Citizenship*, New York, 1968.

4. The best study on Hitler's foreign policy: Klaus Hildebrand, *Deutsche Außenpolitik 1933–1945. Kalkül oder Dogma?*, Stuttgart, 1973 (English translation: The Foreign Policy of the Third Reich. University of California Press, 1974).

5. This term (*Allianz ohne Rückgrat*) can be found in the standard work on German-Japanese relations: Theo Sommer, *Deutschland und Japan zwischen den Mächten, 1935–1940. Vom Antikominternpakt zum Dreimächtepakt*, Tübingen, 1962. See also chapter 8, 'Japan and Germany on the Path towards War', in this volume.

6. The first profound German work on the effects of the Meiji Restoration: Annelotte Piper, *Japans Weg von der Feudalgesellschaft zum Industriestaat*, Köln, 1976.

7. For Japan's policy of aggression as a mobilising factor, see: Bernd Martin, 'Aggressionspolitik als Mobilisierungsfaktor. Der militärische und wirtschaftliche Imperialismus Japans 1931–1941', in: Friedrich Forstmeier and Hans-Erich Volkmann, eds., *Wirtschaft und Rüstung am Vorabend des Zweiten Weltkrieges*, Düsseldorf, 1975, pp. 222–44.

8. Sadako N. Ogata, *Defiance in Manchuria: The Making of Japanese Foreign Policy, 1931–1932*, University of California Press, 1964.

9. Christopher Thorne, *The Limits of Foreign Power. The West, the League, and the Far Eastern Crisis of 1931–1933*, London, 1972. Gabriele Herre, *Das Deutsche Reich und die internationale Krise um die Mandschurei 1931–1933*, Frankfurt am Main, 1984.

10. For Germany's Far Eastern Policy, covering China as well as Japan, see: John P. Fox, *Germany and the Far Eastern Crisis 1931–1938. A Study in Diplomacy and Ideology*, Oxford, 1982; from a Marxist point of view: Karl Drechsler, *Deutschland – China – Japan 1933–1939. Das Dilemma der deutschen Fernostpolitik*, Berlin (Ost), 1964.

11. Roland Felber, 'Die Deutschlandrezeption Sun Yat-sens', in: Kuo Heng-yü and Mechthild Leutner, eds., *Deutschland und China*, pp. 83–96. See also C. Martin Wilbur, *Sun Yat-sen. Frustrated Patriot*, New York, 1978, p. 109 and p. 134.

12. On the German military mission in China, see Bernd Martin, ed., *Die deutsche Beraterschaft in China 1927–1938. Militär – Wirtschaft – Außenpolitik* (The German Advisory Group in China. Military, Economic, and Political Issues in Sino-German Relations 1927–3838), Düsseldorf, 1981. (Half of the articles are in German, half in English.) Jerry B. Seps, 'German Military Advisers and Chiang Kai-shek, 1927–1938', Berkeley, unpublished dissertation, 1972. The article by Billie Walsh, 'The German Military Mission in China, 1928–1936', in: *Journal of Modern History*, 1974, pp. 502–13, does not cover the topic. The typoscript, edited by the Office of Military History, Taipei 1971, on 'A Summary of the Work of the German Advisory Group in China' offers some useful information, but contains errors.

13. These documents, mainly memoranda by the chief advisers and written in German, are supposed to be stored among Chiang Kai-shek's private papers which are not open to the public. They are stored in the Archives of the Kuomintang at Yangmingshan in Taipei but are still (1994) under custody of the Presidential Office. A part of Chu Chia-hua's private papers are kept in the Institute of Modern History which has been preparing an edition of key documents. But neither the papers nor this edition contain anything on the German advisory group (author's visit to Taiwanese archives in April 1994). In Germany, the Political Archives of the Foreign Ministry in Bonn, as well as the Military Archives in Freiburg i. Br., and the branch office of the Federal Archives in Potsdam hold some useful folders.

14. John P. Fox, 'Max Bauer: Chiang Kai-shek's First German Military Adviser', in: *Journal of Contemporary History*, 1970, pp. 21–44. See also the relevant chapters

in the only biography on Bauer: Adolf Vogt, *Oberst Max Bauer. Generalstabsoffizier im Zwielicht 1869–1929*, Osnabrück, 1974.

15. Political Archives, Foreign Ministry Bonn: Folder 'Politische Beziehungen Chinas zu Deutschland', Abt. Pol. IV: Memoranda by Bauer on the reorganisation of the Chinese army (14 December 1929) and on the development of a railroad system in China (28 December 1929).

16. The standard work in German on Kuomintang China was written by Jürgen Domes, *Die vertagte Revolution. Die Politik der Kuomintang 1923–1937*, Berlin, 1969. See also the controversial interpretation by Lloyd Eastman, *The Abortive Revolution. China under Nationalist Rule, 1927–1937*, Harvard University Press, 1974.

17. Fox, *Germany and the Far Eastern Crisis*, p. 141.

18. Ibid., p. 50 and p. 239.

19. Ibid., p. 86, Sommer, *Deutschland und Japan*, p. 21.

20. Hans-Adolf Jacobsen, *Nationalsozialistische Außenpolitik 1933–1938*, Frankfurt am Main, 1968, p. 252.

21. This and the following outline are based on the private papers of Friedrich-Wilhelm Hack. These documents were provided by Hack's nephew, Dr. R. Hack, whom the author wishes to thank for his generosity. These papers together with the notes Hack took during the Second World War in Switzerland, which were transmitted to the Japanese Embassy in Berlin, will be published in 1995.

22. *Documents on German Foreign Policy*, Series C, Vol. IV, Documents Nos. 433, 451, 452.

23. 27 November 1935 (Hack's private papers, note 28 November 1935).

24. Sommer, *Deutschland und Japan*, pp. 30–56 and, for the documents and amendments, ibid., pp. 493–99.

25. 8 April 1936 (*Documents on German Foreign Policy*, Series C, Vol. V, Doc. 270).

26. 30 April 1936 (Fox, *Germany and the Far Eastern Crisis*, p. 169).

27. Martin, 'Aggressionspolitik', p. 232.

28. See the chapter 'Seeckt in China' in the biography on Seeckt written by Hans Meier-Welcker, *Seeckt*, Frankfurt am Main, 1967.

29. Causey, *German Policy towards China*, p. 279: According to the 'Monthly Reports of the Chinese Maritime Customs on the China Trade', 28 July 1937, the figures after the first half of the year 1937 ran as follows: United States, 17.99 percent; Germany, 17.24 percent; Japan, 15.23 percent; Great Britain, 11.9 percent share on total Chinese imports.

30. For trade statistics, see: Causey, *German Policy towards China*, p. 275. Between November 1935 and October 1936, a 57 percent share of Germany's total armament export went to China (Fox, *Germany and the Far Eastern Crisis*, p. 356, note 48). Best accounts on trade relations between Nazi Germany and Kuomintang China by Ratenhof, *Chinapolitik*, pp. 405ff, and William Kirby, *Germany and Republican China*, Stanford, 1984.

31. Walsh, *German Military Mission*, p. 512.

32. Hsi-huey Liang, *The Sino-German Connection. Alexander von Falkenhausen and the Chinese*, Assen, 1978. See also Falkenhausen's private papers, which were returned to the German Military Archives, Freiburg i.Br., late in 1977.

33. Yu-shi Nieh, *Die Entwicklung des chinesisch-japanischen Konfliktes in Nordchina und die deutschen Vermittlungsbemühungen 1937–38*, Hamburg, 1970; for the relevant diplomatic documents, see Joachim Peck, *Kolonialismus ohne Kolonien. Der deutsche Imperialismus und China 1937*, Berlin (Ost), 1961; best account in English by Fox, *Germany and the Far Eastern Crisis*, pp. 251–90.

34. Hartmut Bloß, 'Die Abberufung der Beraterschaft' in Martin, *Deutsche Beraterschaft*, pp. 249–71.

35. Lincoln Li, *The Japanese Army in North China 1937–1941. Problems of Political and Economic Control*, Oxford University Press, 1975; Joyce C. Lebra, *Japan's Greater East Asia Co-Prosperity Sphere in World War II. Selected Readings and Documents*, Oxford University Press, 1975.

36. Sommer, *Deutschland und Japan*, pp. 82–102.

37. See the voluminous report by Alvin D. Coox, *Nomonhan. Japan Against Russia 1939*, 2 vols., Stanford University Press, 1985. For Germany's role in this conflict, see Bernd Martin, 'Germano-Japanese Relations after the Hitler-Stalin Pact and German Reaction to the Nippo-Soviet Rapprochement', in David W. Pike, ed., *The Opening of the Second World War*, New York and Bern, 1991, pp. 228–38.

38. Interviews author – Kuan Te-mau in Taichung/Taiwan on 31 January and 18 March 1977. Kuan Te-mau, Robert Chi, and the newly appointed Chinese military attaché, General Kuei Yung-Ch'ing, were sent to Berlin in April 1940. See also the personal account of Kuan Te-mau (in Chinese) in *Biographical Literature*, vols. 166, 167, 168. The mission failed. On 1 July 1941 the German government formally recognised Wang Ching-wei. This was a mere diplomatic gesture by Foreign Secretary von Ribbentrop in order to please the Japanese and make them attack the Soviet Union (see Bernd Martin, 'Japan and "Barbarossa"', unpublished paper, University of Waterloo, Ontario, Center for Soviet Studies, 18 May 1991). But in response to the German recognition of the Nanking puppet government, Nationalist China severed diplomatic relations with the Reich on 2 July 1941. Finally, China declared war on Germany on 9 December 1941, immediately after the Japanese attack on Pearl Harbor.

39. For the German mediation in the Sino-Japanese war in 1940 within the broader context of the Second World War, see Bernd Martin, *Friedensinitiativen und Machtpolitik im Zweiten Weltkrieg*, Düsseldorf, 1976, pp. 407–24.

40. For a more thorough discussion of Japan's domestic and foreign policies 1939–41, see: Bernd Martin, 'Japans Weltmachtstreben 1939–1941', in Oswald Hauser, ed., *Weltpolitik II 1939–1945. 14 Vorträge*, Göttingen, 1975, pp. 98–130.

41. John H. Boyle, *China and Japan at War. The Politics of Collaboration*, Stanford University Press, 1972.

42. For British-German peace feelers in summer 1940, see: Martin, *Friedensinitiativen*, pp. 234–336.

43. Sommer, *Deutschland und Japan*, pp. 426–49. For the original English text and the secret amendments, see ibid., pp. 514–6. For the Japanese side, see Gerhard Krebs, *Japans Deutschlandpolitik 1935–1941. Eine Studie zur Vorgeschichte des Pazifischen Krieges*, 2 vols., Hamburg, 1984.

44. German government circles, and even Hitler himself, dropped hints to the Japanese about the impending German attack on Soviet Russia. For the telegrams sent by the Japanese Embassy in Berlin to Tokyo in May and June 1941, see Andreas Hillgruber, 'Japan und der Fall Barbarossa', in *Wehrwissenschaftliche Rundschau*, 1968, pp. 312–36.

45. For a more detailed discussion of this, see Bernd Martin, *Deutschland und Japan im Zweiten Weltkrieg. Vom Angriff auf Pearl Harbour bis zur deutschen Kapitulation*, Göttingen, 1969, pp. 37–46.

46. Ibid., pp. 129–51 and pp. 172–4.

47. Ibid., pp. 178–99.

48. Bernd Martin, 'Verhandlungen über separate Freidensschlüsse 1942–1945', in *Militärgeschichtliche Mitteilungen*, 1976, pp. 95–113; Vojtech Mastny, 'Stalin and the Prospects of a Separate Peace in World War Two', in *American Historical Review*, 1972, pp. 1365–88.

49. On the war alliance, see chapter 10 in this volume. Most recent collection of essays on the axis Berlin-Tokyo: Gerhard Krebs and Bernd Martin, eds., *Formierung und Fall der Achse Berlin-Tokio*, München, 1994.

❧ 8 ❧

JAPAN AND GERMANY ON THE PATH TOWARDS WAR
MUTUAL INFLUENCES AND DEPENDENCIES (1930–1940)

*Japan and Germany as National-Totalitarian States:
The Reception and Mutual Influence of Ruling Techniques
and World Power Ambitions*

Contemporary witnesses of the prewar political situation in Japan, such as the American Ambassador Grew[1] or the Far East correspondent to the *Frankfurter Zeitung* Lily Abegg,[2] kept warning the Western world not to judge the Japanese policy by Western standards. The Island Empire had been forced to give up its isolation as a consequence of the treaty of friendship[3] imposed by the United States in 1853. And with Emperor Meiji's accession to the throne in 1868 the Tenno's role had changed, as a result of growing Western pressure, from one of a mere religious cult figure without any real power into one of a worldly ruler, which meant quite a revolutionary political change.[4] Nevertheless, although Japan did thus adopt Western models in the field of public life and institutions, its basic social structure remained untouched. The upper class, especially the court nobility, regarded the Meiji Restoration as an act of self-defence against the 'white' imperialist powers who had forced China into a semicolonial status. Japan's vertical social structure shaped after the family pattern[5] was a

First published in German as 'Das Deutsche Reich und Japan. Zur Rezeption und wechselseitigen Beeinflussung autoritärer Herrschaftspraktiken und spätimperialistischer Weltmachtsbestrebungen', in Eberhard Forndran et al., eds., *Inne- und Außenpolitik unter nationalsozialistischer Bedrohung. Determinanten internationaler Beziehungen in historischen Fallstudien*, Köln-Opladen, 1977, pp. 87–109. Translated by Dr Anne M. Martin.

great help in the adoption of the liberal capitalist economic system and the administrative reforms it involved. National growth, only to be achieved through a modern heavy industry ready to compete with Western standards and through a powerful army, remained the unquestioned political aim until 1945. The oligarchy, though split in rivalling family clans, strongly advocated this policy in order to maintain their status and their privileges.[6]

Therefore, the Japanese political system cannot be compared with either the mutual dependency of domestic and foreign politics – as in the United States and Western Europe – or any fascist system.[7] Nor can it be fully explained with the help of modernisation theories or by any more or less far-fetched analogy to Prussian Germany.[8] Much rather, Japan's singular development can be described as a process that to foreigners looked very dynamic and evoked not a little admiration or fear but that, basically, served the sole purpose of preserving the proper Japanese system. Yet, the 'priority of restorative social structure' meant that the conflict dating back to feudal times between the rural lower class and the small middle class on the one side and on the other side the traditional oligarchy, who made their own good use of the new economic situation, remained unresolved. Japan's economic development together with what was resented as foreign discrimination after the First World War further sharpened class antagonism, which then culminated in upheavals and social instability during the decade between the Manchurian Crisis and the outbreak of the Pacific War (1941).[9] Even if the catastrophe of unconditional surrender (1945) was not historically predetermined and, hence, can scarcely be explained by the orthodox Marxist-Leninist concept of imperialism, the Japanese oligarchy is yet to be blamed for its policy of suppression at home and aggression abroad. To the Japanese ruling élite, who were fixated on Western models, comparisons with the German development seemed only natural; and the apparent political parallels between the two countries during the 1930s induced them to conclude their unholy alliance to challenge the rest of the world. However, the only political action they eventually took in common – though at different times – was yielding to the surrender terms of the victors.

During the First World War, international relations had undergone a fundamental change due to the widening range of direct government intervention. Foreign policy decisions in Western countries were, at least partly, made in much the same way as in

Japan. No longer did the foreign offices, most of whose members stemmed from the traditional ruling classes, bear the full responsibility for international relations. Instead, in fully industrialised countries, new centres of power emerged that had their own conceptions as to foreign political aims. Moreover, in the fields of economics, technology, and transportation, new necessities had arisen – as was made obvious during the world economic crisis – that had to be taken into account in domestic politics, as well as in foreign relations.[10] The conglomerate resulting from inner social processes and international conditions equally influenced bilateral relations, as did the international order of the interwar period. Because of this complexity, evaluating the impact of any single element or process can provide some useful historical insight; it cannot, however, throw light on the whole foreign political scenery – as could be done concerning the days of the European Cabinet Wars by traditional diplomatic history and its comparatively simple pattern of 'challenge and response'.

Shortcomings in historical method together with the comparatively poor source material and scarce literature on Japan's inner development,[11] as well as misunderstandings resulting from the Western outlook,[12] should make it clear that the following attempt at analysing some of those inner political factors that left their imprint on foreign policy can be but incomplete. Trying to examine the 'soil' from which grew the German-Japanese relationship is further hampered by the fact that in any dictatorial and authoritarian system the leaders' actual range of power and influence is difficult to assess and is, in fact, quite often underestimated. Hence, it seems impossible to fully explain all of the unexpected changes of course typical of both countries' bilateral relations and foreign policies in general.[13]

Socialising the Military: Militarising the Political Leadership in Japan (1930–1936)

The unquestioned Japanese predominance in East Asia before and during the First World War was mainly based on overwhelming military victories: firstly, in 1895 during the war against China, and secondly – which caused considerable excitement in the Far East – in 1905 when for the first time a 'white' European world power was beaten by a badly underestimated 'yellow developing country' that had embarked on modernisation only one generation before. According to the constitution shaped after the Prussian model[14] and promulgated in 1889, both the navy and the army were directly responsible to the Emperor and thus could in no way be controlled by either the limited power of the Diet or by the Prime Minister, who himself – as in Imperial Germany – was not responsible to the parliament either.[15] As long as the founding fathers of the Meiji Empire avoided taking any risks by basing their policy on an alliance with Great Britain, the army more or less remained under the control of the powerful Choshu clan personified in Field Marshal Count Yamagata.[16]

However, when the founding fathers retired, which coincided roughly with the end of the Great War, the control over the military weakened considerably. Furthermore, the outcome of the First World War was resented as discriminating against the victorious Japanese. As a result, the officers' corps split into several factions, each of them making their own plans for the future either according to the venerable Japanese traditions or with respect to the total war in Europe. The navy, which in the Washington Treaties of 1922 had not been considered equal to the Anglo-Saxon sea powers, took offence and felt thrown on the defensive. The economic crisis resulting from the breakdown of the obviously oversized armaments industry and the severe cuts in the military budget during the 1920s undermined the self-confidence of the leaders of a military that was still regarded as the strongest in East Asia.[17] While the officers of the Imperial Navy, technologically and strategically orientated towards the Anglo-Saxon model, remained more or less homogeneous and hoped for a peaceful revision of the treaties, as early as 1921 a group of radicals among the army officers accompanying Crown Prince Hirohito on his visit to Germany secretly formed in Baden-Baden in Germany.[18] Most of the officers participating in this meeting had closely witnessed the war in Europe and now considered the worldwide Anglo-Saxon predominance an imminent threat to their own country. Among the leaders were Nagata Tetsuzan,[19] then military attaché to Denmark and later to become a very influential officer within the General Staff, and his classmate from War Academy, Major Tojo Hideki,[20] who was later promoted to the rank of a general and served as Prime Minister during the war.

This group was soon called the 'German faction' not only because they had met in Germany, but also because they adopted the German concept of total mobilisation.[21] What impressed them was not the weak Weimar Republic, but rather Hindenburg's economic mobilisation programme combined with Ludendorff's planning for autarchy during the World War. Since Japan possessed almost no raw materials at all, annexing Manchuria was seen as a prerequisite for establishing an effective line of defence and creating a nation in arms.[22] Moreover, since 1905 Japanese troops had been legally stationed in the southern half of Manchuria, on Chinese territory that is, and Japanese companies enjoyed special economic rights along the railway lines. This situation in Manchuria served as a welcome means of militarising the nation. Therefore, the assassination of the Manchurian warlord Chang Tso-lin in 1928 was, if not ordered, yet fully approved by the 'German Group'.[23]

However, it was not the army itself that threatened the authority of the party cabinets during the 1920s, but rather the fundamental debate on military prerogative that arose as a consequence of the London Naval Conference in 1930. The Chief of the Admiralty, Kato Kanji, in favour of unlimited naval armament modelled on the Tirpitz programme in Germany before the Great War,[24] accused the government of violating Article 11 of the Constitution that laid down the military's direct access to the Emperor.[25] In doing so, he was backed up by the opposition, the Seiyukai party which was traditionally connected with big business and, accordingly, the navy. Yet, Kato failed in his attempt to prevent the ratification of the treaty by the Privy Council. This meant that the Minister of the Navy had won a victory over the Chief of the Admiralty and Japanese inferiority at sea had once again been confirmed. Kato's resignation from office mobilised the rightist nationalists and split the Naval Officers' Corps into a pro-Western majority and a pro-German minority that was, however, to achieve considerable influence among the middle ranks. By openly interfering with politics for the first time in the politically heated atmosphere of 1930, the navy had highlighted a controversy that eventually broke out during the Manchurian Crisis. From then on, most naval officers stationed abroad were sent to Germany to study;[26] at the same time, the Japanese navy tried – in vain – to shake off its technological dependence on the United States[27] by buying technical know-how from the Reich, and in 1933 strove to improve relations with Hitler's Germany.[28]

The army had so far regarded Germany as a model in a rather vague, historical sense. Only under the impact of the Manchurian incident on foreign politics did it turn towards National Socialism. The Japanese army considered itself the 'school of the nation' and, during the 1920s, had organised the rural population and the young into paramilitary groups within the traditional village community and its hierarchical structure.[29] The impoverishment of Japanese agriculture due to the world economic crisis[30] expressed itself by politically radicalising the army officers, fifty percent of whom came from the countryside, and the masses of conscripts, most of whom were the sons of farmers.[31] The anger of the rural population directed itself against the corrupt alliance of the industrial oligarchy – the *zaibatsu* – with the political leaders. The programmes of the different officers' circles ranged from Soviet communist planned economy to fascist mass demagogy and authoritarian forms of government which, from 1933 on, resembled the German system.[32] The 'Showa Restoration' with its agrarian romanticism seemed to offer an alternative to the masses who had been morally destabilised and materially deprived by industrialisation. This programme can best be described as a national identification pattern on the basis of racial and social homogeneity.

Its irrational antimodernism was aimed at mobilising the masses. But for its claim for expansionist policy, it did not have much in common with the technocratic aims of the German Group in the General Staff. In his memoranda, Nagata, head of the Department for Economic Mobilisation since 1927, had pointed at the Manchurian raw materials as indispensable for a war which in those days seemed conceivable only against Soviet Russia.[33] Consequently, the group surrounding Nagata did most of the planning for the Mukden incident but, unlike the other army officers, it disapproved of revolutionary military dictatorship.[34] Instead of staging a coup d'état, thereby running the risk of instability and unpredictable difficulties in foreign relations, Nagata advocated a policy of gradually and legally transforming the country into a national defence state.

Likewise, the Nagata group did not hold with political murder, such as the assassination of some members of the old élites[35] by fanatical officers,[36] which brought an end to parliamentarian government in Japan. The two wings of the officers' corps were temporarily united by their common aim to form a national government independent of the political parties and by their claim for a Japanese Monroe Doctrine[37] concerning East Asia. The navy, too, by taking a large part in the battle of Shanghai in 1932[38] supported southward expansion, so that both the government and the nation declined the peace efforts of the League of Nations. Japan's leaving the League of Nations was considered tantamount to throwing off the yoke of Western interference.[39]

The leadership, however, deeply disagreed on how to bring about the militarisation of the country and, in particular, where to direct the expansion. Disapproving of the army's concept of fighting communism, the navy together with heavy industry preferred the way south, which was supported by the Tenno's counsellors and Hirohito himself. The civilian government, on the other side, most of all the *Gaimusho*, could not make up their minds between the two positions. The Foreign Office in Tokyo, however, did not completely reject the military's large-scale planning. As early as in April 1934, a spokesman of the *Gaimusho* officially announced that Japan would not tolerate any foreign interference in China[40] and thus openly challenged the Western powers. Three months later the Cabinet decided to abrogate the Washington and London Naval Treaties at the earliest possible date, i.e., in 1936.[41]

By 1934 the civilian government had already given in to the army's and the navy's demands concerning foreign politics. Yet, the question of how to reorganise the country itself remained controversial. Nagata, by now Chief of the Military Affairs Bureau – the army's political centre – vehemently stuck to his theories of establishing a defence state, but, as he depended on the support of heavy industry, rejected any change by means of violence. Thereupon, his opponents accused him of 'perverting the truly national principles'[42] and denounced his propositions – one of them concerning a professional army with modern technical equipment – as fascist and National Socialist, of all things. The skirmishes between the two wings in the army came to an end – though only for a short time – when Nagata was assassinated[43] by one of his subordinates, a singular event in the history of the modern Japanese army.

The social revolutionary officers immediately turned the murder trial into a revolutionary tribunal.[44] This was the starting point for the mutiny of the Tokyo garrison in February 1936.[45] The brutal assassination of several politicians and the rebellion of regular army units under the command of middle-ranking officers was the peak, and at the same time the turning point of the rightist offi-cers' movement. So far, the Tenno had silently approved of the inner radicalisation and the foreign policy of expansion. Now, however, with a rebellion from below, the whole traditional polit-ical system as well as the privileges of the upper class were at stake. Hence, Hirohito personally insisted on unconditional sur-render and the execution of the ringleaders. The attempt at estab-lishing a kind of 'army fascism from below' had failed.[46] Instead, in accordance with the traditional leading élite's beliefs, 'authori-tarian government from above' was imposed; delusions of national grandeur and the sacrosanct Tenno cult helped to keep the masses quiet.

The militarisation of the leadership and, from 1935 on, of all society in Japan at first sight looked very similar to the German development. Yet, the Japanese did not simply imitate German revisionist politics. Much rather, the parallels between the two countries derived from the necessity to build up a strong defence without an adequate economic and technical basis. In both coun-tries, the military tried to compensate for the deficiencies by irra-tional visions of unlimited war and a total *levée en masse*.

Racism and Foreign Relations: Japan in National Socialist Foreign Policy, 1933–1935

By now it is a generally acknowledged fact that Hitler's foreign policy was based on his racist assumptions and his ideas of the worldwide mission of the Germanic 'master race'.[47] Equally well known is the fact that Hitler personally insisted on and carried out his plan of approaching the Japanese, notwithstanding massive opposition from highly influential circles in Germany. In *Mein Kampf* he had already accorded to the Japanese the status of a 'cul-turally receptive' race, thus ranking them second only to the 'cul-turally creative' Germanic races.[48] Likewise, as early as 1924 he put down the conflict between Great Britain and Japan to the machinations of the world Jewry who, in his eyes, were out to destroy Japan as well as Germany.[49]

In Hitler's eyes the two countries were the only bulwarks against a worldwide Jewish empire, the nuclei of which he spotted in what he called the 'Bolshevist-Jewish subhuman species' and the 'Western-Jewish plutocracy'. No doubt, Hitler, who had always admired the fighting spirit of the Japanese, was deeply impressed with the success of the Imperial Army in Manchuria.[50] On the one hand, the German government had voted with the League of Nations for the Lytton-Report, i.e., for rebuking the Japanese;[51] on the other hand, from a geopolitical or anticommunist point of view, the Japanese invasion of Northern China seemed to make sense not only to Hitler himself, but also to the National Socialists. Alfred Rosenberg, who was considered the ideological head of the 'movement', had pointed in his writings to the Asians as potential allies to stamp out the 'Bolshevist fire'.[52] The same view was held among politically minded German academics, especially those who accepted the then topical geopolitical theory that Japanese aggression was veiled as a geostrategic necessity,[53] all the more so since from 1931 onwards, Japan pretended, in her propaganda, to defend East Asia against the tide of communist infiltration. To the geopolitical point of view, an opportunity now presented itself, for the first time since the Russian Revolution, to form a Eurasian block across Russia – once Russia was 'liberated' from communism – and, at the same time, to break the supremacy of the Anglo-Saxon sea powers. Thus, a reorientation of the German Far Eastern policy towards Japan seemed to suggest itself. What stood in the way of a rapprochement to the former victorious power – with whom the Weimar Republic had been on politely distant terms – were the National Socialists' racial doctrines on 'Aryans' and 'Non-Aryans', as well as the massive interests of German industrialists and armament producers in China, together with the traditionally pro-Chinese leanings of the *Wilhelmstraße* and the German public in general.

German foreign policies – especially with respect to the two Asian countries 'free' from Jews – were hampered far more by the National Socialists' racial politics than by the fact of Hitler's dictatorship.[54] The Japanese and the Chinese alike had deeply resented the discrimination expressed at the Versailles Peace Conference. There, with respect to their own colonies, the Western powers had denied racial equality to the Chinese and the Japanese, and the restrictive immigration laws of the British Commonwealth and California[55] further aggravated the discrimination. The National Socialist racial doctrine by far exceeded the measures taken by the Anglo-Saxon powers and, consequently, after Hitler's seizure of power, caused Asian diplomats to intervene in

Berlin. At the same time, trade with China decreased at once because of the unresolved racial issue.[56] The German *Reichswehr* had found in China a field adequate to the one it had lost in Soviet Russia for testing new weapons and tactics and, furthermore, was under obligation to the deliverers of the raw materials essential for armament production.[57] The *Reichswehr* objected to the official race definition of the Party, as did the industries who were interested in business with China, the Foreign Office, and even the Ministry of the Interior.[58]

Official circles in Japan – except for some pro-German groups within the navy – kept their distance from National Socialism. If Hitler wanted to gain Japanese support against the Soviet Union – which in 1933 he had already asserted to the newly appointed ambassador to Tokyo, von Dirksen,[59] and to Rosenberg and Ribbentrop, his then closest advisers on foreign policies[60] – the race question had to be resolved first. The Japanese mistrust was not to be overcome by mere friendly gestures, such as a formal reception for the president of the upper house of the Japanese Diet[61] or by giving an interview to the Japanese press[62] and admonishing the German press to report in a pro-Japanese way.[63] In order to set aside the race question for the time being and to outmanoeuvre the pro-Chinese attitude of the government, Hitler, in his next move, planned – with the help of Party circles and the (as yet) pro-National Socialist tycoon Fritz Thyssen – to create a *fait accompli* by officially recognising Manchuria and increasing trade relations with the Japanese puppet state, Manchukuo. This scheme, too, failed because of the China lobby's united resistance.[64] Even the Ambassador to Tokyo, von Dirksen,[65] despite his strong Aryan leanings could not help repeatedly informing Berlin of the negative response to National Socialism in Japan.[66] All of the German government's official statements defining the race question as a merely inner German problem were in vain.[67] An inquiry by the Foreign Office concerning the Japanese attitude towards 'new' Germany produced rather a meagre result: so far the National Socialist movement remained alien to the Japanese.[68]

The Foreign Office had repeatedly tried to define the term of Non-Aryan in such a way that it sounded acceptable to Asian ears in particular. The Party, however, to whom any compromise seemed unthinkable, stubbornly opposed all suggestions to promote the Japanese to 'honorary Aryans', as it were. Yet, for practical reasons, even the Party eventually had to consent to the

Ministry of the Interior's proposal to henceforward classify only the Jewish as Non-Aryan.[69] The Nuremberg race laws proclaimed on 13 September 1935 used the very same definition, thus – at least on the surface – removing the main obstacle to Hitler's intended rapprochement with Japan.

Nonetheless, the 'Führer's' ambivalent attitude towards the 'yellows' remained unchanged. Hitler was ready to overlook racial factors while he was trying to win the Japanese over for a coalition; but whenever it came to dealing with concrete questions to be discussed among equal partners – e.g., during the war alliance – he backed out. To him, the Aryan 'master race' should much rather meet its doom heroically than conclude a contemptible blood alliance with the 'racially inferior yellows'. In decisive moments Hitler – quite unlike those surrounding him – always sacrificed tactics to dogmatism.[70]

Foreign Policy as an Instrument of Military Strategy: The Anti-Comintern Pact, 1936

Militarising the Japanese political leadership as a step towards total mobilisation was an equally important precondition for the rapprochement, as was the superficially resolved race question. However, both factors – the internal political development in Japan, and the National Socialist policy concerning Japan – cannot be directly connected with the preliminary talks and the conclusion of the Anti-Comintern Pact. The complex international system, the specific foreign political situation of the two countries, and the competence and, not least of all, conceptions of the individual participants must be taken into account as well.[71]

Despite the pro-German attitude of the Japanese navy, it was Hitler who took the first step towards closer relations. Fighting communism in Germany implied giving up the traditionally pro-Russian policy of the Weimar Republic and, at the same time, shifting the foreign trade relations that had existed so far between Germany and the Soviet Union. The Soviet government itself had reacted to the clearly pro-Western policy of the Brüning and Papen presidential governments[72] by approaching its pre-war ally France.[73] After Japan quit the collective security system of Versailles, Soviet Russia turned to the League of Nations, which it had formerly attacked,[74] and even eventually took up diplomatic relations with the United States.[75] Under the trauma of encirclement, the Soviet politicians suspected secret German-Japanese talks long before anybody else was thinking of them.[76]

Not only Soviet propaganda, but also the Western media exaggerated the apparent parallels between Germany and Japan and drew erroneous conclusions as to secretly existing treaties threatening the world order.[77] Overestimating any kind of conceivable alliance between the two 'have-nots' did not only result from both their authoritarian government systems and revisionist programmes in foreign politics. What made the German-Japanese rapprochement seem equally, if not more, dangerous to Great Britain and the United States was the threat that it might impose on their own newly established economic spheres of influence.[78] To the as yet merely rhetorical proclamations of German-Japanese unity, the governments in London and Washington reacted in a rather extreme way, mingling their own national interests with postimperialist conceptions of a new world order.

Sending Eugen Ott, a high-ranking officer of the Ministry of Defence, to Japan in the spring of 1933 was nothing but a precaution to protect Colonel Ott who had compromised himself by his talks with the National Socialists before their seizure of power.[79] He was let in on the treaty only after the decision had been finalized in Berlin.[80] Likewise, appointing Colonel Oshima, a known Germanophile, as Japanese military attaché to Berlin[81] did not serve the purpose of preparing the ground for talks, but was a result of the army's claiming of as many attaché posts as the navy. Neither Oshima nor even less Ott can be regarded as the spiritual architects of a 'worldwide conspiracy'; instead, they both served merely as tools to carry it out. Nor did the Foreign Offices in Berlin and Tokyo take any part in the preliminary talks; both were known to strongly oppose a German-Japanese rapprochement and were, consequently, left out on purpose.

The traditional leading élites of the Reich turned a deaf ear to Hitler's ideas of an alliance with Japan. For fear of risking their loyalty, the 'Führer' could not dictatorially impose his views on them. He, therefore, turned to Ribbentrop and his office, which had been created especially for the purpose of bypassing the traditional political establishment. Starting his talks with the Japanese, Ribbentrop used Friedrich-Wilhelm Hack,[82] an arms broker who was engaged in trade with the Japanese navy, to approach

Admiral Yamamoto, who was then staying in London. The Admiral did not belong to the pro-German navy faction, and in any case, his plan of visiting Berlin was thwarted by the Japanese diplomacy.[83] The Imperial Navy, on the whole, stuck to its Anglo-Saxon orientation and showed little interest in talks with the Germans.

It is probable that the navy's rival, the Imperial Army, got to know about those failed contacts and, for its part, picked up the threads, all the more so, since friendship with Germany seemed useful in two ways: it could help to neutralise the German influence in China, and it might mean gaining an ally against the Soviet Union. Consequently, in September 1935 Military Attaché Oshima addressed Hack for the first time and, after Ribbentrop had been consulted, on the 4 October 1935 presented a first, handwritten draft of the treaty.[84] Then Admiral Canaris and the German Minister of War Blomberg were taken into confidence. Canaris wholly agreed to the treaty that originally comprised Great Britain, the Netherlands, Germany, Poland, and Japan; he did so not so much as Head of the Military Intelligence Service, but as a member of the navy which could achieve worldwide influence only in an alliance with other sea powers. Blomberg, on the other hand, insisted on including China.[85]

The Japanese had doubts only about Poland as a partner, but tried hard to integrate China and, therefore, asked Ribbentrop for Germany to act as an intermediary.[86] The Chiang Kai-shek regime, too, repeatedly showed its interest in German mediation.[87] Thus, wooed by both Asian countries, the political influence of the Reich in East Asia by the end of 1935 by far exceeded that of the Western powers. Instead of realising such a promising alliance between Germany, China, and Japan, Hitler expressly forbade German mediation in East Asia[88] and, as early as on 27 November 1935, decided to conclude only a German-Japanese treaty.[89] In doing so, the German dictator for the first time revealed the merely strategic aim he pursued by this alliance. He just wanted to make sure of the Japanese Empire temporarily supporting the Nordic-Aryan race on its way to worldwide predominance. The decision concerning German Far Eastern policy was made by a single person – Hitler – more or less regardless of the concepts of the traditional centres of political and economic power. Hitler's dictatorial decision met with considerable German and Japanese opposition, which – together with the change in world politics – explains the delay of almost one year until the treaty was finally signed in Berlin on 25 November 1936. In Hitler's eyes, the agreement – meaningless anyway because of its secret amendments[90] – was nothing more than a propaganda means to let the world know about National Socialist Germany's claim to worldwide power. The Japanese, especially the army, interpreted the pact as an anti-Soviet defence alliance that would enable Japan to strengthen her position in Manchuria and Northern China and would foster turning the country itself into a 'nation in arms'.[91] Both countries connected differing and actually incompatible expectations with the Anti-Comintern Pact. Contrary to the suspicions of the Western powers and the Soviet Union, it was a temporary stratagem that had sprung from military thinking much rather than being the first step on the way to a solid military alliance.

Authoritarian Structures and Military Aggression: The Mobilisation of Japanese Society, 1935–1940

In May 1934 the German ambassador, in his report on nationalist and socialist-communist movements in Japan, analysed the different political groups and came to the conclusion that the common ideological classifications of 'rightist' and 'leftist' were completely mixed up. 'What is missing', he wrote, 'is an outstanding personality who would tear down the barriers and melt the different factions and groups into one mainstream'.[92] This man could obviously not be chosen by a plebiscite but, in Japan, had to be the godlike Tenno. After parliamentarian government had been forcibly ended and industry had been intimidated, nationalist army officers set to work on the central issue of the Showa Restoration programme: depriving the Tenno of his 'evil counsellors' and pushing him into the role of a mere sacramental cult figure.[93] Because of his sacrosanct position, which had been laid down in the constitution, the Emperor had always been compelled to 'rule through the curtain'.[94] Now he was to be prevented from making political decisions at all, so that in case of criticism the rivalling armed forces could always hide behind the lofty institution of the monarchy. For officially, all political decisions were made and proclaimed in the Tenno's name, which meant that disobedience or even the slightest criticism could be regarded as *lèse-majesté* and be drastically punished.

The dispute between court and army over the question of how to change the structure of the Japanese state was of decisive importance for the interior development of the country. Far from functioning as a puppet, Emperor Hirohito managed to defend the palace as a bulwark against 'fascism from below' as well as 'army dictatorship from above'.[95] Joining with the traditional élites and meeting the wishes of the industry and the navy, the Tenno succeeded in directing southward the expansion initiated by the army in Manchuria.[96] The army, after trying in vain to impose its concepts on the court, mobilised society outside the palace walls.

After orthodox communist organisations had been smashed with the help of the Peace Laws, the most dangerous adversaries that remained by the end of the 1920s[97] were liberal, Western-orientated intellectuals who might stir up criticism, some of them openly confronting the usurped power of the military. The army particularly tried to turn to its own advantage the influence of some renowned university professors of constitutional and international law, whose widely known reasoning sprang from Western or fascist sources. The chairholder of international law at Tokyo Imperial University – the most famous university of the country – on the basis of Kelsen's work on 'Pure Law' (*Reine Rechtslehre*) criticised the actions of the army in Manchuria and their legal camouflage.[98] His colleague, the most famous professor of international law, Minobe Tatsukichi, who for his merits had been awarded a seat in the upper house by the Emperor himself, attacked a memorandum by the technocrat Nagata; realising the concepts of the memorandum, Minobe argued, would most certainly lead to war against the Western powers and risk the security of the Empire.[99]

What might look like a scholarly dispute at first sight[100] was at once turned into a propaganda campaign under the slogan of 'Clarifying the National Policy', and Minobe's so far unquestioned teachings on the Japanese constitution were damned as dangerous heresies.[101]

According to the liberal propositions of Ito Hirobumi, the creator of the modern Japanese constitution of 1889, Minobe had integrated the Emperor into the constitution as an organ of the state. The military, on the contrary, in order to reinforce their dictatorial ambitions, demanded that the Tenno be placed above the written constitution as a sacrosanct person. The debate was opened by conservative members of the upper house in February 1935 and induced a retired general to indict Minobe for *lèse-majesté*.[102] Minobe was finally outmanoeuvred by a campaign of the army veterans' union demanding the government to officially distance itself from his teachings and to forbid his books.[103] From then on the Tenno was placed in a position *supra leges*. By this manipulated campaign, that according to a report of the Tokyo Police Bureau caught the public like 'wildfire', the Western liberal element was weeded out in the universities and in the media.[104] Though shaken by the February Incident, the army had succeeded in bringing public opinion into line. In the upper house, Prime Minister Hirota, who like most politicians and the Tenno himself still adhered to Minobe's theories,[105] was for the first time presented with Hitler as a model of 'great force of decision, of enormous will power, and of untiring effort'. Hitler, it was hinted, had long since expelled the Jewish liberal scholars from Germany.[106] From now on, the doctrines of the German professor of international law, Carl Schmitt, especially his 'Law of the European Hemisphere' (*Völkerrecht des europäischen Großraums*) were generally adopted in Japan and, like in Germany, helped to legalise violence.[107]

After eliminating the opposition by the summer of 1936, both the navy and the army could lay open their war aims in their political memoranda and strategical expertises: the navy propagated southward advance and rearmament in order to confront the American sea power from a superior position.[108] The army, in accordance with the late Nagata's views, demanded the totalitarian state in arms where there would be no room for either political parties or special economic interests.[109] The programme of 'Fundamental Principles of National Policy'[110] that was adopted by the Five Ministers' Conference[111] on 7 August 1936 was generally looked upon as the blueprint of preparations for war. Its demands were expressed in comparatively moderate terms, but as to foreign politics clearly resulted from the aims of the navy. While the army was busy working at internal war preparations and, especially after the Anti-Comintern Pact had been concluded, frequently used the German 'Führer-State' as a model, the navy was planning its expansion towards Southeast Asia with its lucrative sources of raw materials.

The Hirota government finally legalised the political conformity brought about by the army. Two laws were passed, both of them influenced by the German practices to direct public opinion and eliminate political opposition, both of them, however, adapting their contents to the specific Japanese situation. Formal establishment of a ministry of propaganda was postponed until later (1940); in its stead, an information office of the cabinet[112] took care of censoring in advance all radio broadcasts and of postcensorship of the press.[113] The other law 'for the protection against, and control of persons harbouring dangerous thoughts'[114] offered to the police a means of violating the individual's civil rights and of severely restricting the journalists' freedom of speech. Any offence against this law was punished by protective custody. But instead of being sentenced to forced labour in inhuman concentration camps like in Germany, the Japanese delinquents, for the purpose of 'moral betterment', were sent to traditional institutions such as shrines or hospitals, there to serve their time.[115] This kind of compulsory reintegration into Japanese society usually lasted two years, which was quite enough to make those liberal or even communist intellectuals abjure their dangerous thoughts[116] and, once returned to the large Japanese family, fight for their Emperor and their country on the battlefield.

Some opposition, however, was left among intellectuals and, in particular, among the agrarian proletariat whose situation had not improved at all after the army had taken control of domestic politics. This became obvious in the 1937 elections – the last before the outbreak of war – when the 'Social Mass Party' doubled its votes.[117] Such an unexpected success of the 'Left' was considered 'a serious warning' in a report by the German Embassy,[118] all the more so since the winner, the Minseito Party, had clearly revealed its antagonism against 'military fascism'. What was needed was another international conflict like the Manchurian Crisis that would unite the country, including the opposition, in an upsurge of nationalist emotions. Consequently, the army in July 1937 widened one of the usual local skirmishes in Northern China[119] into a 'conflict' that was supposed to achieve autonomy for Northern China after the model of Manchukuo.

The new government that had been in office for one month under Prime Minister Konoe, a protégé of the court, did next to nothing to end the war by political means. Unlike during the Manchurian Crisis, the political fronts in Tokyo changed sides.

The Imperial Army, after demonstrating its power, was in favour of what it called a 'Bismarck Peace', a mild peace treaty, and of mediation by the German government.[120] Konoe, on the other hand, advocated a prolonged war on the Asian continent, which would neutralise the politically restless officers on the battlefield and enable the civilian government to work out its expansion programme of a 'New Order of East Asia'.[121] This was to be established not only against the strong position of the Soviet Union in the Far East, but against the Western powers as well. Therefore, the German mediation failed, not because of the intransigence of the military, but because of the Japanese politicians' exorbitant demands. Chiang Kai-shek was even prepared to renounce Chinese claims on Manchuria, provided peace was guaranteed by third powers.[122]

Building up a war economy after the German model in the First World War, together with Five Year Plans to foster special branches important for war (such as synthetic petrol production)[123] and the mobilisation laws[124] passed unanimously by the Diet in April 1938, gave the state almost complete control over the nation.

Only the questions regarding political parties and bureaucracy were to remain unsolved. Much as Konoe shared the demands of the army and the navy to abolish political parties, which were considered outdated, and to replace them with a single mass movement, he shrank back from military dictatorship. As a protégé of the court, the upper house, and of 'political capitalism',[125] the Prime Minister objected to suspending the Meiji Constitution. Instead, he preferred that the existing parties be combined into one. For the most part, it was this dispute about the constitution that in 1939 brought down the Konoe cabinet which, under the cover of national policy, had served the interests of the traditional oligarchy.[126] Only at his next attempt, after forming his second cabinet in July 1940, did Konoe succeed in solving the problem of political parties in his way by overriding the radical reformers whose model was the German National Socialist Party.[127] On 12 October 1940 an 'Imperial Rule Assistance Organisation' was founded with Konoe at its head. After the parties had dissolved themselves, Konoe's new institution gathered the members of parliament into one seemingly uniform organisation. However, Konoe did not succeed in tearing down the traditional party barriers nor in ending the rivalries among their different factions. Much to the regret of the German Embassy, he made a clear distinction in a public statement between his organisation, under the slogan 'one sovereign – one people', and the plebiscitarian mass movements in Italy and Germany.[128]

Neither the National Socialists nor the authoritarian Japanese leaders managed to integrate the bureaucracy, which through performing the reforms from above had in both countries achieved an indispensable position of its own.[129] Nor could the two systems, both of which were, to a large extent, the products of a strong bureaucracy, dispense with the support of their traditional civil servants, much as they tried to create new administrative institutions.[130] The Japanese bureaucracy, shaped after the Prussian model, successfully counteracted any attempt of the military to usurp civil competence. In October 1939 the Abe cabinet tried to establish a new Ministry of Foreign Trade to be controlled by the army. At once, 130 civil servants of the Foreign Office resigned, which forced the cabinet to cancel its decision.[131] Later on, during the Pacific War, the military imposed the institution of a 'Greater East Asia Ministry'. This, too, generated protests from the administration, and Foreign Minister Togo resigned.[132] In Japan, neither the bureaucracy nor the court were to be brought into line until 1945. Mobilising the people proved much easier for the military radicals. All that needed doing was the perversion of traditional moral values for the purpose of total war. Its aims, however, were fixed by the traditional oligarchy, i.e., the court nobles, industrial circles, some navy groups, and most of the civilian politicians.

Declamations in the Face of a Dead End: The Tripartite Pact of 1940

The mobilisation of the Japanese nation is not to be connected with a military alliance with Germany and in fact did not play any part in the futile talks about such a treaty in 1938–39.[133] On the way to war, Japan stuck to her own policy of confronting Great Britain and the United States over the China conflict, rather than forming an alliance with the European Axis powers. Hitler, too, ruthlessly pursued his own interests. His concluding the Nazi-Soviet Pact of Non-Aggression came as a surprise to the Japanese, who regarded it as a contradiction to the Anti-Comintern Pact. It showed that

Hitler was quite capable of joining his worst domestic enemy – the communists – when it came to pursuing his international political aims. While Foreign Minister Ribbentrop was advocating a Eurasian continental block which would include the Soviet Union and, in the long run, be directed against Anglo-Saxon supremacy, Hitler regarded the pact, like all other international treaties, merely as a temporary alliance to serve his own purposes.[134]

The Japanese government took offence at the German move and looked for a means of coming to terms with the Western powers. But its total domestic mobilisation, as well as its aggression against China, blocked the road back into the liberal Western camp. Instead, the *blitz* victories of the German *Wehrmacht*[135] renewed the army's admiration of the German model. When the Netherlands and France surrendered leaving their colonial possessions in Southeast Asia unprotected, the second Konoe cabinet decided to reapproach Germany.[136] What enforced the renewed rapprochement was not so much domestic pressure and the war aims of the navy or the army, but much more the European theatre of war and the impact that it had on the political situation in Southeast Asia.[137] In order not to miss her chance at taking part in those worldwide changes, Japan took the opportunity that offered itself in the politically open situation in Southeast Asia to win back her formerly unquestioned predominance. The political instability of those colonies in the summer of 1940 seemed to coincide luckily with the navy's war aims in exactly those regions. And it made the rapprochement with Nazi Germany easier to the traditional Japanese leaders who kept their doubts about German domestic policies and, from their own racist point of view, considered the 'Yamato Race' and its historical mission[138] superior to the 'white', that is to say inferior, Germans.

Hitler ignored the Japanese approaches and spoke of the Japanese as mere opportunists ('Johnny Come-Latelies').[139] After his victory over France, he was hoping for Great Britain to give in. Together with England, worldwide 'white' predominance might have been established even against the massive interests of the 'yellow' Japanese.[140] Only the failure of the Battle of Britain and the American engagement in favour of the British Isles made Hitler fall back on the 'world political triangle' between Rome, Berlin, and Tokyo – his Foreign Minister Ribbentrop's long cherished idea – that was, at least temporarily, to integrate the Soviet Union into a worldwide anti-British front.[141] When his *blitz* strategy came to a momentary standstill, Hitler fell back on diplomatic means. In no time a 'preventive defence alliance'[142] was drawn up and eventually concluded on 27 September 1940. However, with its secret amendments undermining its contents, the alliance was as hollow as the Anti-Comintern Pact had been. A mere declaration of power, the pact was meant to prevent the United States from a two-ocean war, to isolate Great Britain, and to make Russia join the hazardous tripartite powers.

The Japanese expected the alliance to ease the tensions with the Soviet Union and to force the United States to disengage in Eastern Asia.[143] Yet neither the German nor the Japanese hopes were fulfilled: the Soviet Union insisted on being considered an equal partner. Hitler refused and, after Molotov's visit to Berlin in November 1940, returned to his original plan of an anti-Bolshevist war of annihilation.[144] The Japanese were supposed to take a defence stance during this campaign in the East, i.e., they were to keep the Anglo-Saxon powers from intervening.[145] However, the Western powers, particularly the United States, felt provoked by the tripartite conspiracy of the three 'have-not' countries and from now on openly sought confrontation with the totalitarian nations.[146]

Within a world dominated by Anglo-American liberal capitalism, it was partly a matter of course for the two authoritarian countries to link arms. Because of their different historical roots, social structures in both countries obviously differed; but Germany and Japan did resemble each other in their specific development towards domestic repression and unlimited aggression abroad. It is difficult, if not impossible, to trace the connections between the centres of domestic political power, which in both countries militarised society and created a nation in arms, and the decisions of those in charge of foreign politics. For obvious reasons, the incapability of cooperation between the two countries was predetermined, as was the collapse of the two societies based on premodern norms. In the liberal democratic and capitalist countries of the West, political issues ranked second to economic ones. On the other hand, in authoritarian interventionist states, economic and individual interests had to submit under the common good of national defence. As long as both camps were unequal in political and industrial strength, two such incompatible systems could not peacefully coexist. Certainly, Hitler's personal impact before and during the war is not to be underestimated. But, to a certain extent, Hitler's radical programme as well as the

Japanese oligarchy's concepts of world domination also were an answer to the supremacy of the Anglo-Saxon powers. British and American world hegemony, often asserted in a lofty and arrogant way, was resented as discrimination by the three 'have-nots'. The sociohistoric interpretation[147] – that unconditional surrender was necessary for Japan as well as for Germany to open up their way into the Western world – still deserves some credit. Yet, what with social inequality and instability in Britain and the United States, let alone the medium powers' growing aspirations for greater independence from American predominance, one may entertain doubts as to what is really meant by the term of 'Western world' today.

Notes

1. *Foreign Relations of the United States, Diplomatic Papers (FRUS)* Vol. V, The Far East, Washington 1956. Report from 3 November 1941.

2. Lily Abegg, *Yamato. Der Sendungsglaube des japanischen Volkes*, Frankfurt a. M., 1936, and, by the same author, *Chinas Erneuerung. Der Raum als Waffe*, Frankfurt a. M., 1940. Furthermore, see her excellent analysis of January 1938, to be found in the Political Archives (*PA*) of the German Foreign Office (*AA*) in Bonn, Büro Unterstaatssekretär, Politische Beziehungen Japans zu Deutschland: Report German Embassy Hankow, No. 65, 31 January 1938.

3. Bernd Martin, 'Aggressionspolitik als Mobilisierungsfaktor: Der militärische und wirtschaftliche Imperialismus Japans 1931–1941', in Friedrich Forstmeier and Hans-Erich Volkmann, eds., *Wirtschaft und Rüstung am Vorabend des Zweiten Weltkrieges*, Düsseldorf, 1975, p. 222.

4. Paul Akamatsu, *Meiji 1868, Revolution and Counter-Revolution in Japan*, New York, 1972; Joseph Pittau, *Political Thought in Early Meiji Japan 1868–1889*, Harvard University Press, 1967; Kenneth B. Pyle, *The New Generation in Meiji Japan. Problems of Cultural Identity 1885–1895*, Stanford University Press, 1969.

5. Standard works for analysing Japanese society of the interwar period: Kazuko Tsurumi, *Social Change and the Individual. Japan before and after Defeat in World War Two*, Princeton University Press, 1970, and Thomas R. H. Havens, *Farm and Nation in Modern Japan. Agrarian Nationalism, 1870–1940*, Princeton University Press, 1974; Richard J. Smethurst, *A Social Basis for Prewar Japanese Militarism. The Army and the Rural Community*, University of California Press, 1974.

6. See Bernd Martin, 'Japans Weltmachtstreben 1939–1941', in: Oswald Hauser, ed., *Weltpolitik II, 1939–1945. 14 Vorträge*, Göttingen, 1975, pp. 100ff.

7. For the validity of analysis of fascism theories as to the Japanese development see chapter 6, 'Three Forms of Fascism: Japan – Italy – Germany', in this volume.

8. For modernisation theory, see Hans-Ulrich Wehler, *Modernisierungstheorie und Geschichte*, Göttingen, 1975; Barrington Moore, *Social Origins of Dictatorship and Democracy. Lord and Peasant in the Making of the Modern World*, Harmondsworth, 1969, pp. 228–313; David S. Landes, 'Die Industrialisierung in Japan und Europa. Ein Vergleich' in: Wolfram Fischer, ed., *Wirtschafts- und sozialgeschichtliche Probleme der frühen Industrialisierung*, Berlin, 1968, pp. 29–117; Reinhard Bendix, 'Preconditions of Development: A Comparison of Japan and Germany' in: Bendix, *Nation Building and Citizenship*, New York, 1968. Wehler's summary remains somewhat incomplete since even in its bibliography and annotations Japan is almost not mentioned at all. Moore and Landes are not very convincing. Bendix succeeds in assessing the historical differences.

9. For economic development, see Martin, 'Aggressionspolitik'.

10. For the following, as with the first paragraph ('Socialising the Military'), I will rely on and transfer to the situation in Japan the methodological approach of Michael Geyer, *Aufrüstung oder Sicherheit? – Die Reichswehr in der Krise der Machtpolitik 1924–1936*, Wiesbaden, 1980. James B. Crowley, despite his apologetic tendency, gets closest to Geyer's approach. See James B. Crowley, *Japan's Quest for Autonomy. National Security and Foreign Policy 1930–1938*, Princeton University Press, 1966.

11. Between the proclamation of the armistice (15 August 1945) and the official signing of the surrender document (2 September 1945), Japanese officials had more than two weeks to systematically destroy their files. (The author's interview on 13 August 1969 in Tokyo with Nishiura Susumu, Colonel ret., head of the historical archives of the Japanese army.) In James William Morley, ed., *Japan's Foreign Policy 1868–1941. A Research Guide*, Columbia University Press, 1974, p. 115, the lack of profound Japanese studies on militarism in Japan is regretted. For Japanese research into contemporary history, see Martin Broszat, 'Zeitgeschichte in Japan' in: *Vierteljahrshefte für Zeitgeschichte*, (1974), pp. 287–98, which does not offer much insight either.

12. For a rather well-balanced view, see Morley, *Japan's Foreign Policy*, and, extremely rewarding, Dorothy Borg and Shumpei Okamoto, eds., *Pearl Harbor as History. Japanese-American Relations 1931–1941*, Columbia University Press, 1973.

13. For the bilateral relationship and the background of international relations, see Bernd Martin, 'Die deutsch-japanischen Beziehungen während des Dritten Reiches', in Manfred Funke, ed., *Studien zur Außenpolitik Hitler-Deutschlands*, Düsseldorf, 1976.

14. See George Akita, *Foundations of Constitutional Government in Modern Japan 1868–1900*, Cambridge, Mass., 1967; and Johannes Siemes, *Hermann Roesler and the Making of the Meiji State*, Tokyo, 1968.

15. See the standard work based mainly on the documents of the Tokyo war tribunal, Yale Candee Maxon, *Control of Japanese Foreign Policy. A Study of Civil-Military Rivalry 1930–1945*, University of California Press, 1957. Reprint Westport, Conn., 1973.

16. Albert M. Craig, *Choshu in the Meiji Restoration*, Cambridge, Mass., 1961; Roger F. Hackett, *Yamagata Aritomo in the Rise of Modern Japan 1838–1922*, Cambridge, Mass., 1971.

17. For the 'Taisho period' (1912–1925), see Bernard Silberman and H. D. Harootunian, *Japan in Crisis. Essays on Taisho Democracy*, Princeton University Press, 1974; for the international situation, see Akira Iriye, *After Imperialism: The Search for a New Order in the Far East 1921–1931*, Harvard University Press, 1965.

18. Not always reliable: David Bergamini, *Japan's Imperial Conspiracy*, New York, 1971, pp. 322ff; and Ben-Ami Shillony, *Revolt in Japan. The Young Officers and the February 26, 1932 Incident*, Princeton University Press, 1973, pp. 43f.

19. Nagata Tetsuzan, 1884–1935, in 1904 graduated from the Military Academy (where he took his officer's training), in 1911 General Staff Officer, in 1913 Language Officer in Germany (which means he must have spoken Germany fluently), in 1915 Language Officer in Denmark, in 1921 Military Attaché to Sweden, from 1923 on member of the Army General Staff in Tokyo.

20. Tojo Hideki, 1884–1948 (he was hanged), in 1919 was stationed with the Swiss army, in 1921 with the German army at Leipzig.

21. See Crowley, *Japan's Quest*, pp. 202ff. Besides Nagata, this group included Tojo, Umezu (Yoshijiro, in 1944 Chief of the General Staff), Suzuki (Teiichi, in 1941 Chief of the Cabinet Planning Board), Yamashita (Tomoyuki, General of the army, in 1941–42 Commander in Chief of the campaigns in Malaya and in 1944–45 on the Philippines), Okamura (Neiji, in 1944 Supreme Commander in China).

22. See Crowley, *Japan's Quest*, pp. 88 and 113.

23. See Gravan McCormack, *Chang Tso-lin in Northeast China, 1911–1928. China, Japan and the Manchurian Idea*, Stanford University Press, 1977.

24. See Borg/Okamoto, *Pearl Harbor*, pp. 227ff, and Crowley, *Japan's Quest*, pp. 52ff.

25. See Crowley, *Japan's Quest*, pp. 66ff.

26. See Borg/Okamoto, *Pearl Harbor*, p. 229. This aim was pursued especially by Kojima Hideo, who later was naval attaché to Berlin (from 1936 to 1938, and again in 1944 to 1945).

27. PA, Personalien japanischer Militärpersonen: Telegram AA – Embassy Tokyo, 27 August 1932. With the help of the German export tradesman Dr. Friedrich-Wilhelm Hack, the Japanese Admiral Komaki bought some complete aircraft from the German firm Heinkel.

28. PA, Innenpolitik Japan: Unsigned memorandum of a conversation with the Japanese Naval Attaché Yendo and his personal secretary Sakai on 4 October 1933.

29. See the excellent survey by Smethurst, *Social Basis*.

30. See Martin, 'Aggressionspolitik', p. 229.

31. See Shillony, *Revolt in Japan*, p. 22; and PA, Innenpolitik Japan: Report German Embassy, Journal No. 867, 3 March 1936, p. 6.

32. For editions of source material, see Tsunoda Ryusaku and Wm Theodore de Bary, eds., *Sources of Japanese Tradition*, New York, 1961, pp. 760ff; and Joyce C. Lebra, ed., *Japan's Greater East Asia Co-Prosperity Sphere in World War Two. Selected Readings and Documents*, Oxford University Press, 1975.

33. See Crowley, *Japan's Quest*, p. 88, studies on a 'Plan for General Mobilisation' and on a 'National Defence State'.

34. See Crowley, *Japan's Quest*, pp. 100ff and pp. 132ff.

35. See Martin, 'Die deutsch-japanischen Beziehungen', note 13.

36. PA, Innenpolitik Japan: Report German Embassy, Journal No. 1651, 23 May 1932.

37. PA, Innenpolitik Japan: 'Notes on the military movement in Japan' by Michelsen, addressed to State Secretary von Bülow, on 24 May 1932.

38. Local skirmishes were escalated into undeclared war by Admiral Shiozawa, Commander of the Japanese navy troops. See Crowley, *Japan's Quest*, p. 160.

39. See Bergamini, *Imperial Conspiracy*, pp. 516ff; and John Fox, *The Formulation of Germany's Far Eastern Policy*, Phil. diss., London School of Economics and Political Science, 1972, p. 41. Before the decisive vote in Geneva took place, the leader of the Japanese delegation, Matusoka Yosuke, stayed in Berlin from 3 March to 6 March in order to promote German economic investment in Manchuria and to influence the German attitude at the Geneva conference. Nevertheless, the German delegate voted against the Japanese aggression in China.

40. See Borg/Okamoto, *Pearl Harbor*, pp. 135ff. The so-called 'Amau-Declaration', named after the press officer of the Japanese Foreign Ministry, was issued on 17 April 1934. Also see PA, Japan. Faszismus: Report German Embassy, 11 May 1934, Journal No. 1549 II on 'Communist and nationalist movements in Japan'.

41. See Crowley, *Japan's Quest*, p. 199: Decision taken by the Okada Cabinet on 14 July 1934.

42. See Crowley, *Japan's Quest*, p. 265.

43. See Bergamini, *Imperial Conspiracy*, pp. 613ff. (12 August 1935). For the official version given by Military Attaché Oshima in Germany, see PA, Ministerien Japan: Special bulletin issued by the German-Japanese Society on 13 August 1935.

44. PA, Innenpolitik Japan: Report German Embassy Tokyo Journal No. 867, 3 March, 1936: 'Causes and effects of the Tokyo mutiny of 26 to 29 February 1936'.

45. Ibid., and, most detailed, Shillony, *Revolt in Japan*.

46. Shillony, *Revolt in Japan*, and PA, Militärputsch Tokyo: Notes by German Foreign Minister von Neurath on his talk to Japanese Ambassador Mushakoji on 6 May 1936.

47. See, unsurpassed, Andreas Hillgruber, 'Die "Endlösung" und das deutsche Ostimperium als Kernstück des rassenideologischen Programms des Nationalsozialismus', in: *Vierteljahrshefte für Zeitgeschichte*, No. 20 (1972), pp. 133–53.

48. See Adolf Hitler, *Mein Kampf*, München, 1938, p. 318.

49. Ibid., pp. 722f.

50. See Erich Kordt, *Nicht aus den Akten ... Die Wilhelmstraße in Frieden und Krieg. Erlebnisse, Begegnungen und Eindrücke. 1928–1945*, Stuttgart, 1950, p. 122.

51. See note 39.

52. See Alfred Rosenberg, *Der Mythus des 20. Jahrhunderts*, München, 1930, pp. 655ff and pp. 675f.

53. See Ernst L. Presseisen, *Germany and Japan. A Study in Totalitarian Diplomacy 1933–1941*, The Hague, 1958, pp. 13–24: 'Geopolitical Plans'; and Karl Haushofer, ed., *Zeitschrift für Geopolitik*, issues published in 1932.

54. For the following, see John P. Fox, 'Japanese Reactions to Nazi Germany's Racial Legislation', in: *The Widner Library Bulletin*, 23 (1969), pp. 46–50.

55. See Roger Daniels, *The Politics of Prejudice. The Anti-Japanese Movement in California and the Struggle for Japanese Exclusion*, University of California Press, 1962.

56. See, Fox, *Formulation*, p. 94.

57. See chapter 7, 'Germany between China and Japan', in this volume.

58. See Fox, *Japanese Reactions*, pp. 47f.

59. Theo Sommer, *Deutschland und Japan zwischen den Mächten 1935–1940. Vom Antikominternpakt zum Dreimächtepakt. Eine Studie zur diplomatischen Vorgeschichte des Zweiten Weltkrieges*, Tübingen, 1962, p. 21 (conversation on 18 October 1933).

60. See above note 59.

61. See Presseisen, *Germany and Japan*, p. 46 (October 1933).

62. PA, Personalien, japanische Staatsmänner: Letters from Reichskanzlei to Foreign Office No. 11330 of 25 September 1933 and No. 11354 of 13 October 1933 on Hitler's reception of the Japanese member of parliament Nakamura. The interview published in the *Japan Advertiser* on 15 December 1933 was the first friendly report on Hitler in the Japanese press. See PA, Report, German Embassy Tokyo, Journal No. 3529, 19 December 1933.

63. See Frank William Iklé, *German-Japanese Relations 1936–1940*, New York, 1956, p. 26.

64. Martin, 'Die deutsch-japanischen Beziehungen', p. 459.

65. In his political reports on the inner political situation in Japan, Dirksen tended to overrate the impact of the German 'Führer-State' model.

66. For instance, see PA, Innenpolitik Japan, Journal No. 4691; The annual report of the German Embassy in Tokyo of 31 December 1934.

67. See Frick's (minister of the interior) statement in *Ostasiatische Rundschau*, 16 December 1933, p. 521.

68. PA, Soziale Verhältnisse in Japan: Report German Embassy in Tokyo (on request from Berlin) from 13 March, Journal No. 1220, 23 August 1935.

69. See Fox, *Japanese Reactions*, pp. 49f.

70. See Bernd Martin, *Deutschland und Japan im Zweiten Weltkrieg. Von Pearl Harbor bis zur deutschen Kapitulation*, Göttingen, 1969. Especially for Hitler's attitude towards the Japanese entering the war against Russia.

71. For details, see Martin, 'Die deutsch-japanischen Beziehungen'.

72. See Hermann Graml, 'Präsidialsystem und Außenpolitik', in: *Vierteljahrshefte für Zeitgeschichte*, No. 21 (1973), pp. 134–45; especially for Papen, see Bernd Martin, 'Friedensplanungen der multinationalen Großindustrie (1932–1940) als politische Krisenstrategie', in: *Geschichte und Gesellschaft*, No. 2 (1976), pp. 66–88.

73. See W. E. Scott, *Alliance Against Hitler. The Origins of the Franco-Soviet Pact*, Durham, N.C., 1962. (Non-aggression pact of 29 November 1932)

74. See Christopher Thorne, *The Limits of Foreign Policy. The West, the League and the Far Eastern Crisis of 1931–1933*, London, 1972, and – from the Western outlook – the standard book by Max Beloff, *The Foreign Policy of Soviet Russia 1929–1941*, Vol. 1, 1929–1936, London, 1968.

75. On 16 November 1933.

76. See Fox, *Formulation*, p. 52: Such rumours were first spread by *Izvestia* in January 1934.

77. For the misconception about Japan in the American press, see Borg/Okamoto, *Pearl Harbor*, pp. 511ff. An example of German misconceptions about Japan is to be seen in the dispute between the German Embassies of Tokyo and Hankow (China) about Lily Abegg's statements in early January 1938. Mrs. Abegg was correspondent to the *Frankfurter Zeitung* (see note 2).

78. See the Ottawa agreements on preferential duties within the Commonwealth of July and August 1932. For Japanese-American economic relations, see Borg/Okamoto, *Pearl Harbor*, pp. 261ff. and pp. 341ff.

79. PA, Militärangelegenheiten Japan: Notes of the Foreign Office from 22 March 1933. Schleicher's adjutant Ott had, from approximately mid-1931 on, engaged in talks with the National Socialists. See Thilo Vogelsang, *Reichswehr, Staat und NSDAP – Beiträge zur deutschen Geschichte 1930–1932*, Stuttgart, 1962; also see the author's (Bernd Martin's) interview with Eugen Ott on 11 January 1966, in Munich.

80. In detail, see Sommer, *Deutschland und Japan*, pp. 23ff.

81. See Presseisen, *Germany and Japan*, p. 69 (in March 1934).

82. For the Hack papers and their evaluation, as well as for the following in general, see Martin, 'Die deutsch-japanischen Beziehungen'.

83. Ibid., Hack's notes of 25 September 1935.

84. Ibid., Oshima's draft of 4 October 1935.

85. Ibid., notes of 25 September 1935.

86. PA, Geheimakten Ostasien, Erdmannsdorff's notes of 18 November 1935.

87. Ibid.

88. PA, Geheimakten Ostasien: Telegram Ribbentrop/Dieckhoff – Consul General Kriebel Hongkong of 7 December 1935.

89. Hack papers: Note of 28 November 1935.

90. Printed in Sommer, *Deutschland und Japan*, pp. 494–500.

91. See PA, Innenpolitik Japan: The German Embassy's annual report of 27 Dec. 1936.

92. PA, Japan Faszismus: Report German Embassy, Journal No. 1549 II, of 11 May 1934.

93. See the writings of the agrarian romantics, e.g., Seikyo Gondo's, in Havens, *Farm and Nation*, also see Smethurst, *Social Basis*.

94. See the fundamental work by David Anson Titus, *Palace and Politics in Prewar Japan*, New York, 1974.

95. See above: the Tenno's personal intervention after the Tokyo Mutiny in February 1936.

96. See Martin, 'Aggressionspolitik'.

97. See Robert A. Scalapino, *The Japanese Communist Movement 1920–1966*, University of California Press, 1967. The so-called 'Peace Laws' of 1925 and 1928 forbade any group or individual activity aiming at 'changing the national policy or the system of private property'.

98. Professor Yokota Kisaburo. See Borg/Okamoto, *Pearl Harbor*, pp. 577f. (Hans Kelsen, 1881–1973, an advocate of positivist law theory, according to whose views state and law were identical. His 'Pure Legalism' was edited in 1934.)

99. See Crowley, *Japan's Quest*, pp. 204ff. In general, see the monograph by Frank O. Miller, *Minobe Tatsukichi. Interpreter of Constitutionalism in Japan*, University of California Press, 1965.

100. See Borg/Okamoto, *Pearl Harbor*, p. 499: in 1934 Minobe was for the first time attacked by rightist colleagues.

101. For the activities of the Tokyo Veterans' League against Minobe, see Smethurst, *Social Basis*, p. 18, and Bergamini, *Imperial Conspiracy*, pp. 590ff.

102. See Borg/Okamoto, *Pearl Harbor*, p. 499.

103. Ibid., and Bergamini, *Imperial Conspiracy*, pp. 592ff. For the National Socialists' interpretation, see the article 'Nipponismus. Die Weltanschauung des jungen Japan. Der Fall Minobe', in: *Berliner Börsenzeitung*, (15 May, 1935). (PA, Japan Innenpolitik)

104. See Borg/Okamoto, *Pearl Harbor*, p. 501: extract from a report of the Police Bureau.

105. Hoover-Library, Stanford, Calif.: Saionji-Harada Memoirs, p. 1207.

106. PA, Japan-Deutschland: Report German Embassy Journal No. 1737 of 13 May 1936 (speech delivered in the upper house by Baron Sonoda).

107. See Borg/Okamoto, *Pearl Harbor*, p. 593; especially Carl Schmitt, *Völkerrechtliche Großraumordnung mit Interventionsrecht für raumfremde Mächte*, Berlin, 1939.

108. See the April 1936 Navy memorandum, 'General Principles of National Policy', excerpts of which in Lebra, *Greater East Asia*, pp. 58ff.

109. See Borg/Okamoto, *Pearl Harbor*, pp. 329f.: Army memorandum, 'The renovation of all aspects of government', 21 September 1936.

110. See Crowley, *Japan's Quest*, p. 290ff; and Borg/Okamoto, *Pearl Harbor*, p. 244.

111. The Prime Minister, the Foreign Minister, the members of the navy, the army and finance (Prime Minister was Hirota Koki a former career diplomat).

112. PA, Innenpolitik Japan: Report German Embassy, Journal No. 1807, 25 May 1936: '… the Embassy has repeatedly been asked by officials and private persons for detailed information about the "Reichsministerium für Volksaufklärung und Propaganda"'. At the same time the government founded the official news agency *Domei*. (Borg/Okamoto, *Pearl Harbor*, pp. 543ff).

113. Ibid., p. 536.

114. Ibid., p. 537.

115. PA, Innenpolitik Japan: Report German Embassy Journal No. 2197, 16 June 1936 on the law issued on 29 May.

116. See Tsurumi, *Social Change*, p. 42: 95 percent of the leftists (i.e., socialists and communists) abjured their 'heresies'.

117. Robert A. Scalapino, *Democracy and the Party Movement in Prewar Japan. The Failure of the First Attempt*, Berkeley, 1953, p. 386.

118. PA, Innenpolitik Japan: Report German Embassy Journal No. 808/37, 5 May 1937.

119. Because of the 'Boxer Protocols' of 7 September 1901. Japan had stationed 2,000 soldiers southeast of Peking. For the outbreak of the conflict, see Crowley, *Japan's Quest*, p. 320 (partly apologetic); and Bergamini, *Imperial Conspiracy*, pp. 684ff and pp. 3ff (somewhat overevaluating the Tenno's personal responsibility).

120. See Crowley, *Japan's Quest*, pp. 358ff: the military advised a peace treaty modelled after the ones of 1866 and 1870–71.

121. 22 December 1938. Konoe's statement is printed in Lebra, *Greater East Asia*, pp. 68ff.

122. For the Trautmann Mission, see Sommer, *Deutschland und Japan*, pp. 56ff., and Presseisen, *Germany and Japan*, pp. 124ff.

123. See Martin, 'Aggressionspolitik', pp. 232 and 235.

124. Ibid., p. 235.

125. PA, Ministerien Japan: Reports German Embassy Journal No. 1010/37, 22 June 1937, and Journal No. 762 II, 31 March 1938, on Konoe (considerable excitement was caused when Konoe turned up masked as Hitler at a fancy dress party and even had his photograph taken).

126. At least this is how the German Embassy had it. See PA, Ministerien Japan: Report German Embassy Journal No. 42/39, 1 February 1939. Probably the unresolved China question was equally important for the resignation of the first Konoe cabinet.

127. The strongest supporter of this group was Admiral Suetsugu the former Minister of the Interior of the first Konoe cabinet. For the internal discussions, see PA, Deutschland-Japan: Report German Embassy Journal No. 510/40, 10 June 1940.

128. PA Deutschland-Japan: Report German Embassy Journal No. 880/40, 13 November 1940.

129. For the German development, see the overview by Wolfgang Sauer, 'Das Problem des deutschen Nationalstaates', in: Helmut Böhme, ed., *Probleme der Reichsgründungszeit*, Köln, 1972, pp. 448–74; and the standard work on Prussia by Hans Rosenberg, *Bureaucracy, Aristocracy and Autocracy. The Prussian Experience 1660–1815*, Harvard University Press, 1958.

130. See Hans Mommsen, *Beamtentum im Dritten Reich*, Stuttgart, 1966.

131. See PA, Deutschland-Japan: Report German Embassy Journal No. 716/39, 16 October 1939.

132. See Bernd Martin, 'Japan im Krieg 1941–1945', in: Oswald Hauser, ed., *Weltpolitik II, 1939–1945. 14 Vorträge*, Göttingen, 1975, p. 144.

133. For details, see Sommer, *Deutschland und Japan*, pp. 94ff.

134. For the differing conceptions, see Martin, *Deutschland und Japan im Zweiten Weltkrieg*.

135. Ambassador Oshima resigned. But a Japanese army delegation under General Terauchi, war minister when the Anti-Comintern Pact was signed, that had originally been invited for the NSDAP Party rally, were shown the effects of the German war machinery in Poland. See Paul Ostwald, *Deutschland und Japan. Eine Freundschaft zweier Völker*, Berlin, 1941, pp. 116ff.

136. Michael Libal, *Japans Weg in den Krieg. Die Außenpolitik der Kabinette Konoye 1940–41*, Düsseldorf, 1971, and Sommer, *Deutschland und Japan*, pp. 324ff.

137. Martin, 'Japans Weltmachtstreben', pp. 115f.

138. Chief ideologist was Professor Okawa Shumpei. Excerpts from his programme in Tsunoda/de Bary, *Sources*, pp. 785ff; quite interesting, too, is the plan on how to achieve Japanese leadership drawn up by the army headquarters in 1942, where a distinction is made between master peoples, foreign peoples, and guest peoples. (See Lebra, *Greater East Asia*, pp. 118ff.)

139. See Martin, 'Japans Weltmachtstreben', p. 116.

140. For Hitler's notions about Great Britain, see Bernd Martin, *Friedensinitiativen und Machtpolitik 1939–1942*, Düsseldorf, 1974.

141. See Hillgruber, *Hitlers Strategie, Politik und Kriegführung 1940–41*, Frankfurt am Main, 1965, pp. 192ff.

142. Ibid., p. 204.

143. See Martin, 'Japans Weltmachtstreben', pp. 117ff.

144. See Hillgruber, *Politik und Kriegführung*, pp. 351ff.

145. See Martin, *Deutschland und Japan*, pp. 94ff.

146. For the American embargo policy towards Japan, see Borg/Okamoto, *Pearl Harbor*, pp. 280ff., and William L. Langer and S. Everett Gleason, *The Undeclared War 1940–1941*, New York, 1953; also see Martin, *Friedensinitiativen*, especially pp. 207ff. (the Welles Mission).

147. See Ralf Dahrendorf, *Gesellschaft und Demokratie in Deutschland*, München, 1966, pp. 430ff.; and Andreas Hillgruber, 'Eine Bilanz des Zweiten Weltkrieges aus der Sicht der kriegführenden Mächte', in: A. Hillgruber, *Großmachtpolitik und Militarismus im 20. Jahrhundert*, Düsseldorf, 1974, p. 53; and Bernd Martin, 'Restauration – Die Bewältigung der Vergangenheit in Japan', in: *Zeitschrift für Politik*, N.F. 17 (1970), pp. 153–70.

PART IV

THE WAR ALLIANCE

❧ 9 ❧

GERMANY AND PEARL HARBOR

Introduction

The problems which we face are so vast and so interrelated that any attempt even to state them compels one to think in terms of five continents and seven seas.[1]

President Franklin D. Roosevelt used these words at the beginning of 1941 to describe to his Ambassador to Japan, Joseph C. Grew, the complexity of the prevailing international situation and resulting dangers facing the United States. It was self-evident to American (and also British) politicians and military leaders at that time that Hitler's aggressive politics of armed expansion and the foreign adventures of Germany's Asian ally Imperial Japan posed a threat to American interests throughout the world. Similarly, everyone expected the European theatre of operations and Japan's war of annihilation in China to be connected together. After the end of the Second World War, however, most historians forgot this very important Allied concern – the Axis link between Europe and Asia. The prehistory of the attack on Pearl Harbor was depicted as a bilateral Japanese-American phenomenon,[2] and the Pacific War as a tragic confrontation between the two powers on the shores of that ocean. Experiencing the war as a threat to their national existence led to describing it in the following histories from the point of view of one nation, the United States, or belatedly Japan. The global nature of the conflict and, particularly with regard to the theme of this essay, the cooperative efforts of the two 'provocateurs' – Germany and Japan – have not received adequate attention.

This article was published in Japanese translation in Chihiro Hosoya et al., eds., *Taiheiyosenso*, Tokyo, 1994.

The revisionist powers, Germany, Italy, and Japan,[3] tended during the 1930s to separate themselves ever more from the democratic nations in the West, and also from the communist-internationalist camp led by the Soviet Union. This was especially so after the signing of the Anti-Comintern Pact in 1936. These 'young, aspiring nations',[4] as they saw themselves, strove to create a supposedly better world based on an authoritarian, folkish, inner national order. As a result of each country's expansionist policies and the realities of war, this developed into an egoistic, extremely brutal power-political system based on separate spheres of influence. To the revisionist power with the most advanced economy, technology, and military – the German Reich, led by Adolf Hitler – fell automatically the leader's role in formulating and enacting worldwide fascist policy. The supremacy of the Third Reich was accepted reluctantly by the Italians due to their geographic proximity; the distant Japanese, who were very sensitive about preserving their special national identity, conveniently overlooked it.

Nevertheless, Japan's fate was, in fact, linked to that of Germany.[5] This was a consequence of Japan's own foreign policy – manoeuvering exclusively in a three-cornered world, Berlin-Moscow-Washington, and isolating herself internationally. As Japan became increasingly bogged down in the war in China, her leaders reacted with growing sensitivity to Hitler's moves in Europe and, finally, were lured into a confrontation with the United States. Though basically reactive, one cannot say the Japanese government formed national policies and decided on offensive military measures in tow behind the Germans. Quite the contrary. The policies of Japan's hopelessly divided and quarreling political oligarchy, with respect to the concrete enactment of her expansionist plans, hardly agreed with the wishes of Germany's leaders, also noted for their lack of consistency. This was equally true for the proposed strike north against the Soviets, and the enticing prospect of striking south and procuring the raw materials of the European colonies in Southeast Asia.

However, the uneven balance of power and influence between the two 'partners' should not be disregarded. On the one hand, Hitler unleashed his war in Europe largely independent of developments in East Asia. On the other hand, the Japanese war in China and its expansion into a conflict with the United States was, among other things, a reaction to events in Europe. Moreover, Japan was to a certain extent doubly dependent on Germany, in terms of *Realpolitik* and historically. The success of Imperial Japan's programme of expansion was contingent upon the German power potential. At the same time, this programme was historically a result of misconceived modernisation, a process strongly influenced in the late nineteenth and early twentieth centuries by German models.[6] This predilection for German archetypes can also be seen in the events leading to Pearl Harbor.

Japan and the National Socialist Model: The Conclusion of the Tripartite Pact

The negotiations for a German-Japanese alliance began immediately after Joachim von Ribbentrop took office as Foreign Minister in early 1938.[7] His efforts to replace the 'wooden bridge' (Anti-Comintern Pact) with a 'steel bridge' were well received by one of his Japanese associates in Berlin, the Military Attaché Oshima Hiroshi.[8] Representatives of the Japanese armed forces had already proposed such a military alliance during the talks preceding the signing of the Anti-Comintern Pact. Ribbentrop became a proponent of this alliance, and after its conclusion in September 1940 he was responsible for its enactment. The National Socialist Party, despite racist reservations, also stood for the most part behind the idea of a military alliance between Germany and Japan. On the Japanese side, its principal supporters were the representatives of the Imperial Army. After General Oshima was appointed ambassador in October 1938, the relationship between Germany and Japan until the end of the war was mainly a product of negotiations between him and the German Foreign Minister. Still, each had his own, in part, very different conceptions of the concrete form this cooperation should assume. Furthermore, each was able only sporadically to receive a hearing within his respective government. Plans and ideas which both advocated often were not suited to political realities, and their talks, especially in the last years of the war, often bordered on the fantastic. Oshima, when he simply proposed a military strategy – a German-Japanese attack on the Soviet Union – hardly took into account the opposition of the navy and imperial court advisers in Tokyo. Ribbentrop, since the time of the international crisis over the Sudetenland, wanted to bring Japan into a general defensive alliance directed mainly against Great Britain. The Foreign Minister promoted his concept of a Eurasian landblock,[9] which would include the Soviet Union after the conclusion of the nonaggression pact with the Soviets. This, however, was diametrically opposed to Hitler's basic conception of the planned war for the extermination of 'Jewish Bolshevism'. For Hitler, the agreement with the Russians was never anything more than a temporary expedient.

The Japanese had become increasingly isolated internationally by their pursuit, since July 1937, of the fierce war in China, which was causing them heavy casualties, and basically they were prepared to conclude a pact with the rising, greatly admired German Reich. However, they did not want to become involved, as a result, in a conflict with the Western powers, particularly not the United States. The latter's industry and technology were superior to that of the Japanese. Moreover, a confrontation with the United States could involve Japan in a two-front war.

With the escalation of tensions in Europe, the alliance was promoted with increasing urgency by the German side. In 1938–39 it was a topic of discussion in more than seventy Liaison Conferences between military and civil leaders in Tokyo,[10] without achieving a consensus. Japanese foreign policy during the period between the Munich Conference and the conclusion of the Tripartite Pact was clearly centered on Germany, and the importance of the relationship with the United States was deemphasised. Domestic sentiment also did not favor an arrangement with the Western powers. The people, who had been mobilised into a chauvinistic defence fraternity as a consequence of the China War, demanded an alliance with the European fascist camp. Nevertheless, the leaders of the Japanese government were unable to arrive at a clear decision.

The Japanese dilatory attitude could only be interpreted as a refusal of his proposal, and Ribbentrop distanced himself, for the time being, from the idea of a world-encircling alliance. He turned instead to constructing a temporary substitute in order to localise the planned war against Poland. The impromptu 'Pact of Steel' of 22 May 1939 and the likewise hastily concluded treaty with the Soviet Union (23 August 1939) were merely makeshift measures designed to fill the gap resulting from Japan's delay in joining in a world political alliance. Which is to say, Japan's refusal to conclude a pact with Germany had an important effect on the political situation in Europe at the time of the outbreak of the war.

However, the treaty between the Soviet Union and Germany threatened Japan, then involved in heavy fighting with the Red Army on the border between Manchuria and Mongolia, with total international isolation.[11] A reorientation of Japanese foreign policy could only be considered, after September 1939 when Hitler took the initiative militarily, in the wake of the events unfolding in Europe.[12] Japanese leaders, insofar as they were not inclined to resign their posts, were left with no choice but to follow the complete change in German foreign policy with an equally radical course change of their own. A Eurasian block, as propagated untiringly by Ribbentrop, offered the best possibility of ending the war in China and neutralising the Western powers in East Asia. On the domestic front, the reformists, who wanted to restructure Japanese society together with the army as a garrison state, received support from the German victories in Europe. National Socialist Germany, from this radical perspective, was not only a worthy example of successful armed *Revisionspolitik*, it was also seen as a model for the desired domestic revolution. The hesitant attitude of the cabinets led by General Abe Nobuyuki (August 1939–January 1940) and Admiral Yonai Mitsumasa (January–July 1940) was, from the Japanese point of view, the reason for their brief terms in office: the problem of the war in China and the question of a new, definitive approach to Berlin could not be separated from one another.

The unexpected, rapid German victories in Western Europe finally led the Japanese to reach the decision which had been pending for over two years. The prospect of taking over the colonial possessions left behind by the European powers in Southeast Asia and including them in the Greater East Asia Co-Prosperity Sphere vaguely planned in Japan was too great an enticement for the Imperial Army.[13] One can well imagine that the German statement on 20 May 1940 renouncing claims to these colonies – a sort of blank cheque for Japanese operations in the area – accelerated army planning. By the end of May 1940 the Imperial Army General Staff prepared for the first time a memorandum on the occupation of Southeast Asia. It included the demand that the British bastion in Singapore be taken. The Philippine Islands were to be excluded from this offensive in order not to draw the United States into the war. This latter aspect of the plan was soon abandoned, because the illusory character of separating the United

States and Great Britain in the event of a war was acknowledged due to pressure from the navy.

The army and also the *Gaimusho*, Foreign Ministry, were united in their demand for open solidarity with Germany and Italy and an improvement in the relationship with the Soviet Union. This would enable Japan to revamp her society at home and effect a new order abroad. The persons best suited to bring about this expansionist national policy appeared to the reformists to be the team of Konoe Fumimaro[14] as Prime Minister with Matsuoka Yosuke responsible for foreign affairs. Since the time of his first cabinet (June 1937–January 1939) when he escalated the war in China, Prince Konoe was regarded as being sympathetic with the reformists, though indecisive and personally too sensitive to be a politician. His political ideals were greatly influenced by socialist theories and had many similarities with the concept of a national socialist folk community. He was a declared opponent of Western supremacy and a silent admirer of Germany since the Versailles Peace Conference, in which he had participated as an observer. A politician who belonged to the oldest, most prestigious noble house in Japan, the Fujiwara, he advocated national power politics in foreign affairs and an authoritarian, basically old-style feudal order at home. His Foreign Minister, Matsuoka,[15] influenced by his early experiences in the United States, was self-assured in a very unJapanese way. He disregarded the traditional, protracted ritual of Japanese decision making which was orientated toward achieving a consensus, often shocking cabinet colleagues and military leaders. Through his many years of employment on the South Manchurian Railway, he became convinced that the experiment in state socialism (unification of all political parties, a planned economy, politisation of the Tenno cult) pursued there by the Kwantung Army since 1933, was the right model for restructuring the Japanese fatherland. The new minister, following his diplomatic debut in Geneva in 1933, had personally experienced the 'national revolution' in Germany. He became, with his gushy enthusiasm for National Socialism, an eloquent advocate for, and finally the executor of the alliance with Germany.[16]

Diplomatically, the Germans had courted the Japanese in 1938–39 without success, but now the shoe was on the other foot. When the Japanese sought an audience with the victorious Germans, at first they were shown the door. Hitler expected a positive echo to his recent peace gestures from the British.[17] The 'white' man's dominance of the globe was to be reestablished based on a division of the Euro-Asiatic world. In the meantime, the Konoe-Matsuoka cabinet formulated their government programme in line with the army's concepts. The alliance with Germany was given the highest priority. It was seen as a prerequisite to ending the war in China and constructing a new political order in Japan. Matsuoka summarised these thoughts in two long memoranda prior to announcing on 1 August 1940 in a radio broadcast that the goal of the new politics was a Greater East Asia Co-Prosperity Sphere for the future. Mindful of the chilly climate in Berlin and the reservations still prevailing in the navy and among court advisors and business leaders about close ties with the fascist powers, the Foreign Minister did not mention at first the sought-after alliance with Germany which was necessary for Japan's expansionist foreign policy. With the German ambassador, on the other hand, he first brought up the prospect of a military pact and inquired about future German strategic and political intentions.

Still, Berlin continued putting off the Japanese. On 10 August 1940 Matsuoka publicly revealed the plan for a pact, but only three days later did Ribbentrop find time to take up negotiations. The change in German policy can probably be explained by the United States' growing concern for the British, and the latter's firm rejection of all German peace feelers. A Japan obligated by treaty ties seemed better than an isolated one possibly open to a new compromise with the Western powers. This would serve in part, at least, as a diversion in the Pacific for the Anglo-American coalition coming into being, with its mighty industrial and military potential. Matsuoka immediately snatched up the proposal brought by Germany's Special Emissary Heinrich Georg Stahmer from Ribbentrop: mutual recognition of spheres of influence, a defence agreement against the feared American intervention, and the integration of the Soviet Union in the Euro-Asiatic Block. The navy, which was, after the first American embargo, more dependent than the army on the raw materials in Southeast Asia, also declared itself in basic agreement with such a pact. Automatic entry into a possible war, however, was still unacceptable.

During the negotiations with the Germans, the Japanese side was unable to avoid marking off the borders of the planned spheres of influence, which were to extend from India to Australia and were to include the far-eastern provinces of the Soviet Union. Even before the signing of the treaty, the government in Tokyo pushed the Vichy Regime into allowing troops to be stationed in northern Indochina and began with the occupation of the area. The expansion of the American embargo to include steel and scrap metal, as well as Washington's financial help for the beleaguered Chiang Kai-shek regime, did not induce the Japanese to renounce the alliance with Germany. The agreement was signed on 27 September 1940 in Berlin and was officially presented as a pact for the defence of peace. Nevertheless, for both Matsuoka and Ribbentrop it was above all a power political design to isolate the United States. However, due to a lack of trust between the partners, the eventuality of war was not provided for, and up until the Japanese attack on Pearl Harbor, there were no joint consultations on strategy.

Instead of retiring into their own hemisphere as the Berlin-Rome-Tokyo agreement was supposed to bring about, the United States felt threatened by the fascist powers.[18] They imagined themselves confronted by a 'world conspiracy' of the 'have-nots', as Secretary of State Cordell Hull was inclined to put it. Instead of hindering the United States' entry into the war, the pact strengthened the Roosevelt government's resolve to use force if necessary against the revisionist powers. Among German leaders, for example, Navy Chief Erich Raeder, discussions ensued about the strategic alternatives of a massive attack on British positions in the Middle East, showing a willingness to point their activities geographically in the direction of Japanese interests.[19] In addition, an attack on Singapore as soon as possible was urged on the new treaty partner. Domestically, after the conclusion of the agreement, warlike tones came from the pages of Japan's many newspapers for the first time, and the German newspaper *Völkische Beobachter* commented on the alliance with the striking words, 'The sun is going down on the plutocratic gods'.[20] Fashioning the world according to fascist-folkish basic principles, overcoming what was regarded as demoralising individualism, and the corresponding liberal democratic economic order were the common goals of the three signatory states. Matsuoka's urging of such an alliance was not a peace policy. It was a policy leading to the brink of war. However, before an occasion arose which would have required action according to the terms of the alliance, both parties assumed different, basically incompatible positions which made the Tripartite Pact, practically speaking, superfluous.

German Aggression in Russia and Japan's
Final Move South

Hitler's basic plan for Operation Barbarossa, dated 18 December 1940, did not include a single word about Germany's strongest ally, Japan.[21] By contrast, Germany's European partners were assigned roles in the coming offensive against the Soviet Union. Hitler believed the annexation of territory in the East should be carried out exclusively by the German 'master race'. Trapped in traditional concepts of a contained land war, the German General Staff also omitted Japan from their plans. Due to his ideological prejudices Hitler could not comprehend the global aspects of prosecuting a war in a coalition, and the highest ranking officers of the army were not open to this possibility due to their own one-sided expertise. Only the relatively small German navy, always on the lookout for strong comrades-in-arms at sea, regarded the alliance with Japan positively.

Japan was referred to in Hitler's directives to the *Wehrmachtsführungsstab* (German High Command) solely about promoting a strike against Singapore, and finally in his 'Führer Directive', 'Collaboration with Japan' (5 March 1941): the Japanese were to rout the British with a combined land-sea operation on the Malayan Peninsula.[22] In this way, the United States would be restrained from further helping her ally Britain in Europe as well as in East Asia. Hints to this effect, however, fell on deaf ears in Japan at this time. The Imperial Navy thought the idea of separating American and British military interests illusory, and had long planned accordingly. Nor was this request welcomed by Foreign Minister Matsuoka. He wanted to force the Americans to withdraw from East Asia from a position of overwhelming strength. At the beginning of April 1941, during his talks in Berlin,[23] Matsuoka was told repeatedly by Hitler and his Foreign Minister Ribbentrop that this was a once-in-a-lifetime chance to take Singapore. Though diplomatically open to the Germans' arguments, he still had to admit that he did not rule alone in Japan. In early 1941 a consensus among the leaders of Japan approving such an operation was not to be expected.

Hitler's strategy was summarised succinctly by Foreign Minister Ribbentrop in a discussion with his Japanese counterpart; should war break out between Germany and the Soviet Union,

Japanese participation would be unnecessary. Instead, the best assistance would be a Japanese attack on Singapore. The double guarantee given by Hitler and confirmed by Ribbentrop that Germany would support Japan, should either the Russians or Americans attack her, obviated the risks involved. With the beginning of the German offensive, which was originally planned for May 1941, the Japanese were to attack Singapore. Britain would then be involved in a war in the Far East making retaliation against Germany impossible in Europe or North Africa during the campaign in Eastern Europe.

The relationship between Germany's surprise attack on the Soviets and the proposed Japanese attack on Singapore was not entirely clear to the latter, due to a lack of information from Germany about the coming operations. Matsuoka's report to the Liaison Conference, as well as to the Privy Council, about what German leaders had told him regarding a possible war between Germany and the Soviet Union was correct. In the Privy Council he even put the eventual probability of such a war at fifty percent and for the first time proposed deliberating if, in this event, Japan ought to participate in subduing the Soviet Union. The United States' inflexible posture in the negotiations with Japan – Secretary of State Hull insisted in his 'four principles' on Japan's withdrawal from China – meant that there was no doubt that the United States would react militarily to a Japanese assault on Singapore. Matsuoka for the first time pleaded, therefore, for a German-Japanese military union and extolled Germany as a worthy model for the final transformation of Japan into an authoritarian state.[24] The Foreign Minister's display of independence violated the Japanese 'holy principle' of governing by consensus. Matsuoka expounded his ideas ceaselessly with the result that he isolated himself in the cabinet and came to represent himself personally, and not Japanese foreign policy. The traditionalists around Minister of the Interior Hiranuma regarded Matsuoka simply as a fascist whose public statements were quite correctly redlined by the censors.[25]

Japanese foreign policy lacked clear direction due to the diverging ideas of the country's individual leaders. This confusion and cacophony came to a head during the negotiations with the United States when, against the Foreign Minister's will, Japan appeared ready to distance herself from the Tripartite Pact while at the same time this Pact was being praised as fundamental to

Tokyo's entire foreign policy. Matsuoka then attempted to acquire a clear picture of German intentions, and at the end of May he sent his ambassador to Hitler and Ribbentrop to advise against a *coup de main* in Eastern Europe. The German leaders, who were not at all happy about the Japanese-American negotiations, because they were contrary to the German policy of isolating the United States, sought anew to bind Japan closer to Germany. Therefore, at the beginning of June they informed the Japanese leaders of the upcoming offensive in the East.[26] Hitler left it up to Tokyo to decide on Japanese participation in this conflict, but Ribbentrop came out clearly in favour of Imperial Army collaboration. He proposed a coordinated pincer operation against the Soviet Union. This fundamental dissension among German leaders concerning Japanese participation in the Russian campaign lasted until January 1943 when the *Wehrmacht* came to their Waterloo at Stalingrad. Finally, Hitler adopted the line of his Foreign Minister and called unequivocally for Japan to intervene militarily in Russia.[27] However, by this time Japan was likewise on the defensive on all fronts and was in no position to respond. This open difference of opinion between the leader of the government and his foreign minister is difficult to imagine in a democracy, and it completely discredited the reports to Tokyo from Ambassador Oshima in Berlin. Not even the Japanese, long accustomed to factional feuds, could imagine a head of state tolerating such contrariety in a key minister.

In fact, before the German offensive began, the Japanese decided in a Liaison Conference, during which Matsuoka presented the newest information from Germany, not to attempt to pursue a two-front war. Instead, from that time onwards, in the shadow of Germany's successes, Japan would venture into Southeast Asia as originally desired by her European 'ally'. This began with the nonviolent occupation of southern Indochina. Even the army explicitly acknowledged in a memorandum the priority of the southern operation and communicated this to their German partners. In the Liaison Conference of 16 June 1941 Matsuoka read the reports from his ambassador in Berlin. They revealed that the war with Russia would begin within a week. Matsuoka stood alone with his request for a change of policy. The representatives of the army and navy would not consider abandoning their hard-won compromise. The ponderous character of collective leadership in Japan, faced with the necessity of reacting quickly and adequately to a new situation, is clearly evident. 'However, it is not good to alter what was decided the other day', stated the Navy Minister. To which Matsuoka could only retort sarcastically, 'I'm not very intelligent ...'[28] The shock over the Hitler-Stalin Pact had not been forgotten, and on 21 June 1941 Prince Konoe, head of the government, attempted to resign due to the most recent change in Germany's Eastern Europe policy. Lord Privy Seal Kido, the Emperor's political advisor and the most powerful bureaucrat at court, informed the Prime Minister, however, that the German government had correctly informed Japan of their plans and they had in no way objected to them.[29]

With the onset of the German assault, Ribbentrop assailed the Japanese ambassador in Berlin, and in Tokyo Matsuoka implored the Emperor and court officials to immediately join in the German operation. Both argued from the basic standpoint of the Eurasian block concept which they had previously advocated. Since the peaceful integration of the Soviet Union into this block was not possible, the continental landbridge necessary for a military coalition against the Western powers was now to be constructed by force. However, neither of the Foreign Ministers was able to gain acceptance of this policy among the leaders of their respective governments. Ribbentrop's exhortations were unconvincing as long as Hitler, for ideological reasons, did not support him. Matsuoka, on the other hand, was unable to break through the united opposition of the army, navy, and imperial court to a Japanese expedition in the north. Only Hiranuma's traditionalist anticommunist camp, with their Bolshevik phobia, changed their evaluation of Matsuoka and seconded the Foreign Minister.

In a total of six Liaison Conferences the question of a Japanese operation against the Soviet Union was the central topic of discussion. Foreign Minister Matsuoka argued, convincingly from our point of view fifty years later, that a quick attack in the north would forestall American intervention, but a strike south would surely bring the United States into the conflict. He also stated that there was the danger that the war in China might have to be put on hold, should Japan venture northward. This latter comment aroused the premodern, prestige-oriented leaders of the army. Army Minister Tojo immediately voiced opposition to any cutbacks in the China war effort.[30] The Japanese Imperial Army was so preoccupied with the stalemated war in China that it rejected any strategic alternatives and, later, possible political solutions. The continuing conflict in China and the inability of the army leaders to accept some sort of compromise with respect to this thorny issue, eventually brought Japan onto an inescapable collision course with the United States.

Matsuoka's position was further weakened by the lack of an official request from Germany for Japanese participation in the war with Russia. Clearly, Ribbentrop did not wish to openly disagree with Hitler. Hitler appears to have purposely waited for the initial victories of his army before he approved a corresponding *démarche* by his Foreign Minister. Thereafter, Japan's retarded entry into the conflict could not diminish the great achievements of the 'Aryan Race' in the battle against the 'subhuman Slavs'. Finally, one week after the surprise invasion an official request from Ribbentrop was sent to the Japanese side requesting that Japan enter the war against the Soviet Union without delay. In a personal message[31] to Matsuoka, Ribbentrop indicated that a Japanese push to the north, contrary to his earlier recommendation, was now a prerequisite to a subsequent, successful strike south. German recognition of the puppet government under Wang Ching-wei in Nanking was regarded as a demonstration of German-Japanese unity. However, the Imperial Army would not consider even a six-month delay of the southern operation, and it frustrated the Japanese Foreign Minister's last attempt at achieving a compromise.

On 2 July 1941 an Imperial Conference, the highest government council in the land, approved a plan for the occupation of southern Indochina.[32] Japan reserved for itself the possibility of participation in the German war against the Soviet Union, should the German operations go well, and increased the strength of Japanese forces in Manchuria from four hundred thousand to seven hundred thousand men. The following day, Matsuoka communicated this historic decision to the Germans. Japan and the Axis Powers had squandered, fortunately, their best chance of winning the war. From this point onwards the independently chosen paths of the German and Japanese war machines diverged, even before the Japanese challenged the United States militarily in the Pacific. All that remained for Foreign Minister Matsuoka to do was to seal his complete defeat with his own resignation.

In mid-July 1941 the collapse of the Soviet Union appeared imminent. Even the United States government had written off Stalin. With this turn of events, the possibility of a combined German-Japanese offensive briefly reemerged. On 14 July 1941, when

German forces were at the height of their seemingly unstoppable march on Moscow, Hitler received Japanese Ambassador Oshima, who had been sent to make a tour of the front, at his headquarters in East Prussia. Exalting in the string of German victories, Hitler exhorted the Japanese to participate in the destruction of Russia so that afterwards they could embark together upon the battle between the continents – the struggle with the United States.[33] This vision of German-Japanese world hegemony, never again proposed by Hitler in this form, was enticing for the Japanese up until the first week of August. They seriously considered taking advantage of this suggestion, now coming directly from Hitler. Even the Japanese General Staff, in talks with the highest-ranking representative of the German military in Tokyo, spoke of the imminent unleashing of the Kwantung Army in Manchuria. Similar reports piled up in Berlin – Japan would invade the Soviet Union in October at the latest. The Japanese Foreign Ministry, in its diplomatic negotiations with the Soviet Union, also assumed that the latter would be ultimately defeated. Matsuoka had remained purposefully unclear about the Japanese position *vis-à-vis* the neutrality treaty, but the Ministry under his successor Toyoda wanted to use it to force the Russians to cede Amur Province and northern Sakhalin to Japan through diplomatic measures.

However, the course of the war along the middle of the Eastern Front, which the ambassador in general's uniform Oshima reported in detail to Tokyo, prompted a revision of the Japanese estimate of the situation. Bitter defensive fighting by the Russians in the area of Smolensk had stalled the middle of the *Wehrmacht* line, and the Japanese General Staff began to have doubts about a quick victory over the Soviet Union.[34] An order sent to the units stationed in Manchuria on 6 August strictly prohibited them from engaging in border skirmishes of any sort.[35] Three days later the leaders of the Japanese army decided not to intervene in the German-Soviet conflict of 1941. Instead, they intensified their preparations for the strike south.

On 24 July 1941 Japan began the occupation of southern Indochina. The northern half had already been occupied one year earlier. The move further south was answered by the United States two days later with a total trade embargo. The government in Washington froze all Japanese assets in the United States and banned oil deliveries to Japan. Britain and the Netherlands joined this embargo, and the Japanese were able to calculate, based on their oil reserves, when the fleet would be forced to give their sailors permanent leave ashore. Matsuoka's warning that a strike south would result in an intractable conflict with the United States was confirmed within a few weeks. On 6 September 1941 the decision was taken in an Imperial Conference that Japan would go to war with the United States if the situation did not improve dramatically within a month.[37] This was to take place regardless of what happened on the Russian front. The Japanese still hoped for a German victory, but no longer expected the rapid destruction of Stalin's régime. Shortly thereafter, an internal discussion began in the Foreign Ministry and among leaders of the military about the possibility of Japan providing mediation in the conflict between Germany and the Soviet Union. Displaying rare unanimity, the Japanese leaders returned to their position of 1940 – the building of a continental block against the Western powers. With the ever increasing probability of war with the Allies, Japanese leaders wanted to secure access to German technology, vastly superior to their own at the time, and eventually to military help.

Just as the final German assault on Moscow had started (2 October 1941), the Japanese military brought up the possibility of a political solution to the war in Russia with German diplomats in Tokyo.[38] In order to emphasise the proposal, they also communicated to the Germans their decision made two months earlier not to join in the war against the Soviet Union that year. Hitler, who had never insisted on Japan entering the war, and with his confidence in a quick victory restored, returned to his former position: the Japanese should be restrained from entering the war so as to increase the chances of making peace with Britain. German and Japanese interests diverged before the alliance between them was of any practical consequence. The Germans were transfixed by the war with Russia in the east, the Japanese by the conflict in the Pacific with the United States.

Pearl Harbor and the Partition of the World Between Germany and Japan

Japanese foreign policy, even under Matsuoka's successor, the moderate Admiral Toyoda, gradually leaned towards formally withdrawing from the negotiations in Washington. Viewing the dark war clouds gathering over the Pacific after the United States had imposed a total embargo on Japan, the leaders in Tokyo once again looked to their two potential allies in Europe. During the three months prior to the opening of hostilities, Japanese leaders made their decisions about the coming war independently of promises of aid from their German and Italian partners. However, the Japanese sought and received assurances from Berlin and Rome that they would not have to stand alone against the United States. Thus, the Tripartite Pact had no direct influence on the Japanese decision to go to war, but may have reassured the Japanese leaders indirectly in their conclusion that war was inevitable.[39]

During the decisive Imperial Conference of 6 September 1941, in which, for all practical purposes, war against the Western powers was decided upon, Chief of Staff Sugiyama Gen specifically referred to the two allies: Germany and Italy should be informed in due course of the decision to go to war, and it should be ensured contractually that they would not conclude a separate peace.[40] The final resolution stated that Japan, to be sure, would have to rely on her own resources, but close ties with Germany and Italy were to be established. Japanese diplomacy remained true to this policy up until Japan entered the war.

After Prime Minister Konoe had worked himself into a hopeless situation politically – the great war appearing ever more probable – he resigned. The Emperor then approved the formation of a government by General Tojo Hideki, telling him not only to review the 6 September decision to go to war, but also reminding him of Japan's German ally.

Although the Japanese plans for the war,[41] first completed on 20 October, did not provide for a coalition with Germany to direct the war or corresponding consultations on strategy, representatives of the navy brought up this possibility in the next Liaison Conference. According to the admirals, the British placed a high priority on the defence of Singapore and the Suez Canal. A German advance in the Middle East would turn it into a battleground, opening up the possibility of a maritime connection between the two war zones across the Indian Ocean. A few days later, the conference decided on this strategic proposal of united action in the Middle East together with the demand that Germany immediately declare war on the United States and not agree to any separate peace accord. Because this plan came from the army, the navy relinquished the hoped-for collaboration with their German counterparts and proposed to agree to a division of operational areas along a line extending north-south through Colombo.

Japanese deliberations about bringing Germany into the war against the United States coincided with the German navy's desire to move the German Reich in the same direction. A conflict with the United States, an acknowledged power at sea, was deemed inevitable, and it would be better to enter the war together. A navy memorandum to this effect, which may have accelerated reconsideration of this possibility, circulated through the high command of the armed forces and the Foreign Ministry. Hitler's original principle of avoiding any provocation of the United States during the campaign in Russia in order to keep Washington out of the war at least temporarily became untenable with the collapse of the *Blitzkrieg* on the Eastern front. The German dictator revealed for the first time, in a secret conference on 19 November 1941, his doubts about a German victory.[42] At the same time, he began to reconcile himself to the United States' entry into the war, and within ten days in mid-November opinion in Berlin reoriented itself completely.[43] At the beginning of November, Ribbentrop had reacted as before to the first reports from Tokyo about the approaching war in the Pacific: the American threat against Japan was simply a bluff. The Axis allies should persevere and preferably begin an attack on the Soviet Union which involved no risks. But on 21 November Ribbentrop suddenly changed course and moved in the direction of Japanese wishes.

In Japan, after giving the German ambassador in Tokyo advance warning and reendorsing the agreement in the event of war which had been reached at the Liaison Conference, the Japanese officially approached, for the first time, the German military attaché on 18 November and requested that Germany enter the upcoming war. The ambassador immediately reported this unanimous wish of the Japanese armed forces to Berlin. He asked for new instructions covering these 'situations not included in the scope of the Tripartite Pact'. Ribbentrop at once sent the desired directives which, however, were to be transmitted discreetly and only verbally to the Japanese. The German Reich would stand by Japan and sign the agreement not to settle for a separate peace treaty, 'if Japan or Germany, regardless of the grounds, becomes involved in a war with the United States'.[44] This new tune from Berlin sounded so unusual to the Japanese that the German ambassador was requested to reconfirm the promise. This he did, and when the

United States' rejection of Japan's latest compromise proposal arrived in Tokyo, Japanese leaders already had an oral promise from Germany to enter the war. Two days later Ribbentrop underscored Japanese-German shoulder-to-shoulder cooperation in a talk with Oshima, and encouraged the Japanese directly to take up the fight with the Americans.

Japanese soundings in Berlin corresponded with the timing of enquiries in Moscow about the neutrality treaty.[45] Would the Soviet Union grant foreign powers the use of air bases – in Vladivostok, for example? The answer from Moscow was also positive: No. As a result the Japanese were strategically well prepared. They need not fear an attack from the rear in a war with the United States, and they had obliged the Germans to accompany them in their risky venture.

With these assurances in hand, Japanese leaders decided irrevocably on war in the Imperial Conference of 1 December 1941.[46] Now, for the first time, the Japanese ambassador in Berlin received formal instructions that he should have the oral promises reconfirmed in written form. The no-separate-peace agreement proposed long ago by the Japanese, and accepted by the Germans, should be quickly concluded and ratified by the Tripartite Pact signatories. When Ribbentrop delayed the proceedings because he wanted first to consult with Hitler who was touring the Eastern front, the Japanese turned to the Germans' junior partner, the Italians. Leaders in Rome were flattered and, without equivocating, immediately agreed. In Berlin, where Mussolini was obliged to report the entire course of action, Ribbentrop followed suit after consulting with Hitler. On 5 December at four o'clock in the morning, the German Foreign Minister handed the Japanese ambassador the German-Italian counterproposal for a no-separate-peace agreement.[47] Thereby, some sixty hours before the surprise attack on Pearl Harbor, the European Axis Powers had committed themselves in writing to entering an eventual war with the United States. Of course, at the time they had no idea when and where this war might break out.

The role of the German-Italian no-separate-peace promise in Japanese decision making is very difficult to ascertain. It is doubtful that this reassurance from their pact partners was meaningless to the Japanese, but it seems finally to have had little influence on their decision for war. Dwelling on possible Japanese reactions to a clear refusal from Germany and Italy to join in such an agreement is, therefore, mere speculation. Basically, German leaders had already reconciled themselves to the inevitability of a war with the United States, and this agreement can be viewed as acknowledging a self-evident situation. It hardly implies, as Cordell Hull thought, the spawning of a worldwide conspiracy.

After Japan's successful air attack on the US Pacific Fleet at Pearl Harbor, which the Germans first heard about from the enemy over the BBC, the German leaders delayed declaring war on the United States until after the no-separate-peace agreement was signed on 11 December. Despite the initial unexpected military success, Hitler, ever distrustful, wanted to be sure that the Japanese would steadfastly stand by the other two Axis Powers in what Berlin was sure would be a long, protracted war.

The military negotiations[48] begun at this time in Berlin were also marked by mistrust. The first meeting of the military commission ended without positive results. Immediately afterwards, the Japanese proposed to clearly delineate between German and Japanese zones of operation, instead of forming a coalition of commands at sea via the Suez Canal, Indian Ocean, and Singapore. Despite serious doubts about this proposal by everyone consulted in the German government, from the Foreign Ministry to the navy, Hitler opposed them and prevailed. The 'Führer' – as with Japan's entry into the war against the Soviet Union – was not interested in military collaboration with the Japanese. Hitler's doctrinaire racism would not allow sharing the victories of the 'German master race' with the 'yellow' Japanese. A division of military zones of operation and similar spheres of influence at 70° longitude (around the mouth of the Indus River) concurred with Hitler's ideas and also those of the Imperial Navy General Staff in Tokyo, each, of course, with very different motives in mind. The revisionist Axis Powers divided the world, excluding the Americas, exactly between themselves, but neither was able to subdue militarily or rule politically their respective areas.

Conclusion

The Germans under Adolf Hitler's leadership continued to be the main enemy from the point of view of Washington and Moscow. Even after the outbreak of war, all military measures were first and foremost directed toward destroying the German Third Reich.

Despite their unexpected military successes, Japanese power and ingenuity were again underestimated – and not for the last time. In Washington on the evening of 8 December, the prevailing mood was one of relief.[49] At last the opposing fronts were now clear. Thanks to 'magic', the Americans were intercepting and reading all diplomatic transmissions between Tokyo and Berlin. They were aware, as a result, of the two European Axis Powers' acceptance of the no-separate-peace agreement requested by Tokyo. A declaration of war was expected any time from the Germans, who were regarded as the real enemy and the wirepullers behind the scenes. The Japanese surprise attack on Pearl Harbor provided the excuse many American leaders had hoped for – it opened the back door to participating in the war in Europe. Stalin, too, could simply not imagine that Japanese strategists, who in the Nomohan Incident of 1939 had demonstrated their inflexibility and incompetence, could devise such a clever undertaking.[50] The Soviet dictator obviously believed the Germans were capable of anything. After all, they had stood only a short while ago on the war-ravaged outskirts of Moscow. He therefore assumed that there were German military experts and pilots behind Japan's surprising success. Within a short period of time this situation changed. The Allied Powers came to greatly overestimate both their German and Japanese opponents, largely due to their bombastic propaganda.

However, the realities of war were something else again. The separation of their areas of operations, which implicitly meant limiting each country's geopolitical sphere of influence, was a result of the different directions German and Japanese military offensives took. Coordinating their military efforts against one adversary or agreeing on priorities was impossible for both parties. Premodern prejudices in Germany, as in Japan, in the end prevented their coming together. Hitler's racist reservations about the 'yellow' Japanese were requited in kind by Tokyo. The hoped-for liberation of East Asia from the white man's yoke left little room for an alliance with a white man's nation. Each strove with criminal megalomania to become a world power and thought they could forgo the help of the other. The 'young, aspiring nations' of the fascist alliance were much less able to agree to a basic equality among themselves than the disparate members of the opposing coalition. Germany and Japan arrogantly appropriated the world for themselves, divided it, and marched separately to a common defeat.

Notes

1. Letter from Roosevelt to Grew from 21 January 1941 in Detlef Junker, *Kampf um die Weltmacht. Die USA und das Dritte Reich 1933–1945*, Düsseldorf, 1988, pp. 129f. For Roosevelt's policy of intervention, see Waldo Heinrichs, 'Franklin D. Roosevelt and the Risks of War', in: Akira Iriye and Warren Cohen, eds., *American, Chinese, and Japanese Perspectives on Wartime Asia (1931–1949)*, Wilmington, Del., 1990, pp. 147–78, and Bernd Martin, 'Les Relations êntre les États-Unis et les Démocraties occidentales de 1938–1941. La Prétention Américaine au "Leadership Mondiale"', in: *Guerres mondiales et conflits contemporains*, vol. 163, Juillet 1991, pp. 33–50.

2. For a classical example of the bilateral approach, see Dorothy Borg and Shumpei Okamoto, eds., *Pearl Harbor as History. Japanese-American Relations 1931–1941*, New York and London, 1973.

3. For a comparison of the three fascist powers, see chapter 6, 'Three Forms of Fascism: Japan – Italy – Germany', in this volume.

4. 'Die jungen, aufstrebenden Völker', expression frequently used by the German Foreign Minister Joachim von Ribbentrop (1938–45).

5. On German-Japanese relations before the outbreak of the Pacific War, from German sources: Ernest L. Presseisen, *Germany and Japan. A Study in Totalitarian Diplomacy*, The Hague, 1958, and Theo Sommer, *Deutschland und Japan zwischen den Mächten. Vom Antikominternpakt zum Dreimächtepakt*, Tübingen, 1962; from Japanese sources: Gerhard Krebs, *Japans Deutschlandpolitik 1955–1941. Eine Studie zur Vorgeschichte des Pazifischen Krieges*, Hamburg, 1984, and Tokushiro Ohata, 'The Anti-Comintern Pact, 1935–1939', in: James W. Morley, ed., *Deterrent Diplomacy. Japan, Germany, and the USSR 1935–1940*, New York, 1976, pp. 9–12.

6. For Germany as a model for Meiji Japan, see chapter 2, 'Fatal Affinities: The German Role in the Modernisation of Japan in the Early Meiji Period (1868–1895) and Its Aftermath', in this volume.

7. For the shift of German Far Eastern Policy from China to Japan, see John P. Fox, *Germany and the Far Eastern Crisis 1931–1938. A Study in Diplomacy and Ideology*, Oxford, 1982.

8. On Oshima, see Carl Boyd, *The Extraordinary Envoy: General Hiroshi Oshima and Diplomacy in the Third Reich, 1934–1939*, Washington, 1980.

9. On Ribbentrop's foreign policy, see Wolfgang Michalka, *Ribbentrop und die deutsche Weltpolitik 1933–1940*, München, 1980.

10. For the discussion in the Hiranuma government, see Krebs, *Japans Deutschlandpolitik*, pp. 221–305.

11. For the Japanese position at the outbreak of the war in Europe, see Masaki Miyake, 'Die Lage Japans bei Ausbruch des Zweiten Weltkrieges', in: Wolfgang Benz and Hermann Graml, eds., *Sommer 1939. Die Großmächte und der europäische Krieg*, Stuttgart, 1989, pp. 195–222. See also Akio Nakai, 'Die Haltung Japans gegenüber dem europäischen Konflikt am Vorabend des Zweiten Weltkrieges', in: Johann Schmidt, ed., *Deutsch-japanische Freundschaft*, Preetz,

1980, pp. 63–87, and for the strenuous relations with Germany, see Bernd Martin, 'Germano-Japanese Relations after the Hitler-Stalin Pact', in: David W. Pike, ed., *The Opening of the Second World War*, New York, 1992, pp. 228–38.

12. For the diplomatic correspondence of the period from 1 September 1939 until 7 December 1941, see *Akten zur deutschen auswärtigen Politik (ADAP)*, series D, vols. 8–13, Baden-Baden, 1961ff., Bonn, 1964–1970. English translation and publication, *Documents on German Foreign Policy*, series D, vols. 8–13, London, 1949–64.

13. On the origins of the Pacific War, and the memoranda of the Army General Staff, see Akira Iriye, *The Origins of the Second World War in Asia and the Pacific War*, London, 1989.

14. For the politics of the second and third Konoe cabinet, see Michael Libal, *Japans Weg in den Krieg. Die Außenpolitik der Kabinette Konoye 1940–41*, Düsseldorf, 1971. See also Krebs, *Japans Deutschlandpolitik*, pp. 438–575. On Konoe's political outlook, see Gordon M. Berger, 'Japan's Young Prince. Konoe Fumimaro's Early Political Career, 1916–1931', in: *Monumenta Nipponica*, vol. 29, no. 4, 1974.

15. John Huizinga, 'Yosuke Matsuoka and the Japanese-German Alliance', in: Gordon A. Craig and Felix Gilbert, eds., *The Diplomats 1919–1939*, Princeton, 1953, pp. 615–48.

16. On the Tripartite Pact, see the detailed study, including documents, by Theo Sommer, *Deutschland und Japan zwischen den Mächten 1935–1940*, Tübingen, 1962. See also Chihiro Hosoya in: Morley, *Deterrent Diplomacy*, pp. 191–258 and Ian Nish, ed., *The Tripartite Pact of 1940: Japan, Germany and Italy*, London, 1984. From Japanese sources, Masaki Miyake, *Nichi-Doku-I sangoku dōmei no kenkyū*. With an English summary, Tokyo, 1975.

17. On the peace issue, see the detailed study by Bernd Martin, *Friedensinitiativen und Machtpolitik im Zweiten Weltkrieg 1939–1942*, Düsseldorf, 2nd ed., 1976.

18. For the American reaction upon the conclusion of the Tripartite Pact, see Paul W. Schroeder, *The Axis-Alliance and Japanese-American Relations 1941*, Ithaca, 3rd ed., 1963. For the Japanese southward expansion, see James W. Morley, ed., *The Fateful Choice. Japan's Advance into Southeast Asia, 1939–1941*, New York, 1981.

19. Bernd Martin, *Deutschland und Japan im Zweiten Weltkrieg. Von Pearl Harbour bis zur deutschen Kapitulation*, Göttingen, 1969, p. 129.

20. 'Die Dämmerstunde der plutokratischen Götter ist aufgezogen', in: *Völkischer Beobachter*, 28 September 1940.

21. A basic study on the origins of the German attack on the Soviet Union is Andreas Hillgruber, *Hitlers Strategie, Politik und Kriegführung 1940–41*, Frankfurt a. M., 1965. For Hitler's war directives, see Walter Hubatsch, ed., *Hitlers Weisungen für die Kriegführung 1939–1945. Dokumente des Oberkommandos der Wehrmacht*, Frankfurt a. M., 1962.

22. For the deliberations about a Japanese attack on Singapore, see Jun Tsunoda, 'Matsuoka und Singapore', in: *Wehrwissenschaftliche Rundschau*, vol. 19, 1969, pp. 68–74.

23. Records of all diplomatic talks Matsuoka had in Berlin, in: *Akten zur deutschen auswärtigen Politik*, series D, vol. 12 (see above).

24. Records of the Liaison Conferences in Nobutake Ike, ed., *Japan's Decision for War. Records of the 1941 Policy Conferences*, Stanford, Cal., 1967.

25. Krebs, *Japans Deutschlandpolitik*, p. 534.

26. For Japanese reports from Berlin, translated into German, see Andreas Hillgruber, 'Japan und der Fall "Barbarossa"', in: *Wehrwissenschaftliche Rundschau*, vol. 18, 1968, pp. 312–36. Furthermore, see Gerhard Krebs, 'Japan und der deutsch-sowjetische Krieg 1941', in Bernd Wegner, ed., *Zwei Wege nach Moskau. Vom Hitler-Stalin-Pakt zum 'Unternehmen Barbarossa'*, München, 1991, pp. 564–83, and Bernd Martin, 'Japan and Barbarossa', paper, University of Waterloo, Ontario, Center for Soviet Studies, 18 May 1991.

27. Martin, *Deutschland und Japan*, p. 173 (Conversation Hitler-Oshima, 21 January 1943).

28. Ike, *Decision for War*, (Liaison Conference, 16 June 1941).

29. Krebs, *Japans Deutschlandpolitik*, p. 541.

30. Ike, *Decision for War*, (Liaison Conference, 27 June 1941).

31. *Documents on German Foreign Policy*, D XIII, Doc. No. 53, telegramme from Ribbentrop to Ambassador Ott (Tokyo), 1 July 1941.

32. Ike, *Decision for War*, pp. 77–90

33. For the meeting between Hitler and Oshima on 14 July 1941, see Andreas Hillgruber, *Der Zenit des Zweiten Weltkrieges Juli 1941*, Wiesbaden, 1977.

34. For the political repercussions of the battle of Smolensk, see Andreas Hillgruber, 'Die Bedeutung der Schlacht von Smolensk in der zweiten Juli-Hälfte 1941 für den Ausgang des Ostkrieges', in: Inge Auerbach et al., eds., *Felder und Vorfelder russischer Geschichte. Studien zu Ehren von Peter Scheibert*, Freiburg i. Br., 1985, pp. 266–79.

35. For the attitude of the Japanese army, see Takushiro Hattori, *The Complete History of the Greater East Asia War*, Tokyo, 1953 (American translation, unpublished, copy on microfilm), vol. 1, part 1, p. 153.

36. On the origin of Pearl Harbor, see the recent anthology by Hilary Conroy and Harry Wray, eds., *Pearl Harbor Reexamined. Prologue to the Pacific War*, Honolulu, 1990, and the papers from the International Conference, 'Fifty Years After – The Pacific War Re-examined', Lake Yamanaka 14–17 Nov. 1991, edited, in Japanese, by Chihiro Hosaya, Tokyo 1993.

37. Ike, *Decision for War*, p. 158.

38. Martin, *Deutschland und Japan*, p. 110.

39. See Krebs, *Japans Deutschlandpolitik*, and Peter Herde, *Pearl Harbor, 7. Dezember 1941. Der Ausbruch des Krieges zwischen Japan und den Vereinigten Staaten und die Ausweitung des europäischen Krieges zum Zweiten Weltkrieg*, Darmstadt, 1980; on Italy's Far Eastern policy, see Valdo Ferretti, *Il Giappone e la Politica Estera Italiana 1935–1941*, Roma, 1983. Most recent anthology, stressing cultural relations:

Gerhard Krebs and Bernd Martin, eds., *Formierung und Fall der Achse Berlin – Tokyo*, München, 1994.

40. See note 37 above.

41. Takushiro Hattori 'Japans Operationsplan für den Beginn des Pazifischen Krieges', in: *Wehrwissenschaftliche Rundschau*, vol. 7 (1957), pp. 247–74.

42. Hillgruber, *Hitlers Strategie*, pp. 551–52 (Hitler in a conversation with General Halder and other military leaders).

43. For the German decision to declare war upon the United States, see Jürgen Rohwer und Ernst Jäckel, eds., *Kriegswende Dezember 1941*, Frankfurt a. M., 1981 and Martin, *Deutschland-Japan*, pp. 34ff. With special regard to the topic of this article, Gerhard Krebs, 'Deutschland und Pearl Harbour', in: *Historische Zeitschrift*, 253 (October 1991), pp. 313–70.

44. Martin, *Deutschland und Japan*, p. 34 (Telegramme Ribbentrop – Ambassador Ott in Tokyo from 21 November 1941).

45. On Japanese-Soviet relations, see Hubertus Lupke, *Japans Rußlandpolitik von 1939–1941*, Frankfurt a. M., 1962, and George A. Lensen, *The Strange Neutrality. Soviet-Japanese Relations during the Second World War*, Tallahassee, Florida, 1972.

46. Ike, *Decision for War*, pp. 262–83.

47. Key documents in Martin, *Deutschland und Japan*, pp. 224–28.

48. For the no-separate-peace treaty and the military agreement, see Martin, *Deutschland-Japan*, pp. 46–54, and for the reproduction of the documents, pp. 229–34.

49. For the atmosphere in Washington, see the diary of Harry Hopkins, 7 December 1941, quoted in Rohwer/Jäckel, *Kriegswende Dezember 1941*, p. 40.

50. For Stalin's remark, see Peter Lowe, 'The Soviet Union in Britain's Far Eastern Policy 1941', in: Ian Nish, ed., *The Russian Problem in East Asia*, London, 1981.

❧ 10 ❧

THE GERMAN-JAPANESE ALLIANCE DURING THE SECOND WORLD WAR

The shock attack of Japanese carrier-based aircraft on units of the U.S. Pacific battle fleet in Pearl Harbor on 7–8 December 1941 converted the German war in Europe and North Africa and the Japanese localised conflict in China, the 'Chinese incident', into worldwide conflagration.[1] In the American view, such global war had become inevitable after the two nationalist totalitarian states – National Socialist Germany and the equally totalitarian Tenno Empire – and their junior partner fascist Italy signed the Tripartite Pact on 27 September 1940, signalling fundamental agreement of the three states on political and military issues.[2]

Neither the Reich's revisionism, officially contained within Europe, nor Japan's aggressive pursuit of a new order in East Asia would necessarily have led to global war. Nevertheless, the political strategies of both Germany and Japan in the 1930s to create their own self-sufficient spheres of influence threatened the security of the victorious powers of the First World War. In restructuring their societies on authoritarian patterns by recourse to nationalist ideologies, both Germany and Japan sought to become world powers – by force, if necessary.[3]

Throughout the interwar years the doctrinal communism of an externally and internally enfeebled Soviet Union was far less of a challenge to the liberal capitalist Western democracies and their much postulated individual freedoms than the united front of a transnational fascist system, in which the individual was

The first two sections of this chapter are a revised version of a translation from the German by Ursula Watson which was first published in Saki Dockrill, ed., *From Pearl Harbor to Hiroshima: The Second World War in Asia and the Pacific, 1941–45*, London, 1994, pp. 153–73.

superseded by communal interests and the omnipotent state regulated all public and economic matters. When, therefore, the Western countries united against fascist provocations, they acted essentially on sociopolitical principles, as well as for power and economic interests; conversely, internal political norms and deliberations of power were fundamental to the joining of forces of Germany, Japan, and Italy.

The former socioimperialism of the Western colonial powers (the United States included) was being restated in a new, more radical form in the revisionist states, which still felt dissatisfied with the outcome of the last worldwide conflict. Of these, fascist Italy – economically backward, a 'latecomer' if compared to Britain and the United States – was the first to attempt to realise a premodernistic state concept by applying rigid, repressive methods internally and adopting an aggressive stance externally. Germany and Japan, socially and economically in near collapse after the Great Depression, followed suit. It is, therefore, far more likely that the German-Japanese understanding in the Second World War was the result of internal political parallels and not of international diplomatic movements. In Japan, an affinity with Germany had been consciously sought since Meiji times, culminating in the widely promulgated fascist 'kindred spirit', which came to an abrupt end in 1945.[4]

World War and Combined Warfare: Incompatible Military and Political Aims

The Japanese global strategy was not produced until 20 October 1941 and proved to be no blueprint for global domination.[5] Hastily drawn up, the strategic plan incorporated defensive elements: military opposition to the United States' overwhelming political and economic force; shock attacks against the fleets of hostile nations; elimination of American, British and Dutch military bases; occupation, as security, of certain territories; defensive measures against repossession of their holdings by former colonial powers; the determination of the as yet unspecified demarcation line of the area under occupation; enforced American recognition, by a peace settlement, of the East Asian Commonwealth Sphere. The planners excluded possible American counteroffensives. Britain was –

in accordance with the German view – already defeated and its empire on the point of collapse.[6] Logistical agreement with Germany was, therefore, superfluous. The hostilities simultaneously started at various and widely distant fronts, from the Pacific island of Guam, to British Malaya, and the exhilarating initial victories were demonstrative of such overwhelming Japanese strength that outside help could be dispensed with. Within a few weeks phase one of the plan – the conquest of American positions and the reversal of the British forces – had been achieved. In a second phase, the key British fortress of Singapore was to fall, and the Dutch East Indies and British Burma would be occupied.[7]

The triumph in the Far East suited the German leaders, who were preoccupied with their own problems at the Russian Front and readily agreed to meet Japan's wishes, although these negated the concept of combined warfare.[8] Hitler's determination not to invite Japan into his Russian war was unchanged, despite the first ominous setbacks to his Russian campaign and despite the representations of his foreign minister. In addition, the army command was unwilling to fight the Russian war with the help of a country that was totally outside its own continental orbit. Only the navy devoted some thought to integrated strategies and revived its old alternative strategy – a concentration of forces against British positions in Suez and the Near East – but, being the weakest and least influential arm of the three services, the navy remained unheard. Torn between admiration and envy of Japan's successes the German leaders themselves were little inclined to effect military agreements with the Japanese.

Both the actual military situation and the ideological power concepts – to create a great Germanic empire in Europe and a Greater East Asia Co-Prosperity Sphere – suited the purpose of both powers, particularly the Japanese, which was to achieve a contractual definition of each sphere of dominance. Within a week of the successful raid on Pearl Harbor, General Oshima (who had returned as ambassador to Berlin) had submitted a draft agreement of firmer military cooperation, which in reality amounted to division rather than cooperation. According to Japanese notions, the dividing line between the two zones of operation (or zones of influence) should coincide with longitude 70 degrees east, at approximately Karachi/the Indus estuary. This was rejected by the German Foreign Office and by the German navy. Division at this geographical point allocated India to the Japanese and precluded naval operations in that area. But clear separation met the wishes of Hitler, who was then deeply involved in his war on the Eastern front. The treaty was consequently signed in Berlin on 18 January 1942.[9] The negotiated boundaries were soon to prove an insurmountable obstacle to coordinated political decisions – on the liberation of India[10] or on naval strategies in those waters. Even the crossing of this boundary line by supply cruisers or blockade runners required tedious prior consultation. Japan, Germany, and Italy had set out to give the world a new order. They had loudly publicised their claim and had confirmed it in secretly negotiated pacts. However, when it came time to do it, the three 'rising young nations' had neither the will nor the strength to redesign the existing world order.

The first half of 1942 was perhaps best suited to combined military operations in the form of either a joint campaign against the Soviet Union or, alternatively, a naval pincer-type operation against British Middle Eastern and Indian positions, which had recently been reinforced with American troops. The operations together would have overstrained even their combined resources, but a concerted effort in the first half-year at either one or the other front might well have succeeded. However, on strategic deployments of this kind, the opinions of the respective upper echelons of Germany habitually clashed, and decisions of the 'Führer' had to paper over the differences. In the absence of an all-powerful dictator, the discord among Japanese leaders was apt to result in strategic half-measures and empty compromise. Quite unlike their adversaries – the chance alliance of Western capitalism and eastern communism – the 'fascist' powers were unable to compromise internally or cooperate externally. The 'prerogative of the strongest', contained in the National Socialist and Italian fascist ideologies, as well as in the missionary fervour of the Yamato race (*kokutai*), produced in all three nations egoistic, compartmentalised thinking and *sacro egoismo* guidelines in foreign policy. Inability to compromise internally and to cooperate on a rational basis became the hallmarks of all three 'fascist' states.

The issue of a united front against the Soviet Union is a case in point:[11] in Berlin the foreign ministry untiringly propagated Japan's entry into war against Russia to Japanese diplomats and military attachés. Not an unreasonable course of action for Ribbentrop to take, in view of the critical war situation, but it was a view shared by no one else. Hitler himself continued to dislike the idea of the 'yellows' fighting in his own Germanic war of destiny in the east. In fact, he even warned Japan not to dissipate its strength by joining the war with Russia. Hitler's growing detachment from his Japanese partner is evident in the infrequency of his contacts with Japanese representatives: the 'Führer' saw the Japanese ambassador perhaps twice on formal occasions after the Japanese declaration of war and then not again for a whole year. However, on 21 January 1943, with the Stalingrad disaster at near-culmination point, Hitler once again summoned the Japanese ambassador to convey the urgent request that Japan should finally enter the war against the Soviet Union,[12] to which Tokyo replied belatedly in March and predictably in the negative.

In view of the disparity within the German leadership – Hitler's attitude was fully shared in Berlin by the army supreme command and supported by the navy, eager to introduce its own alternative strategic plans – Tokyo did not feel particularly obliged to launch an attack against the Soviet eastern provinces.

To the Imperial Navy, bent upon its southward strategy, the British and American navies remained the major adversaries. Military alliance against Russia was therefore incompatible with the primary Japanese war aim of driving the Western powers out of East Asia. Since the German war of attrition in Russia was diverting German resources from the war with the Anglo-American powers, the naval command had consistently urged its cessation. For the sophisticated technology of the Japanese carrier fleet, the free transfer of war materials and technology with the highly developed armament industry of the Reich was of vital importance in order to prevail against the equally highly technologically sophisticated American forces. Furthermore, in the wake of the defeat in the Midway aircraft carrier battle in June 1942, an American counteroffensive, and hence an extended war, loomed larger.

Japan's maritime *Blitzkrieg* concept had failed after seven months of victorious advance, and global defensive policies against the Americans regained significance. The Japanese navy – supported by the Foreign Ministry and, after autumn 1942, by the army – consequently became the driving force behind a German-Soviet peace settlement.[13] The entire Japanese leadership made this the main element of its foreign policy for the remaining three years of the war. In numerous official and unofficial initiatives, Japan attempted, in both Berlin and Moscow, to bring the combatants to the conference table, to reestablish the Eurasian bloc, and at least reach a balance of power with Britain and the United States in this battle of the continents. However, the Japanese efforts were disregarded; moreover, since Moscow regularly informed the Western powers of each new initiative, the coalition between the United States and Soviet Russia was strengthened rather than weakened. On the German side, Hitler clung dogmatically to his decisive racist war in the east and refused even to discuss a negotiated peace in Russia. Even Russia's readiness for talks, and there had been several feelers in this direction in Stockholm,[14] were diverted on Hitler's instructions, whilst Ribbentrop, and later Goebbels and Himmler, saw ending the war in the east as the only chance of rescuing the Reich and National Socialism. The question of the Soviet Union was to be decisive in the defeat of both Germany and Japan, the differing, ideologically founded strategies of the Tripartite Pact powers towards the Soviet Union being primarily responsible for the collapse of the German-Japanese alliance.

The failure to cooperate across the Indian Ocean[15] was, in the face of this, of secondary importance. Ten days after the start of war in the Pacific – regarded with envy by the German navy – high-ranking Japanese naval officers met with Commander-in-Chief Admiral Raeder to discuss mutual plans for the first time. Important naval officers in Tokyo were also positively inclined towards a liaison of the two powers in the Indian Ocean. Plans, studies, and reports were made in Berlin and Tokyo. When the British stronghold of Singapore capitulated in February 1942, and it was apparent that Japan would succeed in occupying Burma and the Dutch Indies, questions in Tokyo concerned further expansive strikes. The naval staff officers had three main alternatives to choose from: an offensive in the Indian Ocean, towards Australia, or towards the American Midway Islands. As the Germans would not commit themselves to an attack by Rommel's *Afrikakorps* on Suez, the most promising alternative was only partially pursued.

At the beginning of April a Japanese task force arrived in the Indian Ocean. The presence of heavily armed Japanese units opposite Colombo, Ceylon and the ensuing bombardment on 5 April 1942 caused panic reactions among the Western powers. The British Eastern Fleet relinquished the ocean area and sought protection from the superior might of the Japanese fleet in the harbours of East Africa. The Indian Ocean, even India itself as the jewel of the British Crown, lay open to the Tripartite states. However, the Japanese force turned back as its ships were needed for scattered attacks against Australia and Midway. When, two months later, the Germans, after the fall of Tobruk on 20 June 1942, opened their offensive against Suez, the Japanese fleet had suffered defeats at Port Moresby (New Guinea) and Midway and was in no position to undertake any extensive naval operations. The attempts at combined maritime warfare foundered in Germany primarily through Hitler's obstinacy and the absolute priority given to the land war against Russia. On the Japanese side, carelessness and the lack of a strategic concept, leading to a wastage of potential and then to the first naval defeats of the Imperial Navy, were responsible for the failure of the Singapore-Suez connection.

Separation of the respective zones of warfare and influence in the Indian Ocean by the line of 70 degrees longitude was a further, more strongly political, hindrance to German-Japanese cooperation. The German navy and foreign office kept jealous watch against any disregard of the demarcation line by the Japanese fleet. When the Japanese wanted to launch an offensive against Madagascar, which lay in the sphere claimed by Germany, it was stifled in the planning phase by massive German objections.[16] In addition, with regard to the question of the future role of India, the demarcation agreement proved to be a hindrance to cooperation.

However, German foreign and military policy maintained strong interest in the Indian subcontinent,[17] despite its allocation to the Japanese. One of the most prominent Indian politicians, the leader of the radical wing of the Indian independence movement, Subhas Chandra Bose, was in German custody; with his help it was possible to found an Indian exile organisation and Indian armed units. A declaration of freedom prepared by the Germans was wrecked by the distrust of the Japanese. When, however, somewhat later the Japanese wanted to garnish their successful naval offensives in the Indian Ocean with a political declaration on future freedom for India, the German side found such action premature, and refused. In August 1942 the worst internal rioting in India's colonial history broke out, during which Congress demanded that Britain relinquish the country. But the Japanese were no longer capable of encouraging the disturbances by spectacular military actions. Germany, too, whose troops at this time were held north of the Caucasus, was incapable of influencing the internal situation in India. The possible dislodgement of India from the British Empire through the concentrated combined operations of the Tripartite states failed due to their own egoistic power interests.

Trade Relations and Technological Transfer

The exchange of industrial goods and raw materials between the German Reich and the Japanese Empire was regulated by the Commercial and Shipping Treaty dating back to 1927.[18] All attempts to renew this agreement according to the new political situation and the changing demands of industry during the 1930s failed, even while communication lines – the Trans-Siberian Railroad and merchant shipping – were as yet undisturbed by war activities. It was not until January 1943 when surface transportation, even by blockade runners, had almost ceased, that a new 'Treaty on Economic Cooperation' was signed, to no real effect. As with all of the political agreements, such as the Anti-Comintern Pact of 1936, the Tripartite Pact of 1940 and the No-Separate-Peace Agreement of 11 December 1941, which were mainly designed to bluff the adversaries of the fascist New World Order, all commercial arrangements and technical contracts were designed to have similar propaganda effects. Lacking real substance, these treaties were supposed to cover up weaknesses and shortcomings on both sides. Mistrust, envy, and even treachery, together with an outspoken feeling of racial superiority, were characteristic of German-Japanese trade relations, especially for the period of combined warfare. The greediness of the 'have-nots' and their inability to agree to terms, or even to communicate in a frank way, were best revealed in their commercial talks during the war.

As both countries lacked natural resources for their industry, which was highly developed in Germany, but less so in Japan, they could hardly be regarded as complementary trading partners. Since the nineteenth century German industry had been looking towards China as Germany's future market for exporting commodities in exchange for the import of raw materials, for example, special ores and foodstuffs, such as soya beans. While German-Chinese barter trade boomed on the eve of the war in 1937, with Germany ranking second in China's overall foreign trade,[19] commercial relations between the newly allied nations of Hitler's Germany and Imperial Japan made up about 0.6 percent of all German imports, while, on the other hand, the share of German exported goods to Japan was 1.8 percent of Germany's total export volume.[20] German merchants complained continually about Japanese bureaucratic restrictions and trade limitations. 'Receiving a lot of friendship, but very few import licences', was quite a common saying with the German residents in Japan.[21]

The situation did not change for the better, as German politicians had hoped, when the Reich gave up its dominant trade position in China, acknowledging the special necessities of Japanese warfare on the Asian mainland. Even German diplomatic recognition of Japan's puppet state Manchuria in March 1938,[22] with the intention of improving trade relations with this region of agrarian surplus, brought nothing. The New Order of East Asia was to be dominated politically and economically by Japan. Tokyo planned to become the hub of a closed economic sphere[23] where no Western nation, not even the befriended Germans, would be granted special privileges. This stubborn Japanese attitude, to expel German trade from all Japanese controlled or occupied areas of the Greater East Asia Co-Prosperity Sphere, as well as Japan's constant refusal to compensate German firms for their losses, prevailed until September 1943.[24] Finally Japan, with her industry almost wrecked, invited Germany, who was suffering severe military setbacks on all fronts, to participate in the reconstruction of East Asia, an area that by this time had developed into a 'Greater East Asia Robbery Sphere'.

Despite the low volume of bilateral trade, some significant technical cooperation did exist between the two countries. As Germany's industry during and after the First World War was far more advanced than that of Japan, which basically remained an agrarian country, this exchange soon turned into a unilateral technical transfer from Germany to Japan. Although Japanese industry had been modernised following English and American patterns during the Meiji period (1868–1912),[25] the Island Empire was forced from 1930 onward, due to rising tensions with the Western powers, to rely on Germany as a model for technical and industrial development.

The high standard of German armaments had attracted Japanese army and navy groups from as early as during the First World War. As one of the victors, Japan requested and was granted German reparations in the form of captured weapons and naval units. Seven German submarines, several different aeroplanes, and one complete airship, as well as sets of motors and samples of special equipment were delivered free of charge to the Japanese side. In most cases the equipment, for example, the planes and the submarines, were dismantled for the purpose of studying their construction and then reconstructed with some improvements. The Japanese navy even managed to acquire the latest construction plans for submarines which were no longer to be built in German shipyards and engaged five German civilian experts and one former German submarine commander for about six years at the naval station in Kobe. From there, the first Japanese submarine cruisers (I-1 to I-4) were eventually launched at the Kawasaki shipyards.[26]

German aviation greatly influenced the development of Japanese planes during the interwar period. Under the Treaty of Versailles the construction of fighter planes and bombers was forbidden to Germany, so German aircraft pioneers welcomed the Japanese engineers and shared their knowledge with the visitors from the Far East. All of the prominent German aircraft firms, such as Messerschmitt, Junkers, Heinkel, and Dornier, provided technical help to the Japanese. Dornier and Kawasaki even went so far as to conclude a ten-year partnership agreement which allowed the Japanese to construct and build German planes under licence. German engineers and technicians helped with the construction of the first Japanese all-metal aeroplane which was built with duraluminium.[27]

After the abrogation of the Versailles Treaty by the National Socialist government, the new and highly advanced German air force attracted the Japanese. An order of more than seventy dive bombers of the Heinkel 111 type had finally to be cancelled as the German authorities refused the required export permit with reference to the priority of German rearmament. Japanese proposals for a joint construction plant in Japan, in order to produce a revised model of the German fighter plane Me-109, were declined for the same reasons. Despite this, in both cases plans and blueprints reached construction bureaux in Japan, often with the help of industrial espionage, and greatly influenced the development of the respective Japanese models. From 1936 onwards, Junkers sold their models to Japan and as late as 1941 managed to have four planes (Ju-86) transported via the Trans-Siberian Railroad to Germany's ally in the Far East. Japanese aircraft engineers were trained in Junkers' plants. Aircraft engines with fuel injection, such as the famous Daimler-Benz motors, were sold to Japan (a total of 601 units) and were later built under license by the firms of Aichi and Kawasaki.[28]

Furthermore, German expertise helped the Japanese develop lightweight alloys for the fabrication of tin plate, as did German know-how with the introduction of the Thomas process in steel production.[29] Collaboration and technological transfer could also be found in the fields of electronics, radio transmitters, wireless sets, and valves before the outbreak of the war.[30] There is no question that Germany helped with Japanese rearmament. But the German contribution is difficult to assess, since the Western democracies also helped, until the abrogation by Washington of the American-Japanese Commercial Treaty in July 1939. Last but not least, Italian technological help with aircraft production should also be mentioned.

Most prominent as a middleman between the Japanese military, particularly the Imperial Navy, and German firms was a businessman and arms broker from Freiburg, Dr. Friedrich-Wilhelm Hack.[31] His conduct as a businessman was typical of the contacts and semilegal contracts between the Germans and the Japanese during the prewar period. His political influence in shaping the military alliance between the two outcast nations has been almost forgotten. Serving as an adviser to the South Manchurian Railway before the outbreak of the First World War, Hack acquired a knowledge of spoken Japanese. During the First World War the young businessman served as an interpreter with the besieged German garrison at Tsingtao, where he was taken prisoner by the Japanese. During his five-year internment Hack improved his language skills and used them for contacts with Japanese officers and business people. When released, Hack was made head of the first Japanese trade delegation to visit Germany after the Great War. Together with Albert Schinzinger, formerly Krupp's representative in Japan and afterwards His Majesty's Consul General in Berlin, Hack founded an export firm (Schinzinger und Hack) dealing in both legal and illegal export of arms and technical devices.

Hack specialised in military aviation and brought about most of the aforementioned contacts between the German aircraft industry and its Japanese counterpart.[32] It was he, a business go-between and a founding member of the German-Japanese Society in Berlin, who elaborated, together with his Japanese acquaintances, the idea of a closer alliance between the Island Empire and the reemerging German Reich. Eventually, in 1935, Hack introduced high-ranking Japanese military leaders, such as Admiral Yama-moto and Military Attaché General Oshima, to Ribbentrop, then Hitler's personal adviser in foreign affairs. In return for this mediation, Hack was entrusted with conducting the talks on an anti-Soviet military alliance, which he successfully concluded with his Japanese counterparts as early as November 1935. Disappointed with Hitler's politics, he got into trouble with the Nazi regime, was arrested and then released due to diplomatic pressure from the Japanese Embassy, and finally left Germany for Switzerland. There for the duration of the war he again served as a middleman, this time between the American Office of Strategic Services (Alan Dulles) and the Japanese, and in the end helped to mediate Japan's surrender in 1945.

However, in 1939, with the conclusion of the Hitler-Stalin Pact and the outbreak of war in Europe, political and economic relations between Japan and Germany almost came to an end. The discussions for a new commercial treaty, started at the beginning of 1939, were suspended by the Japanese government because of 'undesirable political developments in Europe'. The shipment of urgently needed raw materials, such as rubber, tin and quinine, from Japanese ports to Vladivostok for rail transport to Germany was halted by Japanese authorities. Hampering German trade and helping British commerce became the guideline of Japan's economic foreign policy in those days.[33] This attitude did not change much even after the fall of France. Despite improvements in political relations and the signing of the formal military alliance, the Tripartite Pact, in September 1940, Japan still did not fulfill her obligations with respect to economic aid. Quotas of rubber, granted by the Vichy government to the German side, could not be shipped from Indochina because of Japan's refusal to assist.

Numerous complaints from German firms, diplomats, and military men in Tokyo reached the Foreign Office in Berlin, which, of course, had to react to the unfriendly and egoistic Japanese behaviour. When Japanese delegations from the Imperial Army and Navy visited Germany at the beginning of 1941, an official warning was issued (11 February 1941): 'All Japanese wishes which come close to industrial espionage or look like technological transfer should be declined at once'.[34] Despite this policy of retaliation, the Japanese Naval Mission arriving by special ship in Bilbao (Spain) managed somehow to obtain many samples of weaponry, in particular electronic devices.[35] The shipment in the *Asaka Maru*, which arrived safely at her Japanese home port, was the last transfer of technological hardware from Germany to Japan before land communication was interrupted by the German attack on Soviet Russia.

However, with the arrival of a German trade delegation (the Wohlthat mission) in Tokyo in March 1941 and Matsuoka's visit to Berlin the following month, German imports from East Asia improved. Transit on the Trans-Siberian Railroad[36] reached its peak during the last two months before the onset of war in Russia. Special trains transported huge quantities of rubber from Vladivostok to the German-Soviet border station at Brest-Litowsk. Here, because of different sized railway gauges, the shipment had to be transferred to German freight trains. The amount of rubber transported over the land route was sufficient for tyre production in the following years. With the interruption of this route German-Japanese trade virtually came to an end before the blockade runners started in the darkness of the long winter nights. However, only eleven ships (out of fifteen) starting from Japan reached French ports in the Atlantic, and sailing in the other direction, only five ships managed to reach Japanese waters in the winter of 1941–42.[37]

During the summer of 1942, when sea transportation was once again suspended, expectations about future trade were running high in Tokyo as well as in Berlin. With victory apparently close at hand, the Japanese diplomats in Berlin proposed a type of barter trade on a large scale.[38] Ambassador Oshima handed over a list requesting German credit of over one million yen in order to buy machine tools and samples of technically advanced German weaponry. The Japanese also showed interest in hydrogenation in order to produce synthetic oil, although the oil fields of the Dutch East Indies lay open to them for exploitation.[39] Therefore, the Japanese promise to provide Germany with all the raw materials needed for armament and civilian production did not sound very convincing. Japan obviously lacked the ships needed to transport the riches of the south to the Japanese homeland. This shortage in shipping facilities was revealed to the Germans when the Japanese requested more than one million tons of steel and half a million tons of shipping at the end of August 1942.[40] At the time, hopes of defeating the British in the Near East and establishing a new communication line via the Suez Canal ran high, but in fact there was no existing traffic between the two spheres.

Talks about a new trade agreement were started simultaneously in Tokyo and Berlin. Numerous proposals which appeared utopian, given reality, were made, and many drafts were outlined, but the fundamental differences of the two nations could not be overcome. Gaining victory after victory in Southeast Asia, the Japanese flatly refused to share their booty with their German ally. Tokyo insisted on monopolising the trade with the entire region. Therefore, German firms were to be neither compensated for their losses nor permitted to enjoy special status under Japanese rule. German direct trade with the former colonies of the Western powers was to be eliminated. Once and for all, Western rule was to come to an end. Another issue, the protection of German designs, and licences for production in Japan, could not be resolved either. Claiming an inferior technical status in comparison to Germany, Japan wanted these rights free of charge for military, as well as for civilian production. Sharing the same destiny, the Japanese felt that Germany should demonstrate its generosity by supplying Japanese industry with all the patents and blueprints needed to win the war and to establish Japan's leading position in East Asia. It was only on Hitler's direct orders that these obstacles to an agreement were removed. The 'Führer' blamed the British for the loss of a whole continent to the 'white race' and urged German firms to cooperate with Japan and even to abandon all former special rights in East Asia. Finally, the new trade agreement was signed on 20 January 1943,[41] but had no practical results. While the new fascist nations were struggling over their respective spheres of economic interest and the conditions of future trade, the few blockade runners leaving Europe for East Asia carried less cargo than ballast. German industry did not consent to Hitler's verdict and still refused to send samples and plans to Japan without payment for the licences. As no agreement could be reached, the ships embarked on their last voyage half empty.[42] With these embarrassing results, surface transportation by blockade runners came to an end.

The whole issue of Japanese payment for German rights and patents reached a new dimension when Hitler presented two brand-new German submarines to the Japanese navy the day after the commercial treaty had been signed.[43] The German navy, together with German firms specialising in submarine construction, tried in vain to dissuade Hitler from handing over these samples of Germany's latest technical advancement to the Japanese. It was thought that the Japanese would be unable to copy the submarines for production. One submarine with a German crew arrived safely in Japan, while the second with a Japanese crew was lost during the voyage. The Imperial Navy had the boat dismantled in one of its dockyards where naval experts carefully studied the new German devices – the electronic equipment, the special pumps, the engine, and the design of the periscope. Although Japanese industry at the time lacked both the proficiency and the material to build these types of submarines, they wanted to acquire the patents for military as well as for civilian use. As Hitler wanted to encourage the Japanese navy to take up submarine warfare against Anglo-American communication lines in the Pacific and Indian Oceans, he at once consented to Japanese wishes. All patents and devices concerning the submarine should be given as a further gift from the 'Führer' to the Japanese. There was unanimous criticism from German firms who condemned Hitler's decision as 'sacrificing the whole technical standard of German industry for nothing'[44] and insisted on the Japanese at least paying for other patents and production under licence.

The Japanese attempted to tip the scales in their favour by presenting gifts in return to the German navy. The unwanted presents shipped by Japanese submarines to French Atlantic ports did not fill German naval personnel with enthusiasm for their Japanese comrades. The German admiralty mocked this new method of compensation and drew an unfavourable balance for the Japanese side. The value of the new submarines and licences for special engines and bomb detonators totalled 36 million *Reichsmark*, while the Japanese 'presents' amounted to a mere 90 thousand *Reichsmark*.[45] It was again up to the 'Führer' himself to solve this controversial issue which by this time had become a burden to bilateral relations. On explicit order from Hitler a 'Technical Exchange Agreement' was worked out and finally signed on 2 March 1944.[46] The provisions of the new treaty resembled those of the lend-lease agreements between the United States and her dependent allies. All technical devices and German patents should be given to Japan on request without charge. After final victory, payment would be settled on the basis of a final balance. However, since both countries eventually lost the war, no payment was ever made. Under the obligations of this new treaty, the German chemical trust IG-Farben was compelled to convey all patents regarding hydrogenation of coal, for the purpose of obtaining synthetic oil, to Japanese industry free of charge until as late as January 1945.[47]

Technological transfer, from Germany to Japan peaked there-fore, in 1944 after the signing of the agreement. The Japanese navy now sent transport submarines containing rubber to Europe in order to carry home blueprints and samples of the latest German technical devices. A complete radar set (the *Würzburg* model) reached Japan in 1944, as did new technology for welding met-als.[48] The technique for welding a ship's hull together, instead of riveting the steel plates, which was learned from the Germans, turned out to be of great importance to the Japanese shipbuilding industry after the war. The Japanese were also very much con-cerned about further development of their fighter planes in order to stop American advancement from one island to the next in the Southwest Pacific. The rocket-jet Messerschmitt 163, which could use chemical fuels, and the German turbo-jet fighter, the Messer-schmitt 262, were both revised and rebuilt in Japan. At the end of the war, nineteen prototypes of the Japanese fighter jet *Kikka* were ready for combat use.[49]

With the invasion of the Reich by the victorious armies of the anti-Hitler coalition at the beginning of 1945, German and Japan-ese naval experts worked out a plan to have German top engi-neers of rocket technology (V2) and shipbuilding evacuated to Japan by submarines. This German 'Action Paper Clip' which aimed to benefit the Japanese ally (instead of the American adver-sary) started in April 1945, when a delegation of twenty-seven experts left the doomed Reich for Japan.[50] However, the subma-rine was forced to surrender after German capitulation and deliv-ered the engineers directly into American custody.

A final assessment of German technical help and technological transfer with regard to Japan's industrial development after the war seems almost impossible. The German influence should not be exaggerated but should not be minimised either. Japanese industry was fairly well advanced at the outbreak of the Pacific war and further developed on its own under severe pressure from the United States. While Japan needed 'hardware' from the West during the interwar period in order to compete with Western stan-dards, the armament industry needed 'software' during the war in order to construct and build most modern weaponry, for example, fighter planes, ships, and tankers for oil transportation from the South Seas.[51] The greatest advancements in Japanese industry were stimulated by the Japanese government and industrialists themselves. Structural reforms, such as the establishment of the Munitions Ministry in 1943, a forerunner to the powerful Ministry of International Trade and Industry (MITI)[52] in the 1950s, had a greater impact on Japan's economic miracle than the technological transfer from Germany during the war. However, a final evaluation of this critical topic should be made by Japanese scholars with the help of Japanese source material.

Conclusion

After less than a year of independent fighting, both Germany and Japan were in retreat. Within a further year, the Japanese leaders considered the political consequences of the collapse of the military alliance and declared the East Asian theatre of war to be fully independent from the war in Europe.[53] For both authoritarian systems there remained a separate defeat; the leaders in Berlin and Tokyo were incapable of ending an increasingly forlorn war; and in both, the civilian populations were subjected to great losses and suffering.

Germany and Japan as proponents of new world orders – the one as the saviour of the Occident from the communist threat, the other as the saviour of the colonised peoples of Asia from the 'white man's' yoke – collapsed in 1945; whereas Italy, seen as the unreliable third power in the pact, had already removed itself in 1943 from the unstable fascist alliance. Mercifully for the populations of these countries and for those of their opponents, a successful, pragmatic cooperation on a totalitarian basis which required war, destruction, and subjugation as its means of execution, proved impossible. A combined creed of unscrupulous, arbitrary power politics proved an inadequate basis for united warfare. In almost five years of military alliance, Germany and Japan acted together only once – in 1945 when both aggressor states were compelled to capitulate to their combined adversaries.

However, the world war started by Germany and Japan has not had only negative results for the two countries. In the ruins of the old orders – in Japan the semifeudal imperial system and in Germany the degenerate authoritarian Prussian state – lay the opportunity for both to build new social and political forms. The complete military defeat and moral discredit of their political systems achieved by force what the two latecomer nations could not by their own efforts alone: integration into the Western world.

An epoch of forced sociopolitical change had already begun in Japan and in Germany during the war – the start of a new social structure which, admittedly, could only develop afterwards. The war economy had stimulated innovations – in Japan even more so than in Germany – which were to come to fruition in the following phase of rebuilding. It later proved favourable, too, that during the war mobility and improvisation were demanded from the population in general. The breakdown in 1945 was the necessary, drastic rupture in both countries, the prerequisite for entry into the modern world of mass democracy. The sociopolitical deformations, manifest in rigid perseverance to reactionary social systems, the sociopolitical quarantine in both countries, and the chiliastic expectation of an historical standstill in the thousand-year Reich was first felt by Japan and Germany, with their nationalist totalitarian regimes and internal suppression. The world was drawn into the vortex of a global war before this catastrophic development was forcibly terminated.

Notes

1. For a concise study on the origins of the Pacific War, see Akira Iriye, *The Origins of the Second World War in Asia and the Pacific War*, London, 1989. For Germany's role, see the previous chapter, 'Germany and Pearl Harbor', in this volume. For monographs on the Berlin-Tokyo axis in the Second World War, see Bernd Martin, *Deutschland und Japan im Zweiten Weltkrieg. Vom Angriff auf Pearl Harbour bis zur deutschen Kapitulation*, Göttingen, 1969; Japanese liberal translation by the Air Force Academy, Japanese Self-Defence Forces, Tokyo, 1969, and Johanna Menzel-Meskill, *Hitler and Japan. The Hollow Alliance*, New York, 1966. There is still no Japanese study on the war alliance but only one on the Tripartite Pact by Masaki Miyake, *Nichi-Doku-I sangoku dōmei no kenkyū*. With an English summary, Tokyo, 1975.

2. On the Tripartite Pact, see Theo Sommer, *Deutschland und Japan zwischen den Mächten. Vom Antikominternpakt zum Dreimächtepakt*, Tübingen, 1962; Chihiro Hosoya, 'The Tripartite Pact, 1939–1940' in James W. Morley, ed., *Deterrent Diplomacy. Japan, Germany and the USSR, 1935–1940*, New York, 1976, pp. 179–258, and Ian Nish, ed., *The Tripartite Pact of 1940: Japan, Germany and Italy*, London, 1984.

3. For a comparison of the three 'fascist' countries, see chapter 6, 'Three Forms of Fascism: Japan – Italy – Germany', in this volume.

4. See chapter 2, 'Fatal Affinities: The German Role in the Modernisation of Japan in the Early Meiji Period (1868–1895) and Its Aftermath', in this volume.

5. Takushiro Hattori, *The Complete History of the Greater East Asia War*, Tokyo, 1953 (American translation, unpublished, copy on microfilm). The semiofficial account of an insider – Hattori a was member of the Japanese General Staff. German extract: 'Japans Operationsplan für den Beginn des Pazifischen Krieges', *Wehrwissenschaftliche Rundschau*, vol. 7 (1957), pp. 247–74.

6. Kiyoshi Ikeda, 'The Road to Singapore: Japan's View of Britain 1922–1941' in T.G. Fraser and Peter Lowe, eds., *Conflict and Amity in East Asia. Essays in Honour of Ian Nish*, London, 1992, pp. 30–46.

7. For the military events, see Louis Morton, *The War in the Pacific. Strategy and Command: The First Two Years*, Washington, D.C., 1962, and a more popular account by Edwin Palmer Hoyt, *Japan's War. The Great Pacific Conflict 1853–1952*, London, 1987.

8. On strategic plans for coalition warfare, see Martin, *Deutschland und Japan*, pp. 129–51.

9. Ibid., pp. 46–54. For the Japanese draft and the final text, see: Ibid., pp. 230–34.

10. Ibid., pp. 61–80, and Milan Hauner, *India in Axis Strategy*, Stuttgart, 1981.

11. Martin, *Deutschland und Japan*, pp. 94–121.

12. Ibid., p. 173.

13. Ibid., pp. 110–121 and Krebs, 'Japanische Vermittlungsversuche im deutsch-sowjetischen Krieg 1941–1945' in Josef Kreiner und Regine Mathias, eds., *Deutschland-Japan in der Zwischenkriegszeit*, Bonn, 1990, pp. 239–88.

14. On Soviet-German peace talks in Stockholm, see Bernd Martin 'Deutsch-sowjetische Sondierungen über einen separaten Friedensschluß im Zweiten Weltkrieg. Bericht und Dokumentation', in Inge Auerbach et al., eds., *Felder und Vorfelder russischer Geschichte. Studien zu Ehren von Peter Scheibert*, Freiburg, 1985, pp. 280–309.

15. For the following, see Martin, *Deutschland und Japan*, pp. 135ff.

16. Ibid., pp. 81–88.

17. See note 10 above.

18. Reichsgesetzblatt 1927, Teil II, pp. 1087–100 (27 November 1927). For an overview, see: Erich Pauer 'Die wirtschaftlichen Beziehungen zwischen Japan und Deutschland 1900–1945', in Josef Kreiner, ed., *Deutschland-Japan. Historische Kontakte*, Bonn, 1984, pp. 161–210.

19. William C. Kirby, *Germany and Republican China*, Stanford, Calif., 1984, and Udo Ratenhof, *Die Chinapolitik des Deutschen Reiches 1871–1945. Wirtschaft, Rüstung, Militär*, Boppard, 1985., see also chapter 7, 'Germany between China and Japan', in this volume.

20. Pauer, 'Die wirtschaftlichen Beziehungen', p. 191.

21. Ibid., p. 201 … daß man zwar 'viel Freundschaft erhalte, aber nur wenige Einfuhrgenehmigungen'.

22. Hitler's announcement in his Reichtag speech of 20 February 1938. For the shift in German Far Eastern policy from China to Japan, see John P. Fox, *Germany and the Far Eastern Crisis 1931–1938*, Oxford, 1982, and chapter 7, 'Germany between China and Japan', in this volume.

23. Michael A. Barnhart, *Japan Prepares for Total War. The Search for Economic Security 1919–1941*, Ithaca, 1987.

24. Decision of Liaison Conference of 25 September 1943., see Hattori, *The Complete History*, III (6) pp. 16f.

25. Olivia Checkland, *Britain's Encounter with Meiji-Japan, 1868–1912*, London, 1989, and Foster R. Dulles, *Yankees and Samurai. America's Role in the Emergence of Modern Japan, 1791–1900*, New York, 1965.

26. For the technological transfer from Germany to Japan from 1850 until present times, see the recent collection of essays edited by Erich Pauer, *Technologietransfer Deutschland-Japan. Von 1850 bis zur Gegenwart*, München, 1992. For the forced deliveries after 1918, see Erich Pauer 'Deutsche Ingenieure in Japan, japanische Ingenieure in Deutschland' in Kreiner/Mathias, eds., *Deutschland-Japan*, Bonn, 1990, pp. 289–324.

27. Kreiner/Mathias, *Deutschland-Japan*, pp. 299ff.

28. Hans-Joachim Braun, 'Technologietransfer im Flugzeugbau zwischen Deutschland und Japan 1936–1945' in Kreiner/Mathias, *Deutschland-Japan*, pp. 325–40.

29. Pauer, 'Deutsche Ingenieure', pp. 312ff.

30. Ibid., pp. 306 and 317.

31. Hack was born in 1887 in Freiburg and died in Zürich in 1949. His business transactions are still mysterious. He is better known in Japan than in Germany where only one article – full of mistakes – was written on him: 'Der geheimnisvolle Doktor Hack' in *Frankfurter Allgemeine Zeitung*, 31 August 1965. The account in this text is mainly based on Hack's private papers which the author obtained from Hack's nephew in 1970. Most of these papers which will be published in 1995, deal with the origins of the Anti-Comintern Pact.

32. These contacts are mentioned by John W. M. Chapman, 'Japan and German Naval Policy, 1919–1945', in Kreiner, ed., *Deutschland-Japan*, pp. 235f.

33. Martin, 'German-Japanese Relations after Hitler-Stalin Pact', in David W. Pike, ed., *The Opening of the Second World War*, New York and Bern, 1992.

34. 'Es sind grundsätzlich alle japanischen Wünsche abzulehnen, die einer Industriespionage oder Industrieverschleppung gleichkommen' quoted in Pauer, 'Deutsche Ingenieure', p. 317.

35. John W. M. Chapman, 'The Have-Nots Go to War. The Economic and Technological Basis of the German Alliance with Japan', in Ian Nish, ed., *The Tripartite Pact of 1940. Japan, Germany and Italy*, London, 1984, pp. 25–73.

36. For the transit via the Soviet Union, see: Heinrich Schwendemann, *Die wirtschaftliche Zusammenarbeit zwischen dem Deutschen Reich und der Sowjetunion von 1939 bis 1941 – Alternative zu Hitlers Ostprogramm?*, Berlin, 1993.

37. Martin, *Deutschland und Japan*, p. 158.

38. Ibid., pp. 161ff.

39. Alfred W. McCoy, ed., *Southeast Asia under Japanese Occupation*, Yale, 1980.

40. Martin, *Deutschland und Japan*, p. 166.

41. For the long talks preceding the trade agreement, see ibid., pp. 251–5.

42. Ibid., p. 170.

43. Ibid., pp. 207ff. On the whole issue, see also the file 'German Submarine Materials', Box 370, in the Library of Congress, Manuscript Division, Washington, DC.

44. Note by Wiehl, Head of Economic Department of the Foreign Office, from 29 April 1943 ('Kostenlose Preisgabe des gesamten technischen Entwicklungsstandes der deutschen Industrie'), Martin, *Deutschland und Japan*, p. 210.

45. 'Letter from OKM (German Naval High Command) to Foreign Office from 20 November 1943', in German Submarine Materials, Box 370, (see note 43).

46. Martin, *Deutschland und Japan*, p. 211. For the full text, see ibid., p. 331.

47. Ibid., p. 212.

48. Pauer, 'Deutsche Ingenieure', p. 319.

49. Braun, 'Technologietransfer im Flugzeugbau ...', in Kreiner und Mathias, eds., *Deutschland-Japan*, pp. 337f.

50. Martin, *Deutschland und Japan*, pp. 212f.

51. Bernd Martin, 'Japans Kriegswirtschaft' in Friedrich Forstmeier und Hans-Erich Volkmann, eds., *Kriegswirtschaft und Rüstung 1939–1945*, Düsseldorf, 1977, pp. 256–86, and on social change in Japan during the last war, see chapter 5, 'The End of the Old Order: Social Change in Japan during the Pacific War', in this volume.

52. Chalmers Johnson, *MITI and the Japanese Miracle. The Growth of Industrial Policy, 1925–1975*, Stanford, 1982.

53. Bernd Martin, 'Die Einschätzung der Lage Deutschlands aus japanischer Sicht: Japans Abkehr vom Bündnis und seine Hinwendung auf Ostasien (1943–1945)', in Manfred Messerschmidt, ed., *Die Zukunft des Reiches. Gegner, Verbündete und Neutrale 1943*, Bonn, 1990, pp. 127–46 (Decision of the Liaison Conference of 25 September 1943).

IN PLACE OF A CONCLUSION
THE PACIFIC WAR AND THE TWENTIETH CENTURY
– SOME THOUGHTS –

Fifty years after the defeat of Japan and Germany, the Second World War has been thoroughly reexamined by the international community of historians. Although the United States' declaration of war on Japan (8 December 1941) and Hitler's official declaration of war on the United States (11 December 1941) widened the so far regional conflicts in Europe, North Africa, and China into a global struggle, the different theatres of war are usually dealt with separately at special conferences. Commemorating the beginning and the end of the Pacific War poses difficulties for the countries involved and clearly reveals a national approach, together with a kind of collective memory. The Japanese resent being reminded of their 'sneaky attack' on Pearl Harbor, while the Americans would refute accusations of having bombed innocent civilians at Hiroshima and Nagasaki with arguments about the necessities of war. But both sides, the Japanese as well as the Americans, tend to look on the Pacific War as a bilateral conflict of their own and thereby often overlook the global dimensions and the legacy that this war has left.

The beginning of the Pacific War was commemorated by several international conferences at which the historical roots of this conflict and the contribution it may have made to our world were discussed in a very controversial manner. At the international conference in Japan, which was held near Lake Yamanaka in November 1991, the final panel reflected the traditional approach and the different opinions. Originally reserved for two American and two Japanese scholars, it was opened at the very last moment to the only German guest in attendance, in order to broaden the general view by adding its more European aspects. This gave me the opportunity to present my own views in three steps:

1. Some counterfactual remarks (what might have happened if) concerning the Second World War in the Pacific.

2. Some thoughts on the long-term issues of our century as connected with the struggle in the Pacific.

3. Some comments on today's problems resulting from, or as the legacy of, this last global war.

1. The counterfactual perspective is often regarded as mere speculation by serious scholars. Yet, one must not overlook the fact that, particularly during the course of a war, there is usually a vast variety of alternatives which are neglected for different reasons, such as matters of military prestige, social habits, or ideological convictions. History, however, never follows a predetermined course; there are always different options and open questions which politicians and military men have to decide on. The following three counter-to-fact hypotheses are only a few among an unlimited number. Almost no scenario is entirely implausible, which was proved more than once by sudden shifts during the last war.

A. Japan's really fateful choice was the decision of the Imperial Conference on 2 July 1941[1] to move southward instead of joining Nazi Germany in defeating communist Russia. A joint German-Japanese pincer attack would have been a deadly threat to, or even the end of communism fifty years before it finally dissolved in 1991. The United States would never have intervened because anticommunism was running high in America in those days. And, as the Japanese Foreign Minister Matsuoka (who, by the way, should not be regarded as a maniac, but rather as un-Japanese) suggested in June 1941[2] Japan would have turned south after having gained a victory in the north and would have easily conquered those rich territories without meeting any combined Western resistance. Thus, the Japanese Empire would have become a world power, like the Third Reich. Fortunately, this did not happen, thanks mainly to the inflexibility of the Japanese military, and thanks to the slow procedure of political decision making in Tokyo – *ringisei*.[3]

B. China had to endure a war of annihilation, as did Russia after the German surprise attack, without a formal declaration of war. The communist regime under Stalin's dictatorship was stabilised by the onslaught, as was the Kuomintang under Chiang Kai-shek. Therefore, without the Japanese menace, China's development would have taken a totally different course. Chiang Kai-shek would never have survived on the mainland until 1949. Foreign concepts of modernisation and the reorganisation of the National

Revolutionary Party, the Chinese government, and Chinese society in general failed, as did the Soviet communist concept during the 1920s[4] and the German-inspired adoption, during the 1930s,[5] of modernisation from above, or finally the American help from 1940[6] onward; all of these concepts should rather be taken as signs of the weakness of the Kuomintang. The only choice was Mao's agrarian-based, or rather, Sinosised communist approach to China's social question, i.e., the unsolved agrarian situation.

C. Pearl Harbor: if the Japanese attack had not taken place, there would have been no war in the Pacific and no world war at all. Japan forced this particular issue and Japan, despite the American embargoes, bears the sole responsibility for waging that war. This may have been an even greater mistake than the aforementioned imperial decision not to attack the Soviet Union. There was some chance of compromise with the United States, as Cordell Hull's first draft answer to Japan's Plan B clearly shows.[7] America wanted to enter the war against Germany, not against Japan. Therefore, the Japanese Empire, even a greater Asian one, might have survived the war, and Japan might even have been given a seat at the peace conference.

Be that as it may – the fact remains that the course of history always has an open end. Therefore, even professional researchers might well comment on plausible historical alternatives instead of leaving this task to fictitious writing.

2. As this century nears its end, the long-term issues appear more clearly. The '*longue durée*', as the French annalist school has it, thinks in terms of centuries. Problems of continuity or discontinuity, the emergence of nationalism, and, last but not least, economic processes cannot be fully interpreted or understood with the help of present-day theories. The nationalist bias, too, has to be overcome in order to understand national specifics in their true meaning for the global process of history.

A. There is much more continuity than discontinuity to be found when looking back at the twentieth century. The year 1945, with Germany's unconditional surrender in May and Japan's capitulation, on conditions, in September, even nowadays looks more like a turning point, rather than the final end of an era and the starting point of a totally new development. Continuity prevailed in Japan, especially within the ranks of the bureaucracy, while in Germany the National Socialist government and the Nazi *Volksgemeinschaft* (folkish community) came to an abrupt end. In Germany there was a kind of total collapse, of *'Stunde Null'*, 'zero hour', and more discontinuity may be discerned than occurred in Japan. But eventually, continuity emerged once again in Germany.

B. With the end of this century drawing near, the First and Second World Wars begin to resemble one global conflict, interrupted by an armistice, a cease-fire, of just nineteen years. In Europe the legacy of the Versailles peace settlement has been overcome only in recent times. The situation in Russia – the disintegration of the Union of Socialist Soviet Republics created by the Bolshevik revolution – can be traced back to the turmoils of the First World War. The same applies to the war between Serbs and Croats, who were forced to live in an artificial state by the Paris peace conference in 1919.[8] In the Pacific region of Asia, the consequences of the Washington treaties of 1922,[9] in many respects similar to the Versailles settlements, were mostly overcome during the Second World War, when the system of unequal treaties was finally abandoned. The remaining problems, such as the unification of Korea, the new political order in China, the unification of Taiwan, Hong Kong and the Peoples' Republic, will soon be resolved. Japan's northern issue, the question of the Kuriles Islands, will certainly have been settled before that.

C. The surrender of Imperial Japan should be regarded as the final point in the opening forced upon the island state by Western powers. It all started in 1853, with Perry's black ships arriving in the Bay of Edo, and it ended with the ceremony held on the battleship *Missouri* in 1945. Japan's modernisation, in many respects shaped after Prussian-German models, had, from the very beginning an anti-Western stance, an underlying defensive motif. Over a period of ninety-three years Japan did not achieve the status of an accepted member of the Western-dominated community of nations. Even today, many Japanese have the impression that they have not yet achieved this goal.

D. The myth of the China market, the temptation of unlimited export to a nation with a population of over one billion, dates back to the first unequal treaty, that of Nanjing in 1842 and will certainly survive as long as China remains an underdeveloped country. The China policy of the Western powers, of the fascist 'have-not nations' Italy, Japan, and Germany, and even of Soviet Russia were all, to a certain extent, misguided by wishful thinking. China still appears as a paradise to capitalists, and even the geronts, the old men in Peking, have finally acknowledged this Western obsession.

E. Nationalism has survived during this century, in different forms or in disguise (as in communist Russia). The Second World War, especially in Asia, can be regarded as an eruption of national creeds. The process of decolonisation reached its final stage with the independence of India and Burma in 1947.[10] Japan's role in this process was a prominent one. It should be reevaluated despite the brutal occupation politics which ignorant military men exercised over the different nations of the Greater East Asia Co-Prosperity Sphere, which during the war was named 'Greater East Asia Robbery Sphere' by the victims.

The Asian nations seemed to have found their national boundaries by the end of the Pacific War (China's multinational empire as the eldest state in our world should be regarded as a special case). Therefore, the political order with regard to national thinking seems to have been better stabilised in Asia than in Europe.

F. Strange as it may seem, the role of the historian has not changed much either; as James Morley once put it, 'they either lie or create myths'.[11] In any case, they have always been affirmative in reflecting the current mainstream of public opinion or, in times of war, submitting to censorship. Their so-called critical objectivity can thus be regarded as the real myth.

German historiographical attitudes have changed or have been forced to change several times during this century, as have the Japanese or even the American approaches. The American historiography on Pearl Harbor may serve as an example. Twenty years ago, in the shadow cast by the Vietnam War, there was a deeply rooted feeling of guilt. The war with Japan was regarded as a tragedy. Some Americans, the revisionist camp, even went so far as to apologise to the Japanese. Yet, on the occasion of the fiftieth anniversary of the Pearl Harbor attack, the American public now expects an apology from the Japanese. As times change, so do opinions. Therefore, Pearl Harbor and the Pacific War will have to be reexamined more than once, now as well as in the future.

3. The legacy of the Pacific War with respect to the global conflict is reflected in the world's current political situation and its unsolved issues. The last war was a harbinger of things to come. However, the borderless world and racial equality, which the Japanese losers of the war have been dreaming of and elaborating on in papers, still remains a fiction. The idea of a multicultural society, propagated in the United States and imitated in Germany, has not worked out so far and – perhaps for good reasons – is strictly rejected by the Japanese. The racial war in the Pacific and in Europe fought by the Germans and the Japanese was terminated fifty years ago, but racial thinking and racial prejudices have remained. Our world has become the one world which American interventionists such as Wilson and Roosevelt were striving for during the two world wars, but only in terms of communication. Certainly, the ideological and partly economic confrontation along the lines of liberal capitalism, authoritarian (fascist) state capitalism, and communism was ended with the defeat of the Germans and the Japanese in 1945 and with the collapse of the socialist countries in 1989. The United States and their political, as well as economic, order seem to have finally won. However, they no longer control even those parts of the world which they protected during the Cold War. Suspicion and mistrust against Japan (and Germany) have reemerged in the Anglo-American world, as has anti-Americanism, particularly in Japan. Both attitudes date back to the days of war and can easily be instrumentalised at any time for political reasons.

A. The losers of the war – Japan and Germany – have become the winners of today. Giants in economic respect, they have remained dwarfs in political affairs, an unbalanced situation that is bound to change. Both countries have given up military expansion for peaceful economic penetration. Both have reached their former war aims by different means. Japan now controls the economy of East and Southeast Asia, while Germany dominates the trade within the European Community. The common experience of a fascist alliance, state interventionism in economic affairs, the necessities of a war economy unable to rely on natural resources, and the organisation of trade and industry under the supervision and guidance of victorious United States – all this may be primarily responsible for the economic miracle which both countries began to enjoy as early as in the 1950s, just ten years after having surrendered.

The dominant position they have now reached gives rise to suspicion among their neighbours in Europe, as well as in East Asia. But while Germany is integrated politically and militarily in NATO and the European Community and is considered only one part of a common market without tariff barriers, Japan, by comparison, is isolated. Therefore, the Japanese dominance is resented and suspected much more than the German one. This mistrust is, of course, aggravated by two factors resulting from the last war: cultural misconceptions and the attitude towards a past full of crimes.

B. Cultural differences were used by different political cultures during the last war to mobilise the home front and to raise the fighting spirit of the soldiers. The wars in the Pacific and in Europe were both ideological and racist wars. Mutual disdain and contempt could be found in clichés about the 'sneaky Japs', often referred to as 'lacquered half-monkeys' (a phrase used by both Hitler and American cartoonists!). On the other hand, Americans were pictured as beasts or, by German propaganda, as Jewish-looking monsters.[12] Racial prejudices were inflamed by propaganda and internalised by the population, and can easily be evoked again. The fiction of a potential war with Japan still has a great attraction, as did similar fictions, movies, and novels in the 1920s. Historians should deal with these facts rather than leaving them to sociologists or to the mass media.

C. American suspicion and mistrust of the Japanese seems to be nurtured by the apparent ignorance of the Japanese about the Pacific War. The lack of awareness of guilt in the Japanese people[13] (who do not share the Christian feeling of guilt) arouses deep suspicion in a society such as the American one whose ethical values are based on Puritanical principles of individual guilt. However, I think the blame for suppressing the crimes of the past should not be placed with Japanese historians. Instead, the government and the conservative bureaucrats, who were never politically purged after 1945, should be held responsible for the ignorance of the public.

D. However, I am far from praising the German situation, where there have also been shortcomings. Yet, in general, (West) Germany has managed to make the public accept defeat and the German guilt for the war. German textbooks, written by professors of history, offer excellent information with regard to Germany's recent past, and pupils are supposed to know about the last war and the crimes committed in Germany's name. Of course, in Japan there was never a planned genocide like the Holocaust of the Jews, which has helped make the Germans remember the past and repent. This way of dealing with the National Socialist period has been generally acknowledged by Germany's former adversaries. There are exceptions and the topic is still sensitive, but on the whole Germany is trusted to have faced its own past. The joint visit of President Reagan and Chancellor Kohl to a German military cemetery where even SS soldiers are buried,[14] was seen as demonstrating German repentance and American forgiveness. But the President of the United States and the Prime Minister of Japan are unlikely to make a joint visit to the Yasukuni Shrine[15] in the near future. The entire issue, therefore, deserves proper attention by all historians and should be taken up as soon as possible in Japan.

E. The twentieth century may be called the Anglo-American century, with the Soviet Union playing a dominant role for only about fifty years, from 1941 until 1991. The next century has often been referred to as the 'Pacific century'. The United States' role as leading world power is declining, and there is, despite the success in the Gulf war, a feeling of lack of leadership. Will the liberal-democratic system work, when it is no longer challenged by either the communist or, as it was until 1945, by the fascist model? Looking at the domestic troubles in the United States, one has one's doubts. What may be needed in future to maintain a peaceful world is not the dominance of one region or one country, such as the Pacific or Japan. The new century should be one of peacefully united regions, where national egoism has been sacrificed to the common well-being. Yet, in terms of internationalisation Japan seems to lag behind.

Revenging defeat or forgetting the past will but lead to new disasters. Japan, like Germany, will have to take a lead in the formation of the next century without dominating it.

Notes

1. Nobutaka Ike, ed., *Japan's Decision for War. Records of the 1941 Policy Conferences*, Princeton, 1967, pp. 77–90; Bernd Martin, '*Japan and Barbarossa*', paper, University of Waterloo, Ontario, Center for Soviet Studies, 18 May 1991.

2. Ike, *Decision for War*, pp. 60–70 (Matsuoka on 25, 26, and 27 June 1941).

3. Kiyoaki Tsuji, 'Decision Making in the Japanese Government: A Study of Ringisei', in Robert E. Ward, ed., *Political Development in Modern Japan*, Princeton, 1973, pp. 457–76.

4. Dieter Heinzig, *Sowjetische Militärberater bei der Kuomintang, 1923–1927*, Baden-Baden, 1978.

5. Bernd Martin, ed., *The German Advisory Group in China. Military, Economic, and Political Issues in Sino-German Relations, 1927–1938*, Düsseldorf, 1981.

6. Barbara Tuchman, *Stilwell and the American Experience in China, 1911–45*, New York, 1970; Michael Schaller, *The U.S. Crusade in China, 1938–1945*, New York, 1979.

7. Ike, *Decision for War*, pp. 199–208; Robert J. C. Butow, *Tojo and the Coming of the War*, Princeton, 1961 (Japanese retreat from Southern Indochina – American normalisation of U.S.-Japanese trade).

8. Dimitrije Djordjevic, ed., *The Creation of Yugoslavia 1914–1918*, Santa Barbara, 1980.

9. Thomas Buckley, *The United States and the Washington Conference*, Knoxville, 1970; Wm. Roger Louis, *British Strategy in the Far East*, Oxford, 1971.

10. Bernd Martin, 'Die Verselbständigung der Dritten Welt. Der Prozeß der Entkolonialisierung am Beispiel Indiens', in *Saeculum*, vol. 34, 1983, pp. 165–86.

11. Statement, International Conference 'Fifty Years After – The Pacific War Re-examined', Lake Yamanaka, 1991.

12. John W. Dower, *War without Mercy. Race and Power in the Pacific War*, New York, 1986.

13. Ian Buruma, *The Wages of Guilt. Memoirs of War in Germany and Japan*, New York, 1994; Steven R. Weisman, 'Pearl Harbor in the Mind of Japan', in *The New York Times Magazine*, 3 November 1991.

14. The visit to Bitburg/Eiffel on 5 May 1985 commemorated the fortieth anniversary of the end of Second World War in Europe. Quotations from the official speeches given at Bitburg air base after the ceremony at the cemetery. Translated from the official version in *Archiv der Gegenwart*, vol. 55, 1985, pp. 28732–3.

    Kohl: 'And this our common visit of the graves of Bitburg is also a widely viewed and deeply felt gesture to confirm our reconciliation, the reconciliation of both our peoples, the one of the United States and the German one, a reconciliation that does not try to suppress past but to overcome it together.'

    Reagan: 'On the fortieth anniversary of the end of the Second World War we commemorate the day that ended the hatred, the evil, and all the horrible events, and we solemnly celebrate the rebirth of the spirit of democracy in Germany.'

15. The Yasukuni Shrine is a Shinto shrine in Tokyo, built after the Meiji Restoration to commemorate dead soldiers. It is also a national memorial for all Japanese soldiers (war criminals included) who died in the Pacific War. Regular visits have been made by the Tenno since 1952, and the Prime Minister since 1986.

SELECT BIBLIOGRAPHY

Titles on German-Japanese relations and German literature on modern Japan will be given preference. From the large number of English language publications on Japan only some standard works will be listed. Except for publications marked by an asterisk, the following titles are among those quoted in the footnotes.

Abosch, David. *Kato Hiroyuki and the Introduction of German Political Thought in Modern Japan 1868–1883*. Unpublished Ph.D. thesis. University of California, Berkeley, 1964.

Allen, G. C. *A Short Economic History of Modern Japan*. London, 1972.

Antoni, Klaus, ed. *Der Himmlische Herrscher und sein Staat. Essays zur Stellung des Tenno im modernen Japan*. München, 1994.

Baring, Arnulf, and Sase Masamori, eds. *Zwei zaghafte Riesen? Deutschland und Japan seit 1945*. Stuttgart, 1977.

Barnhart, Michael A. *Japan Prepares for Total War. The Search for Economic Security, 1919–1941*. Ithaca, N.Y., 1987.

Beasley, William Gerald. *The Meiji Restoration*. Stanford University Press, 1973.

———. *Japanese Imperialism 1894–1945*. Oxford, 1987.

Beckmann, George M. *The Making of the Meiji Constitution*. Lawrence, Kansas, 1957.

Bendix, Reinhard. *Nation Building and Citizenship. Studies of our Changing Social Order*. New York, 1964.

Benz, Wolfgang. 'Amerikanische Besatzungsherrschaft in Japan 1945–47', in: *Vierteljahrshefte für Zeitgeschichte*, vol. 26, 1978, pp. 265–346.

Berg, Albert. *Die Preußische Expedition nach Ost-Asien nach amtlichen Quellen*. 4 vols., Berlin, 1864–1873.

Borg, Dorothy, and Shumpei Okamoto, eds. *Pearl Harbor as History. Japanese–American Relations 1931–1941*. Columbia University Press, 1973.

Boyd, Carl. *The Extraordinary Envoy: General Hiroshi Oshima and Diplomacy in the Third Reich, 1934–1939*. University Press of America, Washington, 1980.

———. *Hitler's Confidant. Japanese General Oshima Hiroshi and Magic Intelligence 1941–1945*. Lawrence, Kansas, 1993.

Brooker, Paul. *Three Faces of Fraternalism. Nazi-Germany, Fascist Italy, and Imperial Japan*. Oxford, 1991.

Broszat, Martin. 'Zeitgeschichte in Japan', in: *Vierteljahrshefte für Zeitgeschichte*, vol. 22, 1974, pp. 287–98.

Burdick, Charles B. *The Japanese Siege of Tsingtao*. Hamden, Connecticut, 1976.

Bürkner, Alexander. *Probleme der japanischen Wehrverfassung von der Meiji-Zeit bis in die Gegenwart*. Bonn, Phil. Fak. Diss, 1973.

Buruma, Ian. *The Wages of Guilt. Memoirs of War in Germany and Japan*. New York, 1994.

Chapman, John. *The Origins and Development of German and Japanese Military Cooperation 1936–1945*. Unpublished Ph.D. thesis. Oxford University, 1967.*

Cohen, Jerome B. *Japan's Economy in War and Reconstruction*. Minneapolis, 1949.

Crowley, James B. *Japan's Quest for Autonomy. National Security and Foreign Policy 1930–1938*. Princeton, N.Y., 1966.

Dower, John W. *War without Mercy. Race and Power in the Pacific War*. New York, 1986.*

Drechsler, Karl. *Deutschland – China – Japan 1933–1939. Das Dilemma der deutschen Fernostpolitik*. Berlin (East), 1964.*

Duus, Peter. *Party Rivalry and Political Change in Taisho Japan*. Harvard University Press, 1968.

Duus Peter. 'The Twentieth Century', *The Cambridge History of Japan*, vol. 6, General Editor John W. Hall, Cambridge, 1988.*

Engram, John Henry. *Partner or Peril. Japan in German Foreign Policy and Diplomacy 1914–1920*. Washington State University, 1976.*

Fifty Years After – The Pacific War Reexamined. Papers of the International Conference at Lake Yamanaka, 1991. Japanese edition: Hosoya, Chihiro et al., eds. *Taiheiyosenso*, Tokyo, 1994.

Fischer, Peter. *Buddhismus und Nationalismus im modernen Japan*. Bochum, 1979.*

Fox, John P. *Germany and the Far Eastern Crisis 1931–1938. A Study in Diplomacy and Ideology*. Oxford, 1982.

Gluck, Carol. *Japan's Modern Myths. Ideology in the Late Meiji-Period*. Princeton University Press, 1985.

Hackett, Roger F. *Yamagata Aritomo in the Rise of Modern Japan 1838–1922*. Cambridge, Mass., 1971.

Hammitzsch Horst, ed. *Japan Handbuch*. Wiesbaden, 1981.

Havens, Thomas R. H. *Farm and Nation in Modern Japan. Agrarian Nationalism*. Princeton, 1974.

Hayashi, Kentaro. 'Japan and Germany in the Interwar Period', in: James W. Morley, ed. *Dilemmas of Growth in Prewar Japan*. Princeton University Press, 1971, pp. 461–88.

Hijiya-Kirschnereit, Irmela. *Das Ende der Exotik. Zur japanischen Kultur und Gesellschaft der Gegenwart*. Frankfurt a. M., 1988.

Hillgruber, Andreas. 'Japan und der Fall Barbarossa', in: *Wehrwissenschaftliche Rundschau*. 1968, pp. 312–36.

Select Bibliography

Hunter, Janet E. *The Emergence of Modern Japan. An Introductory History since 1853.* London and New York, 1989.*

Ienaga, Saburo. *Japan's Last War. World War II and the Japanese 1931–1945.* Oxford, 1979.

Ike, Nobutake. *Japan's Decision for War. Records of the 1941 Policy Conferences.* Stanford University Press, 1967.

Iklé, Frank William. *German-Japanese Relations 1936–1940.* New York, 1956.

Iriye, Akira. *The Origins of the Second World War in Asia and the Pacific.* London, 1989.

Ishida, Takeshi. 'Elements of Tradition and "Renovation" in Japan during the "Era of Fascism"', in: *Annals of the Institute of Social Science.* Tokyo University, 1976, pp. 111–40.

Johnson, Chalmers. *MITI and the Japanese Miracle. The Growth of Industrial Policy 1925–1975.* Stanford, 1982.

Kasza, Gregory J. 'Fascism from below? A comparative perspective on the Japanese Right, 1931–1936', in: *Journal of Contemporary History*, vol. 19, 1984, pp. 607–29.*

Kindermann, Gottfried Karl. *Der Ferne Osten in der Weltpolitik des 20. Jahrhunderts.* München, 1970.

Klein, Ulrike. *Deutsche Kriegsgefangene in japanischem Gewahrsam 1914–1920. Ein Sonderfall.* Ph.D. thesis. Freiburg im Breisgau, 1993.*

Kracht, Klaus, Bruno Lewin, and Klaus Müller, eds. *Japan und Deutschland im 20. Jahrhundert.* Wiesbaden, 1984.

Krebs, Gerhard, and Bernd Martin, eds. *Formierung und Fall der Achse Berlin-Tokyo.* München, 1994.

Krebs, Gerhard. 'Deutschland und Pearl Harbor', in: *Historische Zeitschrift*, vol. 253, 1991, pp. 313–69.*

———. *Japans Deutschlandpolitik 1935–1941. Eine Studie zur Vorgeschichte des Pazifischen Krieges.* Hamburg, 1984.

Kreiner, Josef. *Deutschland – Japan. Historische Kontakt.* Bonn, 1984.

———. *Japan und die Mittelmächte im Ersten Weltkrieg und in den Zwanziger Jahren.* Bonn, 1986*

Kreiner, Josef, and Regine Mathias, eds. *Deutschland – Japan in der Zwischenkriegszeit.* Bonn, 1990.*

Libal, Michael. *Japans Weg in den Krieg. Die Außenpolitik der Kabinette Konoye 1940–41.* Düsseldorf, 1971.

Lu, David John. *Sources of Japanese History.* New York/Düsseldorf, 1974.

Lupke, Hubertus. *Japans Rußlandpolitik von 1939–1941.* Frankfurt a. M., 1962.*

Martin, Bernd. 'Deutsche Geschichtswissenschaft als Instrument nationaler Selbstfindung in Japan', in: Gangolf Hübinger et al., eds. *Universalgeschichte und Nationalgeschichten.* Freiburg im Breisgau, 1994, pp. 209–30.*

————. *Deutschland und Japan im Zweiten Weltkrieg. Von Pearl Harbour bis zur deutschen Kapitulation.* Göttingen, 1969.

————. 'Germano-Japanese Relations after the Hitler-Stalin Pact and German Reaction to the Nippo-Soviet Rapprochement', in: David W. Pike, ed. *The Opening of the Second World War.* New York and Bern, 1992, pp. 228–38.

————. 'Japan und der Krieg in Ostasien. Kommentierender Bericht über das Schrifttum', in: *Historische Zeitschrift*, Sonderheft 8, 1980, pp. 79–220.

————. 'Japans Kriegswirtschaft 1941–1945', in: Forstmeier, Friedrich and Volkmann, Hans-Erich, eds. *Kriegswirtschaft und Rüstung 1939–1945.* Düsseldorf, 1977, pp. 256–86.

————. ed. *Japans Weg in die Moderne. Ein Sonderweg nach deutschem Vorbild?* Frankfurt a. M., 1987.*

————. 'Kaiser Hirohito. Eine kritische Würdigung', in: *Das Parlament*, vol. 48, 25 November 1988.

————. 'Restauration. Die Bewältigung der Vergangenheit in Japan', in: *Zeitschrift für Politik*, 1970, pp. 155–70.

————, and Alan S. Milward, eds. *Agriculture and Food Supply in World War Two. Landwirtschaft und Versorgung im Zweiten Weltkrieg.* Ostfildern, 1985.

Meskill, Johanna Menzel. *Hitler and Japan: The Hollow Alliance.* New York, 1966.

Mitchell, Richard H. *Thought Control in Prewar Japan.* Ithaca, N.Y., 1976.

Miyake, Masaki. 'Die Achse Berlin-Rom-Tokio im Spiegel der japanischen Quellen', in: *Mitteilungen des österreichischen Staatsarchivs*, vol. 21, 1968, Wien, 1969, pp. 408–45.

————. 'Die deutsche Nachkriegsentwicklung aus japanischer Sicht', in: *Social and Economic Research in Modern Japan. Occasional Papers*, no. 50, Ostasiatisches Seminar, FU-Berlin, 1984.*

————. 'German political and cultural influence on Japan 1870–1914', in: Moses, John M., and Kennedy, Paul M., eds. *Germany in the Pacific and Far East 1870–1914.* St. Lucia (Queensland), 1980, pp. 156–81.

————. *A Study on the Tripartite Alliance Berlin-Rome-Tokyo.* Tokyo, 1975.

Montgomery, John D. *Forced to be Free: The Artificial Revolution in Germany and Japan.* Chicago, 1975.

Moore, Barrington. *Social Origins of Dictatorship and Democracy.* London, 1967.

Morley, James W., ed. *The China Quagmire. Japan's Expansion on the Asian Continent 1933–1941.* Columbia University Press, 1983.

————, ed. *Deterrent Diplomacy. Japan-Germany and the USSR 1935–1940.* New York, 1976.

————, ed. *The Fateful Choice. Japan's Advance into South East Asia 1939–1941.* Columbia University Press, 1980.

Nish, Jan. *Japanese Foreign Policy 1869–1942. Kasumigaseki to Miyakezaka.* London, 1977.

Nitobe, Inazo. *Bushido. Die Seele Japans*. Magdeburg, 1973. (German translation of "Bushido: The Soul of Japan")

—— et al. *Western Influences in Modern Japan. A Series of Papers on Cultural Relations*. Chicago, 1931.

Oguro, Tatsuo. *Ihr Deutschen – wir Japaner. Ein Vergleich von Mentalität und Denkweise*. Düsseldorf, 1984.*

Pauer, Erich. *Technologietransfer Deutschland-Japan. Von 1850 bis zur Gegenwart*. München, 1992.

Piper, Annelotte. *Japans Weg von der Feudalgesellschaft zum Industriestaat. Wandlungsimpulse und wirtschaftliche Entwicklungsprozesse in ihrer politischen, geistigen und gesellschaftlichen Verankerung*. Köln, 1976.

Presseisen, Ernst L. *Before Aggression. Europeans Prepare the Japanese Army*. University of Arizona Press, 1965.

——. *Germany and Japan. A Study in Totalitarian Diplomacy*. The Hague, 1958.

Pyle, Kenneth B. 'Advantages of Followership: German Economics and Japanese Bureaucrats 1890–1925', in: *Journal of Japanese Studies*, vol. 1, no. 1, 1974, pp. 127–64.

Rauck, Michael. *Die Beziehungen zwischen Japan und Deutschland 1859–1914 unter besonderer Berücksichtigung der Wirtschaftsbeziehungen*. Diss. Wirtschafts- und Sozialwissenschaften Erlangen, 1988.

Schroeder, Paul W. *The Axis Alliance and Japanese-American Relations 1941*. Ithaca, N.Y., 1958.

Schumpeter, Elisabeth Boody, ed. *The Industrialisation of Japan and Manchukuo, 1930–1940. Population, Raw Materials and Industry*. New York, 1940.

Schwabe, Hans, and Heinrich Seeman, eds. *Deutsche Botschafter in Japan (1860–1973)*. Tokyo, 1974.

Shillony, Ben-Ami. *Revolt in Japan. The Young Officers and the February 26, 1936 Incident*. Princeton University Press, 1973.

——. *Politics and Culture in Wartime Japan*. Oxford, 1981.*

Siemes, Johannes. *Hermann Roesler and the Making of the Meiji State. An Examination of his Background and His Influence on the Founders of Modern Japan. The Complete Text of the Meiji Constitution Accompanied by his Personal Commentaries and Notes*. Tokyo, 1968.

——. 'Die Staatsgründung des modernen Japans: Die Einflüsse Hermann Roeslers', in: Joseph Roggendorf, ed. *Das moderne Japan. Einführende Aufsätze*. Tokyo, 1963.

Silbermann, Bernhard, and H. D. Harootunian. *Japan in Crisis. Essays on Taisho Democracy*. Princeton, 1974.

Smethurst, Richard J. *A Social Basis for Prewar Japanese Militarism. The Army and the Rural Community*. University of California Press, 1974.

Sommer, Theo. *Deutschland und Japan zwischen den Mächten 1935–1940*. Tübingen, 1962.

Stahncke, Holmer. *Die diplomatischen Beziehungen zwischen Deutschland und Japan 1854–1868.* Stuttgart, 1987.

Toshitani, Nobuyoshi. 'Japan's Modern Legal System: Its Formation and Structure', in: *Annals of the Institute of Social Science.* University of Tokyo, 1976.

Tsunoda, Ryusaku, and Wm. Theodore de Bary. *Sources of Japanese Tradition.* New York, 1965.

Tsurumi, Kazuko. *Social Change and the Individual. Japan before and after Defeat in World War Two.* Princeton University Press, 1970.

Wagner, Wieland. *Japans Außenpolitik in der frühen Meiji-Zeit (1868–1894). Die ideologische und politische Grundlegung des japanischen Führungsanspruchs in Ostasien.* Stuttgart, 1990.*

Wetzler, Peter. *The Emperor and the Military. Imperial Tradition and Decision Making in Prewar Japan.* Habilitationsschrift (manuscript), Philosophische Fakultäten, Freiburg im Breisgau, 1995.*

Wippich, Rolf-Haral. *Japan und die deutsche Fernostpolitik 1894–98.* Stuttgart, 1987.

Wittig, Horst E. *Pädagogik und Bildungspolitik in Japan.* München, 1976.

Zahl, Karl Friedrich. *Die politische Elite Japans nach dem Zweiten Weltkrieg.* Wiesbaden, 1973.

———. *Der Wandel des japanischen Geschichtsbildes seit dem Zweiten Weltkrieg.* Hamburg, 1983.*

INDEX